To Emil C

With sincere best wishes.

J.H. Doolittle

Doolittle

A Biography

Also by Lowell Thomas

WITH LAWRENCE IN ARABIA

INDIA—LAND OF THE BLACK PAGODA

COUNT LUCKNER, THE SEA DEVIL

THE SEA DEVIL'S FO'C'SLE

RAIDERS OF THE DEEP

LAUTERBACH OF THE CHINA SEA

SIR HUBERT WILKINS, A BIOGRAPHY

BORN TO RAISE HELL

THESE MEN SHALL NEVER DIE

BACK TO MANDALAY

SEVEN WONDERS OF THE WORLD

HISTORY AS YOU HEARD IT

THE VITAL SPARK: 101 OUTSTANDING LIVES

PAGEANT OF ADVENTURE

ADVENTURES AMONG IMMORTALS

THE WRECK OF THE DUMARU

WINGS OVER ASIA

Also by Edward Jablonski

THE GERSHWIN YEARS
with Lawrence D. Stewart

HAROLD ARLEN: HAPPY WITH THE BLUES

GEORGE GERSHWIN

THE KNIGHTED SKIES

THE GREAT WAR

FLYING FORTRESS

WARRIORS WITH WINGS: THE STORY OF THE LAFAYETTE ESCADRILLE

LADYBIRDS: WOMEN IN AVIATION

ATLANTIC FEVER: THE GREAT TRANSATLANTIC AERIAL ADVENTURE

SEA WINGS

THE GERSHWIN YEARS (Revised Edition), with Lawrence D. Stewart

DOUBLE STRIKE

AIRWAR

Doolittle

A Biography

Lowell Thomas and Edward Jablonski

DOUBLEDAY & COMPANY, INC.
GARDEN CITY, NEW YORK

Library of Congress Cataloging in Publication Data

Thomas, Lowell Jackson, 1892–
Doolittle.

Bibliography: p. 350.
Includes index.
1. Doolittle, James Harold, 1896–
I. Jablonski, Edward, joint author.
UG626.2.D66T46   629.13′092′4 [B]
ISBN 0-385-06495-0
Library of Congress Catalog Card Number 75–21247

For Joe, with love

Foreword

Doolittle, as he has been frequently reminded, is hardly the proper name for a man of James H. Doolittle's accomplishments; it is a counterpun, in fact.

Most popularly associated with the fabled Tokyo Raid of the Second World War, Doolittle's contributions to history, and especially to the development of aviation, are solidly based on more than a single, if remarkably heroic, incident. To the man himself the Raid was one event in an eventful career; there were adventures before and more after.

Doolittle, the folk hero of the thirties, the golden age of aviation, was celebrated as a dashing racing pilot, a virtuoso of aerobatics—a man of action, an achiever, a doer. His exploits, naturally, overshadowed the thinking man, analytical, thoughtful, the researcher who was called "a master of the calculated risk." Few were aware of the fact that the apparently cocky pilot with the ready grin had earned a doctorate in aeronautical sciences; the fact that he had mastered the deadly Gee Bee—and won the coveted Thompson Trophy—in 1932, obscured an even greater achievement, though undoubtedly a less colorful one, the first blind flight three years before. This marked the beginning of a new epoch in aviation—man would be capable of flight, through the use of instruments, despite darkness and fog. Aviation had become less a sport and more a science.

Those who associate Doolittle's military career merely with the

Tokyo Raid overlook the important longer stretch during which he served as commanding general of several air forces, closing his wartime military service as Lieutenant General Doolittle at the head of the great Eighth Air Force. In this role he was the Doolittle relatively unknown to the general public: the executive and leader. This image of Jimmy Doolittle, former racing pilot, might disconcert a following accustomed to derring-do, but the decisions he was obliged to make during the Second World War affected his country's fortunes of war and the lives of countless men. These decisions required as much, and probably more, courage than piloting a tricky aircraft around pylons at nearly 300 miles an hour with only one life in your hands.

The postwar Doolittle has remained no less active than the prewar and wartime Doolittle. A great believer in service, he has not only devoted his years since that war to chairmanships and/or memberships of various boards and committees advising governmental agencies, Presidents, the Air Force, and aeronautical agencies; simultaneously Doolittle earned a living in private industry as an executive and adviser. No intellectual, a term he abhors, Doolittle is certainly revealed as the thinking man during those years since the war.

During that memorable, often disruptive, period, he could take pride in the transition of aviation from the jet to the space age and the knowledge that he had participated in it. Events, concurrent with such giant steps in technology, disturbed him; while the machine appeared to be reaching forward, mankind appeared to be slipping back into a dark age. A master of the machine, Doolittle never permitted the machine to master him; he does not wax romantic over vintage aircraft, his eyes do not mist up at the mention of the Gee Bee or the B-25. They were machines designed for a purpose—to serve man—and were either useful or not.

Doolittle deeply believes, and this belief has underscored his life, that man, too, must serve man—although not in the capacity of the machine. "Technology—mechanization—has given man the ability to produce more in a given time and, in addition, has given him more leisure," Doolittle has written.

"This has had a good—and a bad—effect:

"It has enabled man better to serve his fellow man (good).

"It has inclined to make many individuals lazy (bad)."

Associated with the last point is another pungent Doolittle observation, "One of our major problems results from the assumption of unwarranted privileges without proper consideration of the rights and desires of others." Thus did some of the mindless outrages, however justified, of the so-called "permissive generation" trouble Doolittle. Still, unlike many of his own generation and the one following, he refused to make sweeping, categorical judgments, once commenting, "I don't give a damn how long their hair is, it's what's underneath that counts."

He willingly admits to being a "square"; the Doolittles prefer the music of their friend Fred Waring to that of the newest rock group—although their grandchildren keep them up to the moment on that front. The current cinema holds no attractions for them; the Doolittles march to a different drummer.

"I have a very simple philosophy of life," Doolittle once told an audience upon receiving the Horatio Alger Award. "I believe that we were put on this earth for a purpose. That purpose is to make it, within our capabilities, a better place in which to live.

"We can do this by painting a picture, writing a poem, building a bridge, protecting the environment, combating prejudice and injustice, providing help to those in need, or in thousands of other ways. Just so we serve."

That, concisely, is a philosophy which motivated one of the most "useful" lives of our American history. This belief in what might be simplified to the cliché "eternal verities" has produced a unique figure on the American scene, a man who grew out of a raw frontier, serving his fellow man while himself having one hell of a time and, in his eighth decade, who continues to serve and looks to the future.

What follows is the story of the man who has been guided by a "simple philosophy," the events that made him the Jimmy Doolittle of legend. What might also emerge, it is hoped, is a man of wisdom (acquired, he will insist, only with the passage of years), humor (often ironically self-deprecating), and warm humanity.

LOWELL THOMAS
EDWARD JABLONSKI
January 1976

Contents

LIST OF ILLUSTRATIONS

One

A succession of improbable and inexplicable events, circuitous journeyings, chance meetings and unlikely personalities culminated in the birth of James Harold Doolittle, American aviator, boxing champion, prospector, "crackpot pilot" (his own term), scientist, military leader, sportsman, member of the board, and general hell-raiser. His advent could almost be termed accidental, since his parents began their own independent lives on opposite sides of the continent.

Frank H. Doolittle, a restless and ambitious young man, was, in his son's words, "a carpenter by trade but an adventurer by inclination. He sailed around the Horn from Massachusetts in the early nineties." By the middle of the 1890s he had worked his way to the city of Alameda, set on an island in San Francisco Bay nestling up against the mainland near Oakland. It was then a bustling and thriving shipbuilding and shipping center; here Frank Doolittle could ply his trade and dream of Greater Things.

It was in Alameda that he met Rosa Shephard, a beauty with her own strong views, vitality, and ambitions. A common bond was undoubtedly strength of character and, although little is known of their courtship, Doolittle proposed and was accepted. He was then about thirty years old and Rosa twenty-five. Their only child was born in Alameda on December 14, 1896. The birth certificate records him only as "Doolittle," the James Harold being added later. The Doolittles were living at the time at 2426

Buena Vista Avenue and Frank Doolittle's occupation was registered as carpenter and, curiously, his birthplace as Connecticut.
(In later years his son consistently assumed that his father had
been born in Massachusetts; when Frank Doolittle died his obitu-
ary gave his birthplace as Detroit, Michigan. Such mundane details did not particularly interest Frank Doolittle—consequently
his son was never informed of his ancestry and family background
—and he remained, to his small family, a reticent and distant
man.)

Neither marriage nor fatherhood appear to have cured Frank
Doolittle of his love of adventure, his wanderlust, or his dream of
fortune. Within six months of the birth of his son Frank Doolittle
joined the literally thousands of other dreamers and adventurers,
plus scalawags, who also left homes and families to stampede
north to Canada in search of gold. But unlike the dreams of his
companions, Doolittle's were rooted to some extent in reality: for
he took skills and tools with him to the Klondike, in Yukon territory in 1897.

Somewhere along the way luck deserted him, the boat in which
he was traveling on the Yukon River was wrecked, taking all his
tools with it. Doolittle abandoned the search for gold and, staying
with the river, worked his way westward across Alaska. He finally
reached St. Michael, where he went to work for the prosperous
Alaska Commercial Company, which supplied the stampeders
with supplies. Until he could afford his own equipment, or a new
set of carpenter's tools, Doolittle had to content himself with
selling to his rivals in search of gold.

Although between the years of 1898 and 1905 about a hundred
million dollars in gold was scraped out of Yukon territory, primarily along the Klondike River, very little of it seems to have fallen
into the hands of the carpenter from Alameda. Instead, he waited
out his dream, supplying the more fortunate (and in some instances, the less—for many perished in the merciless setting) with
his well-crafted dog sleds. There being nothing for him in the
Klondike, Frank Doolittle by 1899 had worked his way northwestward across Norton Sound to the Seward Peninsula and to
Nome, Alaska, site of a new gold strike and a fulminating stampede.

Just why Doolittle imagined he would find the end of his rainbow in Nome is not known, but once established there he sent for

his family. This probably happened in the fall of 1899, before Nome became locked in by ice. Between November and May all shipping and virtually all mails (except that hauled over the tundra by dog sled) ceased.

Nome in the spring of 1900 was not the garden spot of the earth, or even of Alaska. Set in a barren, treeless tundra, it sprawled and jumbled from the very edge of the sea. The tundra, which turned marshy with the thaw, began just inland from the narrow, sandy beach and extended for about five miles to the gently rolling hills. These hills, green in the spring and summer months, were treeless and marked by streams that flowed into the Bering Sea. Some thirty miles beyond the hills, serrated mountains cut into the monotonous horizon.

When she arrived in May of 1900 aboard the S.S. *Zealandia*, Rosa Doolittle, accompanied by her sister Sarah Shephard, who had come along to assist in looking after "that child," should have been delighted even with the dismal Nomish landscape. A sea journey of nearly two weeks with an active and headstrong three-year-old could not have been a pleasure cruise. Perhaps between them the two young women, headstrong themselves, could have coped with young Jimmy. Sarah, in fact, should not even have been there; just recovering from pneumonia and bronchitis, she had been ordered by her doctor to a warm, dry, climate. Instead, she had chosen to accompany her sister to cold, wet Alaska.

The trip could only have been memorable and seemingly interminable, the voyage from Seattle alone—some 2,350 miles—took about eight days. Thus the first glimpse of Nome might have been welcome.

The first impression would be one of clutter, if the weather was clear enough to provide a view. Tents and varied wooden structures began literally at water's edge. Stacked, piled, and just dumped among these were the necessities shipped in for the stampeders: lumber, mining machinery, food stocks, beer kegs, and whiskey barrels—all of these and more—were strewn along the beach (shippers assumed that their responsibility ended there). Some of these stores ended up eventually in the hands of their rightful owners, but much did not, for the Nome of 1900 was not a center of law and order, and it was a political cesspool. It was a wide-open frontier town, bustling and brawling, peopled with dreamers like Frank Doolittle, good natured and reasonably honest wheelers and dealers like G. L. "Tex" Rickard, and the whole spectrum of humanity, the bulk of it from the darker edges. Saloons and lawyers in Nome proliferated—and there was plenty of business for both.

Seeing Nome for the first time from the ship did not enthrall every newcomer. "Many never left the ship," historian Ethel A. Becker has succinctly stated. "One look at the barren countryside was enough—gold or no gold."

There being no harbor at Nome, nor docks, just getting ashore was an adventure in itself. Ships would anchor off the town and be met by barges to take supplies and passengers ashore. If the ice had not broken up completely and was solid, teams of horses pulling sleds and hordes of people would come out to meet the boat; if the ice was gone by the time the ship arrived, the barges would take the passengers to land where, when the seas were calm, they could walk ashore via gangplank. If the surf happened to be up and tossing, passengers were lifted off the barges, like any other cargo, in a sling by derrick and deposited on the sandy beach.

Newcomers were called, with some disdain, *"chechakos,"* a word borrowed from the Eskimo roughly translated as "greenhorn" or "tenderfoot." According to folklore, it took one season in Nome's harsh environment to transform a *chechako* into a seasoned sourdough—as much a matter of survival as precise definition. It is likely that sourdough Doolittle, though happy to see his wife and child after three years, may have been disappointed with *chechako* Doolittle, who was no strapping boy. He was small, rather delicate, with what might have been considered a "pretty" face, dimpled chin, and long curly hair.

The father-son relationship did not prove to be a congenial one. "I was a miserable, spoiled kid," Doolittle recalls of that period. But it was more than that: the senior Doolittle was not an ideal father, especially of an only child. He had his dream and he had his standards; nothing, or very little, interfered with the dream and few people met his standards—certainly not a runt of a kid who could not even tie a bowline knot.

In time, the youngster learned to use his father's tools, "loved to build things" and to work with his hands. These skills he learned from his father, but the two were never close—"he did everything in the world for me except give me human companionship." Thus early in life was the son instilled with a sense of independence, self-reliance, even defiance. Despite his near-prettiness and the closer relationship with his mother, he was no classic mother's boy.

But then, Rosa Shephard Doolittle was no shrinking violet either; she, as was her sister Sarah, was obviously cut from sturdy pioneer stock. The sisters quickly adjusted to Nome's society and climate and kept constantly busy with various enterprises, including making and selling flowers fashioned from paper (in imitation of those that grew in the States), even beautiful pom-poms for the sled-dog harnesses. Sarah, as attractive as her sister, did not remain unmarried for long and soon became Mrs. Gus Borgen. Her daughter Emily was the first white girl to be born in Nome; she was Jimmy Doolittle's first and favorite cousin.

But it was his mother who was his most constant companion during the first months in Nome; his term for her is "Spartan." He recalled an incident to illustrate the term. One of their chores was to provide the household drinking water, there being no indoor running water. Water could be taken from the running streams nearby or, if these were frozen, from a creek about four miles north of Nome. There they could dig a hole through the ice, lower the five-gallon cans they had brought by dog sled, fill them, and mush back home.

On one of these trips to the creek the dog team had unexpectedly veered, causing one of the sled's handle bars to strike Rosa Doolittle in the side. Uncomplaining, mother—with son—continued on to the creek where they filled their dozen cans with water and then made the four-mile return trip home. Only after she had completed her chores did Rosa go to the local doctor to have her two broken ribs taped up.

The youngest Doolittle eventually learned to survive in Nome, which was noted for its brawling—later channeled by the enterprising Tex Rickard into profitable Saturday-night slugging matches at his Northern Saloon. Self-defense was learned early in Nome.

When he was about five or six Doolittle met a big Eskimo boy on the beach near town. For some reason, the latter began pushing Doolittle around. "Being inexperienced, I was fearless and lit into him . . ." The two tossed, tumbled, and flailed—this being the Doolittle method at the time. During this thrashing of the air, he succeeded in landing a fist on the Eskimo boy's nose and, to the horror of both, a stream of blood gushed forth; neither apparently had seen blood pour from the human nose before. "He thought he was dying," Doolittle recalls. "I thought I had killed an Eskimo. We both ran home to our mothers."

This fistic encounter set the tone of Doolittle's Nome years—and for some time to come. Many of his sharpest childhood memories center around fighting, the need to fight, and his love of fighting. Brawling in the streets of Nome was common and the young who witnessed it undoubtedly assumed it was the normal solution to most disagreements. While there were shootings from time to time in this last northern frontier, sheer physical combat was the most popular form of aggressive self-expression.

For Doolittle this kind of expression began the moment he entered school, followed by an example of his decisiveness. As recalled by his lively cousin, Emily Borgen (now Mrs. Roland W. McNamee), "an unauthorized trip to the barber shop to have his long, beautiful curls cut off reduced his mother to tears. I believe a promissory note was given by Jimmy to the barber for the service."

Though he had rid himself of the curls, the young Doolittle was burdened by two additional handicaps: his reputation in the schoolyard as a fearless scrapper and his size. The latter was painfully demonstrated when his teacher ordered him up to the blackboard to write the sentence: "I am the smallest boy in school." What she thought this would accomplish is a mystery.

Still, Doolittle's size and his pugnacity colored his early school life in Nome. As the smallest boy he was always the first to be challenged by the school toughs. His fighting style soon established him as a courageous, if not too smooth, fighter and after a series of wins (even over heavier and taller upper-graders), little Jimmy Doolittle was regarded with respect by his schoolmates.

This distinction, however, put him in the official role of school champion. As new stampeders arrived in Nome, their children were enrolled in school, and it devolved upon the "smallest boy in school" to initiate the *chechako*. An innocent newcomer, egged on by his schoolmates, would accept the challenge with some amusement and then find himself engaging with a tornado and pummeled to the frozen ground (or mud, depending on the season) until admitting unforeseen defeat. That Doolittle acquired much learning or any vestiges of culture in the combative Nome schoolhouse seems questionable. But he quickly adapted to the environment, its physical and social requirements, and survived. He became a tough youngster in a tough setting.

Not everyone did survive. He recalls, for example, that one of his own schoolmates was killed in the streets of Nome simply because he had stumbled and fell and was attacked by half-wild sled dogs. He himself still bears a scar from an encounter with a husky. Likewise Emily Borgen McNamee remembered being attacked by a dog and only saved by her heavy winter clothing.

She recalls, too, that her celebrated cousin evidenced some talent in school. "When Jimmy was in the fifth or sixth grade, I started school and immediately was able to 'gain much face' as his young cousin; my energetic relative had recently been called to the principal's office, having been caught drawing cartoons in class, one of which was reputed to be a remarkable likeness of the principal, Professor Grimm.

"Frequently during stormy weather Jimmy would take me to his home for lunch, as he lived near school. There was usually a pie, pudding, or eye-bugging dessert cooling on a shelf at the rear entrance outside the kitchen. I could never resist the temptation to run a forefinger over the top for a small sample. Jimmy never told on me even when under suspicion himself."

Tough little Jimmy Doolittle was genuinely fond of his cousin despite her sex and their age difference. "She was my favorite among the little people," he once said. "She was absolutely fearless." This last, of course, would be a quality he would admire. It would be demonstrated in Emily's love of "manly" sports, such as sliding off the roofs of houses into snow banks, dipping into the icy waters of the Bering Sea, or fishing with Eskimos after chopping a hole through the ice.

"There was a wondrous collection of gadgets in Jimmy's closet," Mrs. McNamee recalls. "Electrical wonders powered by batteries, odd shaped pieces of iron, scraps of wood, etc. The one I found most intriguing was a small object with two round long spools or handles which Jimmy would persuade me to hold while he gave me an electrical shock. I'd never refuse this small notice of my existence and always complied, clenching my teeth so I wouldn't cry out. Hero worship at the age of six! The closet was off limits to me unless on an escorted tour (for shock purposes on 'the gadget'), but the lure was sometimes irresistible and then when caught, outcries by owner were loud and clear: 'Make this brat leave my things alone!'

"I wasn't present when our young genius dismantled his mother's foot-treadle sewing machine, but hearsay had it that a trip to the woodshed was postponed if he could reassemble it in good condition. This was done and the machine proved more efficient than before. The woodshed trip was postponed indefinitely."

Though Doolittle tolerated Emily Borgen privately, when he was with the boys he reverted to type. "Jimmy and his friends took a dim view of little cousin following them around and I was known as The Nuisance and That Brat. When things got too unpleasant and my snide remarks and shrill giggles from a few paces to the rear had pushed the lads to the brink of retaliation, I would retreat in haste shrieking, 'All right for you James *Harold* Doo-little Jim,' knowing how he disliked his middle name."

These recollections would indicate that the children of Alaska were not unlike the children of Iowa or Wisconsin in their growing up, amusements, and relationships. The great difference lay in the environment. Mrs. McNamee, for example, did not see a tree until she was three years old (when she was taken to visit Seattle) —"I thought it was tall lettuce" (that being one of the few plants with a short enough growing period to be cultivated in Nome).

Life in Nome around the time Rosa Doolittle and her sister arrived with little Jimmy has been described by James Wickersham, who served as a district judge in Alaska for several years: "A public school building was erected in 1900 from lumber coming by summer ship from Puget Sound, and its rooms were filled with children, who loved their dogs, sleds and snow trails better than they did their books. Dog racing had already been organized as a permanent Arctic sport, and races from Nome to Solomon River and return were run by contesting teams for a fair division of a public purse and side bets.

"[The] Bering Sea was covered with a heavy coat of winter ice; pressure from the sea had driven the ice, many feet in thickness, high upon the shallow shores along the Nome front into huge rough ridges. The surrounding region—the ice fields of the sea, the wide frozen tundra and the nearby rolling Arctic mountains— were covered with a mantle of snow. But not even a north-wind blizzard could cool the ardor of holiday cheer. The great single electric light atop the Catholic church spire guided the Anvil Creek miners to town to enjoy the warmth and comfort of the New Year's festival. Every house in town blazed with the brilliance of newly hung electric light bulbs, crowds of revelers passed along down town streets, the sweet tones of music, sacred and profane, quickened every footstep and a general holiday spirit prevailed. The winter of 1901–02 at Nome was light-hearted, happy and gay."

The human response to the setting and the climate was physical: hard work and hard play. Those who survived were vigorous, high spirited, and in need of somewhat larger-than-life outlets for stored-up energies. The stampeders worked it off in the saloons and the "houses" of the tenderloin and in what appears to be Nome's most popular sport, indoors and out—brawling. However, as Doolittle told his biographer C. V. Glines, the youngsters of Nome held the dog-team drivers and long-distance runners in highest esteem. Wickersham also noted that dog-team races were considered great social events in Nome. "I didn't have any dogs," Doolittle told Glines, "so I ran."

He recalled that an immense gymnasium had been constructed in the town and there the runners prepared themselves for the great summer running event. The distances covered ranged from a hundred to two hundred miles (for the men; the boys covered lesser distances). As a boy, Doolittle participated in one of these long-distance races and "ran until I collapsed." This overexertion as a boy would later cause complications when Doolittle underwent medical examinations, because of an irregularity in his heartbeat.

While Doolittle was a growing young citizen of Nome, a little-reported event—it was certainly not mentioned in Nome—occurred in distant North Carolina. Three days after Doolittle's seventh birthday, on December 17, 1903, two bicycle mechanics named Wright from Dayton, Ohio, succeeded in flying a primitive aircraft off the sands of Kitty Hawk, North Carolina. They achieved both sustained and controlled flight and proved what so many were dead certain was impossible: that man could fly. This epochal demonstration, though the entire population of Nome and much of the rest of the world were unaware of it, would have great impact and significance in the future life of Jimmy Doolittle.

For the moment, however, he was more preoccupied with the

mode of transportation indigenous to Nome. To compensate for the lack of a true dog sled and to eliminate his son from the runner class, Frank Doolittle spent many hours carefully building a miniature sourdough dog sled, such as were used in the racing contests. This beautifully made—but still homemade—sled was to be little Jimmy's Christmas present that year. Christmas morning arrived and Doolittle learned that his friend next door had also received a sled—"a cheap little red coaster sled that his folks had bought at the local store."

Doolittle was desolated; he had received a "homemade" sled and his friend a gaudy "store-boughten" one. He expressed his views and dissatisfaction forcefully. Doolittle senior, who had built the sled with loving care, was crushed. It would be years later before Doolittle realized how thoughtlessly cruel he had been. "We just didn't communicate," he once said, "and it was all my fault."

However deep the psychic wounds, the incident was buried and Doolittle condescended to use the sled, having acquired "a dog team of one dog—oddly enough, its name was Josephine [this aside alluding to the coincidence of names; he would one day marry a Josephine]."

The boyhood world of Jimmy Doolittle, in a drab, featureless setting, was circumscribed by the sea, ice, and snow, the planked wooden main street, the muddy (or icy) lesser streets of Nome, and the marshy tundra of the spring and summer. When he was seven he accompanied his father on a trip to Seattle. The elder Doolittle had to replenish his lumber and replace worn-out tools.

To his son the sight of a great city was a revelation. The contrast between the frontier rawness of Nome and the metropolitan variety of Seattle made a deep impression. Until then he had no idea that the world consisted of other than mud, ice, tundra, and crude structures. The very fact that dwellings were painted was surprising to him. So was the size of the city, the "tall" buildings, the shops, trolleys, and automobiles—all made their impact on the boy.

"My values changed right then and there," he told Glines. "I saw everything in a new perspective and wanted very much to be a part of the exciting life I saw so briefly on that memorable trip."

Shortly after returning to Nome Doolittle went on his first "big-game" hunt. His father presented him with a single-shot .22 rifle and, one day while carrying it on a walk over the tundra, Doolittle spotted a lone teal duck in the middle of a large puddle. He stealthily crawled, Indian style, to the edge of the puddle and shot the duck and then retrieved it from the knee-deep water. It was a proud "big-game hunter" who paraded rather ostentatiously, and repeatedly, up and down the main street of Nome with the game in one hand and his rifle in the other.

The following four years of Doolittle's life were pretty much like the previous four. Life in Nome was a continual struggle for his family: Frank Doolittle managed to make ends meet, helped by the enterprise of his wife and her sister, but his dream—the big gold strike—eluded him; it always would. Nor would those miners he helped finance ever make a strike—or if they did, they never informed Frank Doolittle.

Rosa Doolittle felt that life in a raw, rough-and-tumble, town was having a pernicious effect upon her son. The winters were cruelly bitter and the summers were as much remembered for the mud as for the bright flowers that emblazoned the tundra. There were frightful epidemics (influenza and pneumonia) that decimated Nome's population in the long, cold winters. But with the coming of the new spring's thaw, eager and hopeful *chechakos* arrived in droves to fill the gap.

Nome was the most lawless town in Alaska; it did not even support an organized police force. What law there was—and it was chiefly political—was devoted to depriving the more simple miners of their claims. This came to light with the eruption of the notorious McKenzie-Noyes conspiracy trials in 1901 which resulted in the dismissal and fining of a highly placed judge, Arthur H. Noyes, and the imprisonment of a friend of then President McKinley, Alexander McKenzie. Whether the sharp dealings of these men touched the Doolittles is not known, but it is unlikely for Frank Doolittle certainly had no gold and little property in 1901. That was also the year in which the first hanging occurred in Nome: prospector Fred Hardy had been found guilty in the murder of his three partners.

Gangs often roved through the streets stealing anything—from the town's butter supply (which was then sold to the shops for which it was originally intended, only at higher prices) to an entire house (that is, until the theft was discovered by the rightful owners, two women, who drove the housenappers off with guns).

Gambling was practically a way of life; the man, or woman, who would travel to Nome to make his or her fortune was a born gambler. The saloons were numerous. Emily McNamee recalls that her house was wedged between two of them, one being named "The Bucket of Blood." These and the small cabins of Nome provided the tables and cards, and the prospector, frozen in for the winter, continued testing his luck, if not his skill, until he could get back out into the field again. The hoary story is told by Wickersham of one such prospector who appeared to be losing heavily at faro. When a friend cautioned him that he was undoubtedly being victimized, he replied, "Yes, what you say is probably true, but it's the only game in town."

Rosa Doolittle endured the imminence of a not always wholesome way of life for eight years—but that was enough. Her husband's dream of the Big Strike had not materialized; perhaps it never would. Even her imaginative enterprises with her sister Sarah, by then a mother of two girls, had lost their allure. Meanwhile young Jimmy was absorbing a liberal education in rowdiness, roughhouse, and lawlessness. When they managed to survive through another bitter winter without pneumonia and a summer without typhoid fever, it was considered a miracle. When would they exhaust their quota of miracles?

As far as Rosa Doolittle was concerned, they had no right to expect more. So, when the ice broke in the spring of 1908 and shipping opened up again, the Doolittles boarded one of the ships and headed homeward to California. It was Rosa's wish that son Jimmy be given a better education than the one then being offered in Nome. She wanted him to be somebody.

TWO

As if seeking an entirely new life, the Doolittles did not return to Alameda but proceeded southward to settle in Los Angeles. Their son would one day recall the neighborhood as "unvarnished," but the house in which he lived, at 1235 Catalina Street, was a comfortable two-story structure with a certain post-Victorian charm. Its yard was spacious and provided room for boyish adventures. While the Doolittles brought no Alaskan gold with them, they did manage to live in the "unvarnished" neighborhood in some comfort (certainly more than at Nome, with its pinched little frame house and density of neighbors).

The young Doolittle had no problem fitting himself into the pecking order of his new setting and quickly established himself as a fighter. As for Frank Doolittle, the adjustment was more difficult; when the old restlessness descended upon him, he uprooted himself and returned to Nome. Although he would send money whenever possible, the major burden of providing for their son devolved upon Rosa.

She saw to it that Jimmy went on to complete his grammar schooling. In 1910 he entered the Los Angeles Manual Arts High School, being the classmate of two others who would go on to future fame: Frank Capra, later a film director, and Lawrence Tibbett, who would make a name as a great singer. At the time, however, it was Capra who most impressed Doolittle, for he was top man on the school's pyramid team. Doolittle also revealed himself as an adept tumbler and acrobat, but his first love remained fighting. Thus his education might best be characterized as more physical than intellectual.

He was in his thirteenth year when aviation made its first impression on him. From January 10 through 20, 1910, the first great aviation meet held in the United States took place at Dominguez Field near Los Angeles, a few miles southwest of the city, near the site of present-day Compton. This meet was a sequel to the successful—and, in fact, first ever—one that had made news the previous year at Reims, in France.

The colorful poster for the Los Angeles meet promised "American & Foreign Aviators" plus "Daily Flights," all of which attracted large crowds arriving by streetcar, auto, and even horseback. The American whose name meant most at the meet was Glenn Curtiss, who established a new world's speed record with a passenger, no less than 55 miles per hour; the foreign star was Louis Paulhan, who set a new world's altitude record (4,165 feet) and made a record-breaking distance flight of 75 miles in just under two hours flying time. Paulhan took nearly $20,000 in prize money with him when he returned to France after the meet.

The young Doolittle also watched two local star airmen, Roy Knabenshue and Lincoln Beachey, thrill the crowds with a dirigible race (which Beachey won). The diffident Wright brothers, bitter rivals to Curtiss, were represented by pilot Arch Hoxsey who flew their new Model B, but to no great victory.

Besides the derring-do, the spectators were treated to a cross-section of aviation development of the period: the dirigible as well as different types of aircraft—Paulhan's Farman as well as the Curtiss and Wright designs. Just to see these curious vehicles on the ground and, more astonishingly, in the air, was exciting, even inspiring.

For Jimmy Doolittle, this inspiration tarried for nearly two years till the day, when going through back issues of *Popular Mechanics* magazine, the embryo airman discovered in the January–June 1909 issue an article by Carl Bates entitled "How to Make a Glider." It was, according to the plans, an impressive structure, a biplane with an eighteen-foot wingspan resembling the successful Chanute gliders of the period. It was what was known as a "hang glider," which was literally worn by the pilot like a garment with wings; hanging as he was from the structure, his legs and feet served as the craft's landing gear.

His father's son, Doolittle could foresee no problems with the construction of a glider; raising the money for the materials was a bit more formidable and took time. What little his mother could spare and what he could earn at odd jobs went toward the accumulation of materials for the craft, all of it of first quality such as "straight-grained spruce, free from knots," as well as muslin to cover wings and tail, plus piano wire for strengthening.

With magazine, tools, and materials in hand Jimmy Doolittle began his first lesson in aviation. "A gliding machine," Bates had written, "is a motorless aeroplane or flying-machine, propelled by gravity and designed to carry a passenger through the air from a high point to a lower point some distance away. Flying a glider is simply coasting down hill on air, and is the most interesting and exciting sport imaginable."

Spurred on by that promise, Doolittle quickly completed the glider and was eager for the test flight. It was a beauty, graceful, light, and yet sturdy with all its businesslike wiring. Nearby there was a spot where a street had been cut through a hill and, since he required "a high point" (the hill) and "a lower point" (the street about fifteen feet below), he knew he had his flying field.

In 1912, during the pre-Freeway epoch, the area around Los Angeles had relatively little traffic (though it was, thanks to the Dominguez Field meet, beginning to burgeon as a modest aviation center). So it was that fifteen-year-old Jimmy Doolittle had little to worry him as far as the automobile was concerned as he hauled his handmade glider to the cliff near the road. He carefully surveyed the scene—all clear—then stood back a good running distance from the cliff edge, donned his wings, and "ran like anything, jumped off the cliff, and tried to glide down. Unfortunately, the tail of the glider hit the edge of the cliff and it came straight down and broke the glider up pretty badly. It banged me up a little bit, but not too much."

Upon recovery from the jolt of dropping fifteen feet encumbered by his handiwork, Doolittle gathered up the pieces and dragged them home. Undaunted, he immediately set to work repairing the damage, meanwhile theorizing about the cause of his failure. Obviously he had not been able to run fast enough to clear the edge of the cliff: it was a problem of attaining enough momentum to reach proper air speed. This gave birth to another idea.

"One of my friends," he recounts, "had access to his father's car. So we got out on a nice level stretch, we put a rope on the glider and a rope on the end of the car. He started pulling the glider faster and faster and faster—and I kept running faster and faster and faster. Soon I couldn't run any faster; I leaped up into the air, put the tail down and planned to glide. But again it cracked up, this time rolled up into a ball and there wasn't really enough glider left to build."

Not if the budding aeronautical engineer continued thinking in terms of the original biplane configuration. But then, in yet another issue of *Popular Mechanics,* he came upon plans for the diminutive Demoiselle which had been contributed by the Brazilian air pioneer, living in France, Alberto Santos-Dumont. It was an exquisitely designed high-wing monoplane powered by a small two-cylinder engine. Since there was not enough from Doolittle's second venture into flight to reconstruct the original glider, there was enough in the ball of material to approximate the Demoiselle. The problem of power could be solved by the acquisition of a motorcycle engine. To rationalize the original Santos-Dumont plans with the material on hand, many Doolittle modifications were introduced which might have given even the doughty Brazilian pause.

At best, the Demoiselle was a tricky plane to fly. It may have been this aircraft especially—and there were countless others— that Doolittle had in mind when once describing this swaddling-clothes epoch of aviation: "In those days the pilots would go out, wet their index finger, hold it up, and if it got cool on one side, there was too much wind to fly."

As it turned out, it was in fact an ill wind that blew him good. Having gathered enough bits and pieces from his previous experiment together, he began construction again; he also acquired a pair of bicycle wheels and, after a time, began saving money for the motorcycle engine. One night, however, a strong wind, "probably a fortunate wind," swept through the neighborhood, snatched up the unfinished quasi-Demoiselle, and scattered it over several adjacent backyards. This accomplished fully what the earlier attempts had not; it also closed that early phase of Doolittle's aviation years. "After those three failures," he would observe some years later, "I was out of money, I was out of materials, and a little bit out of enthusiasm."

After he had emerged as one of the great figures in aviation, Doolittle was invited to become a member of the Early Birds, an organization of airmen who had flown before the First World War. Having heard of his early glider "experiments," the group believed that Doolittle was eligible for membership. But he declined "because not even by the most magnanimous stretch of the human imagination could I claim that I had ever achieved controlled flight" in 1912.

Not that he lacked triumphs during this period of his life; he may not have been eligible for membership in the Early Birds, but there were prizes to be won with his fists. In this sphere he was in full control—there were no design intricacies, no theoretic mysteries, just simple, head-on attacks, as he had learned so well in Nome. By the time he entered Manual Arts High School, he was a 105-pound dynamo, cocky, imbued with a love for fighting.

Fortunately for Doolittle, the school's English teacher, Forest Bailey, doubled as boxing coach. He admired the bantamweight's courage and strength, but found him lacking in style. It was Bailey who took the young Doolittle in hand and pointed out the disadvantages of his flailing attack approach and began introducing him to the finer points of boxing. Related to this was some even more wholesome advice: anger was no substitute, however well it had served Doolittle in the past, for a more objective, more "scientific" approach. Under Bailey's tutelage Doolittle was transformed from a street fighter into a boxer.

Not that the transformation was immediately ideal or complete; the ex-Nomite found it difficult to ignore a challenge and now and then this stirred up his mother, when word reached her of his fighting in the street or when he came home in a battered state. Some of this came about honestly—in the school gym or in an amateur bout in which he earned prize money to go into his glider. But there were times when he came home slightly used because of a casual brawl and earned a solid lecture from Rosa Doolittle. The substance of these admonitions, though heeded, were hardly adhered to.

The resourceful Rosa Doolittle ultimately made her point in a manner her son never forgot. The lesson began innocently enough at a Saturday night dance in his fifteenth year. He had accompanied two friends and the sister of one who was the fiancée of the other; the engaged pair were older than Doolittle. The event was a party given by a local dairy for its drivers and was believed by Doolittle and his friends to be an open house. However, some time during the evening a committee began moving among the guests collecting admission fees. This was a surprise to the Doolittle group to begin with, but the asking price impressed them as rather steep. Words ensued and action followed. "Things got a bit rough," Doolittle recalled later. During this phase of the evening's entertainment the sister/fiancée was jostled by one of the fees committeemen and was pushed down a flight of stairs.

Doolittle reacted with gentlemanly outrage, planting a good solid blow upon the man, a truck driver much older than he, with telling force. Before the incident could evolve into a full-scale ballroom brawl, someone with sense intervened to suggest that the contenders repair to the street below. This was done, the crowd followed and, when the two fighters squared off, formed a ring around them. This was not at all good for Doolittle, for in that circle were friends of his adversary so that when he stepped too close to the onlookers, one of the friends would punch him in the side or the back. The first order of strategy was to stay in the very center of the improvised ring.

Soon this problem was cleared up and a modicum of sportsmanship introduced into the fight by the arrival of two policemen. Their presence endowed the rough proceedings with a bit of Queensberry, making it possible for Doolittle, though outweighed and probably not as experienced as his opponent, to hold his own rather well. But what with the noise and the mere fact of a crowd gathering, the curiosity of a police sergeant was aroused and, with his arrival upon the scene, the two spectator policemen turned zealous. They broke up the battle and arrested both contenders.

Their offense, both a petty and fairly common one, required no large fine, so soon the truck driver was free. But not Jimmy Doolittle, who had begun the evening assuming he was going to a free dance. One of the policemen, realizing that their remaining prisoner was a boy of fifteen, decided to call Rosa Doolittle. The conversation went roughly like this:

POLICEMAN: Mrs. Doolittle, I'm calling from the station house—we have your son here.

ROSA DOOLITTLE: What has he done?

POLICEMAN: He was arrested for fighting in the street.

ROSA DOOLITTLE: All right. I'll be around Monday morning
and get him out in time for school.

She was a lady of her word and her combative son, despite the
purity of the motive that had put him on the spot, languished in
jail over the weekend. He also suffered from the cold in his
unheated cell—this despite the issuance of two blankets when he
was locked up. The groans from the prisoner in the adjoining cell
prompted him to give up one of his blankets since his neighbor
complained, through chattering teeth, of the cold. Thus did
Doolittle spend two nights shivering under his single blanket.

On Monday morning, when Rosa Doolittle arrived to release
him, Doolittle learned that the prisoner in the neighboring cell had
slept rather cosily under three blankets. As he pondered the moral
of that fact, he received a running commentary from his mother
all the way to Manual Arts that Monday morning. It was not the
lecture as much the experience itself that chastened the chilled
Doolittle: there would be no more street brawls for him.

The incident did not, however, dampen his enthusiasm for boxing, in which he was encouraged by the interest of Forest Bailey.
Trained by Bailey, Doolittle entered the Pacific Coast amateur
boxing matches in 1912 at the Los Angeles Athletic Club. That
year Jimmy Doolittle, all 105 pounds of him, became amateur
flyweight champion of the Pacific Coast. Perhaps, despite his
mother's objections, he had found his true calling.

He had already joined the St. Joseph Young Men's Club, appearing in its regular boxing bouts and representing it in tourna-
ments. Winning the Pacific Coast championship made him much
in demand for more bouts, a fact which disturbed Rosa Doolittle.
Although he would win some twenty bouts, her son came home
battered from time to time. Realizing that there would be no more
nights in jail for moralizing purposes, she tried simple bribery. If
she bought him a motorcycle, would he give up boxing?

Her reasoning was sound, and young Jimmy accepted the offer
—the motorcycle afforded him the proximity to danger that boxing did, with only his own skill to keep it from coming too close;
and there was the added attraction of speed. There was even
more: the engine which could be worked on and the vehicle itself,

not to mention the fine sound it made wide open as he roared around the countryside. Not being hemmed in by the ropes of the boxing ring exercised his sense of freedom, and he truly loved it.

This interlude came to a grinding halt one day when he collided with an automobile and spent no less than six weeks in a hospital and an additional three on crutches (his most serious injury was a broken foot). Motorcycleless, Jimmy Doolittle returned to the St. Joseph's Young Men's Club. Although his foot had healed, he knew that the nine weeks of enforced inactivity had done nothing for his boxing form. Talked into appearing in an exhibition match —with the concession that it would only be that: a no-decision contest—the out-of-shape Doolittle climbed into the ring and soon proved how right he had been. For three rounds he simply could not keep up with his opponent, which was mortifying enough, but then at the close of the exhibition, the referee raised the hand of the other boxer, and Jimmy Doolittle suffered his first defeat in the ring. The match-makers had also gone back on their word about a no-decision contest, so Doolittle dropped out of the club, feeling that he had been ill-used.

Shortly after, he suffered yet another kind of defeat in connection with boxing. He took a job as sparring partner for the then-champion West Coast bantam-weight, "Kid" Williams. He also did some sparring with Williams' challenger, Ed Campie. In his workouts Doolittle appraised each man and, when the fight came up, deciding to exploit his first-hand, inside information, put his money on the challenger, who appeared to be the smarter, more aggressive puncher. But it was "Kid" Williams who remained the champion by outpointing Campie in the bout. Doolittle had painfully acquired another lesson and never put his money on a boxing match again.

It was during this period while he was a student at Manual Arts High School and active in boxing that Doolittle made what would prove to be a lifetime discovery in the gentle, soft-spoken person of a pretty, slender girl named Josephine Daniels. She and her family had originally come to Los Angeles from Louisiana—she spoke with a soft, Southern inflection that fascinated the infatuated boxer-student. (Parenthetically, it might be noted that when she was born, her parents had expected, indeed, counted on, a boy: Joseph. Since fate had decided against them, the Danielses simply named the baby, Josephine. Their original wish was perpetuated in Josephine's nickname—"Joe," with a final "e.")

The Danielses came from a somewhat higher social level than the Doolittles and though deeply attracted to her, Doolittle regarded Josephine as somewhat snobbish; she, in turn, thought him a roughneck who wasted his time and energies in brawling. Joe Daniels was serious about her schooling, got all "As," and was preparing for a career in library work. What the brash Jimmy Doolittle was getting ready for she could not fathom.

She did join Rosa Doolittle in the campaign against the physical side of his life and in favor of his giving more serious attention to study. Under this influence, Doolittle began talking of going on to college and taking up mining engineering; he might even head for Alaska and succeed where his father continued to fail. He was obviously serious about Joe Daniels, for in their last year at Manual Arts he stunned her by suggesting that they marry. It was, of course, out of the question—her parents would not approve of her marrying a boy whose only skill appeared to be boxing.

Rebuffed but not altogether discouraged, Jimmy Doolittle decided he would show them. Upon graduation from Manual Arts High School, he would go north and seek his fortune. "When I got out of high school," he has said, "I thought I knew about all there was to know." So it was that in the summer of 1914 young Doolittle took his savings and headed for Alaska; at seventeen his sense of independence was highly developed and he managed to reach Seward, in the south, his father having moved there from Nome. Soon after his son's arrival, he moved again—this time to Anchorage, his searching restlessness still very much a part of his nature.

Doolittle senior owned two lots in Seward, a small residential property and a more sizable business parcel. Before setting out for Anchorage, the two, under Frank Doolittle's supervision, built a house—"more exactly, a shack"—on the small lot. (For many years after his father's death, Doolittle paid taxes on the two properties, finally deciding to sell them. The real estate agent, who coincidentally happened to be the tax collector, informed him that the shack was occupied and that the total value of the properties, including shack, was less than the taxes he paid each year. Doolittle decided to give up being a landlord and stopped paying taxes on his Seward properties.)

His arrival and reunion with his father stirred up old and not very pleasant memories for Doolittle. As usual, these had to do with his uneasy relationship with his father. He recalled a particularly unhappy incident that had occurred about half a dozen years before, just before the move to Los Angeles. A boat had been pulled up on the beach at Nome for the winter and a gang of boys proceeded to paint—and thus ruin—the engine, inside and out. Although he had not participated in the vandalism, Doolittle was aware of it.

When the enraged owner sought vengeance, he naturally included the "Doolittle boy" among the culprits. Despite his son's honest denials, Frank Doolittle punished him with a thrashing. When he had finished, his son turned to him and said, "I have never lied to you. You have just whipped me for something I didn't do and as soon as I am big enough I will whip you."

The moment Doolittle arrived in Anchorage, his father recalled the incident. "Do you remember what you said to me when I whipped you?"

"Yes, sir," Doolittle answered. "Are you satisfied I can do it?"

"Yes, I am sure you can."

"Then," his son informed him, "it will not be necessary."

In retrospect, Doolittle is "not particularly proud of this encounter," but it does reveal two lifelong traits: while forgiving, he never forgot an injustice and he had an aversion to lying and the liar. Since a liar was generally ashamed or afraid to admit his guilt, Doolittle believed, he was also "probably a coward."

The reunion of father and son, while still prickly, marked an improvement over their past relationship; perhaps both had matured during the few years of separation. Perhaps the senior Doolittle was impressed with his son's "challenge, although the whipping never occurred," as well as the work he put in on the shack. For his part, Doolittle *fils* soon learned he still had a lot to learn about making his fortune in Alaska.

Prospecting, he found, offered no easy avenue to fortune. He learned something, too, about the complexity of the world economy. Soon after he had arrived and had decided that maybe the search for gold was not for him, the effect of the eruption of war in Europe reached Alaska. British investments were drained away from several Alaskan industries to feed the war machine on the Western Front; there was, then, very little work of any kind to be found in Alaska.

Doolittle's supply of money had been invested mainly in provisions, which eventually dwindled down to some onions, potatoes, and oatmeal. The oatmeal, he found, he was sharing with some

local mice. "You had to pick out the little black oatmeals," he recalls, "and leave the white oatmeals before you could eat it."

That supply eventually depleted and, totally moneyless, Doolittle spent his latter days in Alaska at Six Mile Creek fishing for his
breakfast and, as it turned out, lunch and dinner. "I subsisted
completely on salmon three times a day for, I guess, the better
part of three weeks." (It would be twenty years before he could
bear to eat salmon again.) He finally did get work as a cabin boy
on a ship that took him as far as Seattle. Bent on getting home, he
stowed away aboard another ship, the S.S. *Yale,* to arrive in Los
Angeles in time for the new school semester. Under the urging of
Joe Daniels and, of course, his mother, Doolittle decided to go on
with his schooling and enrolled in courses primarily in mining engineering at Los Angeles Junior College in the fall of 1915.

He resumed his rather one-sided "romance" with Joe Daniels,
announcing that since he had not struck it rich in Alaska, their
wedding would necessarily be postponed for a while. Since she
had never said Yes, let alone set any date, Joe Daniels was more
bemused than disappointed by Doolittle's presumption. She had,
however, more immediate problems to confront. Unable to continue on to college because of her father's business reverses, she
took a job in a department store. Besides, Doolittle was only one
among many young men she was seeing. Sunday afternoons were
generally set aside by Doolittle for visits to the Daniels house on
the East Side. Doolittle was frequently accompanied by his friend
William Downs, who recalls that the Daniels girls, Joe and her
sister Grace, were regarded as "Sunday girls, that is, nice girls," to
be visited at home; Friday night or Saturday night dance girls
were a different matter.

Downs, a life-long friend, recalls his first impression of the
young Jimmy Doolittle. They had met at Manual Arts High
School, from which Downs and his brother John had been ex-
pelled for prankishly clipping the hair of several fellow students.
This marked the Downses as tough guys and thus, in the eyes of
Doolittle, admirable. Bill Downs was not likewise impressed when
he first met Doolittle—"he was little, skinny, and had all that
curly hair." It was only after the Downs brothers were permitted
to return to school and they saw Doolittle in action on the tumbling team, and especially in the boxing ring, that the mutual ad-
miration began.

Downs, a hunter from early boyhood, and Doolittle would often go hunting in the mountains and hills around Los Angeles or fishing in San Diego Canyon. "We were pretty self-reliant," Downs recalls of those days. He lent Doolittle a rifle, and they would take bedrolls and supplies and camp in the wild mountains for days. They would hop a convenient freight train, since neither owned an automobile, and then hike to their campsite.

Downs recalls that in all their sixty-odd years of friendship, he and Doolittle never exchanged a harsh word. During one of their hunting expeditions, however, there was a moment of strain. Their luck had not been good and their supply of food was so depleted they had just about decided to abandon the hunt and return to Los Angeles the next day. They then split up and went off each on his own to have one final try. Doolittle was the lucky one; he bagged a deer and returned to camp. Rather jubilant, he felt he would surprise Bill Downs with dinner.

Generally it was Downs who cooked for them—"I did the cooking, he was the dishwasher"—but Doolittle was anxious to pull off his surprise; which he did in a curious fashion. Rice, he thought, would be good to have, so he got the water to boiling (as he had seen Bill Downs do) and then proceeded to dump their last sack of rice into the water. When Downs, deerless, returned to camp he found his hunting companion struggling with more rice than either could handle, as it came "boiling out of the pot like popcorn."

Gazing upon the mess, Downs could only say, "Damn it, Jimmy, some times I don't think you've got a god-damned bit of sense." With the evidence so overwhelming, Doolittle agreed and returned to dishwashing.

In activities like this he spent his latter teen years, in the mountains and hills, fishing in streams or the ocean—a rugged, outdoor life. This, of course, when he was not in school, where he also led a rugged existence boxing and tumbling. But surprisingly, there was a marked upturn in the direction of scholarship. After two years at Los Angeles Junior College, he continued in mining engineering at the University of California at Berkeley, entering as a junior in the fall of 1916.

It was during his junior year at Berkeley that Doolittle once again took up boxing and also worked out in the gym on the mat and on the horizontal and parallel bars. On the latter he demonstrated a phenomenal sense of balance. But he still preferred boxing, and when he learned that a team was forming he presented himself to the instructor, Marcus Freed. Doolittle, then about nineteen, weighed roughly 130 pounds and was quickly informed that the lightweight and also the welterweight positions on the team had been filled but they didn't have a good middleweight. Undaunted, Doolittle offered to move up a couple of notches, into the middleweight (i.e. 160-pound) spot.

Freed studied him doubtfully and said there were three men contending for that position; Doolittle offered to become the fourth. He was persuasive and Freed permitted him to go into the ring with one of the three, a youth some thirty pounds heavier, several inches taller, and with a longer reach than Doolittle. He studied his smaller challenger with some amusement, they touched gloves, and Doolittle moved swiftly under the other's guard. Two quick blows and the bigger youth was flat on his back. Moments later, the second contender went the same route. And on the following day, though it took longer, Doolittle became the middleweight champion of the University of California, who would represent his school in the match with their archrival, Stanford.

During the week that followed Doolittle was coached by Freed, who took into consideration the problem of weight and reach. But, he pointed out, Doolittle had speed and a remarkable, explosive punch. "You can knock out anyone you can hit," Freed assured him, but reaching the opponent was the problem. Doolittle, in turn, assured Freed that he would move fast. And nothing spurred him on so much as seeing his adversary the following week climb into the ring and smilingly appraise him. The tall man from Stanford, Doolittle imagined, was a bit condescending and his smile either meant that he would make it a brief fight or was a promise not to hurt the little boxer from Berkeley. Whatever the intent, it angered Doolittle, and he rushed from his corner at the sound of the bell, moved in under the taller man's gloves, and planted a solid blow on his chin—and smiling, the man dropped to the canvas.

After some seconds, during which he was counted out, the tall youth regained consciousness and, grinning, walked a little uncertainly across the ring, introduced himself as Eric Pedley, and congratulated Doolittle on his skill.

H's rage abated by his victory and Pedley's uncommon show of good sportsmanship, Doolittle dismissed it all with a remark about a "lucky punch." Pedley assured him it was no lucky punch and that, indeed, the best man had won and deservedly.

(Pedley some years later would become a member of the U. S. International Polo Team. During one of the matches Doolittle, by then a noted aviator, sought out Pedley between chukkers to congratulate him on his polo. "My name is Doolittle," he informed Pedley. Pedley's face lit up. "Ah, yes, I recall we met some fifteen years ago, rather informally.")

After the Pedley bout, on the same day, Doolittle boxed an exhibition match with Walter Gordon, the California heavyweight contender, as his opponent from Stanford failed to appear.

Having returned to boxing, Doolittle earned a little extra money for schooling and fuel for a new motorcycle by participating in exhibition bouts. He even adopted a new name, "Jimmy Pierce," for the role. Freed apparently had high hopes for him and began setting up matches with name boxers, which was fine with "Jimmy Pierce." They had agreed that it would be a good idea to seek a match for Doolittle with Willie Hoppe, a celebrated boxer in the San Francisco area—a bout with him would add luster to the name of "Jimmy Pierce."

Together, Doolittle and Freed visited one of the more celebrated boxing hangouts, a gym where they hoped to discuss their plan with a tough promoter named Jim Griffith. They encountered skepticism upon invoking the name of Hoppe, though Griffith was willing to consider the idea. He then suggested that he would like to observe the young challenger by matching him with one "Spider" Reilly then and there. Reilly was no hitter, but he could move around the ring like a dancer—which is exactly what he did, keeping his distance and tapping away at "Jimmy Pierce," who, in turn, soon became enraged by the performance. Coach Freed's teachings went out the window as Doolittle resorted to his flailing Nome tactics—all the while Reilly deftly danced, eluded, and tapped him.

Griffith had seen enough. He stopped the match and "Jimmy Pierce's" boxing career was over before it had really begun. Humiliated by his showing, Doolittle, in what he still regards as the "wisest decision" he ever made, gave up the ring to concentrate on mining.

Three

Doolittle continued with his studies in mining engineering, particularly enjoying the work with the dean of the School of Mines, Andrew Lawson. He was not only a fine teacher, but also a successful consultant to mine owners and could earn as much as $100 a day in that capacity. This had a fine ring to his pupil. Students were encouraged by Lawson to attain some practical experience by working in mines during the summer vacation period.

During his junior year, in April of 1917, the United States declared war on Germany. But at the moment world events had not quite penetrated into Doolittle's academic world and had no real effect on him. He made plans to head out for the Comstock Lode in Nevada, near Virginia City, as soon as the semester ended.

Bill Downs joined him and the two set off northeastward, in tandem, on Doolittle's motorcycle. Somewhere in northern California they ran into trouble: they were arrested for speeding. The judge, upon hearing they were dashing along at an excessive speed of fifty miles an hour, pronounced them "wicked" (this was the precise word as recalled by Downs) and fined them fifteen dollars. Between them the two culprits managed to raise only twelve, but the upholder of the law would not settle for that. He asked the arresting officer, who was beginning to feel ashamed in the face of official cupidity, if there were anything of value—at least three dollars worth—he could seize off the vehicle of the devil on which the two had breezed into town.

There was a carbide light, the officer told him, but it was worth only fifty cents and, besides, it was out of carbide. The motorcycle was thus left intact, but no argument could persuade the judge to leave them with enough money to enable them at least to return to Berkeley. Whichever way they went now was all the same, so they continued on eastward. They had bedrolls and a rifle, so that sleeping in the hills and desert was no problem and they could live off the land by shooting game and "borrowing" corn and potatoes from farms along the way. They planned to worry about the fuel problem when it ultimately confronted them.

Later, when they had just climbed a hill, they passed an automobile stalled on the highway. As they came alongside they saw an old man seated inside. They turned back to see if he were in trouble and learned that the car had simply stopped functioning. The old man's son had begun walking through the desert to find help—that had been some time before. Doolittle opened up the hood of the automobile and began tinkering; after some time, he coaxed the engine back to life. Bill Downs, who had injured his foot, took the wheel, and with Doolittle following with the motorcycle, they all set off in search of the son whom they found some miles ahead. In the several hours that he had been walking, he had not come across a single person. His father, out of gratitude, presented mechanic Doolittle with two dollars—which solved their fuel problem till they reached Virginia City, where they found work in the Big Max mine in the Comstock Lode.

As newcomers, and college boys besides, they were assigned the more unpleasant jobs. The mine descended nearly 3,000 feet into the earth and was what is known as a "hot mine" because of the proximity of underground hot springs to its shafts and drifts. Downs recalls operating machinery below the earth while seated on a cake of ice. Seepage by boiling water was another problem and pumps were used to drain the mine. It fell to Doolittle on the Fourth of July, when all the other miners had the day off, to remain along with an old timer to man the pump.

The work brought in overtime pay, but it was very monotonous. The old miner merely impressed Doolittle with the importance of maintaining a certain water level and not letting the pump go dry. Whereupon, he settled down for a nap. Doolittle maintained vigilance, but the steady beating of the pump eventually lulled him off to sleep also. As the two men slept, the pump continued its work.

Doolittle awoke suddenly sensing something was not right; the sound of the pump had stopped and the water level in the mine was rising. He awakened the old timer, who immediately muttered a few words, among them "damned dumb college kids," and then informed Doolittle that he—Doolittle—would have to get the pump going again. The pump by then was deep under scalding water.

To reach it he would have to wade hip deep in the steaming seepage, plunge his hands beneath the surface into the sump where the pump was situated and prime it with a hand lever. It was an excruciatingly painful job, but Doolittle managed it under the stern gaze of the old timer. While his falling asleep had not endeared him to his grizzled companion, Doolittle's performance in the boiling water earned him the respect of the old man. His red, swollen arms and legs, however, earned him several hours of agony.

One other experience that summer won Doolittle further respect from veteran miners and at the same time underscored the risks associated with the work he hoped one day to do. Toward the close of the summer while he was working in one of the Comstock "drifts" (an offshoot leading from the main shaft), he—and the others—heard a snapping sound, loud noises, a crash, and then silence. The commotion had come from the shaft and examination revealed that the cable on the cage which was used to bring up the ore had snapped. This was an ominous discovery because the cage also doubled as an elevator to bring the men to the surface.

Doolittle's work crew was then at the 2,700-foot level; the bottom of the mine, where the cage was, lay 200 feet below. There had been two men in the cage when it fell. The question was had they survived and, if so, how badly were they injured? The foreman asked if anyone would volunteer to be lowered by rope to the bottom of the shaft to learn of the fate of the two men. Doolittle volunteered, saying, "I'm the lightest and I know first aid."

Even before he reached bottom his carbide lamp began to flicker; obviously there was not enough oxygen in this part of the mine to sustain the light. Doolittle shouted to the men above and, there being no time to send to the surface for an oxygen line, someone began hosing water into the shaft. This extinguished Doolittle's lamp completely, but it also brought oxygen, besides stirring up the still air which also increased the oxygen supply in the shaft. In total blackness Doolittle eventually found the cage and soon learned that it held the bodies of two dead men. He shouted up again and another miner was lowered down. Together they fastened a new cable to the crushed, and by then very hot, cage which then could be raised with its cargo of living and dead. From that incident on, Doolittle was treated by his co-workers as a real "hard rock" miner and not as a despised "college kid."

The rest of their stay passed without incident and early in September Doolittle and Downs mounted the motorcycle for the return to Berkeley. They had gained the respect of their colleagues and were invited to return the following year. But they were never to return to work on the Comstock Lode again.

The Berkeley campus to which Doolittle returned was not the one he had left several weeks before. Unlike Virginia City, the air was charged with talk and news of the war in Europe. Caught up in the fever, many of his classmates had already enlisted; young men were eager "to do their part." Military uniforms were common on the campus and youngsters wore them with an air of decided smartness in town. With all this bustle, excitement, and promise of adventure, another year of classroom work held little attraction for Doolittle.

Instead of enrolling both he and Bill Downs decided to enlist, the latter in the U. S. Army. Doolittle was a bit more selective; the call to participate in a great adventure was not quite enough. The glamor of no man's land did not impress him; he had other things in mind and decided he would like to try his hand at aviation. This was accomplished in 1917 by enlisting in the Aviation Section of the U. S. Signal Corps, there being no true U.S. air force at the time. Aircraft, in fact, were not taken very seriously by traditional military men. However, the news from Europe frequently reported the exploits of intrepid airmen, some of whose names—Albert Ball, Georges Guynemer, Manfred von Richthofen, the famous "Red Baron"—had become familiar to most Americans.

So it was that Doolittle, pondering what he could do in the war, was again drawn to flying and signed up with the Signal Corps, giving as his preference a desire to serve as a pursuit pilot. Needless to say, perhaps, the most junior of the armed services, practically a stepchild, was a bit disorganized in September of 1917. When the United States declared war on the Central Powers the previous April, one historian noted, the Aviation Section "had 55 serviceable airplanes, of which 51 were obsolete and the other 4 were obsolescent." Great plans were drawn up to swell the ranks of pilots from April's 139 to some 5,000 by 1918.

Once he had enlisted Doolittle was a little disappointed when told to go home for a while; he would be called when needed. This had not been in his plan at all; he had dropped out of school and here he was, adrift again.

"This was a period of, I suppose the term is frugality, because I had no income and a continuing desire to eat." He discovered a little bar with a restaurant where for fifteen cents he could get a very large bowl of bean soup. Each table held two tall stacks of bread slices and, once he had obtained his bowl, Doolittle would sit at a table, have his soup, and eat both stacks of bread. By the third day the manager, immediately upon seeing Doolittle enter, would remove the bread from all the tables. This avenue of nourishment closed to him, Doolittle found a job in a tin-can factory in San Francisco—on the night shift, because women worked the factory during the day. It was a hungry Doolittle who worked his first week there and then expectantly went by to collect his first week's check. He was informed that the company always held out the first week's check until the employee was discharged or quit. Doolittle quit on the spot: "I had to quit to eat."

Unemployed again, though temporarily staving off starvation, he found another job, this time as a hard-rock miner in a quicksilver mine, the January Jones Mine in Napa County, California. In the beginning he operated a water liner, a kind of drill, but when the compressor went out, he was reduced to hand drilling and eventually was demoted to the position of a lowly pusher of a handcar, moving the quicksilver ore out of the mine. When he finally received orders to report to the University of California for ground school training, he left the mine with no regrets.

The ensuing eight weeks were not very exciting and required a minimum of intrepidity, as Doolittle and the other members of his class began learning the techniques of flight and war in the air. There were courses in aerodynamics, navigation, radio telegraphy, meteorology, as well as the mechanics of aircraft, from the propeller to the intricacies of the ignition system. There were even less rewarding subjects for the man of action, such as administration, military life, even close-order drill. Chafing, Doolittle endured what at times impressed him as sheer inactivity and survived his first phase in the Aviation Section. By the Christmas–New Year holiday season, he had completed his ground schooling and graduated into the cadet class for pilot training. Before he began flight training he was granted Christmas leave.

Doolittle immediately set out for Los Angeles to confront Joe Daniels with his perpetual question. He hoped that the fact that he was in uniform would have a beneficial effect upon her decision, but it was Mrs. Daniels who most seriously questioned the question. Why marry this young tough who wanted to be an aviator? Even his own mother, who dearly loved Joe, suggested that she "shop a little longer."

It is unlikely that either the uniform or her mother's objections influenced Joe Daniels' decision, but in any event, after seven years—since Manual Arts High School—she finally answered Yes. They were married on Christmas Eve 1917 at Los Angeles City Hall. Joe paid for the license with her Christmas money (a gift from her mother); this left them with roughly twenty dollars —hers also, for the embryo cadet had nothing and his cadet pay for the month had not yet been received.

The newlyweds boarded a train for San Diego for a few days of frugal honeymooning. They were able to stretch their meager funds, thanks to the patriotic largesse of some of the cafeterias in San Diego where servicemen and their lady companions were served free meals. It seemed an inauspicious beginning to a marriage that would last a lifetime.

Four

Early in January 1918 Cadet James H. Doolittle reported to Charles Todd, a civilian flight instructor, at Rockwell Field, on North Island, at San Diego, California. Their first day together opened ominously. Just as they were about to taxi out in their Curtiss JN-4 Jenny trainer for their first dual instruction session, they heard, louder than the noise of their roaring engine, a sudden confluence of engine sounds, high pitched and straining, and a violent smashing practically overhead. Within minutes two JN-4s which had collided above them, crashed nearby.

Todd and Doolittle shut off their engine and ran to first one Jenny and then the other—one pilot, who had been making a solo flight, was dead and the occupants of the other plane, a student pilot and an instructor, were seriously injured. Once the ambulance had carried the men away and the wreckage was cleared from the field, Todd suggested it was time they got on with their work. It had not been a propitious beginning. Todd was of the old, seat-of-the-pants school of aviation. He may have had his doubts about a cadet who could barely see above the cockpit edge; now he would observe how the cadet reacted to one of the occupational hazards of those wilder days of aviation: the not-so-good landing you could not walk away from.

The two men returned to their Jenny and if Doolittle was shaken (which he was), he did not reveal it to Todd. Accidents happened and it was Doolittle's style to concern himself only when confronted with a specific situation: "I have a simple philosophy: worry about those things you can fix. If you can't fix it, don't worry about it; accept it and do the best you can." It is possible to worry over an issue until one loses his effectiveness. Doolittle was determined to become a pilot, so despite the crash he had just witnessed, he clambered into the forward cockpit of the plane and was ready for his first lesson in the air.

"The training was much different in those days," Doolittle recalls. "We were in a terrible hurry to get pilots trained, and, of course, the airplanes were very simple . . . and we practiced things like grass cutting, which meant holding the plane about three feet off the ground. After seven hours of flying with my instructor, good old Mr. Todd, I soloed. It lasted thirty-nine minutes."

Out of those sessions in the air, Doolittle learned two things: he had the attributes of a good pilot and he loved to fly. In an interview he once defined those attributes, which he himself sought when he later became an instructor. "You look for a chap who has good eyesight, who has fast reactions, who has a good sense of balance, but most important, you look for someone who really loves to fly. It would be very difficult to make a good pilot out of a chap who hated it. We always incline to do best those things that we enjoy doing.

"Another thing you look for is a pilot who can learn his limitations. A poor pilot is not necessarily a dangerous pilot as long as he remains within his limitations. And you find your limits in the air by getting closer and closer and closer and sometimes going beyond them and still getting out of it. If you go beyond and don't get out of it, you haven't learned your limitations, because you are dead."

Doolittle's solo flight was followed by practice in formation flying with those of his classmates who had survived the course and by aerobatics training in maneuvers regarded as crucial in combat. The word "survived" is not used above to imply that crashes eliminated all the unfit. Doolittle recalls few training crashes. "There was a periodic crash—quite frequently a crash occurred because a pilot got into a spin. In those days a spin was referred to as 'the deadly spin,' and it wasn't until I was fairly well along in my instruction that the spin became part of our training. You learned that as the plane begins to spin you push the nose

over, pick up speed, and come out. I remember discussing the
pros and cons of this, wondering why this was. Before this the
tendency was to pull the nose up, which caused the plane to stall,
and that could be fatal."

However, most of the weeding-out process was not accomplished so drastically. Instructors soon recognized a man who
would never make a pilot and that man was washed out. Some ca-
dets even quit of their own volition. Those who remained had a
reasonably excellent survival capability—provided they stayed
distant from the other survivors when flying in formations and did
not become too overconfident—that is, underestimating their and
their plane's limitations—in aerobatics.

Doolittle was endowed with the physical equipment to fly as
well as the emotional: he simply loved to fly and did it so well that
his skill eventually would preclude his getting Over There to become an ace. Anyone who handled a plane as well as he did was
quickly singled out as instructor material. However, upon being
commissioned as a second lieutenant on March 9, 1918, he managed to elude the instructor list and by the twenty-seventh had
been shipped to what was called a "concentration camp" in Texas,
Camp Dick. Doolittle assumed this was the first step on the way to
France; Joe Doolittle remained behind in Los Angeles, where she
had found work in a local shipbuilding plant during Doolittle's
flight training days.

At Camp Dick, where the concentration of pilots supposedly on
their way overseas had converged, Doolittle found himself quartered in a malodorous barracks that had once been used for the
exhibition of livestock. He also learned there were no aircraft at
Dick, nor was there much to do but wait, hoping for an assignment. Among the other newly bewinged second lieutenants concentrated in the former cattle stalls were John Allard, from Boston, and Bruce Johnson, who was from Binghamton, New York.
All three shared a love of flying and all were eager to "get
across"; in common, too, was their detestation for the fate that
had set them down in Camp Dick.

Tall, aristocratic, and monied, Allard shared with Doolittle a
fondness for scotch whisky; they frequently slipped away from
camp (often through a hole in the fence around Dick) and went
to nearby Dallas, took a room in a hotel, and got quietly drunk.
Johnson, who also came from a family with means, was just a bit

taller than Doolittle and had been a member of the Cornell University boxing team; this was their common meeting ground. He recalls his first encounter with Doolittle at Dick—". . . another pilot officer a mite shorter than I and attired in a fine Stetson, boots, and spurs. (Why in hell we ever wore spurs, no one really knows.)"

As a legitimate dodge to avoid the more unpleasant aspects of being stationed in a camp where there was nothing to do except police the area (picking up bits of paper, etc.) or paint things, Johnson got himself appointed boxing instructor of Camp Dick. Inevitably he and Doolittle met in the ring and boxed three rounds. "After the first lead," Johnson has written, "I knew I had my hands severely full of fight." According to Johnson, they "banged each other around for about ten minutes" without either taking any decision, though both were quite bruised and sore when it was all over. Thus was formed, rather painfully, another lifelong friendship—and Doolittle and Allard found another drinking companion.

But drinking, boxing, and generally trying to dodge unpleasant make-work, was not getting on with the war; it was with some relief that they learned they would be moving on at the end of May. Both Doolittle and Johnson were shipped to Love Field, also near Dallas. It was merely a way station, but at least they had planes to fly there, though Johnson found it all quite frustrating "flying underpowered trainers that wouldn't get airborne in the heat of the day." Soon both men were shuttled off to Wright Field, near Dayton, Ohio, Doolittle arriving on June 12, 1918. The emphasis at Wright was on technical matters and the maintenance of aircraft and engines, with some time for flying. All very valuable but decidedly lacking in action. By this time Doolittle and Johnson had lost track of Allard, who had gone off in some other direction.

Doolittle had begun to wonder if he would ever see France, when word came that his name, along with Johnson's and those of 310 others, appeared on a list that would send them to Hoboken, New Jersey, a port of embarkation. An elated and possibly inebriated Doolittle and Johnson boarded a train at Dayton for the trip east—and, they thought, Over There. But the same gnarled officialdom that appeared to be determined to employ airmen in picking up discarded cigarette butts and painting barracks con-

fronted them at Hoboken. They had not been expected, no preparations made for them, and by the time the red tape had been cut
and they were issued travel orders, there was no ship in the harbor
to transport them to France.

It devolved upon the prospective intrepid pursuit pilots to sit
around Hoboken verbally flagellating The System and growing
more and more restless, to the point of committing an indiscretion: they volunteered. This was a stint of special, if
nonproductive, duty—anything to get out of Hoboken—at nearby
Camp Merritt. Needless to say, while they were there their ship
came in, took aboard 100 men (leaving 210 on the docks—and
Doolittle and Johnson at Merritt). When the two volunteers returned to Hoboken another period of waiting set in. Their combined frustrations were not assuaged when Johnson was sent off to
one assignment and Doolittle another. Each was assured by the
officers in command that soon they would be off to France; meanwhile marking time had become a way of life.

Doolittle soon made another move in August 1918, when he
was sent to Gerstner Field, near Lake Charles, Louisiana, for advanced instruction in combat tactics and aerial gunnery. It was at
Gerstner that he was reunited with both Johnson and Allard. The
aircraft waiting for them was to be the Thomas-Morse S-4C
Scout, a much more complex machine than the forgiving Jenny. It
had a warlike, rakish look to it and must have gladdened the heart
of any young pilot who wished to get into the air to challenge the
Red Baron, but, as Johnson observed, it "was the most miserable
piece of aircraft engineering ever foisted off on an unsuspecting
pilot." Powered by a Gnome rotary engine (or, in some models,
the Le Rhône), it operated at two speeds—in the mordant jest of
the time, on or off. The revolving engine in the nose rendered the
Scout a difficult craft to control because of the centrifugal force it
generated as it raced along at nearly a hundred miles an hour with
the throttle in the "on" position. The larger Jenny, with luck and a
good deal of faith, could be coaxed up to a little over 70 miles an
hour. The transition from the Jenny to the Scout was perilous for
new pilots.

A demonstration of this occurred before Doolittle arrived at
Gerstner. Another new pilot, Major John P. Mitchel, former
mayor of New York City (1914–17), took off in a Scout from
Gerstner, to try his hand at the formidable little plane. Mitchel,

then about forty and rather aged for a pursuit pilot, appears to have earned a reputation for absent-mindedness—at least, he was known to forget to fasten his seat belt before taking off. It was the duty of his mechanics to remind him, advice he seems not to have heeded at least once. Upon climbing to a good altitude for a bit of fancy flying, Mitchel whipped the plane into a sudden maneuver and literally tossed himself out of the cockpit. A parachute in those days was regarded as only fit for balloonists, not intrepid pilots, and Mitchel became another training statistic. His rather unheroic death served to underscore some of the simple rules of safety in the air.

Doolittle maintains that training accidents were remarkably few, considering the equipment, its novelty, and the men, who had much to learn about practically everything. It was during his brief tenure at Gerstner that Doolittle's profession had its initial, frightening impact on his wife, Joe Doolittle. Still in the South Western shipyard on Terminal Island, Los Angeles, she received a phone call from a newspaper reporter purporting to carry the last words to his wife from a pilot, James Doolittle, who had died in a crash, as he had it, in Buffalo, New York. This was a cruel beginning of what the reporter, no doubt, hoped would become a good human interest story.

Instinctively, Joe did not feel that her husband was dead and told the reporter, "I don't believe it." He was firm, there was no doubt, Doolittle was dead. Joe refused to accept this news and as soon as she got rid of the reporter, she wired the commander at Gerstner. Soon she had a phone call from Doolittle himself, assuring her that he was in perfect health. Joe Doolittle's intutition had proved itself, even if she could not have explained why she knew she was right and the reporter wrong. (They were both right in a way: a James R. Doolittle, a former Lafayette Escadrille pilot back from France with battle wounds, had been employed as a civilian instructor at Gerstner Field. It was he who had died in the Buffalo crash.) For Joe Doolittle the incident was an intimation of things to come: her husband's chosen profession—if it could have been called that at the time—was a risky one and she would have to endure the fretful, uncertain life of the airman's wife.

Whatever it was that Gerstner Field seemed to promise for Doolittle's future—and he assumed and hoped it was a trip to France—it all came to nothing that August through an act of

God. A hurricane lashed across southern Louisiana and blew the airfield, literally, off the map. Rain-soaked winds reached a velocity of 180 miles an hour and destroyed nearly every building on the base; some 300 training aircraft were reduced to shreds and splinters; five men were killed and there were numerous injuries. Bruce Johnson recalls seeing six freight cars that had been blown off their tracks and a telegraph pole into which bits of straw had been driven.

The storm was followed within twenty-four hours by myriads of mosquitoes, to compound the miseries of the men who were attempting to clean up in the storm's wake. Gerstner Field had simply been eliminated, and within days the trio of Jack Allard, Bruce Johnson, and Jimmy Doolittle were transferred to Rockwell Field, at San Diego.

Ostensibly, he and his companions were sent to Rockwell for work in pursuit aerial gunnery; this they imagined was the final polishing before the port of embarkation. For Doolittle the move was salutary, for it reunited him with Joe.

In command of Rockwell Field was Colonel Harvey B. S. Burwell, a no-nonsense, businesslike airman; most of the training was done at a satellite field, Ream Field, down the bay from San Diego, near the Mexican border. Ream was under the equally businesslike command of Lieutenant Robert Worthington. He obviously taught well—for upon completion of the course, all three, Allard, Johnson and Doolittle, did not go to France but were ordered to remain at Rockwell Field as flight instructors.

To the twenty-one-year-old highly trained pursuit pilot the assignment as instructor, while a tribute to his superior skill, was a bitter development. For three months following that blow Doolittle repeatedly requested a transfer to a combat unit and just as repeatedly was rejected by Burwell. By November 11, 1918, all such requests, demands, and wheedlings became academic, for the war ended and with it all need for hot pursuit pilots. This, too, was, in a sense, disappointing to those who fervently wanted to participate in the glory of air combat. But if the Armistice ended their dreams of glory, it also ended the slaughter and destruction, and there was humane consolation in that.

The advent of peace, which to many minds canceled out any need for a military air service, also forced Doolittle to make a decision about his future. The question was whether or not to return to school and continue in mining engineering or remain in a rapidly shrinking Air Service. In later years, when asked why he decided to stay, Doolittle could merely state, "I had found a great deal of pleasure in flying, and I enjoyed the military life . . . The boys who got out of the service and became barnstormers—they had a rather precarious existence, both from the point of view of eating and living." His decision rested on a sound economic base; as young men were rapidly demobilized, finding work became a critical problem. While his second lieutenant's income, roughly $140 a month, was not much, it came in regularly. This was not true of the barnstormers whose greatest risk, despite their unpredictable aircraft, was starving to death, in the observation of one of them, Dick Depew.

As for enjoying the military life, Doolittle's rather casual approach toward its more formal aspects contributed to his enjoyment, if not to that of Colonel Burwell, who preferred running his base by the book. He was a strict, but reasonably understanding, disciplinarian, but in Doolittle he had a flying maverick who would strain the better part of the colonel's nature.

"I had a great deal of blood in my veins in those days and a certain amount of mischief and I did on occasion utilize an airplane for the purpose of having a little good clean fun," Doolittle recalls, though cautioning that some of the early stories about him might very well be apocryphal.

Having proved to be an exceptional pilot, he enjoyed skylarking —there not being much else to do immediately after the war ended. An authentic incident is one Doolittle remembers with a chill. He was flying one day when he spotted a couple of soldiers walking along a country road. Thinking he would give them a little thrill, he tipped the plane over on one wing and dived. As he swooped a few feet over their heads, they nonchalantly waved to him. Instead of fright, they had registered indifference. "I thought: these folks must be taught that the airplane is more dangerous than they think."

He tipped the nose again and roared down upon the soldiers, judging himself this time merely inches away—that would show them. But to his horror Doolittle felt his wheel strike something and, as he looked back, he saw one of the soldiers flat on the ground—"I was so shocked at having done this that I didn't pull up as rapidly as I should, caught a barbed wire fence on the other side of the road in my landing gear, and, as I pulled up, pulled the fence with me. It quickly stalled the plane and I fell in and crashed. My first thought was whether I had, in my consummate stupidity, killed someone and I rushed back—and here were those two boys, one of them rubbing his head, and he said, 'Lieutenant, I am so glad you weren't hurt!' "

Although relieved, Doolittle realized that his foolishness might have cost a man his life—a wheel had gently grazed his head, enough to bowl him over, but there were no injuries. Nor, for that matter, was Doolittle injured, but he had succeeded in smashing up government property—one former Jenny, about $10,000 worth. This not being the first plane Doolittle had wiped out in a short period, it fell to Burwell to exact punishment. Since the culprit was a valued instructor, Burwell could not ground him— but he could confine him to post; which was done.

Disciplinary action did not necessarily curb the Doolittle exuberance. He formed a partnership with a friend, Lieutenant John McCulloch, who served as pilot while Doolittle engaged in wing walking and other nonmilitary maneuvers. This was generally accomplished out of Burwell's range of vision, except on one occasion. It happened that the film producer-director Cecil B. DeMille was shooting an aviation movie and had received permission to come to Rockwell to film aircraft taking off and landing. As he photographed one plane coming in for a landing, he was rather surprised by what he saw—and so was Colonel Burwell when the day's rushes were screened for him that evening. Blithely seated on the spreader bar of the plane's landing gear as it approached the ground was a man, apparently unaware of the fact that his stunt was being recorded on film. Burwell fumed and snapped to an aide, "Ground Doolittle for a month!"

Since the plane had been photographed from some distance and the figure perched on the landing gear was not truly recognizable, the aide questioned the identity of the culprit. How could the colonel be certain?

"Who else but Doolittle," the colonel stated; it was not a question and the aide understood the logic. The colonel, probably still smarting from some pursuit plane passes Doolittle had made at him during gunnery practice, could not conceive of enough punishment to pile on the maverick. Doolittle was confined to post for a month, he was grounded for a month, and, to contribute fully to the misery, he would serve as officer of the day—for a full month. This was the unkindest cut of all and Doolittle fumed. He could not fly, he could not tinker with engines, since he would have to be in proper uniform. It placed a decided strain upon Doolittle's "enjoyment" of the military life.

Denied the delights of skylarking, he managed to hold on to a cognate element—speed—to ease some of the wretchedness of that mirthless month. He selected as his means of transportation as permanent officer of the day a motorcycle, which he soon began to employ as an earthbound Jenny.

The machine afforded him an outlet for his frustrations and, from time to time, his fancy for mischief. As Doolittle raced about the base, raising clouds of dust and generally adding to the din, Colonel Burwell was never at a loss as to the whereabouts of his officer of the day. On one of his jaunts on the motorcycle Doolittle, skirting along a landing strip, decided to have a little fun with an incoming Thomas-Morse Scout. As the plane made its landing approach, Doolittle swerved into its path. The pilot quickly pulled back on the stick, came in again, only to have the cyclist move again into a collision course. When this occurred for the third time, the pilot pulled away, flew to the distant end of the field and landed. Needless to say, the by-now-extremely-angry pilot was Colonel Burwell.

For engaging in a dogfight—motorcycle v. Scout—Doolittle was given an additional two weeks as a ground gripper. (During the five month period he served as an instructor, Doolittle was confined to base for three months and grounded for one and a half.) However much Burwell was justified in dealing so with his maverick, the maverick himself felt terribly put upon; he even, unreasonably, hoped to challenge Burwell to a boxing match.

Doolittle's scheme, which he placed before the athletic officer, one Lieutenant Barrett, was to provide a little diversion for the troops during one of the evening entertainments. Wouldn't it be splendid, Doolittle suggested, if the men could be treated to a boxing bout in which "their fine C.O., Colonel Burwell," participated? If so, he—Doolittle—would be delighted to serve as his opponent.

Barrett found the idea commendable and brought it to the colonel himself. Burwell, whom Doolittle describes as being "pretty intuitive," smelled a rat. He asked Barrett the name of his opponent.

"Doolittle," he was informed. Burwell had heard of Doolittle's prowess in the ring.

"I'll be very happy to box an exhibition match with Doolittle," he told Barrett, "provided you will also box one with me afterward."

At that point Barrett completely lost interest in the project to Doolittle's great disappointment.

During Doolittle's tenure as constant officer of the day, in the spring of 1919 a group of five pilots (among them Bruce Johnson), led by Major Albert D. Smith, had attempted a cross-country flight from coast to coast which attracted a good deal of attention. The flight was (more or less) accomplished in overloaded Jennies (spare parts plus mechanic), was not nonstop, and was rather haphazard. Bruce Johnson, for example, made a forced landing at El Centro, California, because of a blown spark plug. Trying unsuccessfully to lift the burdened Jenny out of a small field, Johnson cracked the plane up and had to leave the flight. Despite its lack of success, the flight did bring attention to the Air Service—and the other military services then began vying for public attention by initiating a series of historic flights.

"We were constantly trying to think of something to do to keep busy," Doolittle recalled, "and to enhance, we hoped, the public's interest in aviation. The senior people, particularly Billy Mitchell, understood this very clearly. We junior people didn't understand it as well, but we were anxious to participate." Smith had crossed the country from California to Florida; it was Doolittle's idea to fly from San Diego to Washington, D.C., a destination that would lend the effort significance. It would join a major air base with the nation's capital by air. Burwell could understand that and became interested in the idea; besides, it would free him of Doolittle and his shenanigans for a few days.

Doolittle carefully mapped out a flight plan, with various spots noted for fuel stops and selected two other pilots to accompany him, Lieutenants Walter Smith and Charles Haynes. Burwell provided them with three Jennies.

One early morning in the spring of 1919 Lieutenant James H. Doolittle, at the head of his little formation of Jennies, took off—but not exactly into history.

It might be noted that in the spring of 1919, the United States was not covered with a network of airlines; there were, in fact, no airlines. There were few—and far between—military fields and fewer civil airfields. There were, however, cow pastures and roads —all the facilities available to the barnstormers of the period.

With engines throbbing, fabric oscillating, and wires singing, the three Jennies pulled out of Rockwell Field and headed northeast. The first leg of their journey was completed without incident; they flew over the Imperial Valley and set down at Indio, California, about 90 miles from San Diego. The next stop would be Needles, 120 miles farther, still California but bordering on Arizona—and it was here that the incidents began piling up. The second leg had covered more distance than the first and the three planes arrived over Needles with a fuel situation approaching the desperate. Worse: the airfield they had expected to be there, wasn't—there was only the town and plenty of rock-strewn desert. With engines beginning to sputter, Doolittle led his little formation toward a highway and brought his plane down safely on the road; Smith followed, also succeeding in landing his Jenny safely between the telephone lines and fences.

Haynes was not so fortunate; his fuel simply did not last long enough to make the highway, the engine died, and the propeller stopped turning. He had exhausted the fuel in the main tank and could not reach the valve in time to turn on the emergency tank. He had to take what he could get, which was a reasonably smooth stretch of desert unfortunately occupied by a pile of rocks at one end. The Jenny ended up on the rock pile, but luckily Haynes was not injured and headed back to Rockwell by train. That was only the beginning.

The remaining two pilots spent the night at Needles, refueled their planes, and were ready to go the following morning. Doolittle led the way, took off, and circled while Smith began his takeoff from the same stretch of highway. This led to the next incident; as Smith lifted off, a wingtip brushed one of the telphone poles that lined the road and the plane spun in a great cloud of dust. Doolittle quickly returned to the highway to find the Jenny a washout but pilot Smith, though disgruntled, unhurt.

Reporting the loss of two aircraft in as many days to Colonel Burwell was an unhappy chore. Among other things, his commanding officer referred to Doolittle as "a Chinese ace" (the Chinese in those days had earned a reputation for wiping out their own planes) and was ordered to return to Rockwell Field while one plane yet remained. It was an unhappy former transcontinen-tal-flier-to-be who saw Haynes and Smith off on the train, himself took off in the remaining Jenny, and headed back for San Diego.

It was after he had passed over the Imperial Valley, nearly home, that he ran into bad weather in the mountains. Soon he found himself bucking strong headwinds and making very little progress. Downdrifts spilling off the mountain sides caused the plane to drop thousands of feet, his altimeter telling him that he was flying blind at around peak level. Desperately, Doolittle began looking for a hole in the overcast. His luck, such as it had been over the past couple of days, remained with him and he descended safely through the clouds and spotted a little valley with a stream running through it and then some farmland. He selected what he hoped would be a good soft spot—and it was, a freshly plowed field. The wheels of the Jenny had barely settled before it flipped onto its back. Covered with oil, seated in an inverted position, Doolittle snapped his safety belt open and "as I fell out, ripped off the seat of my pants. I got the plane fixed [with the aid of a cou-ple of farm hands, who helped turn the plane over] and flew back.

"When I landed, a mechanic told me to report at once to the colonel. I went to his office, covered with oil, and he gave me a bawling out I was eminently entitled to. When he finished, I sa-luted briskly and did an about-face, exposing considerable bare posterior, which caused him to think that this was my indirect way of expressing *my* opinion. So he bawled me out again, with flourishes. I recall he said something to the effect that I couldn't even keep my ass in my pants."

Thus, rather ignominiously, concluded Doolittle's first attempt at creating aviation history.

Five

While Lieutenant Robert Worthington was Doolittle's immediate superior, he was also a close friend and it was his
idea that perhaps the presence of Joe Doolittle at San Diego might
serve as a steadying influence on the young man who appeared
destined to become Burwell's nemesis. Or vice versa. Consequently, Joe quit her job in Los Angeles, at which, incidentally, she was earning more than her husband, and moved down to
San Diego. With the aid of Worthington and his wife, Louise, the
Doolittles found a house not too distant from the base. The rent,
at $50 a month, was rather steep for the monthly pay of a second
lieutenant, but the resourceful Joe solved that problem. The house
had three bedrooms, so one was rented out to Lieutenant Fonda
Johnson; and since there was a three-car garage, and no Doolittle
automobile, that too was rented.

That was but the beginning for Joe Doolittle. Having worked
since, and even before, their marriage, she had never developed
those skills associated with domesticity. She could make fudge—
divinity and penuche—hardly the basic element of a well-balanced
diet. But with the aid of the slightly more mature Louise Worthington and, later, by studying *Fanny Farmer's Cook Book* she
was able to solve the diet problem as matter-of-factly as she did
some of their financial woes.

The Doolittles then settled down to their first real period of
married life since their wedding about a year and a half before.

(His mother remained in her Los Angeles home.) On the other hand, it would not, could not, be a conventional kind of life—Army life did not lend itself to that. There would be uprootings, moves from base to base, old friends left behind and new faces to get used to, uncertainties, makeshift quarters: there would be no place that could be called "home."

For Doolittle, this seemed to be the normal way of life, but to Joe it could be distressing. A gregarious man, he might show up in the evening, unannounced, with a group of "the boys" from the base and Joe would find herself multiplying Fanny Farmer's advice by three, or four, or five. (While initially these surprises were less than welcome, Joe Doolittle soon took great delight in the camaraderie and learned to enjoy cooking. She became a fine cook, collected a vast library of cookbooks; and, during the nadir of prohibition, emerged as a skilled brewer, providing Jimmy and his cronies with an excellent home brew.)

Absorption in his job created other frictions, for Doolittle might become so engrossed in figuring out a new flying maneuver or in the workings of an engine that, without letting Joe know, he might show up hours late. The aviator's life being what it was in 1919, Joe Doolittle often suffered through fretful moments until her husband came home. He might arrive grease-stained, his uniform requiring rapid cleaning so that he could appear in Burwell's sight a reasonable facsimile of an "officer and gentleman."

Whatever her deeper reasons for leaving Los Angeles—Worthington's entreaty or the simple desire to live a more conventional married life—Joe Doolittle's presence at Rockwell had a minimal influence on her husband's skylarking. Nor was proximity necessarily propitious. In their normal household disputes, Doolittle, with a wicked gleam in his eye, had suggested settlement by the donning of boxing gloves. This method was tried a few times but it only proved that, in the ring at least, the Doolittles were mismatched.

It would be, Joe Doolittle learned early, the same in the air. On one of her first weekend visits to San Diego, during one of those rare periods when Doolittle was neither grounded nor confined to base, Doolittle decided to treat his bride to her first flight; since carrying civilians in military aircraft was taboo, Doolittle had to arrange for a rendezvous out of the range of the beady eyes of the ubiquitous Burwell.

He borrowed a car and came round to the elegant Hotel Del Coronado where Joe was staying, picked her up, and drove out to a stretch of clear beach known as the Silver Strand. Leaving her with a few bananas for lunch, Doolittle drove back to the base for a plane. Although never fond of bananas, Joe became hungry while waiting and ate them. Soon she heard the engine of a Jenny; Doolittle swooped down, indicating a spot where he could land and pick her up.

"I took too long and he was annoyed with me—I had a hobble skirt on," she would one day recall. If covering a stretch of beach was difficult in a hobble skirt, clambering onto the wing and into the cockpit of a Jenny was impossible. Doolittle, of course, could not get out of the plane to help her, so Joe split the skirt and climbed into the plane. ("This was pretty drastic because in those days I didn't have many clothes.")

Once in the cockpit, she found goggles (this was easy, since she sat on them when she got in) and a helmet: so much for her hairdo. Doolittle gunned the engine and they took off. Very soon she was aware of a disagreeable odor—"you wouldn't call it Arpège"—a characteristic redolence of the Jenny caused by the burning castor oil used to lubricate the engine. About this time the thought of the bananas and the fumes of burning castor oil joined in Joe Doolittle's mind and then sent a message to her stomach.

Doolittle blithely took off with a slightly ailing bride in the front cockpit and treated her to all the joys he knew of aerobatics. Joe found it difficult to participate in these joys; she was, in fact, preoccupied with being "violently ill." Her anguished shrieks were mistaken for the delighted outcries expected of all young ladies being treated to their first airplane ride.

The misery, happily, was short lived, because Doolittle was due back at Rockwell, he selected a small field near a factory to set down in. The wings of the Jenny brushed by a tall chimney as he approached the ground. Joe was relieved just at the thought of landing. But then she was assailed by yet another stench—for the tall stack belched fumes from a potash factory.

The wheels bumped the ground and Doolittle brought the Jenny to a stop; Joe climbed out of the cockpit, onto the wing, and joyfully, though unsteadily touched her feet to the ground. With a wave of his hand, Doolittle turned the Jenny into the wind and took off.

It remained for Joe Doolittle to get back to the hotel—this required a trolley ride across town plus a ferry ride and a walk through the hotel's long Peacock Alley, the luxurious lobby where everyone congregated. As Joe moved through the Alley she was conscious of "everybody smiling," which seemed pleasant after her experience. In her room she glanced into the mirror and was shocked. "I looked like I had a horrible disease." Her hair was bedraggled and the area around her eyes was stark white where the goggles had covered her face. A black, horizontal streak cut across her forehead where the helmet and goggles had not quite met. As for her face—"it was pockmarked with oil things." Her dress was an utter mess.

Joe Doolittle threw herself down on the bed and sobbed her heart out. She harbored unkindly thoughts of her husband who had winged his way back to the field delighted with the thought of how he had treated his bride to the wondrous raptures of flight. As she lay crying, Joe Doolittle vowed that she would never again enter an airplane (she kept this resolve for about a month and later even began taking flying lessons, but gave it up because it was too expensive). She would leave flying to Jimmy.

Her first flight had its sequel: when she and Doolittle met again later, Joe told him the tale—including the long disheveled trip across San Diego and through Peacock Alley.

Doolittle laughed—whereupon Joe Doolittle again broke down and "bawled. I guess I didn't have much of a sense of humor in those days."

Joe Doolittle's presence did not really curb the capering of Rockwell Field's chief maverick. Like all individuals with an inventive and inquiring mind, Doolittle also had a highly developed sense of play (scientists and artists frequently fall into this category). Already the incipient scientist, Doolittle wanted to know what was possible when man and aircraft approached their respective limits of performance. He was not, as Burwell generally suspected, always skylarking. He was seeking answers to questions about the relationship between this new machine and man. The one-time rich man's toy had proved to be a deadly weapon during the war, although a much misunderstood one. Its potential as a civil transport had barely been noted in the United States (although in Europe civil air lines had begun springing almost as soon as the war ended, even in defeated Germany).

Doolittle would not claim that in 1918–19 he had a vision of a great network of airlines in the United States or of a great air force. But he was dedicated to his work and its equipment. That his methods frequently upset the more conservative Burwell may have earned him the reputation of the wild man of the base, but Doolittle never attempted any of the maneuvers, or stunts, that set his commanding officer's teeth on edge without a thorough study of its feasibility. He made himself the master of the calculated risk. If aviation were ever to come out of the toyshop, these risks were necessary and inevitable.

An acceptable outlet for Doolittle's winged exuberance was afforded by stunting and precision formation flying. Even the regulation-stickler Burwell approved, aware as he was of what good public relations would mean for the neglected postwar Air Service. Thus Doolittle became the leader of a five-man stunt team which made its initial appearance at a San Diego air show in late November of 1918, a show in which no less than 200 aircraft were airborne simultaneously—Spads, Thomas-Morse Scouts, Jennies. It was an impressive display of air power which the Los Angeles *Times* described excitedly: ". . . they formed a ceiling over the city that almost blotted out the struggling rays of the sun and with majestic solemnity they patrolled the air, magnificent in the perfection of their formation, and while they formed a perfect background at 5,000 feet, the five acrobats below swooped, dived, looped and spun in as perfect unison as though they had been operated by a single hand." The "five daring acrobats" were identified as Lieutenants D. W. Watkins, H. H. Bass, J. H. Doolittle, W. S. Smith, and H. O. Williams.

The team provided the finale to the air show. As the great air armada diminished, the little fighters took over and "the antics and evolutions of the five stunt men increased until finally the skies cleared and the acrobats held the center of the heavens alone, supreme in the mad glory of their thrilling feats."

The next year, a Memorial Day air show was held at Los Angeles and again Doolittle headed an aerobatic team and the Air Service received good press notices. But whether or not this stepchild orphan of the U. S. Army benefited from its excursion into the field of entertainment was questionable. The war was over and of what use were those flying machines except to divert the public? Even the once-eager overintrepid pilots began dropping out of the Service, some of them taking up the uncertainties of the barnstormer's life. Eventually, even one of the original trio of friends, Jack Allard, could visualize no future in the Service, or, for that matter,—aviation, and when his enlistment expired, he left Doolittle and Johnson for a career in business. (Later he would return to both aviation and the Service.)

Doolittle's skill at the stick did not always keep him out of trouble, however. It was possible in the excitement of the testing of man and machine to overlook the limitations of one or the other. Such a test occurred during a cross-country flight in a Jenny; Doolittle was in the rear cockpit flying; his passenger was Bruce Johnson. This was during their instructor phase and, no doubt bored, they were seeking some adventure. Just as they approached a hill they spotted a couple of ducks flying by—Johnson remembers them as geese—and Doolittle banked the Jenny and set off in pursuit of the ducks.

"It was then customary to combat with a duck," Doolittle explained. "You would get on his tail and he'd turn and you'd turn —it was practice in an airplane because the airplane couldn't fly much faster than a duck and the duck tired more quickly. But he could dive away."

The sport proceeded in and around peaks, into and out of canyons, until, indeed, the bird tired of the whole thing and having greater maneuverability than the pursuing aircraft, ducked (so to speak) out of the way and disappeared. To Doolittle's "very great embarrassment" their feathered foe had led them into a cul-de-sac —a ravine, the walls of which "went up steeper than the plane could fly." There was no banking the plane because of the cliffs on either side, so Doolittle pulled back on the stick hoping to get the nose—and if possible the rest of the Jenny—up over the wall approaching with disheartening rapidity. Both men subconsciously tried to raise the Jenny by sheer wishful thinking and by straining upward in their cockpits.

The nose, miraculously, did clear the edge of the ravine but here their luck ran out; the landing gear did not. It sheared off and the plane staggered, a wing brushed some shrubbery, and the Jenny went smashing along the crest of the hill, a confirmed victory for one intrepid duck. With the aid of trees and boulders the Jenny ground to a washed-out stop, and two surprised, because uninjured, and chagrined flying instructors climbed out of the mess.

They stood beside the wreck both cursing and blessing their luck (Doolittle giving considerable thought to how he would explain his latest predicament to Colonel Burwell), when people began to gather, attracted by the spectacular arrival of the Jenny. The plane obviously gone forever, the next point of interest was in the fate of the crew. Upon hearing that no one had been injured, "they went away frankly disappointed."

When the next group of spectators arrived, Johnson decided to make their trip worthwhile. When asked if anyone were hurt, he clutched himself and announced, "Not so it shows, but I'm badly hurt internally." Consequently, Doolittle spent the night with the plane—one of Burwell's Laws—and Johnson spent the night as the guest of an attractive widow who had an even more attractive maid. The next day a somewhat chilled Doolittle once again was warmed by the wrath of Burwell.

The inference might be drawn that the youthful days of what later became the U. S. Air Force were fun-filled and light-hearted, that the boyish pilots and instructors, barely older, reveled in their amusements and thrills and blithely cracked up their planes now and then. That they laughed, walked away to be chewed out by the Old Man, and then back into the cockpit, grinning and seeking out more mischief. This distorts the reality. Planes cost money and someone had to pay for them. And, more sobering, lives were not retrievable.

An anecdotal review of Doolittle's amusing close calls also would distort his early aviation career. He flew often for weeks without incident, which was curious considering the state of the engines then used. Himself a master of the mechanical workings of aircraft, Doolittle undoubtedly suffered fewer unexplained failures than those pilots who left everything to their ground crews.

Doolittle's days as an instructor provided him with several grim incidents, two of them ending in fatalities. During one session he in one plane was taking up a student for instruction in another. They were to take off in tandem: the traffic rules on such takeoffs were clear: the right-hand plane lifted off to the right and the left-hand plane to the left. But inexplicably, the student pilot swerved across the path of Doolittle's Jenny and consequently had his tail section sliced off by Doolittle's propeller. The student's Jenny dived in and burned, killing him.

In another training flight Doolittle had taken up another

student-pilot for dual training in a Jenny. The sky appeared to be clear (though all aircraft had blind spots). Suddenly, and without reason, the Jenny bounced, there were smashing noises from below and their propeller began shuddering so violently that it threatened to rip out the engine. Doolittle snapped off the ignition and began to assess the situation. As he looked below he saw a Thomas-Morse Scout in a twisting, earthward plunge trailing flame and smoke. Apparently the pilot of the Scout had approached Doolittle's plane from below, where the Jenny's wings formed a blind spot; the Scout's upper wing prevented its pilot from spotting the Jenny. He came in underneath, tore away the Jenny's landing gear and damaged portions of the lower wing, then swept upward. The Jenny's propeller, before it splintered, tore away some of the Scout's upper wing, decapitating the hapless pilot, and then the Scout dived, out of control.

Meanwhile Doolittle floated uncertainly with a nervous student in the front cockpit, no power, no landing gear, and a very weak lower wing. He decided to glide the Jenny into as soft a landing as possible on its belly instead of hooking one wing on a tree, as was often the practice then. The condition of the unbuckled upper wing was uncertain so that approach was out; another was to sideslip in on one wing and let the fuselage absorb the shock of the crash. With conditions as they were, the belly landing seemed to be the best possible solution. Luckily, he was able to get back to the field and brought the plane in gently enough so that with a new landing gear, a wing repair, and a replacement propeller, the Jenny was flying again soon after the landing.

The death of the pilot of the Scout earned the incident newspaper space, and it was a shocked Joe Doolittle, who had boarded a trolley (ominously, she had just attended a funeral), and saw a headline: FLIER KILLED IN CRASH/LT. DOOLITTLE . . . , only to have the page turned before she finished reading. Stunned, she left the trolley at the next stop and bought a paper. Only then did she learn the identity of the dead pilot and that Doolittle himself and his student had escaped injury. But it had been a most disturbing trolley ride—the deep certainty that her husband was alive she had had when the newsman had called about the Doolittle death at Gerstner Field the year before had momentarily eluded her. Joe Doolittle was learning to live with uncertainty and headlines.

Irrepressible and sometime jokester though he could be, Doolittle had a reputation as a hard man as an instructor. Once when a student, who had taken off, crashed and burned, Doolittle not so much as glanced at the wreckage; he merely turned, eyed another student, and said, "Next!" A pale youngster acknowledged his position and, after being coolly briefed by Doolittle, took off and performed very well. When another instructor accused Doolittle of having ice water in his veins and asked, "Doesn't that kid's death mean anything to you?"

"I'll think of that kid tonight," Doolittle answered. "But now my job is to make fliers out of these men." Not a callous man, Doolittle was indeed affected by the death of his student. It not only meant the loss of a life but in a sense was an indication of his own failure. Perhaps he had gone wrong somewhere. He was uncompromising in weeding out those young men he believed would not make it—and he tried to do that before the all but inevitable crack up either washed them out or killed them. Taking off immediately after a bad crash was a reminder that they were in a hazardous profession, and merely because now and then the hazards overtook or overwhelmed them did not mean they could stop flying.

By the summer of 1919, however, the need for military flying diminished and, accordingly, so did the need for instructors. Ream Field housed only nine that summer, one of them Doolittle—but that nine represented but a fraction of the wartime quota. In January the Air Service projected plans for a postwar strength of 24,000 men, but was thwarted by a Congress that approved only one third of the required funding; by 1920 the manpower strength would be half of what had been hoped for and Major General Charles T. Menoher, the Chief of the Air Service, stated, "Not a dollar is available for the purchase of new aircraft." What had been in 1918 a burgeoning aircraft industry was all but liquidated in 1919.

The problem was complex: to sustain an Air Service, it was necessary to keep a tight-fisted Congress interested and the few aviators who remained in the Service, interested and busy. Menoher was not an airman (in fact, he had led the 42nd "Rainbow" Division during the war), so his subordinates had to devise the means to keep military aviation alive in the United States. Among these were such pioneering "radicals" as Henry H. Arnold, Benjamin D. Foulois, and particularly the vocal William Mitchell.

Mitchell had returned from France brimming with ideas about the strategic use of air power and expecting to head a new air service, ony to learn that he would be assistant to Menoher. Mitchell was most instrumental in devising the various activities for the remaining Air Service pilots. He initiated a series of historic endurance flights and, in Arnold's phrase, "began a new pattern of national usefulness in peacetime." This took the form of Forest Fire Patrols, begun by Arnold in the West.

There was also a Border Patrol instituted to assist the Internal Revenue Bureau. Air patrols, twice daily both east- and westbound, were established along the United States-Mexico border from Brownsville, Texas, in the East, along the Rio Grande to El Paso, then westward to San Diego. Airfields, such as they were, were set up every 150–200 miles along the border, generally at already existing Army or Cavalry posts. The patrols were supposed to keep their eyes peeled for smuggling, illegal entry, or bandits (Americans had not forgotten the raids of Pancho Villa of 1916). The unstable Mexican government of the time could not prevent border incidents. The precise political definition of this activity would have been difficult to come by, but it did give the floundering Air Service something to do.

Thus it came about, in July of 1919, that Doolittle was transferred from Rockwell Field, via a brief stopover with the 104th Aero Squadron at Kelly Field, Texas, to the 90th Aero Squadron which was stationed at Eagle Pass, Texas, on the Mexican border. The move meant leaving Joe behind, but at the same time it also meant the possibility of action. Both Doolittle and Bruce Johnson were assigned to A Flight, the former as engineering officer and the latter as gunnery officer. Their sector of the border ran from Los Cueves to Del Rio, a desolate, lightly inhabited, uninviting area.

Eagle Pass was no garden spot either, and the 90th Aero Squadron found itself living in pup tents in mid-desert. A large tent served as the mess hall. An old friend, First Lieutenant H. D. McLean, was in command of the patrol at Eagle Pass, which helped to make conditions somewhat more pleasant. The men flew the De Havilland 4, the infamous DH-4 "flaming coffin." Although their guns were loaded and there was a great supply of bombs buried in one corner of the base, they were instructed not to fire upon the Mexicans even if fired upon—and, of course, there were no targets to bomb. It was all a rather frustrating life. "We flew up and down that damn river," Johnson has written, "looking for something to report . . ." and found little more than "sage brush, cactus and a few scrawny cows." One day a dead white horse was spotted and for several days after was meticulously described in the intelligence reports until the vultures and general decomposition removed it from the scene.

From time to time bands of Mexicans were spotted and would fire, generally without effect, upon the the DHs. The location, the time, and the number of Mexicans would be reported but no further action could be taken. Although the firing was usually wild and scattered, an unlucky shot could find a target, as was the case with Fonda Johnson, who had once rented a room from the Doolittles at San Diego. While flying border patrol, a Mexican bullet hit Johnson in the head and killed him.

Except for a few such grim incidents, it was a kind of a musical comedy war. A method was devised to deal with the Mexican snipers. When they were spotted, generally firing from a clump of brush, their targets would fly off seeking herds of cattle, then would round them up, the DHs serving admirably as broncs, and drive them through the brush, flushing out the snipers. As Johnson described it, "The brush would erupt sombreros and into the river they would pile, shaking their fists at us and screaming all manner of Spanish nasties. It made us feel ever so much better."

Bruce Johnson did what he could to improve their way of life on the border. He had had an upright piano hauled in from Kelly Field for after-hours camp entertainment. As gunnery officer he closed his eyes to the fact that the guns of their De Havillands were often fired despite the official order that they were not to shoot back at the Mexican snipers. The pilots had, in fact, poached deer in their DHs. The infraction added a welcome change to the 90th's traditionally dull menu. Grateful, Johnson overlooked the fact that many pilots returned from patrols with fired guns.

Johnson, too, was undoubtedly the mastermind behind the illegal importation of tequila from across the border they so diligently patrolled. Inexplicably, it was a custom at Eagle Pass to issue passes to officers (generally to those who were to be shipped out), enabling them to visit the little town of Piedras Negras and mingle in the bars with those same men who may have been taking pot shots at them during the day.

On one of those across-the-border excursions Johnson over-stayed his pass, arrived at the border station well inebriated and was stopped. The Federal guards apprehended a drunken AWOL officer plus a full case of tequila (which Johnson was unselfishly bringing back to further brighten the life at Eagle Pass: drinking, singing good tunes around the piano, and munching on venison sandwiches). Instead, he found himself in a good deal of trouble.

He was charged with illegally crossing the border (*sic*) and smuggling and shipped to Fort Sam Houston to face a general court-martial. Doolittle, along with others, appeared as a charac-ter witness. Johnson, on his part, was "scared stiff" and if con-victed faced a dishonorable discharge. But he was backed solidly by his squadron mates. And somewhere between the border and Fort Sam the smuggling evidence had been consumed, making it possible for the defense to suggest that the colorless liquid that had been seized just might have been water.

That charge was dropped. Then the curious practice at Eagle Pass of permitting men across the border was convincingly ex-plained and it was not, in fact, illegal (the United States was in slight disagreement, but not at war, with Mexico); it was just a bit impolitic. So Johnson's misadventures were attributed by the sen-ior officers to "boyish pranks" and he was freed.

One of the major problems was boredom. Except for the activ-ity of patrolling, there was little else to do at Eagle Pass but ca-rouse whenever possible. After five months of this, Doolittle de-cided he would send for Joe. With the help of McLean, his commanding officer, he acquired a flimsy house. There being no furniture, Doolittle himself fashioned some chairs and a table and, with the added growth of a reddish beard, awaited the arrival of Joe Doolittle.

When she stepped off the train at Eagle Pass, Joe behaved as if there had been no drastic change; she could read her husband. Doolittle was expecting at least some kind of comment; he was disappointed. A second lieutenant with a red Vandyke was a bit difficult to ignore. "Well," Doolittle asked as they were driving to the base, "what are you going to do about it?"

"About what?"

"This," Doolittle replied, indicating his neatly trimmed beard.

"You know, Doolittle, I thought there was something different about you."

"Well, what should I do about it?"

Joe appeared to give some thought to the query, then brightened and said, "Tweezers!"

Once he had Joe settled in their primitive little house, he shaved.

Joe was making the transition from the housewife to the Army wife: no roots, living out of cartons, friends coming and going (Johnson, as well as Allard, had left the Air Service by then). The little house, as at San Diego, became a favorite gathering place of the squadron, because Joe zealously pursued her hobby of cooking and baking. From the post's chief cook, a Chinese, she picked up pointers as she did also from the Mexicans. The Doolittle cottage became a focal point for the lonely (not to mention the hungry), which helped to make Eagle Pass a bit more livable. Joe Doolittle certainly did not lack for male companionship; the arrival of her sister Grace was a decided improvement for Joe—as well as one of Doolittle's squadron mates, Second Lieutenant L. S. "Andy" Andrews, whom Grace eventually married. Andrews, one of the truly great fliers, would one day become American Airlines first chief pilot.

Andrews recalled one Doolittle prank that gave him pause. He and Doolittle were on patrol one day and Andrews, about to dip a wing for a turn, found the opposite wing would simply not rise. He tried again with the same lack of result. He turned his head and there was Doolittle, widely grinning, with one of his wingtips gently placed over the wing of Andrews's plane, making it impossible for the aileron to work. It was a kind of inside joke that only a pilot could appreciate; the risk was immaterial—it added spice to an existence that seemed to be without direction.

Where lay, or what, was the future? Doolittle loved flying, but he could envisage few expectations in chasing Mexicans in obsolescent aircraft, nor in Joe's following him around from camp to camp, living in tar-paper shacks and baking cookies for the boys.

Six

A change for the better came in the summer of 1920, after a year at Eagle Pass, when Doolittle was transferred back to Kelly Field, Texas, to attend the Air Service Mechanics School. Almost simultaneously he also received his commission as first lieutenant in the Regular Army. For Joe Doolittle this meant uprooting again, although the move would mean better quarters and the promotion a little more money. That would come in handy, indeed, for she was expecting her first child. James, Jr., was born in the Fort Sam Houston Hospital, San Antonio, on October 2, 1920. The second of their two children, John, was also born there on June 29, 1922.

Doolittle's experience at the Mechanics School initiated the advent of the practical theorist, seeker, and scientist. The joy of flight remained, but would grow to include the more esoteric aspects of aeronautical engineering.

The school afforded him the opportunity not only to fly several types of aircraft, including captured German planes, but also to tinker with them and their engines. This coincided roughly with a certain quickening of official American interest in military aviation (there was at the time minimal civil aviation) instigated by activity and statements of General Mitchell. Billy (as he was invariably called) had returned from France certain of the future of air power and an advocate of a separate air force, free of control by Army or Navy men. As mentioned above, he was soon disappointed, and though appointed to a high position in the postwar Air Service, he was subordinate to nonairmen, namely, General Menoher and subsequently Major General Mason M. Patrick. As Assistant Chief, Mitchell contributed much to the discomfiture of his chiefs during the period when he was attempting to create a separate air force.

Firmly believing that a change was necessary in the military structure, Mitchell stated that "changes in military systems come about only through the pressure of public opinion or disaster in war." Unable to accept the second alternative, Mitchell directed his approach to the first, hoping at the same time, perhaps, to catch the ear of the President of the United States. In Mitchell's meteoric and controversial heyday there were two Presidents, Warren Harding and Calvin Coolidge, neither of whom were attuned to the air prophet's vocalizing.

Mitchell felt that the conservatives, the traditionalists, in the War Department were standing in the way of progress; especially obstructive, he believed, were the reactionaries in the Navy Department. It was while Doolittle was stationed at Kelly Field that Mitchell's argument with the War Department came to one of its climaxes: the controversy over aircraft versus the battleship. It was Mitchell's belief that with the advent of the bomber, the day of the big battleship was just about over. This view did not go down well with the Navy, particularly when Mitchell began making public statements to that effect. One of his contentions was that an airplane could sink a battleship and that putting money into battleships (when it could be invested in aircraft) was a great waste. Mitchell's goading of the Navy won him the support of the general public and, consequently, of the Congress and, under such pressure, the Navy very reluctantly made a concession: Mitchell was granted permission to test his claims against a real battleship.

Early in May of 1921 the 1st Provisional Air Brigade was hurriedly assembled by Mitchell at Langley Field, Virginia. Lieutenant Doolittle joined the unit as engineering officer of a DH-4 squadron in which he also served as flight leader and instructor in night flying. The tests were scheduled to take place in June and July off the Virginia Capes, near Hampton Roads. Despite the appearance of haste, Mitchell prepared carefully and, as Doolittle has pointed out, "even had special bombs made by the Ordnance Department, an important part of the whole operation that is sometimes overlooked."

The targets, supplied by a disinclined Navy, consisted of several obsolete Navy vessels and captured German ships, including a battleship, the *Ostfriesland.* Interservice acrimony reached new peaks; even as Mitchell assembled his men and planes at Langley, a former Assistant Secretary of the Navy, Franklin D. Roosevelt, stated that "it is highly unlikely than an airplane or a fleet of them could ever successfully attack a fleet of Navy vessels under battle conditions." His former boss, the Secretary of the Navy during the World War, Josephus Daniels, went even further and offered to stand, in the words of Henry H. Arnold, "bareheaded on the bridge of any battleship during any bombardment by any airplane, by God, and expect to remain safe!" He also expressed the wish that the pilots should be subjected to real battle conditions—that is, with the ships manned and gunned—to show just how "fast the would-be bombers would be shot down by battleships in a real war." It might be noted that Mitchell's pilots did approach Mitchell with requests that the Navy be permitted to shoot back at them, but the usually fiery Mitchell prevailed with a cool head.

The Navy led off the show—for it was to some extent that, complete with an international array of spectators—by sinking a sitting-duck German submarine from the air on June 21, 1921. The following week Navy bombers placed some dummy bombs in and around the battleship *Iowa.* It was the second week of July before Mitchell's 1st Provisional Air Brigade, consisting mainly of Martin MB-2 bombers, began its work: it required forty-four 300-pound bombs to send the German destroyer G-102, to the bottom of the Atlantic. A few days later, on July 18, the light cruiser *Frankfurt* sank within a half hour of attack.

These were followed to the bottom by the "unsinkable" German battleship *Ostfriesland,* an imposing vessel of 27,000 tons, "equal to any ship afloat," in the Navy's view. In fact, the Navy had the U.S.S. *Pennsylvania* on hand to administer the *coup de grâce* with 14-inchers after Mitchell's airplanes had made their attempt.

The test opened with the planes dropping several light bombs on the *Ostfriesland* and then checking the damage—which was slight, there being an inevitable number of misses. It was not until the next day, July 21, that Mitchell unleashed his Martin bombers with 1,000-pound bombs. Of the five dropped, three were direct hits—but the battleship remained afloat and made port despite the damage. Mitchell's next move was to send out a formation of six Martins and a Handley-Page bomber. They each carried the special 2,000-pound bombs that Mitchell had ordered from Ordnance; he instructed the bombardiers to aim for near misses rather than direct hits: let the water pressure do some of the work.

This was the climax of the tests and friend and foe alike (depending which side—Navy or Mitchell one favored) watched the small formation of Martins approach the dreadnought. The first three bombs appeared to do no damage; the fourth, a near miss, caused the big ship to lurch out of the water. The fifth bomb, also a near miss, appeared to be the one, for the *Ostfriesland,* the "unsinkable," began sinking stern first. A sixth bomb hurtled down, but to no visible effect. It splashed harmlessly into the ocean. Then the battleship turned turtle and began churning downward. At this point, the Handley-Page flew over to drop its missile for good measure. Mitchell's bombers had sent the *Ostfriesland* to the bottom.

That Mitchell had proved what he had set out to prove did not settle the issue. An Army-Navy Board evaluated the results of the tests and decided, despite Mitchell, that "the battleship remains the bulwark of the nation's sea defenses." Mitchell disagreed and despite the cautioning of his chief, Menoher, began criticizing the Navy brass and speaking out for a separate Air Force. Mitchell's caustic statements on the Navy were so embarrassing to Menoher that he resigned. The contentious Mitchell went on verbally assaulting the War Department and the Navy so that he finally bad-mouthed himself into a court-martial in 1925.

While it was true that the ships in Mitchell's experiment had been sitting ducks, had not maneuvered nor fought back, a lesson that might have come from it was apparently missed by the hidebound traditionalists. The planes had sunk an "unsinkable" battleship. As Mitchell predicted, the lesson was painfully rammed home years later to firm advocates of the battleship at Pearl Harbor and Midway, where aircraft decided the outcome of both battles.

Doolittle's DH-4s had not participated in the more spectacular bombings and he recalls participating in bombing runs on some small ships and possibly a submarine and one night bombing of little consequence. The point, and what it portended, of the general's argument was not lost on the first lieutenant. That the airplane had unlimited potential as a decisive weapon had been sufficiently demonstrated, despite the Navy's confining stipulations that governed the demonstrations. The flying machine was no longer another sportsman's plaything, suited only to gentlemanly jousting in the blue.

"My feeling then and now is," Doolittle has said, "that Mitchell was right about the basic principles involved. He was ahead of his time in that. His concept of the 1921 bombing maneuvers and their execution was absolutely brilliant." But Mitchell himself was too impatient with those who did not agree with him, too inflexible and abrasive. "Had Mitchell," Doolittle concluded, recalling a Chinese woodcut he had once seen, "more bamboo and a little less oak in his makeup, he might have been more effective in advancing military aviation." That flaw led to Mitchell's eventual undoing.

But to Doolittle the Mitchell tests had more than military implications: if a plane could carry a ton of bombs, could it not also carry a ton of cargo or passengers? It rekindled an idea in Doolittle's mind. After the Mitchell demonstrations were concluded Doolittle returned to the daily Army routine at Rockwell Field; he spent nearly a year at the customary chores—but he also pondered his idea.

With added fuel tanks, it would be possible for planes to cover greater distances—and that was what Doolittle had in mind; he hoped to cross the United States by air in less than a day. Several earlier attempts had ended unsuccessfully (one of them in a fatality) because of mishaps or malfunctions. Doolittle hoped, with careful planning and good flying, to succeed where his predecessors had failed.

Granted official permission to try a transcontinental flight, he acquired a DH-4 which he flew to the San Antonio Air Depot and there removed all excess weight; he also removed the second seat and installed fuel tanks in the cockpit. As an added margin of safety, he made a flight to McCook Field, near Dayton, Ohio, where he obtained one of the latest instruments then undergoing testing—a turn-and-bank indicator, another harbinger of the end of seat-of-the-pants aviation.

By late July 1922, after testing that included a nonstop flight between San Antonio and San Diego, the plane was ready and, by stages, Doolittle flew it to Pablo Beach, near Jacksonville, Florida. A smooth, unobstructed, stretch of hard-packed sand served as a good takeoff spot for fuel-heavy, long-distance aircraft. Word had leaked out that an Army pilot was about to make a historic flight, and soon a crowd, including newsmen, gathered at Pablo Beach. Doolittle found himself rather enjoying the attention of the press and the adulation of the crowd. He began to feel rather intrepid.

By takeoff time, late in the evening of August 6, 1922, he had quite a following. A crowd of about a thousand came down to the beach to watch. He climbed into the DH-4, waved airily to his admiring public, gunned the big Liberty engine, and, with the roar of the engine blending with the cheers of the crowd, headed into the wind. But then his left wheel hit a soft spot in the sand and the plane somersaulted into the water.

With his head submerged, Doolittle unsnapped his safety belt and ejected from the cockpit. In the process, his helmet was pulled down over his eyes and his goggles were pulled down over his nose, the former thus making it impossible for him to see, the latter making it impossible to breathe. Blind and suffocating, Doolittle began thrashing about in the water to save himself from what he imagined would be certain drowning. Somehow he managed to clamber on top of the fuselage of the upside-down aircraft even though he had not been able to straighten out his helmet and goggles. Then, to his chagrin, he realized he had exhibited considerable lack of intrepidity by struggling to save himself from drowning in knee-deep water. "The crowd that had gathered to see me take off thought my desperate antics were pretty funny," he later recalled. "I was very embarrassed."

There being no serious damage done except to his ego, Doolittle requested permission to put the DH back into flying shape so he could make the flight as planned. This required nearly a month so that Doolittle was not ready again until the evening of September 4, 1922. "I was determined to take no chances of failure in this attempt," he has said. "The row of lanterns [which had been set up to mark the beach runway] helped me keep away from the surf and yet stay on the hard beach area."

Doolittle taxied the plane, then applied full throttle; the tail lifted and the DH was soon airborne without incident. He turned the plane over the Atlantic and pointed its great nose, with its pulsating Liberty engine, westward. "A full moon greeted me for about two hours after the start. I was then flying at an altitude of 3,500 feet and at a speed of 105 miles an hour." All was serene and pleasant until he spotted a storm in the flight path ahead; the storm was too massive to skirt so Doolittle plunged into it, "trusting to my compass to steer a straight course." Flashes of lightning permitted him to see the ground from time to time, check his map, and be certain he "was flying high and free and true."

With rain pelting and stinging his face, he recognized New Orleans as he flew over. The rain continued until he crossed over the Texas border, where he veered slightly northward and out of the storm. The weather improved and it "was a wonderful sight to see dawn breaking over the Texas country and to feel the thrill of having successfully completed half of my journey through the long hours of darkness."

At Kelly Field, Doolittle's halfway point, people had begun to gather in the darkness to witness the landing of the "Lone Pilot." By dawn of September 5 some of his brother pilots, concerned about him, began taking off to search for him in the clouds. These extra planes only confused the situation, for as they returned, the crowd mistook them for Doolittle's plane. Finally, however, the DH-4 came in alone, landing at 7:05 A.M., after ten hours and five minutes of flying time.

The cheers Doolittle heard upon cutting his engine were welcome, especially after the jeers he had heard as he stood knee-deep in water in Florida a month before. For the next hour and fifteen minutes, while Doolittle rested and had breakfast, a ground crew went over the plane, refueled it, checked the engine, repaired a leak in the radiator, tightened the brace wires, and generally put the DH in flying trim. At 8:20 A.M. Doolittle again took to the air, on the final leg of his flight.

He had realized he would have at least another ten hours in the air and that after more than twenty airborne hours of listening to the hypnotic drone of the Liberty, the possibility of his dozing off was rather great. He did not drink coffee at the time (he rarely does even today) and found it to be a most effective stimulant. Therefore he had brought along a thermos of hot black coffee he could drink through a tube while in flight. As an added safeguard, he had arranged to be met in the air "either at El Centro, California, or Yuma, Arizona," by two aircraft which would give him "something to think about and, still further, help keep me awake." Doolittle had crossed Texas, New Mexico, and most of Arizona and was feeling the soporific effects of the flight, when in the vicinity of Yuma he spotted two planes circling (they were piloted by Captain William Randolph and Lieutenant C. L. Webber). The presence of the two planes served to hold off his fatigue. They formed into a V, with Doolittle leading the tiny formation.

When they landed at Rockwell Field, in San Diego, 22 hours, 30 minutes had elapsed since Doolittle had taken off from Pablo Beach—he had been in the air for 21 hours, 19 minutes. He had indeed succeeded in crossing the continent, a distance of 2,163 miles—alone—in less than a day.

The feat attracted much attention and the press made him a national celebrity (although it took the Army seven years to present him a Distinguished Flying Cross for the flight); but there was little time to enjoy the prepared reception at San Diego. Orders had already come for Doolittle to report for duty at the Air Service Engineering School at McCook Field. He had completed his flight on September 5; by the eighth he climbed back into his cockpit and headed eastward, landing at Kelly Field in the early evening. There he was accorded an impressive reception: the commanding officer of the base headed the reception committee. Upon landing, Doolittle was escorted to a waiting automobile in which sat both his mother and Joe. The car then led a procession into San Antonio where another reception was held in the mayor's office and Doolittle was awarded the "freedom of the city." It was, of course, all very heady, but Doolittle had spent nearly twelve hours in the air since the takeoff from Rockwell Field and would undoubtedly have enjoyed some rest more than the all the ceremony. After the motorcade passed throught the main streets of San Antonio, Doolittle went home to spend time with his mother and wife —and get some much needed rest.

He was away again the next morning, but no longer—at least for a few miles—the "Lone Pilot." For as he left by train for McCook, several planes from his old 90th Squadron flew overhead to escort him away from San Antonio. Perhaps that was the greatest tribute of all, a salute from his peers.

Seven

The 1922 transcontinental flight marked the emergence of the public Doolittle, whose exploits would be extensively covered in newspapers and whose more solid if less spectacular accomplishments could be obscured by a voracious public appetite for aviation derring-do, particularly during the twenties.

Although in drawing up a list of useful things done, Doolittle placed the flight at the head of the list, where it belongs chronologically, he tended to regard the nonstop transcontinental flight the following year by Lieutenants O. G. Kelly and John A. Macready—New York to San Diego in 26 hours, 50 minutes—as "a much more difficult and justifiably more heralded flight."

Each flight was a substantial contribution to aviation, of course, revealing, one step at a time, what was possible. Thus when Doolittle came to McCook Field in September 1922 it was with the hope that aviation's horizons would be expanded even further with technical development. McCook was the Air Service's great postwar research center and, although directed primarily toward military aviation, its work in design, fuel refinement, and allied fields would be of value in the development of civil aviation also.

While speed and maneuverability (and consequently improved power plants and air frames) were of primary concern in the development of pursuit (later fighter) aircraft, these same qualities would lead to further improvement of all aircraft such as the air liner, still somewhat in the future, and the at-the-moment neglected and generally misunderstood bomber.

Doolittle's assignment to McCook Field was for him like a return to school; he continued to fly, of course, but the stress was on academic courses in the relatively little known field of aeronautical engineering. Getting back into the disciplines of classroom work and reawakening the recollections of the rigors of higher mathematics were initially vexing, but in time Doolittle found himself enjoying the work. Much that he did instinctively in the air could be explained in recondite mathematical terms, but there was much that remained a mystery. He found that fascinating. And he found himself enjoying the challenge of scholarship.

For Joe Doolittle, who followed her husband later, the move from Texas to Ohio was further complicated by the additional little Doolittles. Making a cross-country train trip with a two-year-old and an infant, plus possessions, was an experience. Arrival at the base then meant settling in, but this was considered the lot of the Army wife.

It might be noted that in 1922, in view of his record flight and his work in general, Doolittle received his B.A. from the University of California, despite his skipped final year which had been interrupted by the war. All seniors who enlisted were automatically graduated, according to a special consideration granted by the university. Doolittle, however, enlisted first and then never bothered to register for his final year. This oversight was corrected ("finagled" is Doolittle's term) "by the head of the Army Air Service Engineering School so I could take graduate work at MIT." This opened the way for the next important step in Doolittle's academic career. To bridge the intellectual gap between theory and practice—the aeronautical engineer and the pilot—the Army had decided to sponsor the higher education of six pilots whose grasp of engineering revealed exceptional promise in this generally unexplored field.

As Doolittle recalled, "the idea was to get more rapport between the aeronautical engineer and the pilot. In those days there was a general feeling among pilots that the aeronautical engineers were not quite as competent as they should be. The engineers, on the other hand, felt that the pilots were all a little touched in the head or they wouldn't be pilots in the first place . . ."

About this same time, however, Doolittle had heard of another Air Service project in which he became intensely interested, an around-the-world flight planned for the following year (1924).

Although he tried to get himself assigned to the flight, he was rejected in favor of the aeronautical engineering program. Undoubtedly his two superiors at the Engineering School, Captain Edwin E. Aldrin and his assistant, Lieutenant Samuel Mills, were instrumental in scuttling Doolittle's bid for the global flight. Mills had even approached Joe Doolittle in an attempt to enlist her aid in discouraging Doolittle from the one project and encouraging him in the other. Characteristically she refused to interfere in Doolittle's professional life.

But the Army eventually solved the argument: Doolittle was assigned to the group of six men who would attend the Massachusetts Institute of Technology to study aeronautical engineering. Once again the Doolittles packed and moved, this time, in July of 1923, to Dorchester, on the other side of Boston from the MIT campus at Cambridge. Joe Doolittle found a complete floor in a three-family house for $65 a month, which subtracted considerably from her husband's $160 a month Army check. By the time the semester began, the Doolittles, complete with three-year-old Jimmy, Jr., and one-year-old John, were settled in and Lieutenant Doolittle prepared to plunge into academic life again.

It was a new, hard life for the semigrounded Doolittle (he would fly out of Boston from time to time to keep his hand in) as he contended with the abstractions of higher mathematics and aeronautics in a rather boisterous home atmosphere, enlivened by the sounds contributed by two lusty growing boys. Joe Doolittle managed to keep them in hand; she also ran the household, which as before became a meeting place for Doolittle's friends, even for his instructors, including the brilliant, almost blind mathematician Clarence L. E. Moore and the celebrated aeronautical engineer Edward P. Warner.

Among the courses he would take between October 1923 and June 1925 were Advanced Calculus and Differential Equations, Theoretical Aeronautics, Intermediate and Scientific German, Intermediate and Scientific French (these without either elementary German or French as a base). Also, Navigation, Airship Design, Propeller Design, Vector Analysis, Theory of Functions, Photoelasticity, Advanced Wing Theory, Thesis, and Electrical Engineering (Seminar). While this is not his complete curriculum, it presents a good cross-section of the subjects with which Doolittle would have to grapple during the next two years.

The transition for Doolittle from man of action back to scholar was laborious. The first year, as he took up mathematics after the five-year hiatus since his college days, was especially arduous. He would come home from classes, his mind tired from struggling with abstruse concepts, with a handful of scribbled notes. Joe would transcribe the jumble to a neatly typed paper for review and future reference. This was so helpful that Doolittle eventually bought a special five-shift Hammond typewriter which came equipped with mathematical symbols and the Greek alphabet (to contend with the mysteries of trigonometry and integral calculus).

"I was not a brilliant student," Doolittle would later tell his biographer C. V. Glines, "and I think I passed some of my courses only because of the beautiful typing job Joe did on my term papers."

Joe somehow managed to crowd other activities into her crowded schedule, besides, that is, attending to Jimmy, Jr., and John. For relaxation she began painting on porcelain and, while Doolittle and his fellow students discussed mathematical complexities, Joe would relax quietly touching up their inexpensive china with attractive floral designs. Music was another interest and she found a willing baby sitter (before that term was in use) in the secretary of Professor Warner, Miss Betty Brown, who watched over the two boys in her office while Joe attended a concert of the Boston Symphony.

At around midpoint in the spring 1924 term Doolittle was called back to McCook Field to participate in an Air Service testing program. While it interrupted his courses at MIT, the testing was, in fact, related. Doolittle would be given the opportunity to put some of his new-found theory into practice. The aircraft selected was a Fokker PW-7, powered by a Curtiss D-12 engine. The Dutch-built fighter was greatly respected by the Air Service, particularly because of its sturdy plywood wing structure, despite the fact that an earlier model had suffered wing failure two years previously, killing the pilot.

It was Doolittle's assignment to take his craft to nearly the point of structural failure in order to measure scientifically the effects of acceleration on the plane and himself. For this work he was to receive (again belatedly, in 1929) his second Distinguished Flying Cross. Its citation describes what Doolittle did during the tests:

During March, 1924, at McCook Field, Dayton, Ohio, Lieutenant Doolittle, piloting a Fokker PW-7 pursuit airplane, performed a series of acceleration tests requiring skill, initiative, endurance and courage of the highest type. In these tests a recording accelerometer was mounted in the airplane and the accelerations taken for the following maneuvers: loops at various air speeds, single and multiple barrel rolls, power spirals, tail spins, power on and power off, half loop, half roll and Immelmann turn; inverted flight, pulling out of dive at various air speeds; flying the airplane on a level course with considerable angle of bank; and flying in bumpy air. In these tests the airplane was put through the most extreme maneuvers possible in order that the flight loads imposed upon the wings of the airplane under extreme conditions of air combat might be ascertained. These tests were put through with that fine combination of fearlessness and skill which constitutes the essence of distinguished flying. Through them scientific data of great and permanent importance to the Air Corps were obtained.

The citation does not mention the fact that in pulling out from what turned out to be the final dive of the tests, "the wing failed," in Doolittle's words, "but did not come off." The instrument read 7.8 Gs (that is, the pull of gravity on the plane—and upon Doolittle—was multiplied nearly eight times). At the same time Doolittle studied the phenomenon which enventually became known as "blackout," the loss of consciousness of the pilot during a sudden turn or pulling out of a dive. Very little was known then of the blackout and one of the important factors proved by Doolittle was that, contrary to popular belief, sight was not the only faculty impaired in a blackout. "My experiments indicated that sight was the last faculty to be lost under those conditions. It was considered a very useful piece of work."

Upon his return to MIT Doolittle used the test for his master's thesis, "Accelerations in Flight." This was published as National Advisory Committee for Aeronautics Report No. 203 and was eventually published in every technical language in the world.

He then spent the last semester of 1925 preparing his doctoral dissertation. As his subject he selected one that would disprove another seat-of-the-pants legend. Technically, Doolittle would study "the wind-velocity gradient and its effect on flying characteristics." Most pilots at the time maintained that in flight they could sense the wind direction and that they, at all times, were aware of the flying "attitude" of their aircraft, even in a dense fog when they could neither see the horizon nor the ground. It was Doolittle's opinion that it was the inherent stability of the planes of the time and not "something real lucky in their butts" that made that possible. There were too many inexplicable crashes in fog where it was all too apparent that the pilot, disoriented, flew directly into the ground while assuming he was in level flight.

In his experiments Doolittle had learned, upon questioning twenty experienced pilots, that there was no complete agreement on the effects of the wind on the flying qualities of an aircraft. He found that pilots could "feel" the wind only when there was some visual reference. Blindfolded or in dense cloud or fog, the pilot did not actually "sense" whether he was turning into or with the wind; or, as stated in Doolittle's summary: "A steady wind exercises no measurable effect on airplane performance at altitude except, of course, on speed and direction of flight. Very near the ground, however, the effect of wind-velocity gradient can be serious, particularly in the case of a heavily loaded airplane. The danger is increased by a strong tendency on the part of the pilot to pull the nose up beyond the most efficient angle of attack. This increases any tendency to settle and may even cause the airplane to spin in."

Doolittle presented a first draft of what he would call "The Effect of the Wind-Velocity Gradient" to his advisers and was disappointed when it was rejected. "They said it was not abstract enough," he recalls, "for a doctoral dissertation. So I had to come up with a complicated mathematical derivation—which, by the way, I am not sure was correct—to fit the actual flight results before they would give me my degree."

Doolittle complied but felt that putting the findings of his experiments into recondite language and formulas placed it beyond the comprehension of most of the people it might have benefited, the pilots. However, the total experience was most useful to Doolittle, who could apply his findings in later work. But few others, he felt, would be aware of it, "I rather doubt whether anybody has ever read it."

The paper was accepted and its author became, in June 1925,

at the age of twenty-eight, Dr. James Doolittle; he was among the first in the United States to be awarded an Sc.D. degree in aeronautical science. However, to the Air Service he was still a lowly first lieutenant and, upon completion of his work at MIT, he was ordered back to McCook Field. This meant also moving out of the house in Dorchester and once more finding quarters for himself, Joe, and the two boys at McCook.

Within two months of the Doolittle family's return to Ohio, Doolittle was given a curious assignment: he was ordered by the Air Service to report to the Navy for training in seaplane flight. Since this was temporary duty he left the family in Ohio and packed up for the assignment at the Anacostia Naval Air Station at Washington, D.C.

When he reported in during August, Doolittle found himself engaged in an unusual joint Navy-Army venture, the focus being upon preparing teams from both the Army and Navy for the important Pulitzer and Schneider competitions set for later in the year. The latter had been established to develop seaplanes by a Frenchman, Jacques Schneider in 1913 and its trophy was regarded as the most important internationally. The Pulitzer Trophy had been won for the first time in 1920, was a landplane competition, and, though open to all comers, was generally dominated by American entries.

The United States had won the Schneider Trophy for the first time in 1923, the pilot being the Navy's Lieutenant David Rittenhouse in a Curtiss R-3 racer. This automatically made the United States the host nation for 1924. However, the race was canceled that year because of the withdrawal of the Italian entries and because the British were having problems: one entry was not yet ready when the race was scheduled and another sank after a trial flight. Rather than take the trophy that year by default the Flying Club of Baltimore, the hosts, simply canceled the race in a decidedly gentlemanly gesture.

At Anacostia Doolittle took his training in how to fly a plane from and onto water; an entirely new experience for him. Meanwhile, the Army and Navy shared the expense of acquiring four Curtiss R-3Cs powered with a new Curtiss V-1400 engine. Neither service could afford the total cost of the aircraft, so each put up $250,000 toward the project—"a princely sum at that time," Doolittle has noted. One of the racers was marked for static testing in a hangar, to the point of destruction to see how much stress the plane was capable of withstanding; the remaining Curtisses would be flown in the races in October. Lieutenant Alford "Al" Williams for the Navy and Doolittle for the Army were the test and acceptance pilots for these aircraft.

The Pulitzer race of 1925 was held at New York's Mitchel Field during an Air Service-sponsored air show which ran from October 8 through 13. To publicize the event before the race the Army sent its two pilots, Doolittle and Lieutenant Cyrus Bettis, on Tuesday the sixth to entertain Manhattanites at lunchtime. Besides treating the observers to the usual aerobatics, the pilots played tag with their Curtiss racers among Manhattan's peaks. Winging among the skyscrapers they flew past the Woolworth Building, waving to gapers standing at the windows; they swooped down upon Central Park skimming the treetops; and for a finale before heading back for Mitchel Field on Long Island, they thrilled the crowd gathered at the Battery in lower Manhattan by diving at them.

After dark that night a formation of Army aircraft flew over New York; the planes were wired with lights—red, green, and white—and flew in V-formation over the city. The finale of this spectacle was a great fireworks display which the men in the planes released from around 8,000 feet. All was most exciting, spectacular, and promising for the air show just two days away.

The air show opened badly with a pointless incident. One of the finest pilots of the era, Clarence Chamberlin, had entered his ancient monoplane (originally a Bellanca biplane) in the light plane category, one of the civilian events. The redesigned Bellanca, which had not been thoroughly tested, had a tendency to fly with the right wing low at high speeds. Chamberlin, on his own, could have undoubtedly handled the plane but as he was taking off a spectator dashed from the crowd and climbed into the rear cockpit. The unwelcome passenger was not exactly a stranger—he was Lawrence Burnelli, brother of Vincent Burnelli, designer of the famed "flying wing"—so Chamberlin proceeded with his takeoff. The craft was more unwieldy than ever with the additional weight of Burnelli and was barely 300 feet off the ground when the right wing dropped suddenly and Chamberlin found himself unable to stabilize the plane. Within seconds the plane dropped into the ground, throwing Burnelli 60 feet away, killing him instantly.

Chamberlin was pulled from the wreckage with his right leg broken in two places and a badly sprained back (he recovered and later made record flights).

But the crash and death of Burnelli got the air show off to a poor beginning. However, the performance by military pilots with formation flights helped to moderate some of the public doubt about the safety of aircraft and a Doolittle exhibition of aerobatics in "an amazing exhibition of upside-down flight, slow roll variations, loops, snaps, etc.," in a Curtiss P-1 Army Hawk.

A toss of the coin had decided that the Army participant in the Pulitzer race would be Bettis (with Doolittle as his alternate). He would be pitted against the Navy's famed Lieutenant Al Williams. They would be flying the new Curtiss R3C-1s. Although other Army and Navy pilots would compete, all incidentally flying various Curtisses, it was the contest between Bettis and Williams that excited interest and attention, with the latter as the favorite.

Williams was off first to warm up his engine and shortly after 3 P.M. began racing around the pylons. Bettis followed about two minutes after. Both men flew at an altitude of about 300 feet, not in a race with each other to see who might cross the finish line first, but to see who clocked the faster speeds in four laps. Williams made good time on his first lap but then lost it on the succeeding laps as Bettis gained. In Williams' case it was a matter of his engine going bad after the first lap so that the final result was that Bettis' average speed was 248.99 mph. and Williams', 241.7 mph. The other planes then took off in a more traditional race, with four aircraft twisting around pylons in a dash for a finish line. This was won by the Army's Lieutenant L. H. Dawson, making the Pulitzer an even sweep for the Army.

Doolittle had watched the racing and theorized that speed was invariably lost on the pylon turns. By approaching the turn in straight flight, then banking and turning sharply, a decided loss in speed resulted. Doolittle was certain that if the pylon were approached from above and if the turn were made in a dive, the speed gained in the straightaway would not be forfeited in the turn.

The Schneider Trophy race was scheduled to be held at Bay Shore Park, near Baltimore, Maryland on Saturday, October 24, 1925. Because of the international aspect, excitement had been mounting with the arrival earlier in the month of the British and

Italian teams. There were three British entries and two Italian. The Navy had two planes, two Curtisses—one of those being Al Williams' second-place winner in the Pulitzer—which were to be flown by Lieutenants George Cuddihy and Ralph Ofstie. The single Army entry was Bettis' Pulitzer winner, converted to a seaplane by exchanging the wheeled landing gear for pontoons; this conversion made the plane a Curtiss R3C-2. It would be flown by Doolittle, with Bettis as alternate.

The British brought two familiar biplane racers, Gloster-Napier IIIs plus a new, handsomely designed (by R. J. Mitchell) Supermarine S-4, a beautiful blue-and-white midwing monoplane. The two Italian entries were Macchi M-33 flying boats, which sat low in the water, powered by Curtiss D-12 engines encased in podlike structures mounted on struts almost directly over the cockpits. It was the heaviest, most encumbered entry and compared with the others appeared to have had its day.

Qualification flights began on October 23, the day before the race itself. During these tests the British suffered the worst of two misfortunes. Pilot Henry C. Biard, at the controls of the Supermarine, experienced severe wing flutter in a turn and splashed heavily into the waters of Chesapeake Bay. The impact ripped away the twin floats and the S-4 sank, with Biard unconscious and with a broken wrist in the cockpit. The icy water revived him and he was able to unstrap himself and swim to the surface; he was eventually rescued from the freezing water. Biard recovered from the accident, but the Supermarine was totally written off. (This remarkable aircraft, as history would later record, was the antecedent of Mitchell's later Spitfire.)

The next day the weather turned sour, with lashing rain and gusting winds, and a postponement was called. In the storm several Navy seaplanes were damaged and some destroyed. The poor weather continued and the postponement continued until Monday, October 26. In the morning the British lost another entry. Bert Hinkler, who had not been able to test his Gloster during the initial trials, made an attempt Monday and in the swelling water had his undercarriage collapse. This left but one British entry, another Gloster-Napier with Captain Hubert Broad as pilot.

The Italian pilots, Giovanni De Briganti and Ricardo Morselli were ready for the race, along with the three Americans, two Navy pilots, Cuddihy and Oftsie, and the single Army entry,

Doolittle. During the engine runup Morselli's Macchi was found to be malfunctioning and he too was eliminated from the race, leaving five competitors.

A triangular course, totalling 31.07 miles, was marked by three pylons in Chesapeake Bay; each aircraft would fly seven laps or roughly 217.5 miles (350 km). The five planes were put into the water around two in the afternoon, after the sun had cleared the haze. The water was not smooth, but it was not rough either—and the wind direction was perfect. Doolittle was scheduled to be the first off and taxied the Curtiss into position. The more open water was choppier and when Doolittle began the takeoff run, spectators were certain he would be swamped by spray. But the little Curtiss lifted off the bay and Doolittle began his run, using his new technique of approaching the pylon from above and executing a diving turn. He had taken off officially at 2:38 P.M. The remaining four planes followed in five minute intervals: Broad in the Gloster-Napier, Cuddihy and Ofstie in their Navy Curtisses, and, finally, Briganti in the Macchi.

Doolittle completed his first lap at a speed of 223.2 mph., Broad came by at 194.3, Cuddihy at 211.6, Ofstie at 208—Briganti in his heavy boat was barely in the running. As the planes roared around the pylons it appeared that it would be an Army v. Navy contest, but then Ofstie developed engine trouble and had to drop out. He was followed by Cuddihy, whose engine inexplicably ran out of oil and burst into flame. Cuddihy coolly smothered the flames with a small fire extinguisher and then quickly landed—out of the race and a possible second place.

By this time it was obvious who would be first place winner—Doolittle, whose remaining contender was Broad in the Gloster-Napier. Briganti remained in the race, cutting the pylon corners almost as tightly as Doolittle but in a plane that was hopelessly outclassed.

Doolittle's seventh and final lap was clocked at 235 mph.—his final average being 232.573 mph. a new world's record for seaplanes; Broad was second with 199.169 mph. (itself a record breaking speed), and Briganti came in with 168.44 mph. Doolittle had won the Schneider Trophy for the United States—and, of course, for the U. S. Army. When asked if the Navy had been embarrassed by an Army victory in a seaplane, Doolittle's reply was a laconic "They weren't exactly elated . . ."

Nor was he himself completely content with winning the trophy and requested permission to fly a straight three-kilometer course the next day, a flight that would be supervised by both the National Aeronautical Association and France's Fédération Aéronautique Internationale. The next day he took off again in the Curtiss and made three passes over the course and set the plane down again to learn that he had established yet another record with an average speed of 245.713 mph.

One of the secrets of Doolittle's dual victories was his recently acquired degrees in aeronautical engineering. Before the race he had slightly changed the pitch of his plane's propeller, thus making it possible to obtain optimum speed from the engine. This was before the advent of a true controllable-pitch propeller, although the idea had been around for some time. Doolittle recalled an early (1922 or so) attempt by Muir S. "Sandy" Fairchild. His contrivance was not designed to alter the pull of the engine by changing the angle of attack of the propeller blades, but rather to reverse upon landing as a kind of braking device. As Doolittle recalled the testing of this gadget, "it reversed on takeoff and dropped Sandy into the river and that set back the development of the controllable-pitch propeller about two decades. There was a great lack of interest in something that took control of the plane when you didn't want it to."

Doolittle's adaptation, which contributed to his winning of the Schneider Trophy in 1925, was much simpler—but it worked. His winning meant that the United States had won the trophy twice in a row; a third win would mean that the Schneider Trophy would come into the permanent possession of the United States. Thus Doolittle's record flights attracted a great deal of attention in the aviation industry as well as in the press and the public. He was eulogized on the editorial page of the New York *Times*—at the expense of the Navy; he received a telegram of commendation from the Secretary of War, Dwight F. Davis; and, upon his return to McCook Field, was issued a nautical uniform, complete to the traditional two-pointed hat, and driven through Dayton in an automobile decked out to look like a ship. On the sides were the words: ADMIRAL JAMES H. DOOLITTLE.

Eight

The Army, very quickly relieving Doolittle of his Navy command upon his return to Ohio, assigned him the job of Chief, Test Flight Section, at Wright Field, which by then had become the Air Service's major testing center, supplanting old McCook Field. In keeping with the Depression's fiscal pinch, despite the raise in position, Doolittle remained a first lieutenant.

But the work was congenial and enjoyably suitable, affording him the opportunity to continue being the scientist-flier. At the same time it appears not to have curbed his delight in aerial high jinks; though he was officially a doctor of science and a section chief, he remained the irrepressible Jimmy of yore.

His penchant for high jinks had been revealed during his earlier stint at McCook Field when he served as test pilot for the remarkable Dayton-Wright XPS-1, one of the first aircraft equipped with a retractable landing gear. It was a high-wing monoplane—a parasol type, with the wing raised slightly above the fuselage by struts. The pilot sat tucked under the wing. The configuration, plus the possibility of folding up the landing gear, inspired the Doolittle creativity. A dummy landing gear was affixed to the top of the wing and a stuffed dummy head was attached to the bottom of the fuselage. Nothing could be done to the rudder so it was left in its proper place.

It was during one of the regular air shows at Dayton—the year was 1923—that Doolittle displayed his creation. He took off well out of sight of the stands and the crowd, then flipped the plane and flew by to practically everyone's consternation. No one had ever seen such a plane before, with its strange hanging wing, its rudder projecting from the bottom, not to mention the curious shape of the fuselage. It was obviously an optical illusion and gave rise to much betting as to which side was up.

Then there was the saga of "Hart, Schaffner, and Marx." These were three dummies made of heavy rope, roughly shaped like a man weighing about 150 pounds and used in parachute tests. It was during another air show that Doolittle and friends hit upon what they imagined was a funny idea: "We threw out Hart, Schaffner, and Marx, but we fixed Marx's parachute so it wouldn't open. So these three—supposedly—people jumped; two of them came floating down and one of them would come down *thump!* My job was a very difficult one—it was to notify the Commanding Officer (Colonel Lawrence W. McIntosh) not that we were going to do this, because we knew he'd tell us not to, but to tell him after the thing got started that it was all right and nobody'd get hurt.

"So here I am standing by Colonel McIntosh and out jumped Hart, Schaffner, and Marx: Hart and Schaffner came floating down and Marx came down *thump*. My job as he was saying 'Oh, my God'—wringing his hands—'Oh, my God' was to say, 'Hey, Colonel, it's a joke, it's a joke,' while getting those beady eyes bored right through me." This particular "joke" was never known to have been repeated.

But the "lung tester" was a perennial favorite. This was a gadget consisting of a small can out of which projected a tube into which the subject would blow. Attached also was a small wheel. "The longer you could keep the wheel running, the greater your lung capacity. And you were supposed to do this with your eyes shut, because you could do a better job with your eyes shut —everybody was assured of that: you could blow longer with your eyes shut."

What the subject—or rather victim—did not know was that unless he closed the tiny hole in the tube, he would cover his face with carbon soot. Anyone in on the "test" simply closed the aperture and, of course, succeeded only in causing the wheel to turn.

A public demonstration of the lung tester came about when a traveling Broadway show came to Dayton and the cast was invited

Rosa Shephard Doolittle and Frank Doolittle, about the time of their marriage.
DOOLITTLE COLLECTION

En route to Alaska aboard the *Zealandia,* 1900. Sarah Shephard stands at far left;
her sister, Rosa Doolittle, is at extreme right.. To her right: James Harold
Doolittle, aged three. DOOLITTLE COLLECTION

The *Zealandia* arriving at Nome's ice-blocked waters. DOOLITTLE COLLECTION

Rosa Doolittle and the most efficient means of transportation in turn-of-the-century Nome. She is seated before the entrance to the Doolittle home—No. 301—which had been built by her husband, whose name is over the doorway: F. H. Doolittle. Huskies were never absolutely tamed and could be vicious; Doolittle remembered that one of his schoolmates had been killed by them. DOOLITTLE COLLECTION

James Doolittle, Nome, c. 1902.
ROBERT C. REEVES COLLECTION,
COURTESY C. V. GLINES

Mrs. Staple's fourth-grade class, Nome, 1904. Doolittle, the smallest boy, glowers at the left. DOOLITTLE COLLECTION

Rosa Doolittle models Nome's
springtime fashion. COURTESY
MRS. ROLAND W. MCNAMEE

Doolittle, about twelve, after he and his mother had moved to Los Angeles.
DOOLITTLE COLLECTION

ABOVE: Frank Doolittle in a rare
visit with his family, Los Angeles.
DOOLITTLE COLLECTION
RIGHT: Josephine E. Daniels and
her most persistent high school
suitor, on a Sunday afternoon.
DOOLITTLE COLLECTION

A dapper Doolittle, c. 1914, around the time he was a student at the Los Angeles Manual Arts High School. DOOLITTLE COLLECTION

Doolittle as a college boxer. The formal attire cannot be explained, except perhaps as a tribute to higher education. DOOLITTLE COLLECTION

Doolittle as a high school boxer. DOOLITTLE COLLECTION

Josephine ''Joe'' Daniels and successful suitor, c. 1917. DOOLITTLE COLLECTION

The University of California tumbling team; Doolittle is seated in the middle row, extreme left. Teammate Frank Capra is in front row, second from left. DOOLITTLE COLLECTION

out to tour the field. "One of the chaps," Doolittle recalled, "was a very dignified individual who was the heavy in the show. As the troupe came in it was arranged that we'd be blowing this lung tester.

"So we were trying this and the heavy, who was a rather conceited sort of fellow, came up and said, 'Let me try that, will you?' Now, we didn't tell him to—he wanted to try it. So with all of his friends around we told him to shut his eyes—as we had—so he did and was immediately surrounded in a cloud of lampblack. Of course, he didn't know what had happened because he couldn't see himself, but after his colleagues had gone into hysterics, we finally gave him a mirror—and I must say, he was not a very good sport."

Such were the peripheral amusements of the Flight Test Section; Doolittle's real job was a great deal more useful, though at times hazardous. An idea that General Mitchell had brought back from Europe, later known as the "trim tab," was tested by Doolittle at Wright Field. This was a small portion of the rudder's trailing edge, adjustable from the cockpit, which enabled the pilot to "trim" the controls and compensate for wind or a tendency of the plane to go off course by yawing. The question was how efficient the device might be and what effect it might have in its maximum position.

Accompanied by Lieutenant James T. Hutchinson, Doolittle took off for the test. At 5,000 feet he began trying the tab by placing it in different positions and taking the plane through various maneuvers at increasing speeds. All appeared to go well and the device did its job, but then he set it at the extreme position and severe vibrations afflicted the tail surfaces. Before he could set the tab back to neutral he felt the rudder-control wires snap.

He turned and shouted back to Hutchinson, "Want to jump?"

"Are you?" Hutchinson yelled back.

"No, I think I can bring it down."

"I'll stay," Hutchinson replied.

Doolittle was still at around 5,000 feet without means of directional control, except what could be accomplished with the ailerons. He lowered the speed and gently stalled the plane earthward, making slight turns with the help of the ailerons to keep the field below them. By stages, then, he stalled the plane directly onto the runway for a smooth landing. He had proved two things:

it was possible to fly a rudderless aircraft—though not recommended—and the trim tab required more work before being installed in other planes.

Thus was Doolittle occupied through the rest of 1925 after winning the Schneider Trophy. The year closed on a sour note for airmen with the court-martial of Billy Mitchell in December, resulting in his resignation. The new year began well, however, for Doolittle, who, along with his colleague Cyrus Bettis, was awarded the Mackay Trophy for their contribution to aviation.

In 1926 Doolittle participated in an unusual venture: co-operation between the Air Service and an aircraft manufacturer, the Curtiss-Wright Export Division. The expansion of the American aircraft industry would benefit both the manufacturer and the Air Service with the development of improved aircraft, based in part on the income from planes sold in the foreign market. These were military aircraft already considered obsolescent by the U. S. War Department. So it was that the president of Curtiss Export, Clarence Webster, and of Curtiss-Wright, C. M. Keyes, approached the War Department with a request to obtain the services of a skilled Army pilot who might act in the dual capacity of demonstrator-salesman of their P-1 Hawk fighter plane in South America. The pilot they had in mind was Doolittle, for several reasons. He was familiar with the P-1, he was noted for his skill as a pilot, he was a known name—and he could speak some Spanish. The War Department agreed to grant Doolittle a leave of absence—without pay, of course—for several months; Curtiss-Wright would provide him with expenses and living money.

Joe Doolittle and the boys were to remain in their quarters at McCook Field and Doolittle was to make the South American tour accompanied by Boyd Sherman, a Curtiss mechanic. By April they were in New York, where Doolittle began testing the Hawk they would take with them. They boarded ship, with the Hawk aboard, early in May and arrived, after a leisurely voyage and stopovers in the Canal Zone, at Lima, Peru, and at Arica and Antofagasta, Chile. The ship continued down the coast of Chile to Valparaiso, where they disembarked and set out for Santiago inland. The Hawk was shipped to El Bosque, a military airport, where Sherman attended to its assembly and where the demonstration was to take place. By mid-June they were ready.

Doolittle soon learned he was not the only international sales-man on the scene—there were export models of pursuit planes from Britain, Italy, and Germany. The German bid, Doolittle believed, represented the greatest threat in the form of a Dornier which would be flown by a former Richthofen Squadron pilot, Karl August von Schoenebeck.

Some nine days before the demonstrations were scheduled a party was given at the Officers' Club in Santiago. Doolittle's rule was never to drink anything alcoholic the day before he flew—the timing of the cocktail party enabled him to join in the conviviality. Following the consumption of a few *pisco* sours, a lethal Chilean specialty, the conversation ranged from aviation to the cinema, specifically the swashbuckling acrobatics of the popular Douglas Fairbanks. The Chileans loudly praised his swings, his leaps, and his tumbles—to which Doolittle, feeling the warmth of his *pisco* sour, responded that such antics were in the repertory of every red-blooded American boy.

There were some comments expressing disbelief. Whereupon, Doolittle, former member of his high school tumbling team, flipped over a time or two and proceeded to walk around the room on his hands. This was well received, indeed. The reception was most pleasing and, hoping to be even more Fairbanksian, he hopped onto the window sill (inevitable in every Fairbanks epic). The clubroom was on the second story and Doolittle continued his demonstration with a handwalk on the sill, to further cries of ad-miration. Just below the sill outside the room was a two-foot ledge to which Doolittle lowered himself and then performed his *pièce de résistance:* grasping the ledge, he raised himself so that he pro-jected from the ledge, his body parallel to the ground one floor below.

At this point the Fairbanks script went awry as the ledge began to crumble and, unable to scramble back into the room, Doolittle could only prepare himself for the fall into the courtyard twenty feet down.

Doolittle managed to arch himself in order to land on his feet, which he did—breaking both ankles. This was ascertained by X-ray in the hospital, where Doolittle was informed that he would require at least six weeks of inactivity to recover. It was then that the foolishness of his antics struck him; with the demonstration in the offing, what could he tell Curtiss-Wright? That he had injured himself by disporting on the ledge of a second-story window? His Army superiors, too, would not benevolently regard such exploits of their "fun-loving" Jimmy. He had plenty of time to mull this over in the hospital and as the day of the demonstrations drew closer, Doolittle pressed his doctor for a release from the hospital. This he was granted, both legs in casts, but with one admonition: no flying.

His hospital stay was not without incident. The X-rays had revealed a simple fracture of one ankle and a more complex one of the other. Somehow, someone had gotten the pictures confused and the fractures were improperly set, with the right cast on the left and vice versa. The fractures were not mending properly and it was in this condition that Doolittle hobbled out of the hospital on crutches.

Doolittle contributed some innovations of his own: "My recollection on the broken ankle bit is that I was in traction, and in considerable discomfort—as they tried to pull the broken ankle bones in place—for several days. Finally plaster casts were put on both legs. One was just below the knee and the other came to a half foot or so above the knee.

"On the morning of the ninth day after my fall I had my mechanic come in with a hacksaw blade and we cut the long cast off just below the knee. He also brought my winter flying boots. He had bolted metal clips on the bottom of the boots to help hold my feet on the rudder bars. That same afternoon I got up, dressed, and went out and flew a demonstration. This was on June 24, 1926. I did all 'snap' stunts to the right and the right cast broke in the ankle.

"On June 25 I gave another demonstration this time doing the 'snap' stunts to the left and the left cast broke.

"By this time the hospital people were so annoyed they wouldn't let me back in the hospital.

"I got in touch with a German prosthetic type and he made me two heavier plaster casts braced at the ankles with steel corset stays (the ladies wore them in those days)." These reinforced casts held up through the remainder of Doolittle's South American stay.

When the day of the Curtiss-Dornier competition came, in attendance was no less a personage than the President of Chile, along with members of his Cabinet and the Parliament and a full contingent of military men from the Chilean Army and Navy. Word of the American's disablement had made the rounds and gossip contributed a little spice. And he had not yet arrived at the airfield by the time von Schoenebeck had taken off in the Dornier and had begun his display of aerobatics.

During von Schoenebeck's exhibition an ambulance drove up alongside the Curtiss Hawk. Doolittle, his legs still in casts and further embellished with a strange steel contraption, was helped into the cockpit of the P-1 by Sherman and another man. Von Schoenebeck was still flitting around overhead when Sherman spun the propeller and Doolittle quickly took off. He was certain he had the superior plane: the Dornier's BMW engine was capable of 260 horsepower and his Curtiss, 400. While he respected von Schoenebeck's reputation as a flier and a wartime aviator, he climbed toward the Dornier with accustomed self-confidence.

Pulling his Hawk up alongside the Dornier he waved to von Schoenebeck, who saluted his opponent. Doolittle waggled his wings, gestured that they engage in a mock dogfight, and then made a pass at the Dornier. Von Schoenebeck apparently understood, waved back, and the "air battle" began. It would not be a personal grudge fight, merely a demonstration to show which plane was superior. The Hawk was faster and more maneuverable, which became obvious as the two aircraft circled and dodged above the watching crowd. Nothing von Schoenebeck did kept Doolittle from getting onto his tail or dancing around, over, and above him. The Chileans swore that Doolittle had actually brushed the upper wing of the Dornier.

The excitement of the dogfight took Doolittle's mind off his throbbing ankles, though he was not disappointed when von Schoenebeck pulled away and returned to the field. It was soon noted that the fabric of the Dornier's upper wing had ripped away from the leading edge and the Dornier's salesmen on the ground began to raise the issue of unfair advantage—obviously, they claimed, Doolittle *had* touched the upper wing with his landing gear. But von Schoenebeck disabused him. Doolittle had not touched the plane—the fabric had ripped away during their mock battle, a decided liability in a pursuit plane.

When Doolittle landed he too tried to explain to the Chileans, who were delighted with the exhibition but insisted they had *seen* him touch the Dornier. To have done that would have been irresponsible, Doolittle believed, and could have been dangerous. But the exuberant Chileans preferred their daredevil, and Doolittle, especially with two broken legs, certainly filled the bill. He had also revealed what might have been a fatal flaw in the Dornier, which apparently could not hold up under combat conditions. So he succeeded in winning an order for several Hawks from the Chilean government.

Having proved himself as a salesman, Doolittle decided to proceed with his South American tour as scheduled before his fall. By the middle of August he moved on to Bolivia where his reputation had preceded him from Chile. Unfortunately, relations between Chile and Bolivia were strained because of a border dispute and Doolittle was assumed to be a spy for Chile—and was even so denounced in the Bolivian Parliament.

Consequently, the Strangers Club where he was staying in La Paz was surrounded by a shouting, angry mob of over a thousand. The situation became so heated the Bolivian Army was called in to disperse the demonstrators. The following day Doolittle flew the Hawk for Bolivian military officials who, though impressed with the plane, felt that in light of the previous day's disturbances it would be better not to purchase it. For Doolittle it had been a painful, useless flight.

And so the tour continued, with Doolittle encased in plaster of Paris and steel and moving about on crutches, which, while he flew, he fastened into the Hawk's empty machine-gun mounts. Early in September he was due at Buenos Aires, Argentina, which presented a challenge. It would be his longest flight and would require crossing over the Andes, a rare feat in 1926. Passing over the range would mean flying at an altitude of roughly 18,000 feet —although one of the most majestic peaks, Aconcagua, reared up almost 23,000 feet.

The Andes had been flown before, but several Argentinian fliers had perished in their attempts. Doolittle flew under many handicaps, the major one being his broken ankles. He carried no parachute for the simple reason that, since he was clipped onto the rudder bar, it would have been most difficult to leave the plane if in trouble. And making a parachute landing, provided there was a place to land in the Andes, on broken ankles was unthinkable. But Doolittle, with the engine of his plane properly tuned up, did not foresee any need for a parachute anyway, and on September

3, 1926, he became the first North American to fly over the Andes range. (The unique distinction that he was the first, and to date the only, man to fly the Andes with two broken legs Doolittle has always regarded as a rather dubious one.)

By the end of September Doolittle had covered his territory (Argentina, too, had purchased some Hawks) and he boarded a ship and sailed for New York. From there he immediately proceeded to Washington, D.C. to have his ankles looked at by Army doctors. Some three months of neglect and abuse had taken their toll. New X-rays were taken and the doctors at Walter Reed Hospital were appalled. It was decided that it was too late for corrective refracturing and all that could be done was to immobilize Doolittle for a while and this meant, for Doolittle, imprisonment at Walter Reed.

While this "sentence" may have immobilized the restless Doolittle, it did reunite him with his family, for an extended period. He had been away for nearly half a year, and so when Joe Doolittle heard that he would be confined to Walter Reed for an extended period, she packed up herself and the boys—Jim, Jr., was six and John, four—and left Ohio for Washington, where she found an apartment near the hospital.

Doolittle spent the first month at Walter Reed confined to bed with his legs in casts; another month was spent, once he was permitted up and around, on crutches. After this he walked without the crutches to exercise his ankles. This tedious, often tormenting, process continued for six months and it was spring of 1927 before he was permitted to leave Walter Reed Hospital and return to Army duties at Wright Field.

During his forced inactivity, Doolittle did all of his flying in his head or on paper. During a discussion with fellow patients, the subject of the outside loop came up. There had been speculation on this maneuver for a long time, but no one was known to have ever tried it—at least, not successfully. The inside loop was common practice—this was accomplished with the cockpit facing the center of the loop's circle. Centrifugal force held the pilot tightly to the seat, sometimes at several times the pull of gravity, with a possible resultant blackout when the G-force was at its highest. The forces exerted upon pilot and plane in an outside loop were a mystery. The pilot's feet, instead of his head, would point toward the center of the circle—would centrifugal forces cause the blood to rush to his head as in the inside loop it rushed toward his feet, causing the blackout? What effect would this have on the internal organs? Would the pilot come popping out of the cockpit? What effect, for that matter, would it have on the plane?

Doolittle considered these questions and upon returning to Dayton began seriously working on the problem. He took up a Curtiss Hawk and step by step began working toward the execution of an outside loop. He flew inverted, he often approached the loop itself and then landed to see how the plane had taken the strain and to analyze his own discomfort. His recovery from the unusual stress was rapid and he appeared to suffer no lasting discomfort; and the plane weathered the strain equally well.

On May 25, 1927, just four days after Charles Lindbergh had landed at Paris, Doolittle took up the Hawk determined to try the outside loop. He had quietly informed a few of his friends who, along with a few others, watched as the Hawk leveled out at around 10,000 feet. Doolittle tipped the plane over into a dive and when he saw that maximum speed had been achieved—about 350 mph.—he pushed the control stick away from him. Soon he was in inverted flight and continued with the stick forward. Tremendous pressures drew the blood into his head and Doolittle literally saw red as he maneuvered the Hawk, certain he could describe a great circle before losing consciousness. But the sensation lasted for a fleeting moment as the little plane came over the top and Doolittle, stick still forward, completed the circle.

Once flying normally, Doolittle quickly recovered from the "red-out" and gingerly surveyed the plane for snapped wires or struts; the controls functioned and there appeared to be no structural failure. And, as far as he could feel, all his insides remained in their proper places and no blood cells had burst (two of the most persistent conjectures associated with the outside loop).

Upon landing Doolittle was greeted by his colleagues with jubilation and word soon got out and he was once again page-one copy. When one newsman asked Doolittle how it was he had come to attempt the impossible, Doolittle—conveniently disregarding his days of pretesting—answered jokingly, "Just thought of it on the spur of the moment."

It was not long after that official word came down: there would be no more outside loops flown by Army pilots, whatever their momentary fancy.

Nine

Curtiss-Wright, apparently pleased with Doolittle's flying salesmanship "borrowed" him again from what was now known as the United States Army Air Corps for another South American tour. In January of 1928 Doolittle set out again by ship from New York, this time with two aircraft, the familiar P-1 and a larger two-place O-1 (O for Observation). Accompanying him was a civilian pilot, William H. McMullen, and two Curtiss mechanics.

They debarked at Lima, Peru, and began demonstrating the two Curtisses, using both wheels and pontoons. The O-1 was employed as a good public relations craft, in that its second cockpit could be used to carry officials who might like to be taken up for joyrides. While in Lima he also met two distraught American tourists who had managed to miss their ship. In a surge of chivalry Doolittle offered to fly the two young ladies to the ship's next stop, Salaverry, about 300 miles to the north. With his two passengers crowded into the rear cockpit of the O-1, Doolittle got them to their port on time. The first incident upon his arrival gave him pause: would it set the tone of the second South American tour? He had landed the plane, stepped down onto the beach, and was promptly bitten by a large yellow mongrel, which then, tail wagging, went away.

La Paz, Bolivia, was the next stop and Doolittle was happy to learn that he was no longer regarded as a spy for Chile. Emboldened by warm greetings and general friendliness, Doolittle decided he might interest the Bolivian military in seaplanes (the fact that Bolivia had no seacoast did not deter him). The site for the demonstration was Lake Titicaca (the fact that the lake was situated some 12,500 feet above sea level, the highest big lake in the world, did not deter him either). He hoped that despite the rarefied air at that altitude he would be able to get the little P-1, equipped with floats, off the surface of the lake.

Word of his coming demonstration had gotten around La Paz and public excitement rose; an excursion train was scheduled to bring crowds to Lake Titicaca on the day of the great event. Doolittle had some misgivings and quietly moved the Hawk out to the lake where the mechanics switched the wheels for pontoons and pushed the plane into the water. It was glassy smooth and there was no wind; not a good sign. Doolittle, with engine turning over nicely, pushed the throttle and skimmed along the surface. But not even at full power could he get the Hawk unstuck from the lake. He maneuvered and splashed, he waggled the wings hoping thus to get one pontoon into the air and the other to follow. Rocking dangerously from left to right, right to left accomplished nothing either, except on one of the bounces a strut gave way and Doolittle had to call it a day—the demonstration was abandoned and so were all plans for a Bolivian naval air force.

Before leaving La Paz Doolittle successfully demonstrated the use of the airplane over mountain and jungle, and also acquired a bit of curious anthropological lore. He met a man named Charles Wallen, who managed a large gold mine located about a hundred miles distant, just over the Andes at Tipuani.

Wallen had just made the nine-day journey by mule to La Paz and was exhausted, but about to return right away with medical supplies. He told Doolittle of the problem: the mine employed Indians, locally known as "The Bad Indians," from the headwaters of the Amazon. The name had been earned because of their natural antipathy toward tax collectors, who for about a hundred years had been disappearing in Bad Indian country.

As Wallen explained it, "Things have been rather dull since they stopped sending tax collectors to Tipuani, so they had a little session of their favorite game just nine days ago." This was a game called *probando la suerte,* which Doolittle translated roughly as "trying your luck."

"They play it this way," Wallen continued. "Some forty men stand in a circle just close enough so their outstretched arms will touch. Then they take a quarter stick of dynamite, attach a long fuse to it, light the fuse, and start passing it from hand to hand. They pass it quickly and expertly, but always there is that last man who has it when the dynamite explodes. He is considered unlucky . . ."

The doctor at the mine, Wallen concluded, was keeping about a dozen men alive "with whiskey and quinine." Now he had to get real medical supplies over the mountain to Tipuani.

Doolittle suggested that Wallen get the medicines and meet him at the airport, explaining, "I'll have you there in no time." Wallen pointed out that the Tipuani mine was in the middle of a jungle and there would be no place to land. Doolittle was certain that would be the case and had conceived a plan of swooping down low in the Curtiss O-1, the two-seater, and have Wallen drop the supplies in some clearing near the camp. This was done and he and Wallen were back in La Paz within an hour. The demonstration so impressed Wallen that he made plans to acquire his own Curtiss, have a landing strip cut near the mine, and save himself a great deal of travel time. The following year Wallen bought a small fleet of planes and initiated an embryo airline in Bolivia.

By this time the landing gear strut of the Hawk had been repaired and Doolittle and McMullen were ready to move on to Chile. On July 2 an exhibition for the Chilean Navy was scheduled and the O-1 was fitted with pontoons for the event. At the time British officers were serving as advisers to the Chilean Navy and one of them, Commander Bruce Jones, expressed a great interest in giving the Curtiss a test run himself. He assured Doolittle of his familiarity with the plane and the flight began.

Jones was piloting in the front cockpit and Doolittle sat behind; he began immediately to have misgivings. Jones's handling of the plane during the taxiing was none too adroit, but perhaps he was familiarizing himself with the controls. But then when Jones gave the plane full throttle, Doolittle wondered whether his pilot had ever taken a plane off from water before. The O-1 veered in the water, dipping from side to side, great waves splashing in its twisting, turbulent, wake. Doolittle sat helpless in the controlless rear seat, hoping for the best. It was obvious that Jones was overcontrolling the plane, which at near takeoff speed was clipping through the wave crests. Inevitably, a wing float caught a wave, the left wing suddenly went under, and the Curtiss cartwheeled out of the water for a moment then came down on its back with a spectacular splash.

Almost equally startling to observers was the figure of a man who was flung several yards from the plane into the bay, also landing with a splash (it was Commander Jones, who had neglected to fasten his seat belt). Doolittle, still inside the plane, merely unfastened his safety belt and swam clear of the wreckage. Almost immediately he spotted Jones drifting in the water, obviously unconscious. Doolittle swam to Jones and with one hand held the Englishman's head above water and with the other clung to a drifting pontoon.

While a rescue boat was on its way, Doolittle suffered some uncomfortable moments. The pontoon, obviously punctured, had begun to sink under his and the Briton's weight, their heavy flying boots contributing to the dead weight. However, the rescuers arrived in time and the two men were pulled out of the water. Jones was not injured, only had the wind knocked out of him by his unexpected exit from the plane. Doolittle accepted Jones's thanks with grace, although he mentally kicked himself for having permitted anyone at the controls of the plane, now a complete washout, without being absolutely certain of his ability to control it.

Left only with the little Hawk, Doolittle decided to leave McMullen behind and continue with the demonstration tour alone, dramatizing the plane's qualities by making various record flights. He repeated his cross-Andes flight from Santiago to Buenos Aires and at the same time succeeded in cutting nearly a half hour from the time, setting a new record of 5 hours, 45 minutes for the flight. This feat was followed by an exhibition of aerobatics and a party held in Doolittle's honor by the Minister of War. Doolittle was toasted in Spanish and it pleased his hosts to be answered in their native tongue. It puzzled Doolittle, however, that some of his remarks were greeted with chuckles—he was referring to his flight, after crossing the Andes, over the beautiful green plains—*chatas* —of Argentina (*chata* signifying flat). Doolittle, though quite fluent in Spanish, was not quite up on his idioms and it amused his audience to be informed of how much Doolittle enjoyed flying over the beautiful bedpans (*chatas*) of Argentina.

His itinerary took him to Asuncion, Paraguay, and from there to Rio de Janeiro, a flight of 7 hours, 10 minutes, which took him over the southern part of the uncharted Mato Grosso of Brazil. It was another first for Doolittle, for he was the first airman to cross that great, generally unexplored jungle. "The trees were tremendous," he would later recall of the flight, "laced with vines that must have been six inches thick . . .

"I didn't see one sign of human life in over five hundred miles of jungle, no sign of life at all except flocks of green parrots. I knew they were parrots only when they flew. Otherwise they were green things in a green world, but when disturbed by the noise and the prop wash, they would whirl up below me, the yellows and browns of their wings and feet flashing in a splash of color. It was eerie.

"I flew over great rivers that were on no map and imagined what would happen if the engine of the little Curtiss failed."

As he drew near Rio, Doolittle spotted a railroad and, hoping to ascertain his exact location, dropped down to read the names on the stations, the first being "Mictorio," which was puzzling since it was not a town he had ever heard of. Continuing to follow the track he came upon another station and once again read "Mictorio." He gave up this method of navigation and climbed above the jungle. (It was later that Doolittle learned that "Mictorio" appeared on the west end of every railroad station and indicated the location of the men's room.)

He continued on, still slightly puzzled. "My only navigating instrument was the compass, but I was lucky again: seven hours and ten minutes after takeoff, I hit Rio right on the nose." (For his flight over the Mato Grosso Doolittle was made a member of the prestigious Explorers Club.)

So it was that from July until the late summer Doolittle connected several South American capitals by air, flew his exhibition flights, was dined and feted—at La Paz he was presented with the Bolivian Order of the Condor—and generally spread good will and, of course, sold Curtiss-Wright airplanes. His six-month tour over, Doolittle again returned home by ship.

The tour had been very successful, not only commercially for Curtiss-Wright, but also personally for Doolittle. He had been on his own, selected his own goals, and accomplished them. But once aboard ship he was no longer his own boss but a thirty-one-year-old first lieutenant, with a wife and two young children awaiting him. His family responsibilities and his future in the service weighed heavily on Doolittle's mind during the trip home.

What had once been the Air Service had become by that summer of 1928 the U. S. Army Air Corps. General Billy Mitchell had long since lost his fight to make it an independent service and the mere change in name promised little so far as its future, and, for that matter, the future of its members, went.

However, returning to Dayton meant a reunion with his family; long absences, particularly from his sons, did not help fulfill Doolittle's intention to be more of a father to his children than Frank Doolittle had been to him. His travels, he was aware, placed the burden of his sons' rearing upon Joe Doolittle. His natural tendency was then toward overcompensation, which, to his later disappointed mystification, his sons later rejected to seek out friends of their own generation.

Reunions in the lively Doolittle household were tumultuous as father and sons celebrated in a rough-and-tumble manner. But having barely arrived, Doolittle learned that he was about to enter a new phase in his career. Once again the Army willingly lent him out on an independent project, the first in which the still rather unknown Doctor Doolittle would begin to practice as a professional engineer.

This phase in Doolittle's life had its roots in the founding two years before of the Daniel Guggenheim Fund for the Promotion of Aeronautics. Daniel Guggenheim, the mining magnate, provided the fund with $2.5 million which was administered by an eminent board of trustees in co-operation with the United States Government. The president of the fund was Harry Guggenheim, son of the founder; this was not mere nepotism—the younger Guggenheim was a former Navy flier and devoted to the cause of aviation. His vice president at the time was a Navy loanee, Captain Emory Land. When Harry Guggenheim decided to establish the Full Flight Laboratory at Mitchel Field, New York, for the study of flight under adverse weather conditions, he asked Land who should be approached to head the laboratory. Land, who would become an admiral during the Second World War, in charge of the Maritime Commission, suggested Doolittle, recalling Doolittle's performance during the Schneider Cup races in 1925. "This was my sincere conviction," Land later commented, "and you can realize that it did not make me popular with my Navy associates."

The Full Flight Laboratory was established in 1928; by late September the Doolittles themselves were established in what had been temporary officers' quarters during the First World War— these had been described as "temporary" ten years before. With three and a half of these units assigned to them the Doolittles had plenty of space for the boys to run in and for crowds of visitors. On these occasions caution was required for the quarters had not been designed for the dancing of the Jazz Age; once, in fact, the heavy phonograph fell through the floor.

It was at Mitchel Field during the Full Flight Laboratory stay that Joe Doolittle's renown as a cook and baker flowered; she also brewed, according to those who sampled it, the best beer in the world (and otherwise unavailable because of Prohibition). Her secret lay in the hops friends grew in California and which Doolittle's pilot friends flew in to New York whenever possible.

Doolittle found his laboratory more luxurious than their quarters—and more generously staffed. Assisting him would be Professor William G. Brown of the Aeronautics Department of MIT, whose specialty was in the field of instruments and radio; Lieutenant Benjamin S. Kelsey was also granted detached service from the Air Corps to be flight assistant and safety pilot, and Sergeant Jack Dalton to serve as his crew chief (later, when he left the Air Corps, Doolittle would arrange to "buy out" Dalton to become his mechanic when Doolittle joined Shell. In the peacetime Army it was possible to manage a discharge before one's enlistment had been fulfilled).

"From the first," Doolittle has written, "it was understood that flight safety and reliability were important considerations and that one phase of the Fund's work would be to study means of assuring safe and reliable flights despite weather conditions. With this in mind, a special committee of experts was organized to define the problem. A directive was prepared which authorized a study to include the following: dissipation of fog; development of some means whereby flying fields might be located from the air regardless of fog; developments to show accurately the height of airplanes above the ground, to replace barometric instruments which show height above sea level; improvement and perfection of in-

struments allowing airplanes to fly properly in fog; and the penetration of fog by light rays."

The project began with a study of the work that had been done
before: the use of tethered balloons, for example, for indicating a
landing strip on foggy days—which worked provided the fog was
not too thick and there was no wind. "In both England and
France," Doolittle noted, "the lead-in cable idea was tried out. In
this system, an electrified cable circled the field and led in to a
landing. It required very sensitive equipment in the airplane and it
was necessary to make a precision turn into the field at low altitude. This turn was extremely difficult to make. . . . Actual blind
landings had been attempted with dragging weights and with long
tail skids. These either gave an indication upon touching the
ground or were rigged to actuate the aircraft control."

None of these systems was the complete solution to bad-weather
flying, although there were some existing instruments and certain
radio equipment that, with a refinement or two, Doolittle and his
staff believed could evolve into an answer.

The Full Flight Laboratory was provided with two new aircraft.
The first was a Consolidate NY-2, originally designed as a Navy
trainer. In place of its customary pontoons a reinforced landing
gear had been installed. With its generous wing area, the Consolidated was an extremely stable, slow-landing plane and would be
used for the instrument-landing experiments, as well as for testing
any devices and instruments that might be required. The second
plane was also a Navy plane, a Vought O2U-1 Corsair. It was a
faster plane than the Consolidated and would be employed in
cross-country flying, for quick transport, and for pick-ups and de-
liveries.

Doolittle found that as "the preliminary practice flights progressed, it soon became apparent that even with the very stable
and sturdy NY-2, the available instruments were not adequate.
For determining heading when maneuvering and when landing,
the compass, due to the northerly turning error, was entirely un-
satisfactory and the bank-and-turn indicator, though excellent for
its purpose, was more a qualitative than a quantitative measuring
instrument. Also, at the moment of touchdown in a blind landing,
it was imperative that the wings be level with the ground. This was
not easy to assure, particularly when the wind was gusty."

The two planes were acquired in November of 1928; on the

date the Corsair arrived, November 28, Doolittle and Harry Guggenheim climbed into it and flew up to Boston. Familiarization flights were made in the NY-2 through November and December and then it was grounded for extended periods in Boonton, New Jersey, at the Radio Frequency Laboratory where equipment was installed for blind flying, particularly a device that would enable Doolittle to follow beams and beacons in fog.

During the period of the Consolidated's grounding, Doolittle would use the Corsair for cross-country flights under unfavorable weather conditions. While it carried the most modern flight instruments, it did not have the blind-landing equipment being developed for the NY-2. The need for that instrumentation was rather forcefully demonstrated on March 15, 1929.

"I took off from Buffalo in the O2U-1 [and] headed for Mitchel Field," Doolittle has recounted. "It was night, and the weather was fair and improving at Buffalo, but marginal to the south and east. This was to be a difficult flight but possible, and just the sort of thing required to establish flight 'limitations.' In a pinch I could return to Buffalo at any time up to the point where nearly half of the gasoline supply was used up.

"I well realized that the pilot who flew within his limitations would probably live to a ripe old age, whereas the pilot who flew beyond them would not. I also knew that different pilots had different limitations. This was pointed up in the mid-1920's when I was a test pilot at old McCook Field.

"At that time there were few facilities and little ground equipment to do environmental testing on new airborne devices. It was therefore necessary to test them out in flight, and the test pilots spent many hours flying around the airfield to see how a device held up under the accelerations, vibrations, and changes in temperature and pressure experienced in flight. Lt. Alex Pearson always spent these hours practicing precision flying; for instance, holding constant speed and altitude. As a result he became extremely proficient and could fly a better speed course or do a smoother saw-tooth climb than any of the rest of us.

"I spent the hours flying low in the vicinity of McCook Field and on the main air routes in and out, memorizing the terrain. I knew every high building, tree, silo, windmill, radio tower, and high-tension line in the area. I could therefore fly in—or under—adverse weather safely when other equally experienced pilots did not fly. This was not because I was a better or more daring pilot than my colleagues; constant practice had simply extended my limitations. The trick was to learn your limitations, gradually expand them, but never go beyond them. I thought I was being smart, but the commanding officer, learning that I frequently flew in that area when other pilots did not, thought differently. Unaware of my training plan, he removed me from the job of chief pilot in the flying section, advising me that I did not have judgment enough to be a pilot and assigned me to the airplane section as an aeronautical engineer.

"All these things went through my mind as the weather deteriorated. I planned to fly contact all the way and therefore, in order to avoid the mountains, took the route Buffalo, Rochester, Syracuse, Utica, Schenectady, Albany, and then down the Hudson River. There was no particular problem getting to Albany, but from there on the ceiling and visibility became marginal. Soon I had passed the 'point of no return' and no longer had gasoline enough to get back to Buffalo.

"At one place I found it expedient to slow down and hover with the left wing of the airplane over a brightly lighted southbound passenger train traveling along the east side of the Hudson River. Presently it went through a cut, making its pursuit too hazardous, so I left the train and followed the riverbank. I considered cross-ing the river and landing on the parade ground at West Point, but abandoned this idea as the weather remained flyable—barely.

"Upon reaching the lights and heat of New York City, and finding the ceiling and visibility slightly improved; I flew south to the Battery hoping to be able to get to Mitchel Field from there, but the East River and the area to the south were 'socked in' and I could not go on. I next tried to get to Governor's Island and land on the drill ground, but it was fog shrouded, as was also the Yonkers Golf Course which I next hoped to use for an emergency landing after having turned north back up the Hudson. I then returned to the Battery with the intention of crash landing in Battery Park, but a chap ran out into the middle of the park and waved me off. He apparently thought I mistook it for a flying field.

"It is interesting to note that the George Washington Bridge across the Hudson at 179th Street was under construction at this time. There was as yet no suspension cables or other horizontal structure, and only the great vertical piers on each side of the river had been completed. I had passed the east pier three times without seeing it.

"About this time it appeared that a crash landing in the river might be necessary, so I removed my parachute in order to be able to swim ashore. The water, on closer inspection, looked uninviting, and I decided on a final try—this time for Newark Airport—and headed across the Hudson. As soon as the river was crossed and the lights south of Jersey City appeared, it became obvious that this last chance was impractical. Thereupon I climbed up through the fog, which was only about a thousand feet thick with crystal-clear skies above, intending to fly west until past the thickly populated part of the metropolitan area and then jump. The gasoline gauge had been fluttering on zero for some time. I noted about this time that my parachute harness was off and promptly put it on.

"About over Kenilworth, beyond Elizabeth, I saw a revolving beacon through a hole in the fog and a flat-looking area adjacent to it with no lights. Hoping it might be an emergency field or at least an open area, although realizing that it might be a woods or a lake, I turned the landing lights on and dove through the hole and scouted the area. The bottom of the fog was still very low, and I tore the left lower wing badly on a treetop. The airplane still flew, although almost completely out of gasoline, so I returned to the most likely spot and crash-landed, taking the impact by wrapping the left wing around a tree trunk near the ground. The O2U-1 was completely washed out—quite beyond repair—but I was not even scratched or bruised.

"The moral of the story is that had I been flying the NY-2 mounting blind-landing equipment and with the Full Flight Laboratory radio alerted at Mitchel, this would have been a routine cross-country flight with 'no sweat.'"

However, before they finally developed the solution to the problem of blind flight, various means of coping with fog were tested. For example, as Doolittle put it, "I developed through trial and error a method of literally flying an airplane into the ground. At the far end of the field I had a radio beacon toward which I flew. At the other end I had a fan beacon of lights that marked my approach. On passing the fan beacon at a prescribed altitude, there was a mark on the throttle segment to which I put the throttle. That mark gave me just enough throttle to come down in a very flat glide, and I would just fly right into the ground, and the airplane would scarcely bounce. This technique, along with the new instruments we were able to acquire, allowed me to practice blind landings with a canvas hood over the cockpit."

This technique, needless to say, would hardly work for everyone. The key to the problem lay in instruments.

Since "flying into the ground" was an intricate operation, it was clear that a precise altimeter was required, certainly one much more sensitive than was then in use. Word had come to Doolittle of a man in Brooklyn who had developed a barometric altimeter that might fill the bill. He was Paul Kollsman, a brilliant young German emigré, who had left his job at an instrument company to design his own altimeter, which he was certain would be an improvement. He set up his shop in a garage behind his home on Junius Street in the Greenpoint section of Brooklyn and began work. An indication of his avidity for precision was the fact that he had the gears of his design made by Swiss watchmakers he knew in New York.

Impressed with Kollsman's instrument, Doolittle suggested that they give it a test, so he took Kollsman up for a flight, with the latter holding his new device in his lap. The readings were remarkably precise—within feet—on this and subsequent flights, so that Doolittle was certain he had his altimeter which he regards as "the father of all altimeters used today."

Doolittle next approached another remarkable man, Dr. Elmer Sperry, Sr., famed as an electrician and innovator in the field of gyroscopic instruments. As Doolittle explained, "An accurate, reliable, and easy-to-read instrument showing exact direction of heading and precise attitude of the aircraft was required, particularly for the initial and final stages of blind landings. Two German artificial-horizon instruments, the Anschutz and the Gyrorector, were studied but were not deemed entirely satisfactory." In short, an instrument was required that could inform you that you were headed for a definite point indicated by a radio beam, so that you knew where you were relative to the landing strip. "Attitude" was crucial—it was important to know that the aircraft was on the correct axes as it rode down that directional beam—that you were not coming in nose down or with tail down or a wingtip rather than your landing gear and tailskid in position to strike the ground.

"I sketched a rough picture of the dial for an instrument which

I thought would do the job and showed it to Elmer Sperry, Sr. . . . It was, in substance, the face of a directional gyro superimposed on an artificial horizon. He advised that a single gyroscopic instrument could be designed to meet the requirements, but recommended, for simplicity of construction, two separate instruments. I agreed, and he then assigned his very ingenious son, Elmer, Jr., to work with us and to be responsible for the design and fabrication of the two instruments. We could not have had a better colleague. Elmer, also, soon became a member of the team and spent as much time at the hangar and at the evening 'discussion' sessions in our quarters on Mitchel Field as the rest of us. These evening sessions were frequent and long. The wives joined their husbands and helped in the work. Out of this, as you know, came the Sperry Artificial Horizon and the Sperry Directional Gyroscope which still, with their descendants, are on the instrument panel of every airliner and military airplane today." (Interestingly, after some forty years, the dual-instrument dial that Doolittle conceived and sketched for Elmer Sperry, Sr., is still in fairly common use.)

Before these instruments were devised, other methods were tried and abandoned. One was a sonic device which utilized a kind of megaphone installed on the underside of the NY-2's fuselage. This emitted a tone of a specific frequency toward the ground which bounced back; the time lapse would denote the altitude of the aircraft. "The concept was theoretically sound," Doolittle recalled, "but in its initial form the equipment caused considerable drag and was unduly large, heavy, difficult to install, and complicated. It also appeared that a radio altimeter measuring the phase difference of radio waves reflected back from the ground offered more promise. Several radio altimeters were under development—with fund encouragement—and the sonic altimeter experiments were therefore abandoned."

Another abandoned experiment was a curious fog dispersal idea of one Harry Raeder. A Clevelander, Raeder operated a quarry and had built himself a "large blowtorch type of heater" to break rock. He had observed that on days of intense fog that the area around the giant blowtorch was clear. Hearing about the work of the Full Flight Laboratory, he communicated with Doolittle and was encouraged to bring his "blowtorch" to Mitchel Field.

Meanwhile, Doolittle continued making test flights with the various instruments under development. One of these was called a "vibrating reed homing range indicator" and—to oversimplify— employed an instrument that zeroed in on a radio beam. When the two reeds vibrated equally the aircraft was on course; when too far to either the right or left, the off-course reed would vibrate through a greater amplitude and adjustment could be made to get the plane back on course.

After one of Raeder's heaters was installed at Mitchel Field, a little to the east of the last hanger, Doolittle and his crew waited for months in vain for a dense fog. "Finally, on September 24, 1929, it came. Someone, I think it was Jack Dalton, awakened just before daylight and noted that there was a zero-zero fog covering the area. Our gang was quickly called together. We immediately notified Mr. Raeder, who arrived shortly thereafter. Mr. Guggenheim was also notified, but he had to come from Port Washington and didn't arrive until later. The equipment was fired up, but the fog did not disperse except in the immediate vicinity of the blowtorch. The experiment was a disappointing failure. At the time we considered the concept impractical and the equipment was removed." (The difficulty lay in trying to disperse a moving fog; years later, during the Second World War a similar system, FIDO [Fog, Intense, Dispersal Of] was used in Britain on stationary fog and proved successful. "They had great burners on the sides of the runways, and we saved thousands of men and aircraft that would have been lost by bringing them into tunnels created by FIDO.")

Doolittle recounts what occurred following the failure of Raeder's blowtorch: "Though we were all disappointed, we were there, and the fog was there, so I decided to make a real fog flight. The NY-2 was pushed out of the hanger and warmed up. The ground radios were manned and the radio beacons turned on. I taxied out to the middle of the field and took off. Coming through the fog at about 500 feet and making a wide swing, I came around into landing position. By the time I landed 10 minutes after takeoff, the fog had started to lift.

"About this time Mr. Guggenheim, along with several other people, arrived and we decided to do an 'official,' under-the-hood flight. I had just made a real flight in the fog and wanted to go alone, but Mr. Guggenheim insisted that Ben Kelsey be taken along as safety pilot. The fog had lifted considerably by this time, and he was afraid there might be other aircraft in the vicinity.

"We both got into the airplane, and the hood over my cockpit was closed. The engine was again warmed up and I taxied the airplane out and turned into the takeoff position direction on the radio beam. We took off and flew west in a gradual climb. At about 1,000 feet the airplane was leveled off and a 180-degree turn was made to the left. This course was flown for several miles and another 180-degree turn to the left was made. The airplane was lined up on the left of the radio range located on the west side of Mitchel Field and a gradual descent was started. I leveled off at 200 feet above the ground and flew at this altitude until the fan beacon on the east side of the airfield was passed. From this point the airplane was flown into the ground, using the instrument landing procedure previously developed. Actually, despite previous practice, the final approach and landing were sloppy. This entire flight was made under the hood in a completely covered cockpit which had been carefully sealed to keep out all light. The flight, from takeoff to landing, lasted 15 minutes. It was the first time an airplane had been taken off, flown over a set course, and landed by instruments alone." Not once during the flight did Kelsey touch the controls; seated in the front cockpit, he conspicuously held his hands aloft during the takeoff and landing so that all witnesses could see Doolittle was flying blind.

The flight made the front page of the New York *Times* the next day, noting that the "demonstration was more than an exhibition of blind flying and instrument perfection. It indicated that aviation had perhaps taken its greatest single step in safety."

The evening of that September 24, 1929, was given over to a memorable celebration of the blind flight at the Doolittles. It marked the initiation of a family custom: all who worked on the project signed Joe Doolittle's large white damask tablecloth. She then stitched the signatures into the cloth, with black silk thread, for permanence. This practice continued over the years and the tablecloth became a mass of signatures, among them some of the most glowing names in aviation. It is now ·in the Aviation and Space Museum of the Smithsonian Institution.

Ten

Not all of Doolittle's adventures during the Full Flight Laboratory phase were connected with his work for the Guggenheim Fund. One incident worth recounting occurred about two weeks before the blind flight and might very well have canceled out that historic event.

Doolittle, somewhat reluctantly, let himself be talked into appearing at the National Air Races that were held at Cleveland that year (August 27–September 2, 1929). As noted by Don Vorderman in his study *The Great Air Races,* "By 1929 the National Air Races, particularly since the end of the Pulitzer contests, had degenerated into an annual aerial sideshow." Pulitzer apparently lost interest in the races after the last was flown in 1925. By this time the cost of designing and building high-speed aircraft had become prohibitive for civilian pilots; the final three Pulitzer Trophy races were Army-Navy contests, an extension of interservice rivalry.

The promotors of the 1929 Nationals hoped to get daredevil Doolittle to come out to entertain the crowd with some of his characteristic aerobatics, but he demurred. They persisted, having obtained permission from the Army Air Corps, even had a Curtiss Hawk ready for him. Doolittle had too much to do at Mitchel Field and continued to find excuses. He then received a call from Major General James E. Fechet, then head of the Air Corps, "requesting" him to make the Cleveland appearance; Doolittle warmed up the Corsair and arrived in Cleveland on the morning of September 1. The Hawk, a P-1 like those he had flown so often, had been modified—the nose had been streamlined by moving the radiator to the upper wing, and as a result it probably dived faster than the conventional Hawk.

Since he had been flying the slow Consolidated NY-2 primarily, Doolittle decided to get in a little practice in the Hawk before the scheduled exhibition. As he lifted the plane off the runway perhaps there was a gleam of mischief in his eye. It had been General Patrick, his former chief, present in the stands that year at Cleveland, who had issued the directive forbidding outside loops after Doolittle's successful demonstration. "But the general had not said that you couldn't push a plane under and pull it out. I thought this would be a rather spectacular stunt . . ."

Having gained altitude some distance away from the field, he began maneuvering the Hawk and, satisfied with its response to his handling, began to practice his "rather spectacular stunt." He was at around 2,000 feet when the wings of the little fighter cracked off and folded back. The plane careened through space as Doolittle unsnapped his safety belt and on one of the turns was ejected from the cockpit. He had never had to use a parachute before—although he had made practice jumps—and he dropped 1,000 feet before he pulled the ring and the chute billowed out above him, making him a full-fledged member of the Caterpillar Club (named in honor of the source of the silk from which parachutes were then made. A pilot forced to leave his plane via "the silk" became a member of the club).

Doolittle was soon picked up and driven back to the field and, rather chagrined, walked into the Air Corps' headquarters there with his parachute bundled under his arm. He never forgot the exchange between himself and a friend, Lieutenant Courtland Johnson:

DOOLITTLE: "My airplane broke up."

JOHNSON (*startled*): "Did you get out all right?"

Doolittle assured him he had and made arrangements for another plane, completed his practice flight, and during the same afternoon, gave his exhibition and then returned to Mitchel Field.

The 1929 Nationals had not turned out well for either the Army or the Navy, both of which had planes entered in the Thompson Cup race that took place the day after Doolittle's mishap. The services lost out to a civil aircraft, a Travel Air R, more popularly known as the "Mystery Ship" because of pilot Douglas Davis' penchant for keeping it under wraps until the race itself. As a result, the two services received a bad drubbing in various aviation publications. The gist of the criticism ran: what good were military aircraft designed to protect the nation if they could be outmaneuvered (when Davis missed a pylon, he corrected himself, flew back, and still won the race) and outrun by a civil aircraft? This shocking fact would have some effect upon the future design of military aircraft in the United States.

If the aviation press engaged in close re-evaluation of military planes, Doolittle, with the work for the Guggenheim Fund ended, was also forced to review his own past with the Air Corps and question the future. He not only had a family, but both his mother and Joe's were in poor health and required special medical attention. The closing down of the Full Flight Laboratory at the end of the year would cut off a substantial source of income ($500 a month, more than twice his Air Corps pay); another $100 had been coming in from Sikorsky Aircraft, who paid Doolittle $100 a day as a consultant (Doolittle spent one day a month on this job). That, too, ended because of the Depression. The Doolittles, with their growing boys and ailing parents, would have to subsist on Doolittle's military pay of barely $200 a month.

Just as all the equipment, materials, and data from the Full Flight Laboratory would revert to the Air Corps, so would Doolittle. He had been in the grade of first lieutenant for nine years (not unusual during this period); what with his obligations, he felt he would have to consider the future more objectively than he had before.

Doolittle had, from time to time, received offers from private industry, especially as his reputation grew, thanks to regular press features about his exploits. Late in 1929, before the Guggenheim assignment concluded, Doolittle received an offer from Shell Petroleum in St. Louis (one of three United States-based affiliates of the Anglo-Dutch firm). Seeking new outlets for one of its products, Shell in San Francisco had set up an aviation department under former Air Corps Major John A. Macready, an old Doolittle friend (and with whom Doolittle had once planned an aborted transpacific flight in 1924). Macready, who had made record altitude flights during his Army career, had joined Shell in 1929. He then suggested Doolittle as his counterpart in St. Louis. With the public relations factor in mind, the Shell management went further: they approached Doolittle and James Haizlip, like Doolittle a veteran of the Mexican border patrol days and a well-known racing and stunt pilot. The idea was to furnish the two pilots with aircraft and have them enter races, often competing with each other, thus publicizing Shell products. Both men were widely known in aviation circles also, which would have its public relations effect. Shell's plan was to exploit its aviation fuel expertise which it had begun to acquire in the First World War; with the curtailing of the automobile fuel market because of the Depression, it was hoped that aviation would at least make up for those losses.

Doolittle was cautious; he had known no other life but that of the Army since 1917. Entering the lists of business might have its drawbacks. Using some accumulated leave he had coming, he decided to meet his co-workers and bosses-to-be in St. Louis; if they appeared not to take to him and vice versa, he could remain in the Army. However, hanging heavily over him were the medical needs of his mother and Mrs. Daniels.

Alexander Fraser, vice president of Shell in St. Louis, had been briefed by another member of the firm, Theodore Peck, a Doolittle advocate, and was ready for him. Fraser and Doolittle began on a friendly note of respect; when he was offered his own plane Doolittle was convinced that he had found a place with Shell. The next step was to inform the Army, and thanks to the intervention of the understanding Chief of the Air Corps, General Fechet, Doolittle was placed on reserve status—with the rank of major, skipping the grade of captain altogether.

His final assignment for the Army was an airport survey which began on Christmas Day 1929 and took him cross-country to California, where, at Burbank, he picked up a new $25,000 Lockheed Vega, which he flew back to Mitchel Field. He planned to pick up Joe, the boys, and some of their possessions, leaving the rest to be shipped, and continue on to St. Louis, to report in at Shell. His contract with Shell began on February 15, 1930. The next day all the Doolittles and some odds and ends were loaded into the Vega for the flight to St. Louis.

The weather had been bad; previous rains had softened up the field which had then been cut up by aircraft wheels. Freezing weather then solidified the ruts, rendering the ground rough and unyielding. Doolittle, however, was unconcerned with the condition of the field, which except for the criss-crossing was clear.

Several friends had come out to Mitchel to lend a hand and to see them off. The great Pratt & Whitney Wasp engine was warmed up and with all good-byes exchanged, Doolittle closed the cabin door. With his family squeezed into the packed cabin, he climbed into the cockpit for the takeoff. The engine roared powerfully, but the Vega seemed strangely sluggish. It finally began to pick up speed, then hit a bad bump (which caused the main bulkhead to fail, although at the moment Doolittle was not aware of this). The door directly behind his seat snapped opened and Doolittle fell backwards into the cabin. Shouting at Joe that she must never open the door (which she had not done) when he was in the cockpit, he clambered back into the cockpit. Then came an ominous cracking report and the Vega slumped to the ground: the landing gear had given way and the plane, screeching, scraped on its belly along the frozen earth. The propeller was bent and the plane careened sideways, damaging the left wing.

Although the fuel tank had been ruptured there was no fire—luckily, for the Doolittles were trapped inside by a jammed door. The group that had come to bid them farewell quickly swarmed around the plane and extricated them. Doolittle was in quite a state when he realized what had happened: he had overloaded the Lockheed and the main bulkhead and landing gear had thereupon collapsed. He stood near the plane after everything had been unloaded and unloosed a stream of invective against himself. According to legend, a friend, Captain John McCulloch, came upon the scene and immediately led Jimmy, Jr., then nine, and John, who was seven, away from the profane scene of self-castigation. To Doolittle's further embarrassment, Jimmy, Jr., informed McCulloch, "You should have heard what my father said to my mother—and it wasn't *her* fault he cracked up the plane."

After examining the damages and crating up the plane for shipment back to Burbank for repairs, Doolittle learned that his first day for Shell had cost the company $10,000—not quite half the original price of the Vega. It had not proved to be a very auspicious first day on the job. However, Doolittle was surprised and relieved to learn, when he called St. Louis about the accident, that his employers could be understanding and forgiving. The most ignominious aspect of the incident was the Doolittles' trip to St. Louis by train, not his favorite mode of transportation.

Doolittle had barely settled into his job at Shell when his old Air Service friend Jack Allard appeared upon the scene with a proposition. He had become, by 1930, president of the Curtiss-Wright Export Company. (The other member of the original Rockwell Field trio, Bruce Johnson, had moved from one business venture to another. For a time, through Allard, he had worked for Curtiss-Wright. At the moment Doolittle checked into St. Louis, Johnson was running his own successful business in Rhode Island.)

Allard's plan was to get Shell to permit Doolittle to do in Europe what he had done in South America—promote and sell Curtiss-Wright aircraft. The planes would use Shell products, which made much sense to Shell, and permission was readily granted. An elaborate itinerary, covering some 8,000 miles in nineteen countries, was developed. The enterprise was under the supervision of Curtiss-Wright Export's vice president, William F. Goulding, whose chores, since he was a licensed pilot also entailed demonstrating the Curtiss Robin. Two additional pilots had been lent by the Army, Captain John K. Cannon, who flew the Curtiss Fledgling, and Lieutenant James E. Parker, who flew the Falcon. Doolittle was to fly the fast little Hawk. Also along to assist Goulding with business details was Major Melvin Hall. Two mechanics completed the little group.

They left New York in latter April and arrived at Athens, Greece, in time for Doolittle to give a twenty-five-minute exhibition flight on May 1. For the next two and a half months the Curtiss-Wright/Shell team barnstormed through Europe, from the Mediterranean northward to Scandinavia: Turkey, Bulgaria, Yugoslavia, Hungary, Poland, France, Germany, Austria, Norway, Sweden, and other points between. The several planes were demonstrated for the military representatives of each country and sales were made. At the same time, there being an airman's camaraderie that cuts across national borders, it was possible to view aircraft in the various nations they visited. Doolittle would return to the United States disquieted by some of the developments, particularly in German planes.

Primarily, however, the trip was devoted to salesmanship and flying and, in the latter category, was generally without incident, although Doolittle suffered two minor mishaps—a burned bearing in Poland, a snapped connecting rod in Lithuania. On June 8 he set out from Munich in the Hawk for Bern, Switzerland, and soon found himself enveloped in practically nonnavigable fog. He exploited the first hole he could find and brought the plane down in what appeared to be a pasture. The landing had been a little rough, but there was no damage, but because of recent rains, Doolittle realized he'd never get the Hawk out of the sticky pasture without help. Across the pasture he noticed a somewhat bemused Swiss farmer gazing at him and the Hawk. Doolittle, hoping to find out where he was and to get aid in unsticking his plane, beckoned to the farmer who approached in a leisurely manner.

Knowing the Swiss to be a multilingual people, Doolittle opened the conversation in French, asking his position and that of the nearest airport. The Swiss merely shook his head. Doolittle tried with German and, in desperation, Spanish, each time with the same negative response. Finally, the man said, "Just what the hell are you trying to say?" He was an American, from Spokane, who was tramping through Europe. With his aid, a troop of local Boy Scouts came out to the pasture and tugged the Hawk out of the mud and up to high ground from which Doolittle could take off and continue on to Bern.

Later Doolittle was responsible for a minor international incident in Hungary. The team was given an impressive reception in Budapest by the Hungarian dictator, Admiral Miklos Horthy. The American Minister, J. Butler Wright, reciprocated with a dinner at which Horthy and his twenty-year-old son were guests of honor, along with Doolittle and his friends. Young Horthy suggested a tour of nighttime Budapest, which the fliers appreciated; by dawn they were driving along the Danube, with its low-lying bridges that linked the two sections of the city (Buda and Pest). Young Horthy asked Doolittle, "Could you fly your airplane under these bridges?" Doolittle assured him there was nothing the Hawk could not do—the result being a fast drive to the airport, where Doolittle was left to warm up the engine of the Hawk while the rest of the party sped back to the Danube.

Doolittle took off and soon was heard coming in toward the river, and, for Horthy's edification, he did indeed fly under one of the Danube bridges, the wheels of the Hawk barely skimming the surface of the water. The exploit was the talk of Budapest and inspired the British Minister to write a letter of complaint to Wright about it, reminding him the harm it would have done to international relations if the mad flier had killed himself. Although this was not explained, the letter was notable for its opening line which began, "I would do little to belittle Doolittle . . ."

His most "belittling" episode occurred in Sweden, however. Having flown from Oslo, Norway, to Stockholm, Sweden, he decided to treat his welcoming committee to a fine display of aerobatics. One of the most impressive maneuvers in his repertory with the Hawk was to dive on the field, flip the plane over, and then climb back up for additional twists and turns. Arriving over the airport at Stockholm, where he was to be met by various officials including the chief of the Swedish Air Force and his staff, Doolittle pointed the nose of the plane down, roared toward his reception committee, neatly flipped the plane over on its back, and began rising.

Suddenly he found himself drenched in, inhaling, and swallowing gasoline ejecting from the fuel tank (he learned later that the mechanic in Oslo had failed to replace the gas-tank filter cover after the plane had been refueled). Gallons of fuel had gushed into the cockpit before Doolittle was able to turn the plane right side up and land it. The distinguished committee was awaiting him, probably puzzled over the brevity of the air show. Doolittle queasily approached the group. "I had swallowed so much gasoline that it had completely upset my stomach, so as I walked up to them, the gasoline took over. I stuck my hand out—and regurgitated."

Such an entrance could hardly have been regarded as representative of good salesmanship. Doolittle eventually explained what had happened and the following day treated the Swedish entourage to a full demonstration of what the Hawk and he could do.

By mid-July the Curtiss-Wright traveling circus had concluded its tour and arrived in London for the return trip to the United States. It was welcomed in New York by New York's Mayor James J. Walker and his aviation adviser, Peter J. Brady; it was to the latter that Doolittle first expressed his concern with the development of aviation—and aviation fuels—in Europe. The obvious stress on speed was an indication of a heightened interest in the development of faster military aircraft; this he had observed firsthand when he inspected German-designed Dorniers and Junkers, Dutch Fokkers, and a French Farman. Doolittle was particularly uneasy over the obvious possibility that European aviation was rapidly leaving the United States behind.

The uneasiness caused by his misgivings was moderated by the reunion with his family, which he hadn't seen for nearly four months. Seeing his mother again was not so pleasant, for she was obviously very ill; within two months after his return from Europe she was dead (on September 22, 1930).

His work with Shell took most of his time, and he and Jimmy Haizlip, who had represented Shell in the 1930 National Air Races in Chicago (although Doolittle was present he did not participate), were kept busy flying the refurbished Vega as well as another Travel Air Mystery Ship. Haizlip flew the Travel Air to a second place that year in the first of the Thompson Trophy races, which supplanted the Thompson Cup of the previous year. Haizlip distinguished himself that year also by flying the Shell Vega to a victory in the Transport Race.

Some time after the Thompson race when Haizlip was flying the Travel Air, it suffered engine failure and crashed. Haizlip was not injured, but as far as Shell was concerned, the plane was a washout. Doolittle saw in this plane's design the possibilities for an advanced racer and, after studying the wreckage, decided to buy the remains from Shell and rework it into his own design. To do this he had to dip into the family savings.

During the rebuilding of the plane, Doolittle conceived several modifications; among the first was the change of engine, a new Pratt & Whitney Wasp Jr. He introduced slight changes into the fuselage and some innovations into the wing, these primarily to reduce wind resistance—even the struts connecting wing and fuselage were moved inboard and enclosed in a streamlined housing. A further wing modification altered its configuration slightly, which necessitated changing the usually straight aileron torque tube. To conform to the new wing shape, the tube had to be bent. Between sales, research and exhibition and good will flights for Shell, Doolittle supervised the redevelopment of the Mystery Ship. Finally, it was ready for a test flight on June 23, 1931.

The Travel Air Mystery Ship was a handsome, low-wing monoplane, with its Wasp Jr., housed in a massive cowling, its wheels in "pants"; Doolittle's touches had streamlined it to the maximum. Several friends and colleagues, plus Jimmy, Jr., then ten years old, came out to watch the advent of the new speed ship. The takeoff revealed the promise Doolittle had hoped for and the plane climbed swiftly from the field. He tested its response to the controls, was satisfied, then climbed to put the ship through a few aerobatics. Satisfied again, he dived toward the field to pick up speed to around 100 feet, leveled out to race by the spectators, and saw that his air speed approached 300 miles an hour. There was no time for jubilation, for in an instant he heard a disconcerting metallic cracking sound above the roar of the engine. Then a violent vibration made control difficult and Doolittle barely had time to get the plane away from the crowd, invert it, and gain about 400 altitude before the ailerons snapped off and fluttered away in the slipstream. The wings had begun to disintegrate.

The time lapse from the cracking sound to the instant Doolittle was seen only 500 feet above the earth, dropping from the cockpit was a matter of seconds—as recorded on motion picture film, the Mystery Ship dashed past the crowd, the ailerons blew off, and Doolittle was out. Acutely aware of the proximity of the ground he pulled his parachute ripcord immediately; the chute opened and he hit the ground. Miraculously, Doolittle was not injured, but the plane demolished itself in an open area. Among the first to arrive was little Jimmy, who saw his father standing apparently unhurt. He inquired, with little-boy directness, "Dad, how much money did we have in that airplane?"

"All of it," Doolittle replied. But he was not so concerned with this as the fact that it was obviously his tampering with the original wing design—particularly with the torque tube—that had undoubtedly led to the wing failure. Perhaps there was a valuable lesson in his narrow escape (he had joined the Caterpiller Club for a second time with one of the lowest, successful jumps on record). He took wise little Jimmy—who evidently had overheard the Doolittles discussing the financing of the now defunct Mystery Ship—home.

Joe Doolittle took the news, and their financial loss, with her usual equanimity. Doolittle had gotten out unscathed—and he had been right about the redesign of the plane to a point. That was his business. For his part, Doolittle decided he would leave the more delicate details of design to designers—but his experience did not deter him from seeking the ultimate speedster. Soon after his jump he approached designer E. M. "Matty" Laird, who had built a plane Doolittle hoped to enter in the 1931 Bendix Trophy race, a transcontinental free-for-all, the highlight of the 1931 Nationals.

Laird based his new design on the previous year's Thompson Trophy winner, which had been flown by Charles "Speed" Holman and dubbed the "Laird Solution"; Doolittle's plane would be called "Super Solution." The handsome biplane was built around a powerful, souped-up Pratt & Whitney Wasp engine, capable of over 500 horsepower. A minimum of struts and wiring, an enclosed landing gear, and tiny wings emphasized the plane's function: the Super Solution *looked* like a fast plane. This was especially true when viewed head-on with its painted wheels, enclosed landing-gear struts, and massive engine.

The Bendix Trophy event was initiated by Vincent Bendix, of the Bendix Aviation Corporation, to encourage transcontinental speed flights. In truth, it was not quite that, since the race would begin in California and end at Cleveland, that year's site of the National Air Races. The first Bendix race began on September 4, 1931, at United Airport, near Burbank, California.

Eight aircraft, no less than six of them Lockheed designs, and eight impatient pilots, including Doolittle, were lined up at Burbank awaiting a change in the weather before, in the early hours of the fourth, the word came that the race was on. United Airport blazed with light as the entrants prepared for the takeoff. At 2:35 A.M. the starter flag flashed and the first plane rushed off into the darkness; the rest followed at intervals. The spectators took notice of Doolittle's Super Solution when it zoomed away from the runway within a takeoff run of 400 feet. The speed of the plane was impressed upon pilot Beeler Blevins, whose takeoff had preceded Doolittle's. As he was racing eastward in his Lockheed Altair, Blevins was astonished to see Doolittle's Laird flash by; he quickly glanced at his airspeed indicator, checking to see if he might be slowing up and in danger of a stall.

Within minutes Doolittle had climbed to 11,000 feet to clear the mountains and headed for the first refueling stop at Albuquerque, then to the second at Kansas City, Missouri, and then to Cleveland. A Shell refueling team awaited Doolittle at the two refueling stops and had worked out a method of servicing the plane literally within minutes (140 gallons of fuel at each stop;

eight minutes at the first and ten at the second). The weather, which had finally cleared in California, was perfect for flying and Doolittle made excellent time. Near Cleveland a slight drizzle dampened the plane, but that was no problem.

Doolittle landed in the drizzle 9 hours, 10 minutes, 21 seconds after the takeoff in Burbank—the first to land. It was a full hour later before the winner of second place came in, Harold Johnson in a Lockheed Orion. Having placed first in the Bendix, Doolittle had no intentions of leaving it at that. The same refueling system that had already been employed (an innovation devised by Eugene F. Zimmerman) was used at Cleveland—within minutes the Super Solution had taken off toward the East, leaving behind a rather frustrated group of celebrants—and Joe Doolittle with a sandwich her husband had not had time for during the mechanics of refueling.

Doolittle had taken off from Cleveland into glowering weather and was forced to fight several thunderstorms as well as his own fatigue as he pushed his plane eastward. Within two hours after leaving Cleveland Doolittle set the Laird down at Newark, breaking the old transcontinental record which had been held by Frank Hawks. Shaving over an hour off Hawks's record, Doolittle had flown from Burbank to Newark in 11 hours, 16 minutes, 10 seconds (Hawks's 1930 record had been 12 hours, 25 minutes).

In the nearly half a day he had been flying Doolittle had taken the first Bendix Trophy (and $7,500 prize money) and had established a new transcontinental record (and $2,500). Having done this he had the plane gassed up again, turned around, and flew back to Cleveland to celebrate with Joe Doolittle. There was also jubilation in the Shell camp, as Doolittle learned when he phoned St. Louis later that same day. (Nine years before, on this same date, he had been the first flier to span the continent in less than twenty-four hours; in 1931, he became the first to accomplish this in less than twelve hours.)

The sounds of revelry from St. Louis were too enticing, as was the promise of a memorable celebration party that night by Vice President Alexander Fraser. Doolittle promised to attend—and, in a Shell plane, he blithely took off for St. Louis, arriving around ten that night. He had covered some 3,500 miles by air in a single day. The next morning, with Fraser as a passenger, Doolittle returned to Cleveland to watch the other events of the Nationals.

Doolittle hoped to round off his accomplishments by entering the Super Solution in the Thompson Trophy race, which was scheduled for September 7. On September 1, during the Shell qualifying course, it became obvious that the plane to watch was the strange little stubby Gee Bee Z, designed by the Granville Brothers and flown by Lowell Bayles. During the course Bayles had reached 286 mph., making the Gee Bee the most formidable of the nine entries. (The competitors were reduced to eight on September 6 when Walter Hunter's Travel Air burst into flame during a qualification flight; Hunter bailed out at 200 feet and was burned and badly shaken by his low-altitude parachute jump, but recovered to fly again.)

The Thompson race began well for Doolittle and he was first around the first pylon, with Bayles close behind in the Gee Bee— they were followed by the other participants: Jimmy Wedell in his new Wedell-Williams, Dale Jackson in a Laird Solution (actually the plane of Lee Schoenhair, forced to drop out because of exhaustion), Bob Hall in a Gee Bee Y, Air Corps Captain Ira Eaker in a Lockheed Altair (which had placed fourth in the Bendix), Benny Howard in his own little Pete, and William Ong in a Laird Speedwing.

Doolittle's major competitor was, of course, Bayles, but by the turn into the second lap Doolittle was afflicted with another problem. Bayles, in fact, was in the lead with an average speed of 222.77 mph.; Wedell was also making a tough showing. During this lap a stream of smoke began trailing from Doolittle's Laird, the engine immediately lost power, and Bayles raced further ahead. The Pratt & Whitney, which had stood up so well during Doolittle's flights on September 4, had developed a scuffed piston. Doolittle, however, having calculated the risks, continued in the race until the seventh lap. Then, with his engine overheating, he decided to call it a race.

Lowell Bayles took the 1931 Thompson Trophy in his tricky little Gee Bee, the *City of Springfield,* with an average speed of 236.239 mph., roughly a 35-mph. increase over the previous year's winning average. (Tragically, it was in this prize-winning aircraft, refitted with a more powerful engine, that Bayles met his death. On December 5, 1931, hoping to set a new record over a measured course near Detroit, he took off and zoomed his plane onto the course. He was roughly 160 feet above the ground when inexplicably the Gee Bee suddenly dropped, rolled over, and smashed into the ground, killing Bayles instantly in a spectacular —and filmed—fiery crash.)

Following Doolittle's double Nationals triumph, it seemed good business for Shell to exploit that success with various record flights. The Laird's engine was repaired and soon Doolittle began breaking random records between St. Louis and other convenient points—which was, of course, good for Shell. It was also good for aviation in the sense that the regularity of the flights was an advertisement for the efficiency of engines and the safety of aircraft, as well as for Shell fuels and lubricants. Thus did Doolittle set new records between his home base and Indianapolis, Chicago, and other points.

One of Doolittle's most imaginative flights, dreamed up by the Shell public relations department during this period, was one in which he was to link three capitals of the Western Hemisphere in a single day by air. He flew his Super Solution up from St. Louis and by mid-October was poised for takeoff at Ottawa, Canada. When he left there he had messages from Premier Richard B. Bennett of Canada for delivery in the other capitals; the delivery to President Calvin Coolidge required 2 hours, 20 minutes of flying time. Refueling in Washington was accomplished quickly, but the official ceremonies consumed a half hour before Doolittle could take off on the next leg of the journey which would bring him into Birmingham, Alabama. Within seven minutes he was off again and headed for his final fuel stopover, Corpus Christi, Texas, where Shell trucks and a lunch awaited him. Sixteen minutes later Doolittle was ready for the final leg of his flight, southward along the east coast of Mexico on his right and the Gulf to the left. It was during this portion of the flight that Doolittle suffered the flight's only misadventure.

About midway between Corpus Christi and Mexico City lay Tampico on the Mexican coast—it was at this point that Doolittle planned to climb to around 19,000 feet to cross over the peaks of the Sierra Madre Oriental mountains. Suddenly while over the mountains Doolittle felt faint—"I began I feel that I might pass out." This was an unusual experience for him; lack of sleep should not have been a problem, nor was he up high enough to feel any lack of oxygen. After a second wave of faintness, Doolittle devised a method for keeping himself conscious. He began ask-

ing himself questions—"When did Columbus discover America?"
"When did the United States become a nation?" And so on
through personal questions and mathematical problems. But he
had also decided, "The minute I could not answer, I was going to
jump."

The strange, life-or-death quiz continued and Doolittle, though
fuddled managed to come up with suitable answers. Once over the
mountains he descended to less rarefied air and found that made
no difference at all, so he fought on to keep from slipping into un-
consciousness and somehow managed to find Mexico City. He did
not treat the welcoming committee to the usual Doolittle aerobatics; instead, he set the Laird down as quickly as possible. "I
taxied up to the reviewing stand and was suddenly overwhelmed:
I just threw up pints and quarts . . ."

His arrival, 11 hours, 45 minutes after takeoff at Ottawa, as at
Stockholm, was anything but decorous. Worse, he could not understand the reason for the fainting spells and then the seizure in
the presence of the distinguished committee. The next day, fully
recovered, Doolittle inspected the aircraft; perhaps a break in the
exhaust system could have introduced fumes into the cockpit, but
there was no break. He checked the cockpit, and in a small compartment directly behind the seat, where he stored a change of
clothing, he found the answer.

Doolittle, and others too, habitually carried a small container of
tetraethyl lead. The powerful engine of the Laird required a
higher-octane fuel than was generally available at most airports.
Certain he would have a problem finding high-octane fuel in Mexico, he carried the can to augment the octane number of the local
fuel. Over the mountains, apparently, the container had burst and
the lethal, raw tetraethyl lead fumes entered the cockpit to cause
the anxiety and nausea and faintness that Doolittle had experienced. The incident haunted him—it had been a close call—and
he would meet the problem high-octane fuel again.

After a brief stay in Mexico City, Doolittle closed the circle by
returning to St. Louis. On October 26, 1931, he set a new record
by flying from Mexico City (with fuel stops at Brownsville, Texas,
and Shreveport, Louisiana) to St. Louis in 6 hours, 33 minutes. It
was his final, long, record-breaking flight in what had been an
eventful and, once or twice, harrowing year.

Doolittle, with his wife as company, opened 1932 casually with a flight that served to accentuate the by then accepted safety of flight. They took off early in the morning from St. Louis, in one of Shell's Lockheeds, on January 3, 1932, together with their old high school friend Bill Downs and the then postmaster of St. Louis, A. J. Michener. "It was bitter cold when we left St. Louis," Doolittle recalls. "The Mississippi River was frozen over and there wasn't much heat in the cabin of the Lockheed Vega. (Most of the heat was shunted to the carburetor to avoid icing.)"

They proceeded to fly southward and to warmth in a leisurely eight hours: Jacksonville, Florida, for breakfast, then on to Havana, Cuba, for lunch. After a flight demonstration by Doolittle for Cuban officials, his passengers reboarded the plane for a hop to Miami for dinner. The dramatic aspect of the flight was its total lack of drama.

A few months later, while the Super Solution was in the Laird shop at Wichita undergoing modifications for the coming Nationals (he hoped to participate in both the Bendix and Thompson races), Doolittle made a curiously historic flight in Shell's new Lockheed Orion, fittingly named *Shellightning*. Initially an experimental Altair model, this handsome plane had been converted into the Orion 9C Special (to use its official designation) by eliminating the baggage compartment, making room for passengers, and moving the cockpit forward. It was, to interject a historical aside, the only metal-fuselage Orion built; the wings were constructed of wood.

The *Shellightning* was a low-wing monoplane with a retractable landing gear; it was powered by a Pratt & Whitney Wasp and licensed for racing and long-distance flights. At the time it was the fastest commercial aircraft in the world. Because of the plane's high cruising speed it excited the interest of the National Advisory Committee for Aeronautics and they lent Doolittle an accelerometer which he installed in the Orion. The idea was to keep a record of the Orion's response to the changes in acceleration under the various conditions of high speed flight. (The highest reading Doolittle recorded in the Orion in normal level flight occurred on a very gusty day while he was flying at low altitude over the hills of Arkansas and he noted that the instrument indicated an acceleration of nearly three Gs. The craft withstood an abrupt increase in stress very well.)

Shortly after the Lockheed's delivery in July 1932 Doolittle began preparing for his historic flight, mentioned above. The idea had originated with the U. S. Aeronautical Chamber of Commerce and was willingly seconded by Shell: a dual celebration of George Washington's bicentennial and the 157th anniversary of the United States Postal Service. This was to be accomplished in a dawn to dusk flight by Doolittle over routes traveled by Washington and "dropping mail at many historical places," to quote from the first day cover that he would carry as cargo.

In addition, and to lend piquancy to the event, a descendant— great-great-great grandniece—of Washington was found and invited to accompany Doolittle on his rounds. She was Miss Anne Madison (she also claimed kinship to that family) Washington, then in middle age; she had never flown before. Besides Doolittle and Anne Washington, Shell provided another passenger, Alpheus F. Maple, editor of Shell's company magazine, to serve as mailbag tosser.

At dawn, July 25, 1932, Doolittle lifted the Orion off the runway at Kittery, Maine (Washington's northernmost stopover), and proceeded southward as far as Sunbury, North Carolina, then northwestward as far as Pomeroy, Ohio, and finally eastward to the sites of Washington's Revolutionary commander-in-chief days. For all the pinpoint placement required by some of the maildrops, Doolittle's navigation was impeccable. The last mailbag landed practically at the feet of the postmaster at West Point. Doolittle then followed the Hudson River to Newark where he set the Orion down at 10:15 P.M., 15 hours, 40 minutes after their take-off at Kittery, having covered 2,600 miles.

Miss Washington, when interviewed, announced that she had "enjoyed every bit" of the flight. Besides proving a worthy publicity effort for Shell, the flight had provided some needed stimulus for the U.S. air mail service. Doolittle, with the aid of Al Maple, had delivered the mail on schedule over a preannounced route; this dramatized the practicability of a regular air mail service, which at that time was in doldrums, not much used by the general public, and neglected by congressional appropriation committees.

Having accomplished the George Washington bicentennial airplane flight, Doolittle turned to the project that most concerned him that summer of 1932: the preparation of the Laird Super Solution for the coming National Air Races at Cleveland. It was being fitted with a new, more powerful engine and a retractable landing gear; with these he hoped to beat his own records of the previous year.

Late in August Doolittle went to Wichita, Kansas, to test the Laird in time for the opening of the races on the twenty-seventh. On August 23 he took off in the hopped-up Super Solution, cranked up the wheels, and spent twenty minutes reacquainting himself with the plane. Then, as he made a landing approach, he found that the new retractable landing gear malfunctioned; it would not move into the landing position. Since he was not entirely familiar with the design of the mechanism, Doolittle dropped a note to the engineers and mechanics on the ground:

Something wrong landing gear. Can get 3½ turns each way. If any suggestions, write on side of plane and come up. Otherwise I will run out of gas and stall in.

After a hurried consultation, a message was lettered on the side of a plane—ZOOM RIGHT. ZOOM LEFT. POWER DIVE—and a pilot, Preston Kirk, took off and brought the craft in close enough for Doolittle to read. He then whipped the Laird through the prescribed maneuvers, but the wheels would not budge. The mechanism was obviously permanently jammed. After nearly two hours the fuel supply was practically gone and there was nothing further for Doolittle to do but to bring the plane in on its belly (he could not bring himself to abandon it).

It was a very grim Doolittle who set the little racer down on the Wichita airport and listened to the snap of the slightly lowered gear, the crunch as the propeller bent, and the screeching of the underside of the fuselage. The Laird ground to a lurching halt in a grassy stretch of field, and an unhappy—and unhurt—Doolittle pulled out of the cockpit to inspect the damage. One thing was certain, the Laird would compete in no races that year.

The mishap made the papers across the country and soon Doolittle received several offers from manufacturers willing to supply him with planes. The Bendix race was scheduled for the twenty-seventh (actually, because of delays, it was not held until the twenty-ninth) and it was unlikely that even if he accepted a plane it would be ready in time.

On August 27 Doolittle spoke with Zantford D. Granville, of Gee Bee fame; Granville Brothers Aircraft has just completed two little racers, Models R-1 and R-2. The latter, piloted by Lee

Gehlbach, was entered in the Bendix. (It would come in fourth; first place was taken by Doolittle's Shell colleague, Jimmy Haizlip.) That left the R-1 (with racing number 11 on the side; Gehlbach's had number 7) without a pilot because its intended pilot, Russell Boardman, had spun in in another Gee Bee and was in the hospital. Granvilles' question was, would Doolittle like to fly Number 11 in the Thompson race? and the answer was a speedy "Yes."

The next day he flew to the Springfield airport, near Springfield, Massachusetts, where the Granvilles' little factory was situated. His arrival had been heralded, and the airport had attracted an unusual number of people, including air-minded youths. One of them, L. Fletcher Prouty (later an Air Force colonel), recalls taking the trolley out to the airport to see his hero. "Finally, Doolittle arrived," he has written. "He said little to any of the racing buffs crowding around the small hanger. Instead, he marched right over to the gleaming red-and-white plane and studied it inch by inch."

He was aware of the Gee Bee's reputation as a tricky plane to fly—and the death of Bayles the past December had not been forgotten; the dramatic newsreel film of the crash was, in fact, unforgettable. Almost directly before the camera's lens the Gee Bee appeared to snap out of control, flip over, and smash into the ground (at the time Bayles had been flying at full speed at an altitude of about 165 feet). The plane struck the earth between a road and a railroad track and instantly blossomed into flame. The engine was ripped loose and bounced along the track for about 200 yards before coming to rest against a fence. What was left of the Gee Bee left a spectacular wake of bright flame and thick black smoke. When the wreckage ran its fiery course and ground to a stop, Bayles's flaming body could be seen as it was catapulted 50 feet beyond the still burning wreckage. He was killed instantly.

Doolittle had seen the newsreel before he went to Springfield.

The R-1 was a strange looking craft; chunky, it was called a "bumblebee" by some and "the flying milk bottle" by others—both apposite. The plane measured 17 feet, 9 inches in length and had a wingspan of 25 feet. The cowling housed a Pratt & Whitney Wasp Sr. capable of more than 750 horsepower; at the other end of the plane there was practically no tail. In its original configuration there had been a minimum of vertical fin. A test flight had convinced Boardman that the plane, though fast, was lacking in directional stability. At his suggestion two square feet of area was added to the rudder. The tiny cockpit was located far back on the fuselage and faired (that is, fitted to streamline) into the rudder. The pilot saw very little from this perch while on the ground. The total aspect was unlike any other aircraft of the time. As one observer commented, "That airplane has no center of gravity."

It was an unconventional design, but Doolittle decided within minutes that he would fly it in the Nationals. "We pushed that tiny plane out of the hanger into the hot August sunlight," Prouty recalled in *Air Force Magazine*. "Outside that little package of power looked like a toy . . .

"There had been little flying activity on the airfield that summer, during the depths of the Depression, and the grass was long and billowing in the early afternoon breeze. Doolittle talked things over with the Granvilles. Then one of them took out a screwdriver and opened the tiny hatch. The cockpit was incredibly small, designed originally for Bayles . . .

"Several of us pushed the Gee Bee all the way across a half mile of hot, dusty hayfield. Then Doolittle, before climbing into the cockpit, took one last turn around the plane. Without another word, Doolittle climbed in, and the hatch was closed and fastened securely from the outside, with no way to open it from within. [This bit of folklore is not true.] He started the engine and let it roar. Pebbles and grass flew everywhere. Only the heavy chocks kept the plane from rolling. Then by prearrangement and to give it one final all-out test, we held the wingtips while he revved the 800-hp engine to full power.

"Finally satisfied with it, Doolittle throttled back and gave us the signal to let go. He gained speed across the field and waited for the feel of the rudder so that he could give it full throttle. The Gee Bee cut a swath through the hayfield, throwing buttercups and daisies up in a cloud. In no time, the plane seemed just a toy buzzing across the field. The tail never lifted more than a few inches . . ."

Doolittle, realizing he had a hot airplane on his hands, one that demanded constant piloting, wasted no time after taking off in a cloud of "buttercups and daisies." He did not even circle the field in the traditional manner; he pointed the stubby nose of the Gee Bee toward Cleveland. "It was the 'touchiest' plane I had ever been in," he later recalled, and flying it was a bit "like balancing a pencil on the tip of your finger."

This was forcefully driven home the first time he tested the plane while practicing pylon turns. The Thompson course was triangular, with the three pylons ten miles apart. Wisely Doolittle chose to practice at an altitude of 5,000 feet to get the feel of the Gee Bee. "It's a good thing I did. That airplane did two snap rolls before I could get it under control." Had he been near the ground the flight might have proved fatal.

The qualification flights, known by then as the "Shell speed dashes," began and on Thursday, September 1, he achieved an average of 293.19—a new world's record, except that because a barograph had not been installed in the Gee Bee, it was not accepted as "official." This was a disappointment, but something even worse materialized upon landing after the flights. The cowling of the Gee Bee had begun to pull forward, snapping a few of the fastenings, stretching brackets, and splitting. Also the controllable-pitch propeller (a Smith) was found to vibrate. After repairs and adjustments were made, that same day, Doolittle took the plane up again, with barograph, but was unable to achieve a record-making flight (one that exceeded the previous record by at least five miles an hour). Doolittle announced he was finished for the moment, since racing the engine at high speed could burn it out before the Thompson race.

On Saturday, with the speed dashes continuing, Doolittle took off again (in order to qualify for the Thompson that year, a minimum average speed of 200 mph. was required). Although he had already qualified, Doolittle hoped to make another record. Despite imperfect weather—cloudy, with a heavy crosswind—he whipped the little plane over the course and landed, triumphantly, having averaged 296.287 mph.—a new world's record (with one run at 309.040). The Gee Bee could then be officially hailed as the world's fastest landplane, breaking the record held by French pilot Adjutant Bonnet since 1924.

The great day nearly ended in disaster when Lee Gehlbach, taxiing the sister ship, No. 7, onto the line, was unable to see forward because of the bulbous configuration of the Gee Bee, came close to ramming Doolittle's No. 11 parked at the edge of the field. Only when he realized that the gesticulations of the mechanics and their fruitless attempt to hold the plane back signified that something dire impended, did Gehlbach cut the engine to enable the ground crew to stop the plane from chewing up Doolittle's craft, by a margin of eight feet.

The 1932 National Air Races closed, after ten days, on Monday, September 5, with the Thompson Trophy race as the grand finale. Pitted against Doolittle in his unpredictable Gee Bee were Jimmy Wedell in his Wedell-Williams No. 44, qualifying speed 277.057; Roscoe Turner, Wedell-Williams *Gilmore Red Lion*, 266.674; Jimmy Haizlip, Wedell-Williams No. 92, 266.440; Bob Hall, Hall *Bulldog*, 243.717; Ray Moore, Keith Rider R-1, 237.738; Bill Ong, Howard *Ike*, 213.855; Les Bowen, Gordon Israel *Redhead*, 202.490; and Gehlbach, Gee Bee No. 7, 247.339. Doolittle had an edge in speed on his rivals, but with the cranky Gee Bee who could venture to predict the outcome of the Thompson? The Gee Bees seemed to breed surprises.

The first surprise occurred when Doolittle fired up the big Pratt & Whitney about an hour before the race: in an instant the cowling filled with flame, threatening to engulf the entire plane. Quick action by the ground crew and Doolittle extinguished the fire and a careful check revealed no serious damage; apparently gasoline in the carburetor had flared in a backfire. Satisfied, Doolittle continued with his preparations. He started the engine again and it came to thunderous life without incident. He taxied the plane to the starting line.

Hall was off first, followed in ten second intervals by Doolittle, Moore (who would drop out with engine trouble), Wedell, Haizlip, Gehlbach, Turner, and Ong. Bowen developed engine trouble at the start and never took off. Hall in his *Bulldog* and the two Gee Bees enjoyed the takeoff advantage of a short run, because they were the only aircraft in the race fitted with controllable-pitch propellers. Once airborne, though he had taken off second, Doolittle soon passed Hall—he took the lead and stayed there. The course, around the three pylons, covered 100 miles and Doolittle's average was the winning 252.686 mph., setting at the same time a new speed record for the Thompson race. Wedell came in second, a full 10 mph. slower; Turner was third and Haizlip fourth; Gehlbach came in with his Gee Bee in the last money spot, fifth place.

As he squeezed himself out of the tiny cockpit of the Gee Bee, Doolittle became aware of a tremendous roar—the cheers of a crowd estimated at more than 50,000. A nagging question that had concerned him for some time surfaced: *What am I doing here?* Why the risk to please a mob for glory and money? The Nationals had become an aerial side show.

His feelings, though not yet articulated, were further shaken when he learned from a newspaper photographer that he and his colleagues from the press had deliberately clung to Joe and their children throughout the Thompson race—without taking a single photograph. They had waited, in vain as it eventuated, for that moment when the infamous Gee Bee would crash, to record his family's reactions. Doolittle's victory had denied the photographers a number of dramatic, very marketable pictures—at the same time it had fulfilled, as far as he was concerned, all of his ambitions in one field of aviation—racing.

As soon as the Nationals were concluded Doolittle squeezed once more into the Gee Bee and flew it back to Springfield—"I landed it, taxied up to the line and gratefully got out." His next surprise was to announce that he was finished with air racing, his reason being that aviation was ready to emerge from the "thrills-and-spills" era. Much had been learned from racing aircraft, but at a questionable cost in life. It was time to "give attention to safety and reliability. Commercial and military aviation must be developed so that we become strong commercially and have the best aerial fighting force in the world."

(Some future incidents with the Gee Bees, as well as other racing planes of the period, bore him out. Russell Boardman, flying the modified R-1, Doolittle's No. 11, died after the plane rolled over and crashed on its back during a takeoff at Indianapolis in the 1933 Bendix race; later that same year Jimmy Haizlip, in the R-2—the old No. 7—cartwheeled to a landing at Springfield, wiping out the Gee Bee, though miraculously he was not seriously hurt. Whatever pieces could be salvaged from the two wrecks were assembled into another racer named *Intestinal Fortitude* in 1934. That year the driving force behind the Granville Brothers organization, Zantford Granville, was killed when his Gee Bee Sportster spun in while he was attempting to land at Spartanburg, South Carolina, although the fault could not be completely attributed to the plane. Granville arrived at the airport prepared to land and discovered several workers in his path; his attempt to avoid them led to the stall. Roy Minor, testing *Intestinal Fortitude* for the 1934 Nationals, accidentally ran it into a drainage ditch and ended its career for that year. It was ready for the 1935 Bendix race as the *Spirit of Right* and flown by Cecil Allen, who crashed to his death in a potato field near Burbank during the takeoff. It was the end of the tragic line for the Gee Bee.)

Doolittle himself summed up his feelings after winning the 1932 Thompson Trophy and announcing his retirement from air racing: "I have yet to hear of the first case of anyone engaged in this work dying of old age." He felt, in his own case, that he had "used up his luck."

Eleven

Very few who felt they knew Doolittle well took his renunciation of air racing seriously—except Doolittle. There were tempting offers following his subjugation (unfortunately for others, only a temporary conquest) of the Gee Bee, but he did not succumb. He would say at a conference of the National Safety Congress that "air racing as a spectacle has outlived its usefulness" and conceded that it "originally did promote safety in aviation through testing of materials used in construction of planes and engines, and probably still does. But lately it appears that the value received is not commensurate with the personal risk involved."

It was that concern with element of personal risk that turned his attention to a new project at Shell. Soon after his return from the Ottawa-Washington-Mexico City flight in late 1931 and the near-fatal experience with the tetraethyl lead fumes in his cockpit, he began expounding the idea of the development of a 100-octane fuel for use in aircraft engines. He began at the top at Shell, with Alex Fraser, who cannily wondered who would buy such an expensive commodity. Doolittle's hope was that the Army Air Corps would standardize its fuel to 100-octane and that perhaps the commercial airlines would follow. He had broached the subject with an old MIT friend, Lieutenant Frank Klein, who was specializing in fuel development at Wright Field, near Dayton. While Klein agreed with Doolittle, as a lowly lieutenant he had little

Man with wings: Doolittle as a
flying lieutenant, 1918. DOOLITTLE
COLLECTION

Josephine Doolittle, Army wife.
DOOLITTLE COLLECTION

Doolittle, with beard grown during a
tour of duty with the 90th Aero
Squadron at Eagle Pass, Texas, on
the Mexican border, in 1919.
DOOLITTLE COLLECTION

Doolittle (standing third from left) with various members of the ground crew that worked on his DH-4 in preparation for a transcontinental flight, 1922. DOOLITTLE COLLECTION

LEFT: Refueling stop at San Antonio, Texas, Kelly Field, September 5, 1922, before Doolittle continued on to San Diego to complete the coast-to-coast flight from Pablo Beach, Florida. This was the first time the United States had been crossed in less than a day by a lone pilot. Seven years later Doolittle was awarded the Distinguished Flying Cross for the flight. DOOLITTLE COLLECTION. RIGHT: Doolittle and First Lieutenant Cyrus Bettis, Bay Shore, near Baltimore, Maryland, October 25, 1925. Behind them is the Curtiss R3C-1 racer flown by Doolittle in the Schneider Trophy race. A couple of weeks earlier, on October 12, Bettis flew the same type of plane in a landplane version at Mitchel Field, N.Y., to win the Pulitzer Trophy. U. S. AIR FORCE

TOP: Class of 1923, Engineering School, McCook Field, Ohio. *Standing, left to right:* First Lieutenants Donald L. Brunner, Harry A. Sutton, Clarence B. Lober, John A. MacReady, Bayard Johnson, James H. Doolittle. *Seated, left to right:* Captains Edgar P. Sorensen and Gerald E. Brower; Majors Martin F. Scanlon and Walter G. Kilner; First Lieutenants Horace N. Heisen and Arthur W. Brock, Jr., and Captain S. R. Stribling. U. S. AIR FORCE. ABOVE: A fuller view of the Curtiss racer, the type of aircraft flown by Doolittle in the 1925 Schneider Trophy race. U. S. AIR FORCE

On leave from the Army in 1928, during Doolittle's second South American tour as a salesman for Curtiss. DOOLITTLE COLLECTION

Winner of the Schneider Trophy race, Baltimore, October 25, 1925. Joe Doolittle and Major General Mason M. Patrick, Chief of the Air Service, share the triumph. DOOLITTLE COLLECTION

South American tour, 1928: William
H. McMullen, Curtiss pilot;
Doolittle; and Jerry Van Wagoner,
mechanic. DOOLITTLE
COLLECTION

Doolittle, on upper wing, oversees the delivery of a Curtiss P-1 Hawk, South
America, 1928. DOOLITTLE COLLECTION

TOP: Back in uniform, Doolittle and Lieutenant Wendell Brookley model the latest style of parachute, a device Doolittle would employ three times during his flying career. U. S. AIR FORCE. ABOVE: A classic Navy fighter of the late twenties—a Vought Corsair, a type Doolittle would use for cross-country flights for the Full Flight Laboratory (Guggenheim Fund) in his blind flight experiments. DOOLITTLE COLLECTION

TOP: The wreckage of Doolittle's Corsair after he crash-landed it near Elizabeth, New Jersey, in a fog the night of March 15, 1929. He walked away from the "landing" unhurt, explaining that he took "the impact by wrapping the left wing around a tree trunk near the ground." DOOLITTLE COLLECTION. ABOVE: The demolished Beech Travel Air Mystery Ship. Doolittle had acquired, repaired, and renovated it, hoping to use it as a racer. During a test flight the aileron control malfunctioned and resulting vibration caused the wing to rip off. Doolittle, then only 500 feet above the ground, managed to get the plane away from a crowd of spectators, flipped it over, and made his second parachute jump. DOOLITTLE COLLECTION

Period portrait of intrepid pilot, c. 1930, around the time Doolittle resigned from the Air Corps to join the Shell Oil Company. COURTESY SYSTEMS GROUP OF TRW, INC.

Stellar American trio of the Golden Age of Flight in the late twenties: Lieutenant Alford "Al" Williams, U. S. Navy; Charles A. Lindbergh, whom Doolittle always called "Slim"; and Doolittle. U. S. AIR FORCE power; it would be up to Doolittle to convince Shell to produce and the War Department to buy—not necessarily in that order. At Shell, Doolittle learned that in dealing with the research branch, being Dr. Doolittle was a decided asset. So, deftly moving between St. Louis and Wright Field, Dr. Doolittle began stirring up interest.

Although the War Department remained aloof (Klein, however, continuing his work), Doolittle had impressed Shell, and the company began the erection of a million-dollar plant for the purpose of entering the field of 100-octane fuel production at Wood River, Illinois.

As this risky groundwork was being laid, Doolittle went off again on a joint Curtiss-Wright/Shell excursion, this time one that would literally take him around the world. Having arranged for the care of the boys, Joe Doolittle accompanied her husband; although she carried a typewriter to help with some of the business aspects of the trip, it would be as a tourist that she would best remember it. Early in 1933 they left St. Louis for San Francisco where they boarded ship, and following stopovers in Japan they arrived at their first destination, Shanghai, China, where Doolittle gave his first demonstration of the Curtiss Hawk for one of Generalissimo Chiang Kai-shek's advisers, Dr. H. H. Kung, on April 13, 1933; two days later he demonstrated the Hawk for Chinese Army officials, following on the next day with a similar performance for Harvard-trained T. B. Soong, brother of Chiang Kai-shek's wife. On April 18 Doolittle treated the general public, reported in the papers as the "densest throng" ever assembled at Shanghai, to a flying exhibition. Joe Doolittle was more worried about the possible collapse of the swarming grandstand, especially its people-encrusted roof—which somehow reminded her of an anthill—than with her husband's risks while stunting.

She particularly enjoyed their visits to the various shrines, the pagodas, and the completely different way of life as they moved from city to city in China.

They flew in a small commercial airliner via China Airways to Peiping (Peking) with Doolittle serving in a unique role for him—copilot. The weather turned bad and forced them off course and he was asked to assist in the flying. They landed short of their destination at a small airport and the plane was refueled by hand as the five-gallon cans were delivered by Chinese carrying them on their heads. They took off again and clung to the coastline, affording Joe Doolittle some bonus sightseeing. When the weather worsened and threatened their flight, she suggested to the pilot that they might set down on one of the clear beaches below. He explained that that would be imprudent because it was likely they would be seized by the local warlord and held for ransom. So they pushed on, with Doolittle flying the plane, to land at an emergency airport at Tsingtao—"a wheat field, much of which was knee deep in water."

And so the tour continued from city to city. By June they had arrived at Canton where Doolittle demonstrated the Hawk for the Chief of the South Chinese Air Force, Major General F. Wong and, at his request, gave a lecture on fighter tactics at the base. Wong, appreciative, presented the Doolittles with a beautiful elephant bridge consisting of fourteen carved ivory elephants (Canton was then the heart of the ivory industry). In addition, Wong held a bachelor party for Doolittle at a local "restaurant," which was attended by four others, Doolittle being the only Westerner in the party.

"It was a very interesting place," Doolittle recalled. "There were bunks along the walls with people in them smoking opium. There was a large table in the center, like a tremendous cushion. Around this table were smaller cushions on which we sat. Behind each of us was a *sing-song* girl, what we would call a hostess, who would serve us the enormous number of dishes the Chinese have.

"The Chinese had what was called 'the finger game,' which we all played. The object was for each contestant to hold up from zero to five fingers and then guess the total. The loser would then take a drink of Chinese rice wine. I might say that the hostesses had a remarkable degree of digital dexterity . . .

"After a while, after a few sips of the warm rice wine, one had a tendency to hold up five fingers and guess four.

"The hostess behind me was a most attractive girl and I had had enough rice wine to realize that I couldn't learn Chinese promptly, but not enough to assure me that I couldn't teach her English if I spoke very slowly.

So the English lesson began: "Where . . . are . . . you . . . from?"

The answer was crisp: "I'm from Chicago and wish to Christ I was back there now." (He learned she had been born in Chicago, where her father had been a successful businessman and had accumulated a fortune by Chinese standards. He then returned to his native land only to lose his fortune through poor investments. Thus his daughter was forced to earn a living as a hostess.)

By the end of June the party had moved into the Philippines by ship, then southward to the Dutch East Indies, to Java, with stopovers at Bali, Surabaja, and Batavia (modern Jakarta). Doolittle was asked by the Dutch to "put on a show" and was happy to comply. By this time, since they were traveling by ship and planned to fly westward by commercial airliner, Doolittle no longer had his own Hawk. He borrowed another from the Dutch Air Force for his demonstration. While a similar plane, the Dutch Hawk was powered with a heavier engine; also the airdrome, in the mountains at Bandung, was at a rather high altitude.

Doolittle took the plane up and from about a thousand feet put it into a steep dive, prepared as usual to pull out close to the ground giving the spectators a thrill. It was Doolittle, however, who was unexpectedly thrilled. The combination of heavy aircraft and thin air contributed to his misjudgment of the moment when to pull back on the stick. When he finally pulled back, the plane "mushed" in the thin, hot air and the nose did not immediately come up. Determined, he persisted and was rewarded with the motion of the nose coming up—although the ground seemed terribly close. Just as he fully conquered the dive, he felt a solid thump as the wheels brushed the earth.

Upon landing Doolittle was met by several Dutch officers, some of them fliers, who had witnessed the "feat." Doolittle very honestly turned off their congratulations by declaring that what he had done was "downright stupid flying," that it was a miscalculation on his part, not an example of "the most delicate piece of flying" that the Dutch commander had called it.

They smiled and said: "We knew; we wondered if you would lie about it."

From about mid-July tourism occupied the Doolittles more than aviation. They explored exotic villages, consumed strange foods and attended curious ceremonies. They boarded the noisome ("pigs aft, cattle forward, and coffee in the hold") S.S. *Valentine* at Batavia for Siam (now Thailand). From there a Royal Dutch Airlines plane took them to Burma, then to India, and northwestward to Iraq and Egypt. Asia had blended into Africa in a picture-postcard sequence of pagodas, temples, and pyramids. From Cairo, still flying, they crossed into Europe touching down in Greece, Yugoslavia, Hungary, Germany, and Holland, arriving in London early in August. Air transportation in Europe, Doolittle realized, was a reality, while in the United States it was barely a dream. Even more disturbing was the development of military aviation in Europe compared to that in the United States, which had impressed Doolittle during this round-the-world tour. Because of his reputation, he was welcomed by men in aviation in practically every country that he and Joe visited. The flier in these men overcame their military reticence and they loved to display their aircraft. What Doolittle saw troubled him.

By the middle of August they were ready to go home and they sailed for New York. From there they flew back to St. Louis—for Doolittle it meant getting back into harness for Shell and further agitation for 100-octane fuel. While Shell had proceeded with the idea on Doolittle's urging, the great problem was one of sales: who would buy 100-octane fuel? Armed with the knowledge of the state of aviation in Europe, Doolittle was counting on the Air Corps.

That something was brewing in Germany was revealed in October 1933 by the purchase of two Curtiss-Wright Hawks ostensibly by the Number One living German World War ace, Ernst Udet. "Ostensibly" because he had, in fact, come to buy them for the Luftwaffe. Before the sale was made, however, there were some hours of impasse: Curtiss would not permit Udet to fly the plane until he paid for it—and Udet would not pay until he had flown. The impasse was settled when, by mutual consent, Doolittle was asked to test the plane for Udet. He took it up to 10,000 feet and whipped it into a spectacular vertical dive. As the Hawk, screaming, approached the ground, Udet became apprehensive and said, "My plane, oh, my plane!" One of the Curtiss officials reminded him that Doolittle was *in* that plane. Udet then added, "Oh, Doolittle, too!" Doolittle pulled out of the dive and Udet was completely satisfied with the plane.

An extraordinary pilot and a delightful personality, Udet was instrumental in introducing the "Stuka" (dive bomber) concept into the then-secretly burgeoning air force—the Luftwaffe. This was inspired by the performance of the Hawks and Doolittle's stunt of pulling them out of a power dive chillingly close to the ground. A military romantic rather than an objective theoretician, Udet and his preoccupation with the Stuka close-support use of aircraft inadvertently laid the groundwork for what became a handicap for Luftwaffe.

Not that in 1933 the U. S. Army Air Corps would have been any match for the Luftwaffe. The former continued to harbor dissidents who had agreed with Billy Mitchell on the subject of an independent air force, which unlike Udet's Stukas, would not merely be an adjunct to ground forces. The young "agitators," all disciples of Mitchell, were also proponents of the strategic bomber which, also unlike the Stuka, would not be assigned the chore of tactical operations. To oversimplify, the function of the long-range strategic, or "heavy," bomber was to attack targets well inside enemy borders. Since, as far as anyone knew, neither the potential enemies of the United States nor the U. S. Air Corps had such aircraft, the subject of the strategic bomber was regarded as rather academic by the powerful members of the War Department: if we can't do it to them they reasoned, they can't do it to us. Besides, large bombers cost a great deal of Depression money.

Thus in 1933 the U. S. Air Corps floundered in uncertainty as to its mission and its future. There was talk of cutbacks in equipment and personnel—which did not bode well for Doolittle's efforts in his 100-octane campaign. He shuttled between St. Louis and Wright Field, hoping for the best in an uncertain time.

Then, early in 1934, the worst happened, a tragic turning point that contributed to a further evolution of the Air Corps. Postmaster General James A. Farley concluded that the commercial airlines had acquired air mail contracts through collusion and so convinced President Franklin D. Roosevelt. The result was the cancellation in February of all U. S. Government mail contracts with the commercial carriers. This left a gap in the U.S. mail service, which was soon filled when Major General Benjamin D. Foulois, then Chief of the Air Corps, was asked to fly the mail. Foulois, anxious to bring some needed attention to his service, willingly took on the job. Neither he, nor anyone else apparently, studied the Air Corps' capability at the time in terms of aircraft, training, facilities, and experience.

On February 19, 1934, the Air Corps began flying the mails at practically the same moment that some of the worst storms of the year—ice, winds, blizzards, and squalls—struck the nation from

one coast to the other. Flying in open cockpit planes, without
proper radio equipment and instruments, the Air Corps pilots
demonstrated two things: their legendary intrepidity and the low
level of Air Corps training. On February 22 the first fatal crash
occurred, followed the next day by the second. The luckier pilots
were merely forced down, but a total of four were killed attempting to get the mail through and six others died in training, or related, accidents. The succession of deaths caused a public outcry
which led to the reinstatement of the contracts held by the commercial airlines by the middle of May.

Another result was the formation of a committee by the Secretary of War, George H. Dern, by order of President Roosevelt, to
make a "non-partisan" study of the current difficulties and future
policies of the Air Corps. At the same time, the Federal Aviation
Commission would be making a study under its chairman, Clark
Howell. The War Department committee was to be under the
chairmanship of Newton D. Baker (who had served under President Woodrow Wilson as Secretary of War) and was thus known
as the Baker Board.

During this period, it may be noted, the Air Corps did not lack
for investigative boards; the findings of the Baker Board, it was
hoped, would supplement those of the past summer's (August
1933) Drum Board under the Deputy Chief of Staff of the War
Department, Major General Hugh A. Drum, which had consisted
entirely of military men. The Drum Board had, in a tentative way,
suggested an expansion of the Air Corps and, even more tenta-
tively, had taken a midget step in the direction toward an independent air service with the proposal for restructuring the Air
Corps into a "General Headquarters Air Force" around which
other units would cluster. There was a slight suggestion of au-
tonomy with the proposed establishment of the GHQ Air Force,
but the air arm would remain subservient to the Army. Still the
airmen were happy to take what they could get and began building a strategic striking force around GHQ Air Force.

The Baker Board brought together a group of civilians as well
as military experts. Among the former were well-known fliers
Clarence Chamberlin and Doolittle (Charles Lindbergh had refused to serve on the Board). Others were Dr. Karl Taylor Compton, then president of MIT, industrialist Edgar S. Gorrell, and
George William Lewis, director of research for the National Ad-

visory Committee for Aeronautics. The military members included General Drum and Major General Benjamin D. Foulois, Chief of the Air Corps. Beginning on April 17 and running for several weeks the Baker Board heard more than a hundred witnesses—civilian, military and naval—before issuing a report on July 18.

Airmen had no champion in Newton D. Baker, who could not conceive of an aerial attack upon the United States and who, like many, believed in the U. S. Navy as the first bastion of national defense. While the Baker Board agreed to the establishment of the GHQ Air Force, it was firmly against an independent air force. Mindful of the air mail tragedies, the report criticized Air Corps training methods and recommended more night flying, more beacon and instrument flying, particularly in bad weather, and more emphasis on cross-country flight.

When the Baker Report was finally published in July it contained some strong negative statements: ". . . the limitations of the airplane show that the idea that aviation, acting alone, can control the sea lanes, or defend the coast, or produce decisive results are all visionary as is the idea that a very large and independent air force is necessary to defend our country against air attack." The report pointed out that "the fear that has been cultivated in this country by various zealots that American aviation is inferior to that of the rest of the world is, as a whole, unfounded."

One member of the board appended a dissent to the report. Doolittle, representing a minority of one, said: "I believe in aviation—both civil and military. I believe that the future security of our Nation is dependent upon an adequate air force. This is true at the present time and will become increasingly important as the science of aviation advances and the airplane lends itself more and more to the art of warfare.

"I am convinced that the required air force can be more rapidly organized, equipped and trained if it is completely separated from the Army and developed as an entirely separate arm. If complete separation is not the desire of the committee, I recommend an air force as part of the Army but with a separate budget, a separate promotion list and removed from the control of the General Staff. These are my sincere convictions. Failing either, I feel that the Air Corps should be developed under the General Staff as recommended above."

A realist, Doolittle realized that his dissenting view would have scant effect on the results of the findings of the Baker Report and that the military members would comply with the majority view. It was a compromise between nothing and very little, and he could accept a small step in what he regarded as the right direction—although not without registering his counterviews. A decade later he would find little to rejoice over when a widely destructive world war confirmed his judgment.

Having had his say in Washington, Doolittle returned to St. Louis to continue with his campaign for 100-octane fuel—to encourage Shell to risk its development and to convince the Air Corps and the commercial lines of its merit.

Standard aviation fuel in the early 1930s was 91-octane (as compared to the 50-octane of the First World War and the early postwar period), and aircraft engines were designed accordingly. If a new fuel were developed and accepted, it would improve engine efficiency and performance. At the same time, it would render the airplane power plants of the time obsolete. The Air Corps, all but penniless as the Army's stepchild, could not afford such luxuries. Commercial air lines were buying minimal quantities of 100-octane fuel, primarily for use in takeoffs because of the great surge of power it afforded.

In 1934, it might be noted, it cost about $2.40 to produce a gallon of 100-octane fuel. Standard 91-octane in 1934 cost the Air Corps about 15 cents a gallon. Even if 100-octane fuel was standardized at this time, it would still have cost about twice that of the 91-octane—definitely no bargain by War Department standards.

While Shell proceeded, even going so far as to construct three more plants, Doolittle continued to dream up projects that might contribute to the advancement of aviation. In February of 1934, First World War ace Eddie Rickenbacker had gleaned wide press coverage for Eastern Air Transport (later Eastern Air Lines) and Transcontinental & Western Air (TWA) by establishing a transcontinental nonstop record in a newly designed TWA Douglas DC-1. With Rickenbacker as pilot and TWA's Jack Frye as copilot, the airliner flew from Los Angeles to Newark in 13 hours, 4 minutes. The flight was, in fact, made as an act of protest against the impending air mail contract cancellations and to demonstrate commercial air line capabilities in 1934. The Rickenbacker-Frye exploit occurred during the period of the Air Corps air mail tragedy and proved the point: the necessity for training, planning, and modern equipment.

Later in the year, American Airlines approached Doolittle with the idea of a similar flight from Los Angeles. It was hoped he would break Rickenbacker's record and thus win some space in the press for American.

The plane selected was a standard eight-passenger, low-wing, single-engine Vultee. Upon its delivery Doolittle studied the craft and proceeded to make a small and, as it turned out, fruitless modification. Hoping to reduce drag, with a resultant increase in speed, he cut the engine's exhaust pipes short at the cowling. It did not have the desired effect. He found when he flight-tested the Vultee that he had, in fact, reduced its speed by about 3 mph. In their original state the exhaust pipes had extended well behind the engine's cowling and had contributed to the plane's speed with a slight jetlike thrust. Another function of the original, long pipes was to reduce the engine glare which interfered with a pilot's vision at night. To his chagrin, Doolittle found that he had succeeded in getting himself "a little drag instead of a little help."

Joe Doolittle and Robert Adamson, of Shell, were to accompany Doolittle in the roles of passengers. For some time all three anxiously awaited the word on the weather. Their source was Professor Irving Krick, a meteorologist at the California Institute of Technology and a distinguished specialist who had done valuable work in the field of air-mass analysis. Krick had, as Doolittle saw it, "one minor fault: an enthusiasm that went beyond the realm of technical capability." Krick, in short, had a weakness for predicting weather, with definitive and complete assurance, as much as a month in advance although he did not have the technology for such prognostication.

Doolittle checked in with Krick every day, hoping for "relatively clear weather" in which to take off, and finally on January 14, 1935, Krick assured him, "Tonight's the night."

He also informed Doolittle, "You will climb through a thick low overcast. Once through that, you will find clear air above and will have an absolutely perfect flight to New York with tail winds all the way."

Thus encouraged, Doolittle took off that evening—and began running into trouble immediately. As he tried to get the plane above the overcast, he spun out three times because of icing. On the fourth attempt, he managed to shake off the ice and continued up to an altitude of 16,500 feet, where he came out of the icing overcast. True, it was clear up there, but after a while breathing became a bit difficult (the Vultee had no oxygen system). The coating of ice had rendered their radio useless, but Joe Doolittle had serious reservations anyway about herself as a radio operator. So Doolittle, on instruments, guided the Vultee eastward in the rarefied air. "As we flew along, my wife passed out, the chap with me passed out and flying at 16,500 feet hour after hour, I became goofy, so goofy that I got off course to the south and came out south of Washington, just north of Langley Field, where I saw the ground for the first time since taking off from Burbank—[I was] a couple of hundred miles southwest of my course. I immediately let down, corrected my course, and flew on to New York and landed. I had still made a transcontinental record nonstop." Doolittle had, despite the flight's problems, cut more than an hour off Ricken-backer's record of the year before and had crossed the continent in 11 hours, 59 minutes. (Doolittle's brother-in-law, American's chief pilot, Captain L. S. Andrews, later took the same plane, replaced the exhaust stacks, and, with oxygen, cut a half hour off Doolittle's time.)

Doolittle's record-breaking flight received the customary attention from the press—a man had casually, so it seemed, flown his wife and a friend across the country in less than half a day (it seemed impolitic to mention the unscheduled detour to the vicinity of Washington, D.C.). Doolittle had been quoted as having said to waiting reporters at Floyd Bennett Field, "The old man is slipping; I should have arrived two hours sooner."

One newsman asked Joe Doolittle if she had worn a parachute and quoted her as replying, "Whatever for?" This was in character and so was her comment, "It was an uncomfortable flight—I could hardly sleep."

The flight, in fact, had been miserable, for Doolittle had had to fight through ice storms nearly all the way, was forced to fly blind a considerable distance across the country, and had spent a good deal of time shaking ice off the plane. One of his shakes coincided with his wife's opening of a cockpit ventilator, which resulted in a facefull of ice for Joe Doolittle. She did not think kindly of her (unknown to her, preoccupied) husband, sensing it was another one of his jokes. So was, as far as she thought, Irving Krick. The weather had definitely not been as predicted.

"I was a little annoyed at Krick," Doolittle recalled, "because his weather prognostication, which he had given me with great confidence, was one hundred per cent wrong. So the next time I saw him I chided him a little and his statement was, 'If you had been on course, and hadn't got lost, you would have found it just as I said it was.'

"This annoyed me too. I am an individual who can forgive very readily; I forget with great difficulty. I feel a chap who forgives is tolerant, understanding—a chap who forgets is stupid." Doolittle would not forget Dr. Krick and, indeed, would meet him again.

There was little time to consider the absolution of Dr. Krick, for Doolittle was more concerned with Shell's involvement with 100-octane fuel, which appeared to be reaching some kind of climax. As of now, it had been his preoccupation, off and on between record flights, for about three years.

The history of the development of 100-octane fuel covers a longer period. A now-little-known scientific genius, Thomas Midgly, Jr., discovered a compound composed of lead, hydrogen, and carbon, which he called "tetraethyl lead," while seeking a fuel that would eliminate "knocks" in Delco lighting units which were widely used in rural America in the early years of this century. These were run on kerosene, but after years of experimentation Midgly found that adding the compound to kerosene or gasoline achieved the same desired results: a more efficiently running engine. When Doolittle came to Shell, of course, Midgly's work was known but not widely exploited, primarily because of the enormous costs. By urging Shell to invest in production plants, Doolittle hoped to lower the costs of producing gasoline while raising the octane. The problem was to find the consumer—which, Doolittle continued to hope, would be the War Department. (The Ethyl Corporation some years before had synthesized the first iso-octane, a compound used to establish the octane number of a fuel, in the laboratory of Graham Edgar, at a cost of $4,000 per gallon, certainly no bargain for anyone.)

Doolittle's concern was with a fuel that would increase the efficiency and power of aircraft engines and, in turn, lead to even more powerful and efficient aircraft. The existence of tetraethyl lead had been known since the 1920s, and while there was a need for it, there was no demand. Doolittle hoped to create that demand at the risk of his position at Shell. According to Quentin Reynolds, in his early biography of Doolittle, men in the oil industry considered Doolittle's sponsorship of Shell's 100-octane program the "biggest gamble Doolittle ever took."

According to Reynolds' hypothetical oil man, "Back in the 1930's he [Doolittle] gambled his whole career at Shell on the very thin possibility that the War Department would make 100-octane its standard aviation fuel. He talked the company into building an expensive commercial-size plant to manufacture a fuel that the Army brass said was too expensive ever to be commercial. Jimmy really went out on a limb and the War Department damned near sawed it off."

Doolittle's principal military allies would have hardly qualified as "brass," chiefly Lieutenant Klein of the Fuel and Oil Branch at Wright Field. Klein and his superiors, Lieutenant E. R. Page and the head of research, Samuel D. Heron, were aware of the importance of 100-octane fuel. It was not as if Doolittle were butting his head against stupid bureaucracy or incompetents unaware of the obvious. There was the fact of the Depression and the War Department's preoccupation with economy, as well as an undercurrent of antimilitarism that followed in the wake of World War I and which was particularly strong during the 1930s. Within the War Department itself there were traditionalists who lived in the past and who were unwilling to accept the airplane as a weapon. The horse, in some limited circles, was still regarded as the gentleman's proper mount for war.

Within the Power Plant Branch and the Fuel and Oil Branch at Wright Field, where aircraft were taken seriously in a time when the subject of defense began to insinuate itself on military thinkers, the obvious advantages of the high-octane fuel was never questioned. By the early 1930s the Air Corps used as its standard aviation fuel one in the 90- to 91-octane range—an improvement over the 50-octane of the World War I period.

Under Doolittle's prodding, the U. S. Army Air Corps had made its first purchase of chemically pure iso-octane fuel for use at Wright Field. The order was a small one, for 1,000 gallons—at a rather stiff $2.50 a gallon. The date was April 30, 1934; Shell had built several plants by then and had invested close to $2 million in the enterprise. The initial breakthrough did not promise much. But the fuel was used in testing engine modifications and improvements. It was found, for example, that the standard Army pursuit plane at the time, the Boeing P-26, when fueled with the

100-octane had the engine horsepower raised 25 per cent, speed increased 7 per cent, rate of climb increased 40 per cent, and takeoff run decreased 20 per cent. Not that the 100-octane was a miracle worker, for in order to improve performance by using the higher octane fuels, it was necessary also to improve the power plant. Further experimentation with the P-26 sustained the original findings. Nor were the implications lost on commercial aviation. Doolittle and his little band were vindicated, but the lack of buyers of high-octane fuel canceled out any jubilation.

Klein, in March 1935, made the Wright Field findings and their implications public when he published a brief article in the respected technical *Journal of the Aeronautical Sciences* entitled "Aircraft Engine Performance with 100-octane Fuel." While this may not have had much impact on the general public, its point was not lost on the aviation industry and the military. Curtiss-Wright issued an announcement about developing an engine that would be capable of making the most of 100-octane and members of the oil industry, particularly those who, like Shell, had been investing large funds in the gamble, promised to explore iso-octanes further. Klein, by then a captain, had made his mark but he did not stampede the War Department. Over a year went by before a committee was formed to look into the subject of fuels and engines.

The committee, chaired by Lieutenant Colonel J. T. McNarney, consisted of six military members, its junior member being Captain Klein. Civilian experts were drawn from the several interested engine (Wright, Pratt & Whitney, United Aircraft) and oil (Phillips, Standard Oil, Shell) companies; an additional, non-Army witness was the Navy's Lieutenant L. C. Ekstrom, a fuel and lubricant authority. When the committee met at Wright Field on November 17, 1936, the Shell representative was Eugene Zimmerman, not Doolittle, who happened to be moose hunting in the Canadian woods at the time.

There were panicky moments in the Shell offices in St. Louis when it took four days—a two-day trip, each way, by horse and canoe—to get Doolittle to a telephone. By that time it was impossible for Doolittle to get to Wright Field in time for the meetings of the McNarney Committee and he calmly suggested on the phone that Zimmerman was thoroughly equipped to represent

Shell before the committee. He then blithely returned to his moose hunting.

The case for 100-octane fuel, particularly in aircraft engines, was skillfully presented by Klein, who traced the history of iso-octane fuels and by Zimmerman, who explained the status of Shell in the testing and production capability of such a fuel. The representatives from the engine manufacturers presented their cases, with the major point of their argument being that aircraft engines could only be improved with the adoption of a standard of 100-octane for fuel. Edwin E. Aldrin, a former Army flier, who managed the Aviation Department for Standard Oil, was ready with some sobering news about the fuel and engine development in Europe—Britain, France, Russia, and Germany.

At the hearing's conclusion the McNarney Committee, in a report stamped "Confidential," unanimously recommended "that all engines hereinafter procured, except those for primary training, be designed and tested on a basis of 100-octane fuel; that 100-octane fuel be adopted as standard for the Air Corps effective January 1, 1938."

There was joy in the Shell camp and Doolittle's gamble, all agreed, would pay off after all. Shell had four plants ready to go and $2 million invested in the future of iso-octane fuels. Ironically, after the bids were opened and studied by the War Department, Shell was not chosen to be the supplier.

"As I remember," Doolittle has written, "The Standard Oil Company of New Jersey got the first contract, but my memory is a bit blurred. We soon began to get our share of such business as there was, but for some time at least one of Shell's senior people spoke derisively of 'Doolittle's million-dollar blunder.'

"Of course, 100-octane fuel usage would have been slower without the war, but its advantages—even in commercial aviation —were so great that its eventual use, in large quantities, was inevitable."

The Army's rebuff to Shell, which underscored the "million-dollar blunder" remark, proved to be a temporary setback. Events few understood at the time had begun to enkindle forces that would have an impact on the future, some would even change the mission of the Air Corps. One was the advent of the Boeing B-17 and its implied emphasis on a generally little known concept, "strategic bombing." Another was the ominous stirring in Europe incited by bellicose politics of Germany's Adolf Hitler, Chancellor since January 1933 and Führer and Supreme Commander of the German Army, since 1934. Soon after assuming the triple office, Hitler ordered an expansion of the German army and navy and the creation of an air force (Luftwaffe). The fact was that the Luftwaffe was already in existence, secretly, and had been since the mid-1920s.

In 1936, when the McNarney Committee met, civil war was raging in Spain; on the day after the meeting began (and with Doolittle incommunicado in Canada), Hitler and Benito Mussolini, Fascist dictator of Italy, officially recognized General Francisco Franco's rebel government in Spain. This recognition included military aid, arms as well as men. A week later Hitler signed an anti-Comintern pact with Japan. The depredations of Japanese warlords in China since the early 1930s excited only limited interest in the United States. The Pacific was so vast, so distant; Europe, however, was difficult to ignore.

In November of 1936 Franklin Delano Roosevelt was elected to his second term as President of the United States. Although primarily a Navy man, Roosevelt was not blind to the progress and power of aviation—and when he won re-election the United States was regarded by experts to be sixth in air power among the nations of the world. The anecdote was eventually circulated in the Air Corps that one day Roosevelt was going over Army budget recommendations with his chief of staff. There was a modest appropriation for aircraft among other items, including one for the improvement and enlargement of a fort in Wyoming. The President's comment, perhaps apocryphal but ultimately true, was, "You can't scare Hitler from Wyoming," and he suggested cutting such expenses and investing more in aviation.

Events and personalities would prove Doolittle correct in his hitherto nearly fruitless campaign for the adoption of 100-octane fuel as the standard for aircraft engines. How prescient he had been was not demonstrated until a few years later, with the coming of the Second World War.

Twelve

If he had been agitated after his round-the-world trip in 1933 over the state of European military aviation compared to that of the United States, Doolittle had further jolts in store during his two trips to Europe before the outbreak of the Second World War.

The first, made on the behalf of Shell in the late summer of 1937, was brightened for Doolittle by a renewal of his friendship with Ernst Udet. The ebullient, uninhibited First World War ace (second only to the revered von Richthofen) had been talked into taking a job behind a desk as head of the Luftwaffe's Technical Department. Few who really knew the hedonistic Udet could visualize him in such a role; the theory was that Udet went into the Technical Department in order to promote his Stuka concept and to encourage the manufacture of the most famous Stuka, the Junkers Ju-87. In 1937 he still had the carefree personality that had been characteristic of him during his stunt and movie-pilot career of the 1920s and early 1930s. After failing as a postwar aircraft manufacturer, Udet had made a reputation for himself as a remarkable stunt pilot. He then, rather reluctantly, returned to military aviation as a colonel in the Luftwaffe in 1936 with the title "Inspector of Fighters." In this capacity Udet was able to indulge in his favorite occupation, flying. The following year he took over the Luftwaffe's Technical Department. By 1937, a popular as well as respected figure in German aviation, Udet was able to open all doors for his friend Jimmy, providing him with the services of an aide and a plane for transportation.

During his visit, therefore, Doolittle was permitted into aircraft and engine factories as a representative of Shell and a friend of Udet. At Junkers he saw the Ju-87 being assembled; the ugly, bent-winged craft had already begun to earn an inflated reputation as an invincible bomber in Spain. Doolittle was especially impressed with the speedy and efficient production methods of German industry. The haunting question was: why all these planes?

He sensed a change in mood in Germany since his previous visit, with Joe during their round-the-world trip, four years before. The Depression despondency had been replaced by a quickening of temperament, there was more bustle in Berlin—and there were more uniforms. While he was not afforded a glimpse into munitions factories, what Doolittle saw in the several aviation plants convinced him that Hitler could not be dismissed as a figure of fun.

Not that the frolicsome Udet would have agreed; he had no love for Hitler, nor for his own immediate superior, Hermann Goering, the Chief of the Luftwaffe. He spoke of the latter with general bemusement and the former with a decided lack of respect, as Doolittle learned one evening.

In return for Udet's kindness, Doolittle invited him to dinner, after which they returned to Udet's apartment. A French mission had sent Udet several cases of champagne and drinking some of this appeared a fine way to end the evening. Udet was a delightful host, and while his mistress poured champagne, he and Doolittle talked aviation. Udet spoke excellent English, loved to recite poetry, was a talented caricaturist, loved music, sang well, and was a well-known crack shot with a pistol.

Sufficient champagne being consumed, the result was increased merriment. Udet then suggested that they try some pistol shooting. He had had a small target installed over the mantlepiece in the living room; enclosing it was a roughly ten-inch-square steel box with a sloping back, with sand in the bottom. This caught the spent bullets.

The match began with a small .22-caliber pistol, accompanied by further drinking of champagne, but this impressed Udet as rather unexciting. He brought out a full-sized .455 service revolver (a powerful gun, a bit larger than the American .45). He offered Doolittle the first shot. "By then weaving a little bit," Doolittle aimed and fired, striking a pile of German Luftwaffe papers that lay just below the target on the mantlepiece. Unperturbed by the rain of shredded documents, Udet took his turn with the pistol and missed the target completely, blowing a hole about three inches in diameter through the wall into the next apartment. "We next saw an eye looking through that hole," Doolittle recalled. But there was never any official complaint made, a portent of the power of the military in Germany of 1937.

But what was even more shocking to Doolittle was Udet's irreverent impersonation of Hitler. "He would pull a lock of hair over one eye and he had a little black comb which he put under his nose for a moustache and would go around shouting, 'Heil! Heil!' I was quite worried for fear someone would see him doing that. It was fine that he did not support Hitler, but it was unwise, I felt, to have somebody turn in a report that he was mocking Hitler. Particularly a guy looking through a hole that had just been blown into his apartment."

His business for Shell concluded, Doolittle returned home in October, disturbed by what he had seen in Europe, particularly in Germany. His aviation fuel-selling trips into other countries, such as France and Britain, revealed a strange political complacency and military weakness in the face of Hitler's activities. While war did not appear imminent, it was obvious that something was impending. After his return Doolittle repeatedly brought up the subject when speaking with both military as well as civilian friends and acquaintances—but the general mood was that there was no cause for alarm.

Meanwhile he attended to his work at Shell, lending encouragement to the incipient high-octane program and keeping a wary eye on Europe. In September 1938 Britain's Prime Minister Neville Chamberlain returned from a conference in Munich (attended also by France's Premier Édouard Daladier, Mussolini, and Hitler) and made his infamous "peace in our time" statement. Hitler, who had taken over Austria in March 1938, then sent his troops into the Sudetenland and, by March of the next year, proclaimed that "Czechoslovakia has ceased to exist."

Doolittle returned to Europe, again for Shell, in that same spring of 1939. Chamberlain, by this time, had changed his mind saying that he felt that Hitler "was not keeping his word" in regard to all the Munich promises.

A mere two years, Doolittle found, had brought patent changes, both in Udet and Germany. He was struck by the German military posture; it was difficult to ignore, for he saw uniforms everywhere and heard the rhythmic sounds of marching jackboots almost constantly.

Udet, then Director-General (*Generalluftzeugmeister*) in the Luftwaffe's technical division, was no longer the happy-go-lucky, prankish friend of the previous visit. His command of English had diminished; he fumbled for words and phrases—he had obviously not been seeing as many English-speaking friends as he once had. Nor was Doolittle granted the open-door courtesy vis-à-vis the German aviation industry he had enjoyed in 1937. Instead, he was openly questioned by German aviation technicians, manufacturers, fliers, and Luftwaffe officials about the state of American aviation—especially military. He found their interest too pronounced to be dismissed as mere curiosity.

Doolittle and Udet attended an air show at Frankfurt-am-Main and it seemed to Doolittle that he was the only American present, which contributed to his uneasiness. Generally such shows attracted many foreigners, but not this time. Military aircraft predominated at the show, which impressed him as being ominous. Even so, the event afforded him an unexpected glimpse of current German fighters and bombers—that is, those the Luftwaffe would permit to be seen.

When Udet, with customary courtesy, invited Doolittle to Munich to join him for a ten-day leave, he felt he should refuse. The situation in Germany was so grave Doolittle was certain that before long he and Udet would be enemies in war. He could not bring himself to impose on a long, open friendship to gather military information in Germany. Nor did he feel that it would have been politically wise for Udet to be seen in the company of an American citizen who had at one time been a military flier.

By August Doolittle was anxious to return home; en route he stopped off in London to report his anxiety over the Luftwaffe to the air attaché at the American Embassy—but to no avail, he felt. (He did not know then that Charles Lindbergh had made a similar, though gloomier, report the year before, following a notorious stay in Germany as a guest of Goering and Udet. Lindbergh, too, had been ignored.)

Upon Doolittle's arrival back in the United States he called on his old friend and one-time commanding officer, Major General Henry "Hap" Arnold, Chief of the Air Corps. He made a detailed verbal report of what he had seen in Germany and his estimate of the threat of the Luftwaffe—though imperfect, it was the most potent air force in Europe. Doolittle then offered his services—part time or full time, in uniform or on civilian status. It being peace time, Arnold, though he wanted Doolittle back "full time in uniform," explained that he was unable to recall any reserve officer above the rank of captain back to duty—Doolittle was then a major in the reserves. He would have to wait until the following year when Congress would pass a law permitting field-grade officers to be recalled.

Within days of his return, Doolittle heard the news reports pouring in from Europe. Hitler's forces moved into Poland on September 1, 1939; the Second World War had begun.

The war in Europe was not unexpected, but few were ready for it psychologically or militarily. Hitler had fulfilled his threatening promises, but it was hard to believe. The United States had initiated preparations for the inevitable from around the time of Munich, the year before, when Hitler's methods became self-evident. Roosevelt and his advisers were especially sensitive to Hitler's use of the Luftwaffe as a bargaining weapon in diplomatic relations.

Among various moves made toward United States rearmament was an expansion of the Air Corps. In his message to the Congress on January 4, 1939, Roosevelt had stated, "Military aviation is increasing today at an unprecedented and alarming rate. Increased range, increased speed, increased capacity of airplanes abroad, have changed our requirements for defensive aviation." A week later, in a special message to Congress, he bluntly characterized American air strength as "so utterly inadequate that [it] must be immediately strengthened." By April Congress authorized $300 million to be spent on the Air Corps, the strength "not to exceed 6,000 serviceable airplanes." With this bonanza, the Air Corps planners hoped to double its aircraft numbers within two years and, along with it, personnel and operations equipment. General Arnold hoped for a balanced force, although at the beginning of the Second World War the Air Corps was in fine shape as far as the heavy bomber was concerned, but not too strong in the fighter (pursuit) and medium (attack) bomber categories.

The expansion of the Air Corps was, of course, beneficial to the American aviation industry, which had begun to revive to some extent because of the orders coming in from France and Britain. With the coming of war the United States declared its neutrality, officially concerned itself with the defense of the Western Hemisphere, and also established a policy of "cash-and-carry" for belligerents who could buy anything from the United States except implements and materials of war, provided cash was paid and the purchaser transported his purchase in his own ships. (By 1940 this mood of neutrality would begin to fade in the face of reality and by March of 1941 Lend-Lease aid was initiated and extended to Britain by the United States because, as Roosevelt indicated, the defense of Britain was "vital to the defense of the United States.") The period 1939–41 was characterized by a steady changing of plans as news from Europe worsened and further expansions were demanded for defense—even before earlier plans were complete. The Air Corps grew rapidly and by May of 1940 Roosevelt was asking for an annual production of 50,000 planes (the yearly average then being 2,000.)

Doolittle, aware of the seething activity in the aircraft industry as well as in the Air Corps, restlessly awaited his call to return to uniform. There was some pleasure in seeing his 100-octane plan coming into its own and no longer referred to as one top Shell official had put it, "Doolittle's million dollar blunder." He was honored in January 1940 by being named president of the prestigious Institute of Aeronautical Sciences. But, restless, he found the work at Shell and his duties with the institute left him with time for trouble. This took the form of a young lady, a New York model (Doolittle's work frequently brought him to Manhattan). The affair progressed true to form; after some weeks the young lady demanded a fur coat for, no doubt, services rendered. Doolittle refused; the model threatened to inform Joe Doolittle of her husband's philandering.

What Doolittle resented was the young lady's willingness to apply blackmail. Dalliance and fun and games were one thing, but it disturbed his sense of propriety that she should employ such tactics. Crime, of whatever dimension, he believed should not be made profitable or easy.

Doolittle, characteristically, faced the issue: he discussed his problem with Joe. Her response was equally characteristic; she informed Doolittle fully, and colorfully, just what she thought of him and his liaison and then took pen in hand and wrote to the lady in New York. She referred to the fur coat demand, covering that subject succinctly with a sentence that began, "Well, he never bought me a fur coat . . ." That closed the affair and ended the blackmail threats, but not the strong relationship of Joe and Jimmy Doolittle.

Meanwhile, the news from Europe was bleak; the period that had been derisively termed "the phoney war" came to a cataclysmic end with the German invasion of the Low Countries on May 10, 1940. On that same day Chamberlain resigned and was replaced as Prime Minister by Winston Churchill. By the end of the month British troops were fleeing France from Dunkirk; in June France fell and within a month that phase of the war that would be called the "Battle of Britain"—no phoney war, that—would begin. So would Jimmy Doolittle's war, for on July 1, 1940, Doolittle received a telegram requesting him to return to the U. S. Army Air Corps with the rank of major. He was then forty-three years old, not an unsuitable age for his rank—but a decidedly advanced age for a man who wished to be a military aviator.

Doolittle's first assignment upon returning to the Air Corps was as Assistant Supervisor, Central Air Corps Procurement Center— his specific job being trouble shooting. He was immediately sent to Indianapolis, Indiana, where the Allison Division of General Motors was located. Allison turned out liquid-cooled engines for aircraft, but conversion to the demands of mass production was causing problems, notably by the production of flawed engines; nor could the plant maintain production schedules.

Doolittle came upon the scene, observed the chaos, and began to make his plans. In the meantime, O. E. Hunt, chief engineer for General Motors, came down, viewed the situation, and shut down the plant for two weeks to establish order and efficiency. While this gleaned them few friends, in time better and more Allison engines (being used in the Lockheed P-38, the Bell P-39, and the Curtiss P-40 fighters at the time) began flowing from the plant.

Soon after his arrival in Indianapolis, Doolittle requested a

P-40, with an Allison engine, to be assigned to him as his personal plane so that he could become better acquainted with the aircraft and especially with the capabilities and problems of the engine. Feeling that the request would require some selling to the Air Corps, he carefully prepared a sales pitch. He went to Washington and presented his request personally to Arnold, who promptly said, "O.K."

This had come with unexpected ease and Doolittle continued with his speech, which Arnold interrupted with "Jimmy, are you trying to talk yourself *out* of the P-40?"

When the plane was assigned to him, Doolittle immediately installed a homing device and additional instruments in the P-40. At the time there was considerable difficulty—and some fatalities —when fighter planes were flown in bad weather. Consequently it was ordered that all fighter planes be prohibited from flying in poor weather. Doolittle found this unwise, particularly in wartime. Grounding fighters seemed rather self-defeating. He returned to Washington and again got Arnold's ear: he hoped that with proper instrumentation and the introduction of more sophisticated training methods and operational techniques even the more "skittish" fighters could be flown in any reasonable weather. Arnold again agreed and provided Doolittle with a special letter, dated September 26, 1940, and entitled "Special Authority for Instrument Flying in Pursuit Aircraft":

1. Existing regulations and instructions prohibit intentional flight under instrument conditions in pursuit type aircraft.

2. In your particular case these restrictions are waived, and this letter will serve as authority for you to obtain instrument clearances at your direction in pursuit type aircraft.

3. This authority is granted in recognition of your exceptional qualifications and to enable the Air Corps to obtain valuable information on the behavior and flying characteristics of modern pursuit type aircraft under instrument flying conditions.

4. This letter does not waive instructions contained in Circular Letter No. 39-37, dated July 18, 1939.

Doolittle had a wallet-sized copy of the letter made and carried it with him constantly. When fields were closed down to all other pilots, Doolittle could flash his letter from Arnold and, to general consternation, would have his P-40 pushed out for a flight. When other pilots inquired, "How do you get one of those?" Doolittle would wink and reply, "You have to know the big boss in Washington."

The experiment did bear fruit, for eventually new training techniques were instituted and finally the restrictions were lifted.

By November 1940 Doolittle was assigned to Detroit where the automotive industry was initiating its conversion to the manufacturing of aircraft products. Doolittle was to serve as liaison between the Air Corps and what was called the Automotive Committee for Air Defense.

Neither the automobile industry nor the aircraft industry were particularly happy over the wedding; Detroit hoped to continue turning out its quota of cars and the aviation industry was not anxious to release its patents and tools to strangers, let alone to one another. Earlier in the year, when Roosevelt called for 50,000 aircraft a year, there was plenty of encouragement from Detroit when the industry's veteran mass producer Henry Ford said he could produce a thousand planes a day; William S. Knudsen, of General Motors, echoed Ford, but more realistically, by stating that "possibly" General Motors could turn out a thousand planes a month.

However, before the first plane could take off from a Detroit runway, weeks were spent in talking and planning. The idea was to get the auto manufacturers to become subcontractors to the aviation industry; there being no urgency in 1940 over a real war, the negotiations were complex and frustrating. Sharing of engine production was not so difficult as sharing airframe production, there being a great difference between a truck body and a fuselage. There was the question of facilities: should existing ones be expanded or should new ones be built? Who would underwrite the costs? Automobile manufacturers were unwilling to divert portions of their factories to making parts for aircraft, so that in time, as it became more obvious that the United States might have to go to war, the government agreed to provide new facilities, even the tools, to Detroit. The plan was for Detroit to specialize to a great extent in the production of bombers (within two years Ford's great Willow Run plant would be turning out Consolidated B-24s at a remarkable rate).

In addition to dealing with the problems of the conversion of factions of American industry to wartime production (although the war was still contained in Europe), Doolittle had personal considerations also. When he resigned from Shell, the Doolittles gave up their St. Louis home and moved to Indianapolis. There was no need for large quarters as both their sons, Jim, Jr., then twenty, and John, eighteen, were eligible for military service. Jim, Jr., enlisted in the Air Corps and John was accepted at West Point. Later the family moved to Detroit where Doolittle was preoccupied with transforming Detroit into an aviation manufacturing center.

This unexciting but required work continued slowly on into the next year and, in the summer of 1941, Doolittle welcomed the chance to visit England in order to study British methods of operation, maintenance, and repair of aircraft, especially American-built. The historic Battle of Britain was over, the threat of German invasion appeared to have evaporated, and the night bombings—the Blitz—by the Luftwaffe had greatly diminished. Doolittle's inspection tour convinced him that the British did not regard the war as over. He visited operational airfields, talked with crews and commanders about planes, guns, and tactics. With ground crews he could study the merits of easy assembly and disassembly of planes for rapid on-the-spot repair of battle-damaged aircraft. He was shown through aircraft factories (in some, seeing boys of twelve and fourteen operating machines). Near Bath he inspected the Bristol Aeroplane Company's underground engine plant, which was impressive and perhaps necessary in view of the Luftwaffe's bombing attempts, but the idea of an underground factory in the United States did not seem feasible to Doolittle.

The subject of plant conversion from one industry to another, which had engrossed him for the past several months, was investigated, as was also the dispersal of factories and their repair after bombings. Working conditions were reviewed and Doolittle was interested to learn that smoking was permitted in every factory he visited. He checked into apprenticeship programs, into manufacturing methods and dozens of other topics that he might employ upon his return to the United States.

He had the opportunity to study British warplanes, then operational and being readied for operations—the Spitfire and Hurricane fighters, the Wellington and Halifax bombers in the former category and the Typhoon and Mosquito fighters in the latter. He came away convinced that the experience of the British had proved that American combat planes were undergunned and also convinced of the efficacy of the four-engined bomber, which the Germans had neglected, thanks to his old friend Udet and his pre-occupation with the Stuka principle.

By October, after writing a long report for Arnold, Doolittle returned to his factory circuit, applying what he could of what he had learned firsthand in England. Having visited a center of action, his return to "flying a desk" was unfulfilling. It had become a daily grind, papered over with forms in triplicate—certainly he could be doing something else. But what?

The question was answered for him on December 7, 1941—one week before his forty-fifth birthday—when Japanese aircraft, as if out of nowhere, swept in over Pearl Harbor, Hawaii. The stunning event, from an unexpected direction, prompted Doolittle into action. By the next morning he had sent off a letter to General Arnold requesting a transfer from his Detroit desk to an assignment with a combat unit. He then began working "through channels," furnishing his superior in Detroit, Colonel A. M. Drake, with a memorandum approving his own request. Reluctantly Drake granted approval; Doolittle then flew to Wright Field to acquire the next highest signature, that of Brigadier General George C. Kenney—who proved to be more reluctant than Drake. Doolittle managed to squeeze a single concession out of Kenney—one word: "Forwarded."

By the time Doolittle progressed to the next echelon, represented by Major General Oliver P. Echols, the word had preceded him (the work, evidently, of Kenney) and Echols was ready with an unequivocal "No." An unhappy, frustrated Doolittle retreated to his desk in Detroit, where he entertained unkind thoughts about the fortunes of his war to date.

Suddenly, as the first wartime Christmas drew near, he was summoned by Arnold to report to Washington, D.C. An elated Doolittle left his desk, hastened to the capital, and, on December 24, 1941, was given another desk. He had been assigned to Arnold's staff with the rank of lieutenant colonel and the title of Director of Operational Requirements—a liaison man ("glorified delivery boy," in Doolittle's phrase) between the aircraft manufacturers and the air units. The new assignment was merely a slight variation on his Detroit experience.

There were pleasant differences. Joe Doolittle joined her husband in Washington (both their sons were by then in military training). She also served in Doolittle's office as an unofficial, unpaid secretary. Also, now and then, Arnold handed Doolittle a challenging job that made being chained to a desk more endurable.

Early in 1942 Arnold was informed of serious problems in connection with a highly recommended medium bomber, the Martin B-26 Marauder, which because of a series of accidents had been renamed by pilots the "Flying Prostitute" because of its small wing area and thus "no visible means of support"; it was also known as the "Widow Maker." Doolittle later described the B-26 as "an unforgiving airplane and it was killing pilots because it never gave them a chance to make mistakes." With the influx of embryo pilots into the expanding Air Corps, it was inevitable that a great many would require forgiveness before they could become combat fliers. "General Arnold wanted me to check into the problem and recommend whether it should be continued to be built or not. I checked it over, flew it and liked it."

Arnold's account is less laconic: "Our new pilots were afraid of the B-26," he wrote in his memoirs, *Global Mission,* "and we had one accident after another. Seemingly, all that was necessary was for one engine to go sour on a B-26 while in flight, and it would crash.

"At the time the B-26 trouble was at its height, I called Doolittle to my office, told him I would like to have him go out, take a B-26, fly it under and all conditions, and then go down to the B-26 outfit, take command, and show those boys that flying this ship was no different from flying any other. Doolittle did this, and before he left the outfit he had the boys flying the B-26 on one engine, making landings and taking off with one engine, just as they had formerly done with two."

"The basic problem," Doolittle later explained, "as in the earlier fighter plane weather situation, was primarily one of training. The embryo pilots advanced from a simple primary trainer to a simple basic trainer and then to the unforgiving B-26. It was necessary to have a more difficult plane to fly in the training period before they could graduate to the B-26." Doolittle's recommendation was favorably acted upon and, when the training period was extended, accidents were greatly reduced.

Shortly after the B-26 assignment, about the third week in January 1942, Arnold again sent for Doolittle. Once seated, Doolittle was asked a curious question. What aircraft then available was capable of taking off within a run of five hundred feet with a ton of bombs and fly 2,000 miles? Eliminating the B-26 immediately (because of the restriction on the takeoff run), Doolittle could come up with three possibilities, two Douglas designs, the B-18 and B-23, and the North American B-25. Not absolutely certain of their individual characteristics, he asked Arnold for a day to check on his thinking. This was granted, but with the suggestion that he keep "it under your hat."

A little research eliminated the aging B-18, leaving only the B-25 and B-23, either of which, Doolittle believed, could do the job—with proper modifications. Informing Arnold, he learned of one other restriction: "The plane must take off in a narrow area not more than 75 feet wide." The 92-foot wingspan of the B-23 left only the B-25, with a wingspan of 67 feet, 6 inches, which still left little margin for error. All the strange restrictions piqued Doolittle's curiosity, but Arnold did not enlighten him. But once assured that the B-25 could be modified for the extraordinary mission in mind, he assigned Doolittle the task of overseeing the technical aspects of the job and to train the crews to fly bombers.

That, initially, was to have been Doolittle's sole contribution to that mission that would become popularly known as "Doolittle's Tokyo Raid."

Thirteen

The official designation for the mission was "First Aviation Project" or "Special Project No. 1"; Doolittle usually referred to it as the "B-25 Special Project," specifically in a paper he prepared for Arnold early in February 1942.

The project had been born aboard the *Vixen,* a yacht which served as Fleet Commander Admiral Ernest J. King's "quarters" moored at the Washington Navy Yard. In the evening of January 10, 1942, following a day of meetings with President Roosevelt, Army chief General George C. Marshall, and Arnold, King moodily pondered the major topic of the day's discussions: how to avenge the Japanese attack on Pearl Harbor.

The war news from the Pacific was uniformly bad for the United States as well as its Allies. Following the gloomiest Christmas in American history since the Depression, there was a general demand for striking back, for retaliation. The fact that King had to face was that most of the Pacific Ocean belonged to the stunningly victorious Japanese. With most of the American Pacific fleet crippled at Pearl Harbor, there was little with which to strike back. In addition, there was the problem of Hitler. Just six days before, at a meeting of the Combined Chiefs of Staff, among the topics discussed at the White House in the presence of Roosevelt and Churchill, was the North African situation (General Erwin Rommel, who had been sent by Hitler, had been consistently beating the British armies in the desert) and how this might affect the attitude of the French in North Africa. Ever since the British had attacked French ships at Oran, Algeria, following the French surrender to Germany in the summer of 1940, Anglo-French relations had been poor. The British, of course, initiated the attack to prevent the ships from falling into German hands. Those ships already in British ports were seized; at Oran three battleships and an aircraft carrier were destroyed. The French in North Africa would hardly welcome their former British ally, it was intimated during the meeting.

Plans for invading North Africa were discussed, but the problem of the delivery of troops and supplies was a difficult one. King suggested that carriers be used to deliver aircraft, Navy and Army fighters, as well as Army bombers.

King's proposal raised some objections, the strongest being the vulnerability of the aircraft packed onto a carrier deck, during transportation and especially unloading at docks. But the idea remained with Arnold who, after the conference, returned to his office and wrote a memo for future consideration: "By transporting these Army bombers on a carrier, it will be necessary for us to take off from the carrier, which brings up the question of what kind of plane—B-18 bomber and DC-3 for cargo?

"We will have to try bomber take-offs from carriers. It has never been done before but we must try out and check on how long it takes." The last was a reference to the length of deck necessary for a successful takeoff. The idea of bomber takeoff from a carrier was germinating.

A few days later, on January 10, a member of King's staff, Captain Francis S. Low, a submarine specialist, had flown down to Norfolk, Virginia, from Washington to view the Navy's newest carrier, the *Hornet*. While taking off for the return flight Low spotted the outline of a carrier deck painted on the ground (this was used to train Navy pilots for carrier takeoffs). Almost simultaneously, he saw a couple of Army twin-engined bombers making simulated bombing runs on the carrier outline. As the two elements verged on juxtaposition, the shadows of the bombers running along the "carrier deck," an idea lighted up in Low's mind. That evening he called on King.

Explaining to the mystified and slightly impatient admiral, Low quickly came to the point. What with vengeance so much in the air, the only possibility of striking back at Japan would be by air.

Since carrier-borne aircraft were limited to a striking distance of about 300 miles—well within reach of Japanese bombers—why not employ Army twin-engined bombers launched from a carrier to bomb Japan?

Neither King nor Low were certain that this could be done, but to King the idea had a splendid ring. He told Low to call his air operations officer, Captain Donald B. Duncan, to explore the idea further. The two men met the following day, a Sunday. Duncan dismissed one possibility immediately—it would be out of the question to *land* a twin-engined aircraft on a carrier. Army planes were not equipped with arrester hooks, for one thing; they had rather high landing speeds and they could not be folded up and stowed below decks.

Taking off from a carrier, though it had never been done, as Arnold had noted, was another question. But Duncan did not feel he could make a definite statement without a comprehensive study and computations. Five days and thirty closely written pages later, he came to King prepared to say that it could be done.

The following day, January 17, King sent Low and Duncan to see Arnold with the plan. A joint Navy-Army Air Corps project, particularly one with Japan as its objective, captivated the Air Corps chief; he questioned Duncan on a few technicalities and as soon as the two Navy men left, he summoned Doolittle and presented him with the problem of what plane could perform under the various, mysterious restrictions Arnold outlined. Independently, both Doolittle and Duncan decided that the plane for the job was the B-25 Mitchell.

Once the project was officially under way, speed and secrecy were essential. King placed Duncan in charge of the Navy's contribution to the mission and Arnold assigned Doolittle to oversee the Army's. Within a week, on January 22—on this day American troops were in retreat on Bataan in the Philippines and Rommel enjoyed another victory at Agedabia, North Africa—Doolittle requested that "one B-25B airplane be made available to the Mid-Continent Airlines at Minneapolis, Minnesota, on January 23, 1942, or at earliest possible moment thereafter." An additional seventeen B-25s would follow for the same modifications.

By this time Doolittle had been informed of the objective of the mission; the next day, January 23, he flew to Wright Field to meet with his old boss, General Kenney, and various military and civilian experts, to plan the modifications that would be necessary to prepare the Mitchells for the mission. Neither Kenney nor the other members of the special team were aware of the reasons for the installation of additional fuel tanks, redesigned bomb shackles, and special photographic equipment. The essential extra tanks, one of which was placed in the bomb bay above the racks and another in the passageway between compartments, were made of collapsible rubber, proved to be a major source of trouble. Another source of trouble was the lower gun turret, whose operation was so erratic that Doolittle would have it removed later.

The aircraft ordered and the mechanics of modification under consideration, Doolittle returned to Washington and his office in the Munitions Building. The solution to the problem of manning the planes was fairly simple, there being very few experienced B-25 crews since the aircraft had only recently become operational. The 17th Bombardment Group(M) with its three squadrons, the 34th, 37th and the 95th, plus the 89th Reconnaissance Squadron all then stationed at Pendleton, Oregon, would furnish both the men and the planes.

By January 28 Arnold could state at a White House meeting, although misleading to some extent, that "at present a man is working on this proposition of bombing [Japan] from China or Russia . . ." Three days later a member of Arnold's staff, Brigadier General Carl A. Spaatz, provided Doolittle with a list of industrial targets in ten Japanese cities, including such major centers as Tokyo, Kobe, Nagoya, and Yokohama. Two days after that a curious event occurred: the carrier *Hornet*, after taking aboard two B-25s, left Norfolk, and then, while out to sea, with the captain of the *Hornet*, Rear Admiral Marc A. Mitscher, Captain Duncan, and hundreds of mystified seamen observing, the two Mitchells, piloted respectively by Lieutenant John E. Fitzgerald and Lieutenant James F. McCarthy, were launched from the flight deck of the *Hornet*. As the two bombers, safely off, disappeared over the horizon, Duncan calculated various nautical-aero factors, such as speed of the carrier, wind, and other essentials. There was no doubt in his mind that a battle-ready B-25 could take off from a carrier.

Shortly after, Doolittle set down his ideas concerning the project for Arnold. He indicated at the opening of his memo that the purpose was "to bomb and fire the industrial center of Japan" and he indicated that an "action of this kind is most desirable now, due to the psychological effect on the American public, our allies, and our enemies." He carefully and concisely outlined the myriad of details of the mission: the plan of the mission itself; the landings and refuelings in China (Russia was also suggested as a possible place to land: "Should the Russians be willing to accept delivery of 18 B-25B airplanes, on lease lend . . ."); the bomb loads and types of bombs; the extra fuel; the modification of the planes (which he expected to be ready by March 15); the selection and training of crews, which along with their aircraft, would be ready for boarding of the carrier ("probably the *Hornet*") by April 1. The arrangements in China for landing fields and fuel were covered, as were radio signals, and the weather which Doolittle noted would "become increasingly unfavorable after the end of April." He then slipped in a brief paragraph which must have been news to Arnold:

> Lt. Col. J. H. Doolittle, Air Corps, will be in charge of the preparations for and will be in personal command of the project. Other flight personnel will, due to the considerable hazard incident to such a mission, be volunteers.

On February 3 the B-25 units received orders to fly from Pendleton to Columbia Air Base, South Carolina. The commanding officer, Lieutenant Colonel William C. Mills, informed the departing crews, before they left Pendleton, that volunteers would be needed for an extremely hazardous and equally important secret mission. They were told nothing else, but by the time they reached Columbia Air Base where they refueled, before going on to Eglin Field, Florida, the three squadrons from the 17th Group and the 89th Reconnaissance Squadron had twenty-four crews of volunteers (six of them would be replacement crews if necessary). Doolittle's second in command was to be Major John A. Hilger, of the 89th Squadron, during a great deal of the training phase, since Doolittle would frequently be tied up in Washington (communications by phone or in written form were kept to a minimum). Hilger was the only man in the two dozen crews who had been informed of the mission and its objective. It was Hilger who suggested that a Navy expert be assigned to their unit to instruct the crews in carrier takeoffs. Doolittle agreed, and shortly after from nearby Pensacola Naval Air Station Lieutenant Henry L. Miller appeared at Eglin. He had never seen a B-25 before.

By March 3 all aircraft had been modified by Mid-Continent Airlines and crews, plus ground crews, had arrived at Eglin Field. On that day Doolittle met all the crews for the first time, opening his remarks with the words, "My name's Doolittle," probably the only superfluous words of his brief speech. In it he underscored the need for absolute secrecy (further emphasized when they found themselves quartered—practically quarantined—away from everyone else on the base). Doolittle also informed the men of the dangers of the mission for which they had volunteered and that if any wished to drop out they could and no further word would be said. None dropped out, and Doolittle continued, returning again to the secrecy problem. He explained that many lives besides theirs were involved in their mission (he was thinking of the crews of the Navy ships that would make up what would become Task Force 16) and the wrong word, even the wrong rumor, could be disastrous. Those who were aware of Doolittle's aversion to histrionics found his talk rather sobering and the question arose in many minds: *what in the world are we doing?*

This question was echoed when the training began for the twenty-four crews. At an isolated auxiliary airfield, lines were painted across the runways and marked with flags at distances of 200, 300, and 500 feet. "The idea," wrote pilot Ted Lawson, "we soon found out, was to get into the air in less space and time than we believed was possible for a B-25. We did this by dropping our landing flaps and pouring all the coal we could on the engines." The presence of Lieutenant Miller to drill them in a short-run takeoff, plus his briefing of them in Navy courtesy and lore, indicated to the volunteers that there would be some connection with the Navy.

Soon nearly all of the pilots, "with the exception of a few conservatives," according to Miller, were getting the loaded planes off within a minimal 250 feet. Especially outstanding were, in Miller's estimation, Captain David M. Jones, Captain Robert M. Gray, and Doolittle. Training accidents wiped out two aircraft, but without injury to crews, leaving twenty-two planes and crews.

During the intensive training period the most frustrating "bugs" began appearing in the improvised extra fuel tanks (which had a disconcerting tendency to leak) and the machine guns (which revealed an equally disconcerting tendency to jam). Since the crews were particularly weak in gunnery, the capriciousness of the machine guns was galling. On this problem, Doolittle recalls: "There was no single 'incident.' We tried the bottom turret and found it wanting. The nose gun was natural. It was easy to point and it was fairly easy to figure lead with it. On a dead-ahead incoming or stationary target there was no lead. The top turret was also easy to use and 'normal.' The bottom turret was very complicated and worked 'backwards' to what was normal. It would have taken more time than we had available to master it." Doolittle therefore ordered the offending turret removed, commenting, "A man could learn to play the violin good enough for Carnegie Hall before he could learn to fire this thing."

This, in turn, lessened the over-all weight of the plane. As Doolittle would note, "Another important thing was weight, another space—another fuel. We carried an extra tank with 50 gallons of gasoline. This we couldn't have done without removing the complicated bottom turret. (It was also difficult to keep in working order.) Another good thing was that we could fuel that tank from within the airplane, in flight. This we did with the extra six 5-gallon cans of gasoline that we stowed in the airplane just before taking off the carrier deck."

As a fighter deterrent, two broomsticks, painted black, projected from the tail section, simulating tail guns. These were both light and probably effective. They were the brainchildren of the mission's gunnery and bombing officer, pilot Captain C. Ross Greening, who also devised the simple "Mark Twain" bombsight from about twenty cents' worth of metal. This would eliminate the weight and the risk of carrying the then highly classified Norden bombsight, which would not have been effective at the low altitude at which Doolittle planned to bomb. Since he expected to lose at least one aircraft, he did not wish to carry the Norden sight at all; it was most important that it not fall into enemy hands.

The regulation of carburetors for minimal fuel consumption was also essential. These were adjusted to an extreme, fine setting, but as a precaution Doolittle asked for a representative from Bendix, manufacturer of the carburetors, to come to Eglin. He was picked up at Pensacola by the mission's operations officer, Captain Edward J. York and Greening in one of the Doolittle B-25s and for the first time in his life was treated to a startling short takeoff. The

Bendix man, justly proud of his product, was understandably disturbed by the suggestion that the carburetors required his expert attention.

Upon arriving at Eglin he proceeded to give Doolittle a lecture on the excellence of the Bendix carburetor and how rarely it needed repair work, etc. Doolittle, impatient because the mission's rendezvous with the Navy was impending and with problems with fuel tanks plaguing him, had grown rather testy. He had sent for a top technician and was getting a sales pitch instead of delicate engineering. "What the hell are you," he interrupted, "a salesman? If you're a salesman, get out of here. We've got all the carburetors we need!"

The carburetors were soon tuned up to concert pitch. Around this same time de-icing equipment was installed—de-icer boots on the leading edges of wings and tail surfaces and other equipment for the propellers. This, too, took time away from training, but it was not yet definite whether, upon completing their mission, the crews would fly their planes on into China or to Vladivostok, Russia, so all probabilities had to be covered. A plan to return to the carrier and ditch nearby was rejected, because of the inherent risk in ditching and the exposure during recovery of the carriers to long-range land-based aircraft from Japan, as well as submarines and other surface craft. Had it been possible for the planes to be flown to Russia—where they could have been presented to the Russians on the Lend-Lease plan—at least one chapter of the Tokyo Raid would have been different. However, this was not to be.

Doolittle drove himself and his crews during the weeks left in March before they were to join up with the Navy. Besides the kangaroo takeoffs, the crews practiced flying at near-zero altitude. The Florida coast in the vicinity of Eglin Field thundered to the sound of low-level aircraft dodging trees, hills, buildings, and telegraph wires. Even bombing was attempted in this manner, using Greening's famed "twenty-cent" bombsight. Ted Lawson related what happened to him as he piloted his plane: "The Ruptured Duck laid one of its 100-pound eggs in practice one day from 500 feet. The shock of the explosion on the ground threw me against the roof of the pilot's compartment and raised an egg on my head." Since the intent was to carry 500-pounders on the mission, the incident was cause for alarm until it was learned that bombing altitude would actually be 1,500 feet. It was Doolittle's practice throughout the training period, particularly when a new phase was introduced, to remind his crews that anyone could drop out of the project at any time—no questions asked. At this point, as the bombers appeared to be getting closer and closer to the ground for an unexplained mission, one of the pilots withdrew.

As the training period drew to a close, Doolittle, certain that he had his quota of fine crews, became concerned with his ultimate role in the mission. He had, simply, gotten to know his men and he hoped to go with them all the way. The subject had not really been resolved, both he and Arnold avoiding it gingerly since there were too many other details to attend to and problems to solve without the introduction of another.

However, around the middle of March during one of his several trips to Washington, Doolittle broached the subject. The verbal *pas de deux* that ensued earned him a front seat to the "Tokyo show." He began by sketching the training status for Arnold, slipping in at one point that "it occurs to me that I'm the only guy on this project who knows more about it than anyone else." He praised the crews, their spirit, their response to preparing for a job they could not even discuss, and then, "I'd like your permission to lead this mission myself."

Not yet fully obfuscated by the verbiage, Arnold riposted with a firm, "No," explaining that Doolittle was required on his staff, not leading a hazardous mission. He emphasized his point by stating that he could not let Doolittle lead every mission "you might help to plan."

Summoning up all of his forensic skills and, verbally at least, reverting to his flailing, boyhood, Alaskan combat technique, Doolittle set out to overwhelm his chief. "I launched into my sales pitch," he later told his biographer C. V. Glines, "and finally Hap shrugged his shoulders and said, 'O.K. Jimmy, it's all right with me provided it's all right with Miff Harmon.'" Major General Millard F. Harmon was then Arnold's chief of staff.

"I thought I smelled a rat," Doolittle told Glines, "so I ran down the corridor and burst into Miff's office." He realized that Arnold had simply hoped to pass the buck and have Harmon handle the Doolittle situation. He had not counted on Doolittle's sprinting abilities. He quickly blurted out that he wished to lead the Tokyo mission and that Arnold had told him it would be all right if Harmon approved.

Startled and thrown off his guard, Harmon said, "Sure, Jimmy, it's all yours."

Doolittle thanked him and then, as he hurried from the office, heard the intercom buzz and overheard Harmon saying, "But Hap, he said it was OK with you and I just gave my permission. I can't go back on my word." Doolittle "didn't wait to hear anymore. I beat it back to Eglin and hoped Hap wouldn't order me to stay home. He never did."

Meanwhile, the Navy had been attending to its part of the operation and by mid-March the *Hornet* had begun its long voyage from the East Coast to the final rendezvous point, San Francisco, via the Panama Canal. Duncan was completing arrangements for the rest of the Navy task force in Honolulu. Doolittle was then supervising the final phases of the training of his crews. "Gas consumption was now a primary issue," Ted Lawson would later recall of this time. "During the last part of the training period we made countless flights, mainly for the purpose of testing engineering findings on our best speed at the least consumption. Finally, near the end of March, we had our big test: a quick, ear-splitting take-off, a flight to Fort Myers, Florida, then across the Gulf of Mexico at very low level to Houston, then back to Eglin. That was our final exam in Florida."

Shortly after, with all the Navy arrangements completed, Duncan wired Arnold: "Tell Jimmy to get on his horse." Duncan then left for San Diego, from Honolulu, to board the *Hornet*, still under the command of Mitscher. Another carrier commander, Vice Admiral William F. Halsey, who would bring the *Enterprise* into the mission, also left Hawaii; since he would be in over-all command of Task Force 16, it was his wish to meet with Doolittle before the project got under way. In the early morning of March 23, 1942, twenty-two B-25s took off from the Eglin runways for the last time. Their destination was McClellan Field, near Sacramento, California.

Small formations of the Mitchells headed for San Antonio, their first stop. "We stayed there overnight and the next day we flew on to March Field, on the Coast, refueling only at Phoenix," Lawson recalled. "We were still in training. We were told to hedge-hop our way across the country, testing gas consumption at low levels, and we kept so low we could look up at telegraph wires."

On March 26 Doolittle led his bombers into McClellan for final preparations, such as changing propellers pitted by picked-up gravel from low-level flying, and removal of radios (enforced radio silence would render them useless); the rubberized fuel tanks had to be checked, leakage being a continuing problem. Though Doolittle had been given the highest priority from Arnold, some of the materials required had not yet arrived at the Sacramento Air Depot, where the work was to be done. The engineers, most of them civilians, did not sense the urgency that Doolittle and his men tried to convey to them. To get things done immediately, Doolittle was forced to call Arnold in Washington to get him to impress the base commander to move with dispatch. The Doolittle gang, clannish, close-mouthed, became unpopular at Sacramento within hours of their arrival. Their planes were regarded with almost as much repugnance, with gun turrets removed and their bellies filled with rubber gas tanks, with broomstick guns, no radio, and a strange piece of metal where the bombsight should have been. The planes naturally excited curiosity, which was neither welcomed nor encouraged, also contributing to the tension.

Doolittle was especially emphatic in pointing out that nothing mechanical should be changed—no tampering with carburetors, for example. His chief assistants, Hilger, Greening, and York took to hanging around while the mechanics worked on the planes. "The way they revved our motors made us wince," Lawson recalled. "All of us were so afraid they'd hurt the ships, the way they were handling them, yet we couldn't tell them why we wanted them to be so careful. I guess we must have acted like the biggest bunch of soreheads those mechanics ever saw . . ."

Doolittle was generally regarded as the biggest sorehead of all. An afternoon conference was interrupted by the sound of a backfiring engine which catapulted Doolittle out of an office on the run. A menacing black curl of smoke rose from a B-25 engine as Doolittle bore down upon the plane, yanked a hatch open, and hopped into the cockpit and "restrained" a startled mechanic. When it was possible to talk, the mechanic tried to calm Doolittle explaining that he was running a routine check, something they always did "after the carburetors were adjusted."

Doolittle's entrance into the cockpit was nothing compared to the outburst following that information. All those weeks of fine tuning at Eglin were for nothing. "You mean somebody fiddled with the carburetors without my approval?"

The mechanic explained that the carburetors had been checked and were found to be "way out of adjustment and fixed up." Soon Doolittle had all the crews checking over their planes to learn what else had been "fixed up." Then he was on the phone to Washington again; he also voiced his views to the base commander and engineering officer. While the work proceeded, quite a lot of tension and ill will were generated, not a little because of the absolute need for secrecy.

The best setting for secret discussions being a public place, a meeting between Doolittle and Halsey was arranged for March 30 in a restaurant in San Francisco. The two men met for the first time and, isolated from the rest of the dining room's patrons, discussed the plans and disposition of their mission. Two task groups consisting of eight ships (one in each case being a carrier) would carry out the operation. Task Group 16.2, commanded by Mitscher, would consist of the *Hornet* carrying the Army aircraft and would be accompanied by two cruisers, an oiler, and four destroyers. This group was scheduled to leave San Francisco on April 2.

Meanwhile, Halsey would return to Hawaii and have a similar group (Task Group 16.1) formed: the *Enterprise* and seven other ships, similar in type to those in the other Group; Halsey would leave Pearl Harbor on April 7. Rendezvous for the two groups was planned for Sunday, April 12, to become Task Force 16 under Halsey's command. From that point on, as Halsey simplified the job, "we would carry Jimmy within 400 miles of Tokyo, if we could sneak in that close; but if we were discovered sooner, we would have to launch him anyway, provided he was in reach of either Tokyo or Midway. That suited Jimmy. We shook hands and I wished him luck."

Immediately after, Doolittle phoned Hilger at McClellan and, speaking in a kind of double-talk to confuse anyone who might have overheard him, got preparations under way for leaving McClellan the next day. The planes would be flown the short distance from McClellan to the Alameda Naval Air Station, where the Navy would take over and hoist the Mitchells aboard the *Hornet*. Once loaded and boarded by the crews, the *Hornet* would be moved into San Francisco Bay for departure.

This sounded simpler than it proved to be, for the B-25s were not yet, according to base regulations, ready to go and Hilger found himself embroiled in arguments with various base personnel before he could get the planes released. Doolittle planned to fly his own plane (once flown by Captain Vernon L. Stinzi, who had become ill. Though he recovered to make the voyage on the *Hornet,* Stinzi had relinquished his seat to Doolittle, who refused to give it up). As Doolittle was about to leave for Alameda (his birthplace, though he manufactured no romantic symbolism of the fact), he was handed a formidable report form for his evaluation and signature. This would, after Hilger's arguments, represent the final clearance of his unpopular band of misfits. Doolittle studied the many questions to be answered, the numerous blanks to fill and boiled. His eye caught one sentence asking for his opinion of the work done on his aircraft while being serviced at McClellan and promptly scrawled a single word across the face of the report form: LOUSY.

Sputtering, the base engineering officer demanded a full, detailed report. "Haven't got time," Doolittle replied and headed for his plane. "I won't sign your clearance, Colonel!" he shouted as Doolittle started the engines, cast a baleful look, and took off.

Turning to Hilger the man said with fury, "Who the hell does he think he is? He's heading for a lot of trouble."

"He sure is," Hilger replied in a soft Texas drawl as he smilingly watched the B-25 dip and bank toward Alameda.

Upon landing, Doolittle queried each pilot about the condition of his plane; the slightest mechanical problem placed that aircraft in the reject area. Eventually sixteen planes (fifteen they expected to crowd onto the *Hornet*'s flight deck plus an extra) were towed by Navy "donkeys" to the pier alongside the carrier; all crews, even those whose planes had been left behind, would make the voyage as a source of replacements (while aboard, also, they could not become the source of rumors). The plane crews watched with interest as Navy men swarmed over the Mitchells preparing them for the voyage. Most of the fuel was drained from the tanks and when a plane was towed into position, it was hoisted by crane to the deck of the carrier. They were positioned, one by one at one end of the deck and lashed down and wheels blocked. The last plane aboard, and the first in line for takeoff, was Doolittle's. There was less than 500 feet between the Mitchell's nose and the end of the *Hornet*'s flight deck.

The Army Air Corps crews boarded the *Hornet* in proper Navy style, having been schooled in seagoing etiquette by Miller. "I was proud of those fellows that day," he told Glines, as he watched them go through the prescribed Navy ritual. "They looked smarter in all respects than the Navy personnel that were going to and fro." The fact was that the deck crews were much too preoccupied with getting the Army planes aboard their ship to attend to the niceties of shipboard life; curiosity too was a factor. They had never had an assignment like that before—nor, as it would turn out, again.

Finally the fifteenth plane was lifted aboard and shackled in place; there was still some space on the deck so Doolittle suggested that they fill it with the extra Mitchell. It might be a good idea, he explained, to take the sixteenth plane out to sea and, with Henry Miller as copilot, launch it to demonstrate to the crews that it could be done. Mitscher concurred and the plane was taken aboard and Miller became a captive Tokyo Raider. According to his orders, Miller was to have returned to his home base at Pensacola upon completing his assignment in California, which was to have occurred when the Army crews and bombers were delivered to the *Hornet*. (Once out to sea Doolittle decided that an extra bomber would be an asset to the mission and Miller found himself on an unauthorized cruise.)

Having seen the planes and crews established aboard ship, Doolittle felt his men deserved a little shore leave before they pulled out the following day. Before releasing them he gave a brief lecture on the importance of keeping their mouths shut for security's sake. This formality over, Doolittle too left the *Hornet*.

Joe Doolittle had come to the West Coast to visit her ailing father and had arranged to meet her husband in San Francisco in the afternoon. It was in their hotel elevator later in the day that Doolittle suffered the first premission shock. A man he had never seen before turned to him and said, "I understand you are pushing off tomorrow." Stunned, Doolittle was literally speechless and responded only with a noncommittal stare. Momentarily he pondered calling for the FBI, but dismissed the incident on the assumption the stranger had made a wild, but accurate, guess. It should not have been too difficult: all the planes had been placed aboard the *Hornet* in the bright glare of day and, later, the carrier was moved away from the Air Station dock into San Francisco

Bay and anchored at Berth No. 9. The activity would have been difficult to ignore—and speculation was inevitable. (If Japanese agents were in the area at the time, it is curious that no known report of this unusual operation ever reached Japan.)

The next morning, April 2, Doolittle said good-bye to Joe, telling her only that he might "be out of the country for a little while" and that he would be in touch as soon as he returned. He then left to rejoin the crews aboard the *Hornet*.

By 10:18 A.M. of April 2, 1942, the carrier was under way, preceded by several destroyers and accompanied by cruisers and oilers—a small but conspicuous armada—passing under the Oakland and Golden Gate bridges. Some crew members, recalling Doolittle's security lectures, doubted that their mission could any longer be shrouded in secrecy as they passed under the bridges in broad daylight. Whatever misgivings they felt were dismissed in the excitement of their leave taking.

The mission was sent off auspiciously with the delivery of goodwill messages from Arnold and Marshall, as well as a special one from King to Mitscher. Doolittle, safely aboard the *Hornet* at last, breathed easily for the first time since he had talked Arnold and Harmon into permitting him to lead the mission. All seemed well until a small vessel pulled alongside the carrier and Doolittle was ordered off to return to shore for an urgent call from Washington. He was certain it was Arnold striking back at the last moment; his heart sank.

Upon arriving ashore he approached the phone with trepidation, only to hear the voice of Marshall not Arnold. This would really do it, since he could hardly treat Marshall with the familiarity which his long friendship with Arnold entitled him. Marshall's message was as brief as it was heartfelt: "I just called," he told a somewhat inarticulate Doolittle, "to wish you the best of luck. Our thoughts and our prayers will be with you. Good-bye, good luck, and come home safely."

A grateful Doolittle thanked the general and then hurried back to the *Hornet* heading out through the channel to the open sea. Once aboard he was informed of the preparations under way for the arrival of his crews in China after their mission and all appeared to be well. He was still unaware of the difficulties the Americans were having in making arrangements for this with Chiang Kai-shek, who was not overjoyed with the idea of providing a Chinese haven for American bombers that had attacked homeland Japan. He feared that if the Americans were successful, there would be a savage Japanese retaliation in occupied China (and he was, in fact, right in this).

Another problem in China, the Allies found, was keeping the preparations for the mission secret. During one discussion several servants were discovered eavesdropping behind some drapery. Consequently, only minimal information was exchanged between Chiang and Lieutenant General Joseph Stilwell, the American liaison officer who served as the Chinese leader's chief of staff. Stilwell, no admirer of Chiang, was generally disinclined to reveal too much about the preparations for Doolittle's arrival, fearing it might become the best known "secret" in China. It was unthinkable that Chinese airfields were not being readied to receive Doolittle's men and fuel not flown in for their B-25s to fly them further into China. So, as the *Hornet* moved into the Pacific, Doolittle simply had to assume those essentials were being attended to.

Doolittle and Mitscher had agreed beforehand that they would inform all hands of their mission after the ships were one day out of port. Meanwhile, the Army crews and their Navy hosts were getting acquainted—the traditional enmity (often fought out on the football field each fall) soon surfaced. There was an evident, though somewhat veiled, antipathy in each camp that could have led to the same kind of tensions that had characterized the Army crews' stay at McClellan. Ross Greening sensed a "slightly strained and defensive" coloration in the relationships between the Army and Navy crews. Pilot Ted Lawson recalled being assigned to "a compact little room" he would share with two ensigns. "I was a First Lieutenant then and thus outranked the Ensigns, but that didn't impress them very much. They crawled into their nice bunks and pointed to a cot for me."

At the top level, interservice rivalry—and accommodations—were no problem. Mitscher, the perfect host, had relinquished his quarters to Doolittle—a suite of rooms directly below the flight deck. There was one large "living room" where staff meetings could be held, a small but comfortable bedroom, and a "head," complete with bath. Mitscher slept in a stateroom on the bridge, although he retained one prerogative: access to the head.

Perhaps Mitscher had sensed the Army-Navy estrangement, for

he suggested to Doolittle that they announce their objective instead of waiting for the next day as planned. Doolittle concurred and, as the other ships in the convoy were informed by semaphore, Mitscher proclaimed over the Hornet's communications system that Task Group 16.2 was "bound for Tokyo."

"Cheers from every section of the ship greeted the announcement and morale reached a new high," Mitscher later recalled, "there to remain until after the attack was launched and the ship was well clear of combat areas." The effect upon the crews was immediate. "Relationships improved in a matter of seconds and immediately all hands, Army Air Force and Navy, joined together to accomplish all that was necessary to satisfactorily complete the mission," wrote Greening in his report entitled *The First Joint Action*. And when Lawson returned to his shared quarters that evening "the two Ensigns shook hands with me and insisted that I sleep thereafter in the better of their two soft bunks."

Once the objective of their mission had been revealed, a new intensive training period began. Although his crews had seen little of Doolittle during their stay at Eglin, aboard the *Hornet* they would meet with him every day until mission takeoff time. He made a special point of indicating that Emperor Hirohito's Imperial Palace in central Tokyo was emphatically Off Limits and was not to be bombed under any circumstances. To most of the vengeance-bent crews this appeared to be an odd command at that low moment in the war. With their limited bombing potential, it would seem that the Emperor and the Imperial Palace presented tempting targets.

Doolittle had based this decision on personal experience. He had made a brief visit to Britain in 1940 which happened to coincide with the Blitz, when German bombers had begun dumping bombs into London and other cities rather indiscriminantly. One night the Luftwaffe damaged Buckingham Palace—an incident that infuriated the British more than the greater destruction to their own homes. Commoner united with peer in a determined defiance of the Germans. As the "Imperial Son of Heaven of Great Japan," Hirohito was venerated by the Japanese; he represented royalty as well as divinity. An attack upon his Palace would affront the Japanese militarily and spiritually—and they fought savagely enough without introducing that element. Doolittle impressed the crews with the gravity of this decision—one he numbers among the most important he ever made. He cautioned them, also, about dropping bombs into residential areas which would contribute nothing of value to the mission.

And so it went aboard the *Hornet* for about two weeks, daily meetings with Doolittle as well as helpful indoctrination by Navy officers. Commander Apollo Soucek, the *Hornet*'s air officer, instructed the crews in the technicalities of carrier operations; intelligence officer Lieutenant Commander Stephen Jurika talked to them about various aspects of Chinese and Japanese culture. Their own First Lieutenant Thomas R. White, the one doctor who would participate in the mission, taught a cram course in first aid. The sixteen pilots took a refresher with Navy Commander Frank Akers in navigation. There were also some sorely needed gunnery sessions, since many of the men had never previously fired a machine gun. As Doolittle recalls, the practice shooting was carried out on tethered kites and free-flying balloons.

In between these various sessions, the crews would assemble with Doolittle to go over the finer details of the mission. The crews were permitted, by agreement among themselves, to select their targets, and target folders, with maps, were distributed. These indicated unquestioned military targets in Tokyo, Yokohama, Nagoya, and Kobe. Doolittle stressed the importance of bombing only the targets clearly marked on the maps. Most of the planes would carry three 500-pound demolition bombs and one 500-pound incendiary—and because of the well-known susceptibility of Japanese cities to fire, the question was raised about saving the incendiary bomb for the more inflammable residential areas.

Doolittle rejected the suggestion and again reminded the crews about staying away from the Imperial Palace as well as obvious nonmilitary zones. The demolitions bombs were to be dropped quickly and the incendiary cluster as near to the points of impact as possible—that would have the greatest effect on the targets.

Ten of the sixteen B-25s were assigned to targets in Tokyo. According to the original plan for the mission, Doolittle was scheduled to take off in the vanguard as soon as the *Hornet* arrived within launching distance—about 400 miles, it was hoped. The takeoff was timed to bring Doolittle's plane over Tokyo at around sunset, providing him with the cover of darkness (it would also mean that he would arrive in China in the dark and would have to make a night landing). Doolittle's bombs would ignite the fires that would serve as beacons for the planes that would follow. These were to be launched when sunset had reached the carrier, making it possible for them to drop their bombs at night and to arrive in China after daybreak. This plan was canceled by the intervention of fate.

Fate was to afflict the operation with a number of unpredictable convolutions almost from the beginning. The first occurred when Halsey's return to Hawaii after his meeting with Doolittle in San Francisco on March 30 was delayed by poor flying weather. This, in turn, would set back the rendezvous date of the two task groups from April 12 to April 13.

By April 10 Japanese intelligence was aware of the presence of enemy carriers in the Pacific because of the increase in the exchange of radio messages in the area. The estimate was that there were at least two carriers and, possibly, a third in the American task force. If it proceeded westward, it was estimated at Japanese Combined Fleet headquarters, Tokyo could come under carrier-borne air attack by April 14. This caused no great alarm, for in order to carry out such an attack the Americans would have to come within 300 miles of Japan in order to launch their shipboard bombers (no one at Combined Fleet headquarters entertained the possibility of the more potent Army medium bombers). Another source of comfort to the Japanese was a line of small picket boats 700 miles off Japan's shores—their existence was unknown to the Americans—that would spot the enemy ships long before the Americans could launch their planes. Before that could be done, Japanese land-based, long-range, bombers could deal with the enemy. With preparations under way, the Japanese waited.

Unknown to Doolittle, yet another quirky turn of fate came close to forcing drastic changes. On April 11, three days after Halsey's task group had left Hawaii and two days before the delayed rendezvous, Chiang Kai-shek disconcerted Washington with a request to postpone the mission until some time in May. By then, he promised (or hoped) his troops would secure certain key areas from Japanese control. He continued to be apprehensive about the Japanese reaction to an attack on the Japanese islands Chiang was certain it would unleash a campaign of reprisals in occupied China.

There was another Chinese problem: American efforts to establish landing and refueling facilities for Doolittle's men (two aircraft being lost in the attempts). The Generalissimo vacillated and demurred so that Marshall could only advise his representative in China, Stilwell, and the Air Force's Colonel Clayton Bissell that the mission had progressed too far to consider any change in plans. Marshall offered no further enlightenment, impressing them with the "atmosphere of total mystery" that should envelop the project, still leaving them with the problem of finding landing sites for the Mitchells.

So it was that when the two Navy task groups merged on April 13 to form Task Force 16, no concrete arrangements had been made for the Americans' arrival in China. Unaware of this, the task force sped westward for Japan.

In Tokyo the next day, when the American planes had been expected, there were no planes nor had the picket boats sighted enemy carriers. This brought a sense of uneasiness, even disappointment, in the offices of Japanese Intelligence and a feeling of relief among the military planners; there was no relaxation in preparations, however, but less tension. The nagging question was, what were the Americans up to? It was an indefinite day of limbo; this was reflected aboard the *Hornet* by skipping April 14 completely when the task force crossed the International Date Line.

Meanwhile, Doolittle continued pressing his crews in gunnery practice and indoctrination, for upon crossing the Line directly from April 13 to 15, they were set for takeoff just four days away, April 19. That plan too was fated to be unexpectedly upset.

On April 15 Halsey issued orders for the fueling up of the heavy ships of his force, in preparation for the fast run for Japan; as they drew closer the risks grew greater and Halsey did not want his ships exposed to the chance of aerial attack. On this day, too, an English-language news broadcast from Tokyo was picked up denying a Reuter's report that "three American bombers had dropped bombs on Tokyo." The British news agency's dispatch was dismissed as "laughable." Radio Tokyo then concluded, "Instead of worrying about such foolish things, the Japanese people are enjoying the fine spring sunshine and the fragrance of cherry blossoms."

The broadcast, however inaccurate, did not lessen the tensions among the men on the American ships. Nor were they sharing any "fine spring sunshine" with the Japanese. The weather had become wet and gusty, interfering with the operations of the search planes from the accompanying *Enterprise*. Weather permitting, formations of Navy fighters, torpedo planes, and scout bombers took off and fanned out 200 miles in advance of the task force. On April 16, as the task force plowed into enemy waters, the search planes returned reporting no contacts.

The weather turned increasingly sour and, to further complicate procedures, mechanical problems newly plagued the B-25s. One plane required an engine repair job (no simple task on a rainy deck) and there seemed to be an epidemic of bad spark plugs, malfunctioning hydraulic lines, and leaky fuel tanks. These otherwise minor irritations seemed much greater because of last-minute materialization.

On April 17, with search planes again dispatched (only to return again without sighting Japanese ships or aircraft) and while the ships were being refueled (after which the tankers would leave the task force), Captain Ross Greening supervised the bombing up, fueling, and respotting of the B-25s on the deck, poised for takeoff. The first in line, Doolittle's, had 467 feet of deck for his takeoff run. White guidelines—one for the nose wheel and the other for the left landing gear wheel—were painted on the deck; if the plane was kept properly aligned, its right wingtip would clear the carrier's island by about six feet. Greening and his Army-Navy crews completed their work, as scheduled, by sundown; everything was in readiness for takeoff on April 19, only two days off. "We're in the enemy's backyard now, Jimmy," Mitscher said to Doolittle. "Anything can happen from here on in."

He had in mind the probability of being spotted and attacked; the sooner the Army bombers were launched, the better. Mitscher planned to get away from Japanese waters with his precious carriers as soon as possible. He was, in fact, ready for a premature takeoff, if necessary, the following day, Saturday, April 18.

This would have, of course, thrown off all preparations Doolittle assumed were being made for the B-25s in China, but was unperturbed. Once the bombing had been carried out and the news was released, they would be expected in China. He could understand the Navy's concern over the carriers.

All Mitchells were ready to go by evening of April 17. Some

carried bombs to which Japanese medals had been attached. These were souvenirs of palmier days in Japanese-American relations, representing awards given to American citizens by the Japanese government. It had been suggested to Secretary of the Navy Frank Knox that the medals be attached to bombs and returned "to Japan in that manner" by the recipients. This ceremony was attended to as was the final loading of the Mitchells. Personal equipment was stowed aboard in the standard B-4 bags—including clothing, shaving gear, etc., not to mention a wind-up phonograph, plus recordings and some 160 pints of medicinal rye. As the two carriers and their smaller escorts moved closer toward Japan, the sixteen fully armed and loaded B-25s were poised on the spray-swept deck of the *Hornet*. Below, those members of the plane crews who could, slept.

But not for long. At 3:00 A.M., April 18, 1942, a message was flashed from the *Enterprise*, whose radar had picked up something. "Two enemy surface craft reported."

"General quarters" reverberated throughout the task force as all hands took battle stations and anxious eyes riveted on the radar screens. Within a half hour the screens went blank and eleven minutes after the "all-clear" was sounded, those who could apprehensively returned to their bunks. The big *Hornet*, along with the rest of the ships, tossed restlessly in the miserable early morning sea. Shortly after five, the first search planes—three Douglas SBD Dauntlesses, escorted by eight Grumman F4F Wildcats—bounded off the slippery deck of the *Enterprise*. Three additional Dauntlesses were positioned over the task force as CAP (Combat Air Patrol) as an added precautionary measure. The weather had not improved with the coming of daylight—rain squalls and gusting winds lashed the decks and thirty-foot crests drenched the hapless deck crews.

At 5:58 A.M. one of the CAP Dauntlesses, piloted by Lieutenant O. B. Wiseman, sighted something, studied it momentarily and then dropped a "beanbag" onto the deck of the *Enterprise*. The message was ominous: *Enemy surface ship—latitude 36-04 N., Long. 153-10E, bearing 276 true—42 miles. Believed seen by enemy.*

Halsey immediately ordered the entire task force to swing around, hoping that the Japanese patrol vessel had not spotted the ships nor Wiseman's Dauntless. Doolittle joined Mitscher on the bridge to await developments. For an hour there was more tension than action, then around 7:38 A.M. another patrol boat was sighted from the *Hornet* itself at a distance of 20,000 yards. Soon after a radio signal was intercepted in the *Hornet*'s radio room—it had originated from close by; there was little doubt, the Japanese had spotted Task Force 16.

The boat was the *Nitto Maru*, one of the many little pickets that had been set out in the eastern approaches to the shores of Japan. The message sent by the *Nitto Maru* read: *Three (sic.) enemy aircraft carriers sighted at our position 650 nautical miles east of Inubo Saki at 0630* (Tokyo time; the *Nitto Maru* had seen the *Hornet* eight minutes before the *Hornet*'s crew spotted the picket).

On the *Enterprise* Halsey ordered the cruiser *Nashville* to deal with the *Nitto Maru*. This was accomplished eventually, but it took an hour and the expenditure of no less than 938 rounds of 6-inch shells. Heavy seas, distance, and the smallness of the vessel were responsible for this. Even aircraft joined in the attack, but there was little doubt that the task force had been discovered and a message flashed back to Japan (the Americans had no idea of the content of the message since it had been sent in code, but it was easy to conjecture).

Halsey was consequently forced into an unhappy decision: he would have to order the Army planes off the *Hornet* even though it would mean a flight of 650 miles instead of the ideal 400 miles. It was imperative to get his ships out of reach of Japanese bombers. He ordered a flash to the *Hornet:*

LAUNCH PLANES

TO COL. DOOLITTLE AND GALLANT COMMAND

GOOD LUCK AND GOD BLESS YOU

Doolittle shook Mitscher's hand and hurriedly left the bridge, hurtled down the ladder, and joined his crews. Their discovery so soon would make reaching China a bit more difficult; it was the fuel problem again. So Doolittle ordered ten additional 5-gallon cans placed in each plane. They would also carry dinghies and supplies for survival at sea, as it appeared likely that fuel would be depleted long before they reached China (some estimated as much as 200 miles short of land).

Word of Halsey's decision had spread through the *Hornet* and the flight deck erupted into a frenzy of Army-Navy enterprise. Canvas covers were removed from engines and turrets and the Mitchells were freed of restraining ropes. Fuel levels were checked, planes were rocked to clear bubbles from tanks, and last minute cargo—from sandwiches and rye (two pints per plane) to phonograph and records (inside a cake tin)—was loaded into the B-25s. All of this frenetic activity was accomplished across wet, slippery decks that seesawed in the rough waters. A large blackboard was set on the bridge of the *Hornet* for last minute instructions, plus compass heading of the ship and wind speed. Doolittle was certain that all their compasses had probably gone off because of the proximity of so much carrier metal. They would require setting before heading for Tokyo.

Shortly after Halsey's message, the loud-speakers of the *Hornet* blared: "Now hear this: Army pilots, man your planes!"

Fourteen

Doolittle entered the cockpit, where he found copilot Lieutenant Richard E. Cole beginning preflight procedures, and settled into the left seat of aircraft No. 40-2344. His crew had gotten into their positions: Lieutenant Henry A. Potter (navigator), Staff Sergeant Fred A. Braemer (bombardier), and Staff Sergeant Paul J. Leonard (engineer-gunner). When the signal came, Doolittle and Cole attended to the business of starting the engines. Some 400 feet down the deck on the port side stood Lieutenant Edgar G. Osborne with a signal flag in hand; a seaman, he would best know just the right moment for the takeoff in the rough sea.

As Doolittle peered toward the bow, which tossed dizzily, the sky looked grim—murky, wet, and with a low ceiling at about 1,000 feet. Winds were gusting as high as 27 knots (a little more than 30 miles per hour) as the *Hornet* had turned into them for the takeoffs. The Mitchell vibrated to the power of the engines and the wings fluttered in the gusts that whipped along the flight deck. Once the engines had warmed, the power was reduced; the two men in the cockpit kept their eyes on Osborne and his checkered flag. To Doolittle it promised to be a new experience: for the first time he would take off, with luck, from a moving airport. Would it be luck this time or the old flying instinct? "Luck," Doolittle had once observed, "is something that comes after you've taken every precaution to avoid the necessity for luck."

Osborne, carefully judging the tossing sea, so that Doolittle's plane would reach the takeoff point when the deck was high, began making circling motions with the flag, accelerating the motions, and enlarging the circle—a signal to Doolittle to advance throttle. The wing flaps were completely down and the wheel chocks were pulled away from the straining plane. Slowly, almost in a waddle, the B-25 began moving toward the bow; the *Hornet* had begun its own movement, pitching upward in the waves. The plane gathered speed as it raced into the gale.

"We watched him like hawks," Ted Lawson would later write, "wondering what the wind would do to him, and whether we could get off in that little run toward the bow. If he couldn't, we couldn't."

Doolittle's plane rapidly picked up speed and at the same time kept its nose wheel on the white line which prevented the right wingtip from striking the carrier's island. "Airdales"—the Navy deck crews—were flattened out on the wet deck, out of harm's way. The *Hornet*'s bow had reached the extreme of its pitch and had begun splashing downward, when—yards before he ran out of deck—Doolittle lifted the bomber off the *Hornet*. "He hung his ship almost straight up on its props," according to Lawson, "until we could see the whole top of the B-25. Then he leveled off and I watched him come around in a tight circle and shoot low over our heads—straight down the line painted on the deck."

Having checked the compass against the *Hornet*'s heading, Doolittle turned the nose of the Mitchell toward Japan. Five minutes after Doolittle had lifted off the deck, the second plane, piloted by Lieutenant Travis Hoover—his eye also on Osborne—started his run: brakes off, flaps down, and engines up. His takeoff was not quite as uneventful as Doolittle's; for some reason—perhaps in his anxiety to get off the deck as soon as possible—Hoover held the nose of the plane up too long and for a second, just as the B-25 was tossed off the deck by the heaving swell, with nose up and tail down, the plane sank a little and appeared on the brink of a stall. But quick action in the cockpit corrected that and Hoover and crew were also on their way to Japan. The remaining aircraft left the *Hornet,* with two additional incidents. To correct for what might have happened to Hoover, Miller chalked onto the blackboard: STABILIZER IN NEUTRAL. There were no further nose-up takeoffs, but in his excitement Ted Lawson had forgotten to lower the flaps on his plane, though he managed the takeoff with no problem.

Three other planes awaited the takeoff signal with flaps up, a condition corrected through various signals from the deck crews. One plane, piloted by Lieutenant Donald G. Smith, caught in an unexpected roll of the deck, rammed into the tail of the preceding aircraft, Hilger's, resulting in cracked plexiglass in the nose section. This appeared to present no problem, so Smith took off, but not before noting that the airdales had forgotten to remove the wheel blocks which were pulled and he took off, following Hilger. Smith's plane carried Dr. White, who was doubling as a gunner.

The final, most serious, incident occurred when the sixteenth and last plane, piloted by Lieutenant William G. Farrow, took off immediately after Smith. As the last plane in line, its tail section projected over the fantail of the *Hornet* and all the crew could not enter the plane until it had been moved forward because of the midsection fuel tank. A half dozen airdales assisted in holding the B-25 in position on the wet, gusty deck, and just as Smith, in the plane ahead, gunned the engines for his takeoff, the sudden blast caught one of the Navy men, Seaman Robert W. Wall, who stumbled into the left propeller of Farrow's plane. Wall's arm was so mangled that he eventually lost it. Lieutenant George Barr, the navigator, in the nose of the plane would later write: "This accident unnerved me and it was all I could think about as we lined up for our takeoff. I hoped it wasn't going to be a taste of worse to come. Little did I realize how tragic our mission was to become." (The crew of Farrow's plane was captured, and both Farrow and the engineer-gunner, Sergeant Harold A. Spatz, were executed by the Japanese.)

The moment Farrow's plane left the *Hornet*'s deck Halsey ordered the task force to turn about for the race back to Pearl Harbor. In the week it took to get there, no real encounters with Japanese forces occurred; although radar spotted search planes and ships, only the latter were engaged, resulting in the sinking of a total of three Japanese picket boats and the taking of five prisoners, the first of the war. The *Hornet* lost one search plane, which sank before it could be reached, taking its crew, Lieutenant G. D. Randall, and his radio operator, T. A. Gallagher, with it. Two other Navy craft were lost, but without loss of life and a landing accident resulted in an injury. The cost to the Navy was minimal, considering the risks, and as Task Force 16 pulled into Pearl Harbor, Halsey sent his command a hearty "Well done." It was only then that he would learn what had happened to Doolittle and his men the week before.

The log of the *Hornet* notes that Doolittle had lifted off at 8:20 A.M. and the sixteenth and last plane, Farrow's, exactly one hour later. For the first time, an American striking force was headed for the Japanese homeland. Roughly thirteen hours later after his takeoff, Doolittle would become a third-time member of the Caterpillar Club.

Doolittle's narrative of this historic venture is a characteristic model of succinct understatement:

Took off at 8:20 A.M. ship time. Take-off was easy. Night take-off would have been possible and practicable.

Circled carrier to get exact heading and check compass. Wind was from around 300°.

About a half hour after take-off, was joined by A/C 40-2292, Lt. Hoover, pilot, the second plane to take off. About an hour out passed a Japanese camouflaged naval surface vessel of about 6,000 tons. Took it to be a light cruiser. About two hours out passed a multimotored land plane headed directly for our flotilla and flying at about 3,000—2 miles away. Passed and endeavored to avoid various civil and naval craft until landfall was made north of Inubo Shima.

Was somewhat north of desired course but decided to take advantage of error and approach from a northerly direction, thus avoiding anticipated strong opposition to the west. Many flying fields and the air full of planes north of Tokyo. Mostly small biplanes apparently primary or basic trainers.

Encountered nine fighters in three flights of three. This was about ten miles north of the outskirts of Tokyo proper. All this time had been flying low as the terrain would permit. Continued low flying due south over the outskirts of and toward the east center of Tokyo.

Pulled up to 1,200 ft., changed course to the southwest and incendiary-bombed highly inflammable section. Dropped first bomb at 1:30 (ship time).

Anti-aircraft very active but only one near hit. Lowered away to housetops and slid over western outskirts into low haze and smoke. Turned south and out to sea. Fewer airports on west side but many army posts. Passed over small aircraft factory with a dozen or more newly completed planes on the line. No bombs left. Decided not to machine gun for reasons of personal security. Had seen five barrage balloons over east central Tokyo and what appeared to be more in the distance.

Passed on out to sea flying low. Was soon joined by Hoover who followed us to the Chinese coast. Navigator [Henry A. Potter] plotted perfect course to pass north of Yaki Shima. Saw three large naval vessels just before passing west end of Japan. One was flatter than the others and may have been a converted carrier. Passed innumerable fishing and small patrol boats.

Made landfall somewhat north of course on China Coast. Tried to reach Chuchow [the air base for which the raiders were headed] on 4,495 (kilocycles) but could not raise.

It had been clear over Tokyo but became overcast before reaching Yaki Shima. Ceiling lowered on coast until low islands and hills were in it at about 600'. Just getting dark and couldn't dive under overcast so pulled up to 6,000' and then 8,000' in it. On instruments from then on though occasionally saw dim lights on ground through almost solid overcast. These lights seemed more often on our right and pulled us still further off course.

Directed rear gunner [Paul J. Leonard] to go aft and secure films from camera. (Unfortunately, they were jerked out of his shirt where he had put them when his chute opened.)

Decided to abandon ship. Sgt. Braemer, Lt. Potter, Sgt. Leonard and Lt. Cole jumped in order. Left ship on A.F.C.E. (automatic pilot), shut off both gas cocks and I left. Should have put flaps down. This would have slowed down landing speed, reduced impact and shortened glide.

Left airplane about 9:30 P.M. (ship time) after 13 hours in the air. Still had enough gas for half hour flight but right front tank was showing empty. Had transferred once as right engine used more fuel. Had covered about 2,250 miles, mostly at low speed, cruising but about an hour at moderate high speed which more than doubled the consumption for this time.

Certain that all of the crew had left the plane, Doolittle had set the AFCE (automatic flight control equipment) for level flight, adjusted his chute, and leaped into nothingness. For the third time in his flying career he made an emergency jump, experienced the snap of an opening parachute, and began the descent to earth. In this instance, however, he had no idea of what lay below—was it land or water? At least, as he had once expected, it would not be the sea, thanks to an unexpected but providential tailwind.

Silently Doolittle descended through the black drizzle; if there was earth below, he could not see it. His concern was landing in the dark on terrain he could not assess; a hard landing on his once broken ankles could bring his part in the Tokyo raid to a pretty definite conclusion. Sensing the rapid approach of the ground he doubled up slightly to lessen the impact—and suddenly found himself sitting up to his neck in a fetid rice paddy (it having been fertilized with "night soil," i.e., human excrement). Unhurt in the soft landing, Doolittle freed himself of his parachute, retaining, as was the custom, the inspection card placed there by the packer. (Later Doolittle would send J. H. Patton at the Sacramento Air Depot a box of cigars—this was also a custom.)

Having seen a light about a hundred yards away, Doolittle sloshed his way out of the paddy and approached what appeared to be a small farmhouse. Knocking on the door he called out the phrase all had been taught by the *Hornet*'s Jurika, *"Lushu hoo megwa fugi"* ("I am an American"). There was movement inside the house; he heard the door being bolted, the light was snuffed out and then utter silence. The magic phrase, repeated, did not work, and teeth chattering from the cold, Doolittle moved on until he found a lane, which he followed, hoping to find shelter. Shivering and odoriferous, Doolittle came upon an unusual structure after he had a walked a short distance. Two sawhorses held a large crate covered with planks; it wasn't much but it was shelter from the chilling wind. He removed a couple of planks, clambered onto a sawhorse and dropped into the crate—and soon found he was not alone. He was in someone's coffin, for his companion was an elderly dead Chinese. This was not as disturbing as the fact that the coffin did not really shield him from the wind, nor did it afford him room for movement to keep up his circulation. Doolittle sought shelter elsewhere after carefully replacing the planks over the coffin.

The rain had increased; while this did not contribute to his comfort, it did at least wash off some of the night soil. In further exploration he found a water mill, which protected him from the rain, but not from the penetrating cold. Unable to sleep except in restless snatches, Doolittle spent most of the night at calisthenics to keep from freezing.

With morning—April 19, 1942—the rain had stopped, although the sky was still overcast and the weather bleak. Miserable and tired, Doolittle left the mill; he was determined to learn about his crews. He had spent what had been physically and emotionally the most wretched night of his life; he had no idea of the fate of the seventy-nine men he had led in the raid. Of the total of eighty, he only knew where he was—wherever that was. And of the sixteen aircraft, knew only about how his own had ended up, rolled up somewhere in China, a total wreck. He could not even use the signal he and his crew had agreed upon to assemble after their jump; a single pistol shot by Doolittle. His copilot had caught his chute harness while leaving the plane and by the time he had worked himself free, the previous jumpers were miles away, out of the sound of a pistol shot—and Doolittle was even more distant.

For the first time in his life Doolittle was near despair, certain he had failed in his mission. But he could not dwell on that; he had to find his crews.

He set out along the road again and came upon a lone farmer who regarded him with curiosity; he apparently spoke no English, nor did *Lushu hoo megwa fugi* appear to have any meaning for him. Taking a pad out of his pocket, Doolittle attempted to draw a locomotive on it, adding a question mark. Perhaps if he found a railroad he could also find a nearby town and, once making himself understood, could begin the search for his crews. The farmer nodded affirmatively, beckoned, and Doolittle followed.

Instead of a railroad they came upon a Chinese military installation where he was not exactly greeted with open arms. The Chinese major, apparently in charge, indicated that he would relieve Doolittle of his .45. Doolittle attempted to explain—the major appeared to understand some English—that he was an ally of China and would retain his weapon. There were sharp glances exchanged and the three soldiers with the major cradled their machine guns menacingly. Doolittle attempted to explain more fully about the bombing of Tokyo, about the jump from the B-25, and he offered as proof the parachute he had left in the fragrant rice paddy. Surely, the occupants of the farmhouse would remember their nighttime visitor. The major and his surly crew did not appear to be convinced, but Doolittle persuaded the officer to go with him to the farmhouse and rice paddy.

To Doolittle's chagrin, there was no parachute and the farmer and family denied having heard any aircraft or rappings in the night. A great uneasiness overwhelmed Doolittle; he carried no real identification (and unknown to him, the Chinese troops had not been alerted to the impending arrival of the American airmen). It was all but impossible to explain to the skeptical major and his muttering gunmen how it was that an armed man—neither Chinese nor Japanese—was wandering about the Chinese countryside.

Meanwhile, two of the soldiers entered the farmhouse and returned smiling—carrying the great silken parachute (the farmer evidently could have put it to good use and did not want to turn it over, even at the risk of Doolittle's life). The major's attitude immediately changed and he and Doolittle returned to headquarters, while search parties were sent out for the rest of Doolittle's crew.

In his report Doolittle had written, "All hands collected and ship located by late afternoon of the 19th." That concise sentence contained the seeds of a longer, harrowing narrative. Navigator Potter and Bombardier Braemer fell into the hands of guerrilla-bandits, were robbed and tied and were being marched off until a youngster, who could speak English, was able to explain to the chieftain who the Americans were. Freed, they then set out in search of the rest of the crew and came upon Sergeant Leonard who had just had a run-in and shooting match with four men (no one was hit, and the four men had retreated apparently to get reinforcements). The four men too may have been from the band of guerrillas; but before there was any more shooting Leonard met the group that had "befriended" Potter and Braemer.

Doolittle, meanwhile, had been taken to the governor of the Chekiang province, General Ho Yang Lin, and was able to initiate the massive search throughout the province and all along the sea-coast for his scattered crews. He was joined at the governor's house by the rest of his crew later in the afternoon; except for Potter, who had injured his ankle in the jump, all were unhurt. For Doolittle it was small consolation; there were seventy-five others to find. By evening word had come in that Chinese search parties had located the wreckage of his plane, about eight miles away in the hills.

In the morning Doolittle and Leonard set out for the site of the crash. The plane had hit just below the crest of a hill; one wing panel was a quarter of a mile away and one engine had been ripped away and had rolled downhill and nested among some rocks. What remained had already been worked over by scavengers—nothing of value remained. Poking in the wreckage, Doolittle did find his oil-soaked Army OD blouse—all the buttons had been torn off.

An overwhelming sense of depression filled him. Doolittle sat down, head in hands, studying what was left of the one plane in sixteen whose location was known to him. *He had failed.* The first time he had undertaken a real combat mission he managed to lose his own aircraft and had no idea where the others were. Dejectedly he studied the debris of what had once been a B-25 while Paul Leonard took a few photographs.

Then Leonard sensed Doolittle's mood.

"What do you think will happen when you go home, Colonel?" he asked.

"They'll send me to Leavenworth, I guess."

"No, sir," Leonard consoled. "I'll tell you what they'll do. They're going to make you a general."

Doolittle managed a weak smile at this preposterous notion. Leonard tried again, "And they're going to give you the Medal of Honor." This amused Doolittle even more and he managed a more generous smile. But Leonard persisted. "Colonel, they will give you another airplane and when they do I would like to be your crew chief."

This was, among airmen, the greatest compliment of all and for some moments Doolittle had a difficult time controlling his emotions; his eyes glistened and he managed to assure Leonard that should the Air Force ever entrust him with a plane again, Leonard would indeed be his crew chief (the promise, incidentally was kept). The two men returned to the governor's house, where word had come through that four additional crews had been found—that left eleven to be accounted for. From the governor's house Doolittle wired Arnold, through the U. S. Embassy at Chunking: TOKYO SUCCESSFULLY BOMBED. DUE BAD WEATHER ON CHINA COAST BELIEVE ALL AIRPLANES WRECKED. FIVE CREWS FOUND SAFE IN CHINA SO FAR. The thought of eleven still missing was discomfiting.

When word came through that some men had fallen into the hands of the puppet government near the China coast, Doolittle authorized the payment of ransom and then tried to talk a local warlord into sending troops to rescue them. His efforts, tragically, proved useless and eight men, the survivors of Lieutenant Dean E. Hallmark's crew (three men) were turned over to the Japanese, and all of Lieutenant William G. Farrow's crew (this was the last hard-luck plane) were captured by the Japanese.

Another plan to rescue the crews that had fallen into the hands of, or were turned over to the Japanese was considered. Colonel Merian C. Cooper, former Hollywoodian who had produced *King Kong* some years before, was in Chungking at the time of the Doolittle raid, suggested forming a commando-like group to swoop down on the captors and rescue the Americans. The idea was rejected because it was most likely the Japanese would have murdered the prisoners before they would have permitted them to be freed.

Doolittle, preoccupied with the fate of his crews, and cut off from all news from the United States, was of course unaware of the impact the raid had had at home. The raiders made headlines across the country and throughout the world (the newspaper accounts in Japan were highly censored or inaccurate, or both). Headline writers, reflecting the elation that swept the United States, attempted to outdo themselves with clever banners: DOOLITTLE DO'OD IT (with a nod to Red Skelton's obnoxious "Mean Little Kid") and, from his boyhood home town: NOME TOWN BOY MAKES GOOD! The lift to the nation's morale after a series of defeats was incalculable but undeniably extensive. A new wave of hope swept the country.

With his crew Doolittle made his way to Chuchow (their original destination where, supposedly, a reception and fuel were awaiting them, but in fact were not). There he was reunited with several other crews, namely, those of Hilger, Greening, Captain David M. Jones, Lieutenant William M. Bower, and Captain Robert M. Gray. On April 22 word came from Russia that one of the planes, Captain Edward J. York's, had landed in Vladivostok and the entire crew had been interned.

On April 26, upon arriving by rail, bus, and boat in Chuchow, Doolittle found that the first of Leonard's predictions had come true. Doolittle, to his surprise, learned that he had been promoted to the rank of brigadier general, skipping the intermediary rank of full colonel, a rare practice even in wartime.

There was no supply of star insignias in Chungking so Clayton Bissell, recently promoted to the rank of brigadier general, presented him with a set. Bissell had also greeted Doolittle with the traditional "swallow" when he landed in Chungking. Bissell's eyes bugged at the size of the swallow, as Johnny Walker Red Label was $80 a fifth at the time—and Black Label was going for as high as $100. Doolittle estimated he had taken "about a ten-dollar-gulp" of Bissell's welcome whiskey.

There was little time for jubilation, for Doolittle continued his unremitting search for his crews. When he and Hilger compared notes, he learned that the phrase they had been taught on the *Hornet* was in the wrong dialect for the province in which they had landed; no wonder no one understood them at first. He was distressed to learn that they had been unsuccessful in their efforts to bribe the Chinese puppet government that had captured the crew of Farrow's plane. When he went through the ceremony of being decorated by Madame Chiang, he rather brusquely brushed aside her pleasantries with questions about what was being done about the two crews that had fallen into the hands of the puppet troops. Her assurances, however, came to nothing. Within two days of that ceremony Doolittle was ordered to return to Washington, and on May 5, 1942, he left China without knowing the fate of all his crews.

In time Doolittle would learn about the other crews. In summary: of the sixteen planes that left the *Hornet*, only one, York's, made a three-point landing; eleven crews bailed out and four made crash landings. Fifteen planes bombed their targets and one, piloted by Lieutenant Everett W. Holstrom, with leaking fuel tanks and useless guns, was forced to jettison its bomb load when under attack by several fighters.

Not counting Doolittle, who served as the mission's pathfinder, there were five flights of three planes each, although before take-off Doolittle made it clear that each pilot was in command of his plane and would make all decisions pertaining to his aircraft and crew. It was, in a sense, every plane for itself, unconstricted by any hard and fast regulation (except one: not to bomb the Imperial Palace). Considering the weather, this proved to be a sensible decision. Only three of the planes did not complete the mission, in the expression of the time, "as briefed": one jettisoned its bomb load before reaching its target, one landed in Russia instead of China, and one bombed a secondary instead of its primary target.

The plane which took off after Doolittle, piloted by Lieutenant Travis Hoover, accompanied Doolittle to the target area in Tokyo, bombed, and then rejoined Doolittle out at sea and followed until they approached the China coast. Hoover elected to crash-land his B-25, bringing in the bomber skillfully without injury to any of the crew. They then burned the plane and the entire crew eventually made its way to Chungking, with the aid of a young aeronautical engineer, Tung-Sheng Liu (now an American citizen and an honorary member of the Tokyo Raiders). By this time Doolittle had left China.

Captain Robert Gray followed Hoover in the takeoff sequence, bombed targets in the Tokyo area, and, like Doolittle, decided to order a bailout over China. Four members of the crew landed safely; the engineer-gunner, Corporal Leland D. Faktor, died in the fall—although his parachute had opened, the jump may have been made too close to the ground. Copilot Lieutenant Jacob E. Manch was weighed down by several guns and his windup phonograph; when his chute opened with an eye-popping jolt, he lost all but one of his guns and found upon landing that all that remained of his phonograph was the handle which he had held onto all the way to earth. The four survivors also made their way to Chungking via their original destination, the airfield at Chuchow.

The third plane in Hoover's element was that of Lieutenant Everett Holstrom, who never reached Tokyo. Fuel leakage, jammed guns, and a concentrated fighter attack forced Holstrom into the unhappy decision of jettisoning the bomb load into the water before racing for China. The same weather problem afflicted his plane, as it did the others—darkness and heavy rain. Holstrom ordered the crew to bail out; with the aid of Chinese civilians and soldiers they were eventually transported to Chuhsien, where they were reunited with four other crews and then with General Doolittle. In time, they arrived in Chungking for reassignment.

The second element of three B-25s was led off the *Hornet* by Captain David Jones and, except for a brief encounter with a twin-engine Japanese land plane (which flew off immediately), flew unchallenged to Tokyo. Although a little off course for a few moments, Jones found his targets (he claimed a direct hit on an oil storage tank) and continued on to China. Unable to raise any radio response from their assigned destination, Chuchow, Jones ordered a bailout. The entire crew landed without serious injuries and were rapidly brought together with the aid of sympathetic Chinese. They were treated like heroes by the Chinese, who moved them from one city to another until they arrived at Chuhsien, where they were able to communicate with Doolittle. Eventually Jones and his crew were transported to Chungking.

Jones had been followed off the deck by Lieutenant Dean Hallmark, whose plane took its position (No. 3) in the formation; Lieutenant Ted Lawson, took off, and fitted into the No. 2 spot in York's element. Unfortunately, these last two planes ran out of fuel over water and did not quite make landfall. The Hallmark crew bombed its target in Tokyo but ran low on fuel before reaching China and Hallmark set the plane down in the water just off the coast. The impact threw the pilot through the windshield. Two crew members were so seriously injured that they were unable to get to shore: bombardier Sergeant William J. Dieter and engineer-gunner Sergeant Donald E. Fitzmaurice. Their bodies were washed ashore the next morning. Both Hallmark and copilot Lieutenant Robert J. Meder were so badly injured they were unable to travel; the other survivor, navigator Lieutenant Chase J. Nielson had suffered lesser injuries. All three were captured by the Japanese four days later—only Nielson would survive. Following a mock trial (as well as months of torture and abuse) Hallmark was executed. Meder succumbed to the abuse and general maltreatment, the major direct cause of his death being beriberi. Nielson was freed after the war ended.

Ted Lawson's plane also landed wheels-up in the water after bombing Tokyo. The massive shock of the B-25 striking the rough water propelled four of the crew through the windshield and nose of the plane; only engineer-gunner Sergeant David J. Thatcher, the least injured was left to tend to those who were in serious condition. How Thatcher managed to sustain his injured crew mates and, with the aid of the Chinese, to elude Japanese search parties is a saga in itself (and graphically told by Lawson in *Thirty Seconds over Tokyo*). Lawson, the most seriously injured, eventually lost his left leg, which was amputated by the sole medical man to fly the mission, Lieutenant Thomas White, from the crew of Lieutenant Donald Smith. Navigator Lieutenant Charles L. McClure, who had been hurled through the plexiglass nose, was also seriously but not so drastically injured but would need hospitalization even after his return to the United States.

The lead plane in the third element was under the command of Captain Edward York and had lifted off the *Hornet* thirty-five minutes after Doolittle. The flight into the Tokyo target area was reasonably uncomplicated—only one attempt at interception by a Japanese fighter and no antiaircraft at all; but as the flight progressed it became worrisomely obvious that fuel consumption was inordinately high. The carburetors had been replaced at Sacramento, counter to Doolittle's explicit orders, and at too rich a setting were literally swallowing fuel. (The change had been discovered only after they had boarded the *Hornet;* York decided nevertheless that they would attempt the mission. He had not counted on the early takeoff.) After dropping his bombs, York headed for China but it soon became apparent they would never come within 300 miles of the coast. York instantly made another decision and changed course for Russia. Doolittle, he reasoned, had not exactly ordered them *not* to go to Russia (no agreement had been reached with Stalin), he had merely stressed that it was not a good idea.

York landed the B-25 on a Russian airstrip about 40 miles north of Vladivostok, hoping to get fuel to enable them to continue on to China. Instead, he, his crew, and the aircraft were interned. The five men were fated to become unwilling guests of Russia for a year. They were moved from one internment camp to another in various parts of Russia, eventually ending up at Ashkhabad, near the Persian border. With the help of a Russian not above a little capitalistic bribery, they all managed to escape into Iran, where they turned themselves in to the British Consul and were finally sent back to the United States in May 1943.

York's plane was followed by that of Lieutenant Harold F.

Watson, who was also plagued by leaking fuel tanks. Although the plane came under heavy fighter and antiaircraft attack, the bombs were dropped in Tokyo and Watson set out for China. After over fifteen hours in the air (Watson had conserved fuel remarkably and his plane reached further inland than any other; he made the decision to bail out. Setting the plane on autopilot after the four others had jumped, Watson took to his chute also; somehow he got an arm entangled in the shroud lines which resulted in a wrenching dislocation of his right shoulder. Even landing in an icy creek and lying there for hours did not revive Watson from the shock—nor could anyone reduce the dislocated shoulder. Enduring excruciating pain, Watson had to wait weeks before he was flown to Walter Reed Hospital in Washington, where he required surgery to correct his condition.

Five minutes after Watson took off, Lieutenant Richard O. Joyce gunned his Mitchell down the *Hornet*'s bouncing deck. After bombing a steel mill in Tokyo, Joyce's plane was attacked by a formation of nine Zeros, among others, and took an antiaircraft burst in the rear fuselage. Arriving over China, Joyce flew past Chuchow to assure their being over friendly territory and ordered the crew to jump. The penultimate jumper, gun-turret expert Sergeant Edwin W. Horton, Jr., delighted pilot Joyce with, "Here I go and thanks for a swell ride." Joyce followed and within a day was reunited with his crew, all of whom had landed in friendly hands without serious injury.

The last two flights were assigned targets not in Tokyo proper but in its industrial outskirts. Captain Ross Greening led the first three aircraft; his plane and that piloted by Lieutenant William Bower bombed targets in Yokohama. Both crews bailed out over China and eventually, with the help of the Chinese, rejoined the other raiders. The last plane of the element, "lucky thirteen," was piloted by Lieutenant Edgar E. McElroy and struck a naval base at Yokosuka; the crew bailed out over China and eventually was helped to Chungking.

The final element was led by Major John Hilger, Doolittle's second-in-command, with targets selected in Nagoya, Kobe, and Osaka. Hilger's bombs fell into a military barracks, a fuel storage station and arsenal, and an aircraft factory [Mitsubishi]. As it had the others, bad weather awaited Hilger over China, and after more than thirteen hours in the air, he ordered bailouts, estimating that they were somewhere near their destination, Chuchow, and away from Japanese-occupied China. Like so many other of the raiders, Hilger experienced a bailout misadventure.

"When I pulled the ripcord," he later wrote in his diary, "I thought someone had dropped the ceiling on me. My breath was knocked out of me and I saw enough stars to keep the movie industry running for ten years. I fought to recover consciousness and when I did I found I had lost my musette bag with all my rations, matches, and whiskey but still had my gun and canteen full of water. I had a terrific pain in my left groin and soon found that in crawling between the armor plate [in leaving the cockpit] I had unfastened my right leg strap. As a result I had slipped down in my harness and the breast strap had socked me under the chin and then hit me in the nose so that I had a bleeding nose along with my other worries."

Among Hilger's worries was the location of his crew, which had been gathered up by some nameless but remarkable Chinese. The bombing and jump had occurred on a Saturday; by Sunday night all five men had been found and given shelter at the mayor's house in the small, ancient city of Kuang Feng. By Tuesday they had been transported, by car and train, to Chuchow where they were reunited with several other crews. Doolittle and his crew arrived on the following Sunday and together he and Hilger continued the assembly and disposition of the various crews. By that Sunday, April 26, a dozen crews had been gathered at Chuchow and it was known that York and company had been interned in Russia. Eventually all were sent to Chungking and, upon Doolittle's return to the United States, Hilger remained in command of the raider crews—many of which remained in the East to continue fighting the Japanese.

Lieutenant Donald G. Smith followed Hilger off the *Hornet* to bomb a steel plant in Kobe. Upon arriving at the China coast in a heavy mist, Smith decided not to continue inland when he caught a glimpse of a mountain top jutting out of the sea directly ahead of him. He banked to the right and headed out to sea with one engine sputtering and the other losing power. He splashed the B-25 into the sea about four or five hundred yards offshore. The plane remained float for about eight minutes, long enough for the crew to inflate a dinghy and fill it with supplies, including the medical kit of Lieutenant Thomas R. White. (When he later heard of the hard landing of Lawson and crew, White remained behind to join up with them to treat them, while Smith and the rest followed the same path as the others to the safety of Chungking.)

Lieutenant William Farrow's plane was the last to leave the *Hornet.* After bombing oil storage tanks in Nagoya, Farrow spotted another target—presumably an aircraft factory—and deposited the rest of the plane's bomb load there. (These were both secondary targets; by the time the plane reached Osaka, where the primary targets were located, Farrow bombless, set out for China.)

Farrow continued flying until the fuel warning lights flashed, having hoped before that to receive some message from Chuchow which never came. He then ordered the crew to bail out—and all five men fell into the hands of the Japanese. Navigator George Barr summed up the fate of Crew No. 16: "During the night [Lieutenant] Bob Hite was brought in and the following day we learned that Farrow, [Sergeant Harold] Spatz and [Corporal Jacob] DeShazer were also captured. There were forty months of hell waiting for Hite, DeShazer and me. Spatz and Farrow were spared that. They were executed."

Doolittle found it difficult to regard the mission as a success. Although he did not yet know what had befallen all the crews when summoned back to the United States, he knew that Farrow's crew had been captured (although he was still unaware of their ultimate destiny), he did know all sixteen aircraft were lost. Eventually he would learn the total cost: nine dead (including those who died or were executed in Japan and the two Navy airmen), four seriously wounded, and all the planes. The cost to the Chinese was even greater. The Japanese unleashed a savage, three-month ground and air assault throughout the province of Chekiang, which had provided a haven and escape route for most of the raiders. Chiang Kai-shek informed the United States in a cable:

AFTER THEY HAD BEEN CAUGHT UNAWARE BY THE FALLING OF AMERICAN BOMBS ON TOKYO, JAPANESE TROOPS ATTACKED THE COASTAL AREAS OF CHINA WHERE MANY OF THE AMERICAN FLYERS HAD LANDED. THESE JAPANESE TROOPS SLAUGHTERED EVERY MAN, WOMAN AND CHILD IN THESE AREAS—LET ME REPEAT—THESE JAPANESE TROOPS SLAUGHTERED EVERY MAN, WOMAN AND CHILD IN THOSE

AREAS, REPRODUCING ON A WHOLESALE SCALE THE HORRORS
WHICH THE WORLD HAD SEEN AT LIDICE . . .

Japanese troops penetrated some 200 miles into China, razing entire villages and killing their populations, committing unspeakable atrocities at the slightest provocation (especially if some hapless Chinese had saved some little souvenir of the Americans' passage, whether a bit of parachute, a coin, or article of clothing). The airfield at Chuchow was completely destroyed—by 4,000 Chinese forced laborers. Nothing, no one, was spared: even most of the American church missions (twenty-nine out of thirty-one) were demolished and their churchyards desecrated.

After the three-month Japanese rampage—to what military end was never determined—some 250,000 Chinese civilians and soldiers had died. As one missionary observed, "Cannibalism is the only terror they spared the Chinese people of Kiangsi."

The immediate cost of the raid to Japan was, as expected, militarily slight. The official Japanese line, broadcast for home consumption, minimized it and propagandized it even more. Admitting, after a period of silence, that "several enemy planes" had attacked the Tokyo-Yokohama area, the radio announcement also noted that antiaircraft and air units had driven the attackers away "in retreat." It also claimed: "The number of known enemy planes downed at present is nine. Damage to our side appears to be slight. The Imperial Household is safe."

Later there would be claims of wanton American bombings and even strafings of schools and schoolyards. While in disorganized flight from attack, later newspaper reports had stated, "the enemy planes chose innocent people and city streets as their targets. They did not go near military installations. They carried out an inhuman, insatiable, indiscriminate bombing attack on the sly, and the fact that they schemed to strafe civilians and noncombatants demonstrates their fiendish behavior."

What had the raid actually accomplished? The First Demolition Ministry reported that about ninety buildings had been completely burned out, among them undisputed military targets such as the Japanese Diesel Manufacturing Company, Factory No. 1 of the Japanese Steel Corporation, a warehouse of the Yokohama Manufacturing Company, the Mitsubishi Heavy Industrial Corporation, the Nagoya Aircraft Factory, a naval ammunition dump, and an army arsenal, among others. Although those who could see were aware of the damages done to these targets, these damages were not admitted publicly.

However, among the targets struck were the homes of civilians and schools in the vicinity of the targets—also several wards of an Army hospital in Nagoya. The toll was about 50 dead and 250 wounded; among the dead, according to a contemporary news-paper account, was fourteen-year-old Hinosuke Ishibe, who was purportedly killed by a deliberate strafing of the school. These tragic, almost always inevitable accidents of war were employed to stir up the Japanese to "move forward on the road to smashing and annihilating England and America."

Parts of the wreckage of Farrow's plane were brought to Japan to be exhibited as a sample of the "nine" planes that had been de-stroyed and as proof that the raid was ineffectual. But there was an uneasiness in Japan, which was not relieved by one newspaper account that observed, "we must imagine that, as the enemy did not achieve his objectives in the first air attack, he will make sev-eral more vain attacks."

This was a chilling point. While the general populace tended to believe the propaganda, the higher military authorities were not deluded. They were deeply embarrassed that they could have per-mitted enemy aircraft to sully the air over the Imperial Palace; much face was lost and they felt compelled to act. While the dam-age to Japanese industry had been slight, the raid had proved it could be done; the raid had raised American moral and distressed the Japanese. There is no doubt that the long-run result of the Tokyo Raid was the rather precipitate decision of the Japanese high command to launch an offensive that would become the bat-tle of Midway, which marked the beginning of the end of the war for Japan.

When he left China—prematurely, he thought, for he did not yet know the fate of all of his crews—Doolittle gave no thought to the larger dimensions of his mission. The practical point that gnawed at him was that he had lost all of his planes; it was not his idea of an auspicious mission.

He had been ordered "by any means possible" and "in the shortest possible time" to report in Washington. This was also to be accomplished with absolutely no publicity. There not yet being the great air network that would be developed as Air Transport

Command, Doolittle found his "means" of transportation rather catch-as-catch-can: consequently, though he traveled by air, it took him nearly two weeks to get to Washington.

Doolittle boarded a Chinese National Airways transport in Chunking on Tuesday, May 5, his first stop on the homeward flight being Kunming, roughly 300 miles to the south and west. At about the halfway mark, word came through that Kunming was under air attack by the Japanese and, until the all-clear, the plane was set down in an emergency field. Upon his arrival at Kunming Doolittle was greeted by an old and admired friend, Claire Chennault. Because he was located at the extreme end of the supply line, Doolittle felt he had accomplished more with less than any commander in the Second World War.

Chennault had been promoted to brigadier general on the same order that had carried Doolittle's promotion, but was still wearing his colonel's eagles. "Where are your stars?" Doolittle asked.

"I don't have any here," Chennault answered.

Doolittle then presented Chennault with his set, explaining that since he was heading home he could very readily replace them. What he did not tell Chennault was that they had come from Bissell, who was not one of Chennault's favorite people.

At Kunming, the CNA plane was refueled and headed for Burma—again harried by the ubiquitous Japanese. Doolittle continued westward, eventually arriving at Calcutta. During his stay he decided he would acquire a change of clothes; the flying clothes in which he had arrived in China were beginning to get tattered, what with his encounter with night soil and his wide-ranging travels in search of his crews.

Calcutta was very British; the only uniform available was, while dashing, not quite Doolittle. His choice was simple, either he could be the shabbiest general or the most ludicrous; it would be the latter. There was something grand in the idea of greeting Joe Doolittle after more than a month's absence attired in pith helmet, bush jacket, shorts, and knee-length stockings.

From Calcutta Doolittle continued westward and homeward, with stops in Iran and Egypt; from Cairo the course veered southward to Khartoum in Sudan, then across Africa to Dakar, Senegal, the jumping off spot for the transatlantic flight to Natal, on the bulge of South America. Following a stopover in Puerto Rico, the flight proceeded on to Washington, D.C. The date was May 18,

1942—a month and a half since he had shipped out on the *Hornet*.

His friend and chief, Hap Arnold had already begun to arrange for the reunion of the Doolittles—although he would inadvertently cancel out the sartorial surprise for Joe. After her father's death Joe had decided to remain in Los Angeles with her mother until she had some definite word from her husband. She had finally learned along with the rest of the country where Doolittle had been heading after their evening together in San Francisco in April, but she had not heard from him since. Early in the morning of May 18 her phone rang; it was Arnold asking her to return to Washington. As soon as Joe Doolittle consented to the trip (there being no explanation offered), Arnold had his staff arrange for her reservation on a commercial airliner for that afternoon.

By the next morning the plane had landed in Pittsburgh. She had not spent a comfortable night; the only woman passenger aboard the crowded plane, she had found it virtually impossible to get into the lavatory, which seemed to be constantly occupied. So it was with a great sigh of relief that she heard the announcement that there was to be an hour stopover in Pittsburgh.

As she stepped from the plane she was met by an Army officer who informed her that a military plane was waiting to whisk her off to Washington.

"How nice," she gritted through clenched teeth, "but first do you mind . . ."

She was assured that her baggage was being attended to and that they would be off immediately. She had to settle for visions of the restroom at Washington airport. But that was not to be either. Upon landing, she was hurried into a waiting Army vehicle and informed that they "would have to hurry."

Rather acidly, Joe countered with, "I've got to hurry, too. No matter where we're going it can't be as important as where I need to go."

The officer gave her an uncomprehending look and said, "Mrs. Doolittle, we are due at the White House in ten minutes."

Doolittle's original homecoming plans were also thwarted, though not with quite the same discomfort. He too had been met at the Washington airport with the words, "General Arnold wants you to report at his quarters at once."

Did he detect an amused glint in the man's eye when he noted the uniform Doolittle wore? And then it struck him: what would Hap think of the strange garb?

The fact is that when Arnold saw Doolittle, in pith helmet and shorts, he wondered what a Boy Scout was doing coming up to his office. Then he realized it was none other than Brigadier General James Doolittle. The two old friends, after warm greetings, discussed the raid—Doolittle still unhappy over the loss of all the planes. Arnold assured him of the impact of the mission on the homefront and that no one regarded it as anything but a success.

The next day, properly uniformed, Doolittle was taken by Arnold to see General Marshall; something appeared to be up and Doolittle could not disguise his curiosity. It was Marshall who informed him that the second of Paul Leonard's predictions, made beside the wreckage of 40-2344, was about to be fulfilled: "The President is going to give you the Medal of Honor."

Stunned only momentarily, Doolittle replied with what must have seemed shocking and ungrateful candor, "General, I don't feel I'm entitled to the Medal of Honor." He tried to explain his feelings about the decoration—the highest possible award the nation could bestow upon anyone—and that he simply did not feel he had earned it. Marshall by this time had turned quite ruddy; Arnold was becoming angrier by the moment. Marshall made it clear that he did not recommend anyone for the Medal of Honor lightly. (Doolittle intimated that he believed some recipients had been awarded the medal too readily and had thus tarnished it; receiving the Medal of Honor for losing several men and all his planes would not add to the luster.)

Marshall conceded to a degree, but Doolittle had earned the Medal of Honor in his estimation and in the estimation of many others. His acceptance could very well place the medal back upon the level where it belonged. Doolittle had had his say ("I have never gotten into any trouble keeping my mouth shut") and relented under Marshall's words and Arnold's hostile stare. He had one more thing to say, "General, I will spend the rest of my life earning the Medal of Honor."

They then drove to the White House; in the anteroom the two Doolittles were reunited.

"Hello, Doolittle," Doolittle said to Joe, "how are you?"

"Fine, Doolittle," she replied, "how are you?"

They had little time to talk, although Doolittle managed to ask about their sons, Jimmy, Jr., in the Air Force awaiting shipment overseas and John attending classes at West Point.

The little group was ushered into President Roosevelt's office; his mood was jovial—the enemy had been struck from his mythical "Shangri La" (his special code name for the *Hornet*) and the President reflected, at that moment, the temper of the people. Marshall read the citation then handed the scroll to Joe Doolittle; the President then pinned the medal itself onto Doolittle's shirt. Joe Doolittle appeared to take the ceremony in characteristic stride, but Marshall told her later that he had been tempted to snatch the citation scroll away from her because she unconsciously rolled and twisted it to near destruction. However, she calmed down and the ceremony closed with a brief story of the raid by Doolittle at Roosevelt's request.

The news of Doolittle's return quickly spread and letters and telegrams began piling up. He had an amusing telegram from his friend, flamboyant racing pilot Roscoe Turner (who had early in the war suggested to Doolittle that they form a military unit of the Old Time fliers, but Doolittle demurred knowing at the time that the Air Force already had plans for him). Turner's postmission communique read simply,

DEAR JIMMY:

YOU SON OF A BITCH.

ROSCOE

There were many letters to read, but there were letters to write, too. He wrote to some member of the family—parent, wife, or close relative—of every man that had followed him in the Tokyo Raid. By the end of May all crews had been accounted for, including the one that had been interned and the two captured. The bulk of the letters were relatively easy to write and reassuring, informing the relative that when Doolittle had last seen "Edwin" or "Jack" or "David" he had looked well "and happy although a little homesick." He touched on the importance of the mission and mentioned the Distinguished Flying Cross all the men had earned.

The letters to the families of the known dead were more difficult, as were those of the captured crews, although their ultimate fate would not be known until much later. Doolittle believed at the time that the captives would be treated more or less humanely, according to the Geneva Convention rules on the treatment of prisoners of war. He was mistaken on this point when he wrote to the father of captured Dean Hallmark, who would be executed. Although the Russians offered scant if any information about York's interned crew, there was little concern about their safety at least, since Russia was an ally of sorts of the United States.

Once these letters had been sent, he turned to the others he had received, some of which contained donations ranging from a few to thousands of dollars; these sums were turned over to the United Service Organization (USO) and other worthy causes. One letter writer even offered to adopt all of the raiders for the duration.

He and Joe were again established in a Washington apartment during that summer of 1942; while the Army was deciding what he should do next, Doolittle would occasionally travel up to New York to meet with his old friends, Jack Allard, then working for Curtiss-Wright, and Bruce Johnson, then doing rather well as a businessman at the head of his own firm. Both, suspecting that Doolittle would be given a command, hoped that he would find a place for them in it.

Doolittle remained noncommittal until he could make his own judgments; the United States was gearing for total war. The national mood had grown more warlike and more businesslike. It was one of the first impressions he had received upon arriving back home after the raid. One day, in uniform, he walked into a drug store and asked for a tube of toothpaste. The druggist, in turn, asked for his empty tube (then a required metal-saving measure). The general had not brought an empty tube: thus no full tube. He asked for another item which was not available because of a shortage.

He finally managed to buy something and then commented on the rather stiff war tax.

Exasperated by the general, the druggist replied, "Don't take it out on me." Then he riposted further with a popular phrase of the time, "Don't you know there's a war on?"

"Sorry," the general replied, "I didn't know. I've been away," and he left the store.

Fifteen

R eunions over, Doolittle was dispatched by the Air Force to visit defense plants to keep various speaking engagements (including some on radio) on a morale-building tour. Having employed their latest hero to the fullest, the Air Force then was at a loss as to what he should do after the tour.

Arnold found that some resentment had grown around Doolittle's promotion, particularly among career officers who had felt slighted when Doolittle was jumped to brigadier general. He was readily accepted as a daredevil flier, but as a general officer who had "deserted" the service in peace time: No. The first official rejection came soon enough. When Arnold offered to send either Major General George Kenney or Doolittle to Australia as a replacement for Lieutenant General George H. Brett, who had been feuding with his chief, General MacArthur, MacArthur turned down Doolittle and chose instead career officer Kenney. ("Wisely," Doolittle has often said.)

Arnold then turned his eyes to Europe and finally came up with a solution: he placed Doolittle in command of the 4th Bombardment Wing, a medium bomber unit which theoretically would be using the Martin B-26 Marauder. Once trained and up to full strength, group by group, the wing would be assigned to the Eighth Air Force then forming in Britain.

Some time in June 1942 Doolittle met for the first time at Bolling Field, near Washington, D.C., with his staff, which included Lieutenant Colonel Jack Allard. Although the 4th Bombardment Wing(M) existed merely on paper (it would not become truly active until May 1943, and then as a heavy unit flying B-17s), Doolittle began holding organizational and staff meetings. He hoped to use the B-26, still a problem to many new pilots, for the mission for which it was intended, as a short-range medium bomber. The Air Force had already begun to think of it as a long-range medium bomber. This would mean sacrificing bomb load for fuel (used properly, the B-26 could carry as large a bomb load as some of the four-engined heavy bombers of the time).

Doolittle introduced another idea: that staff officers would be expected to fly missions enabling them to experience, and therefore to understand, the pressures under which crews operated in combat.

All of which proved, temporarily at least, academic. Late in May he was in Detroit—at the great Willow Run airport, having flown in in a B-26. He planned to test the B-26 and compare it with the B-25. His old friend "Slim" Lindbergh was on hand, then employed by Ford in its massive aircraft production program. Lindbergh noted that Doolittle was "looking somewhat tired." Doolittle found Lindbergh, as usual, friendly but distant and courting anonymity.

Doolittle continued with his preparations, feeling that eventually he would be sent to England for service with the Eighth Air Force. Currents and forces of which he was unaware by midsummer of 1942 were at work that would change that. The Russians were clamoring for a "second front," meaning a cross-channel attack from Britain into Europe to ease the pressures on Russia, reeling under the German blitzkrieg. Allied commanders saw no wisdom in a direct assault upon Europe at the time—they were just not prepared for an attack across the English Channel. However, with German troops tied up in France, embroiled in Russia and, since February of 1941, concerned with bailing out Axis partner Mussolini in North Africa, it seemed the wiser decision to open a lesser second front in the Mediterranean first. Europe could be invaded only when supplies and troops were available. Hitler's Germany would come under attack by a combined bomber offensive once there was an Eighth Air Force ready to co-operate with the RAF Bomber Command (the first American heavy bomber raid would not occur until August 17, 1942—a mere handful of B-17s striking at a rail target in France, but a beginning).

Meanwhile, the planning for an invasion of North Africa continued at the high command level while Doolittle worked at whipping a B-26 unit together. By June decisions had been made and plans initiated. Major General Dwight D. Eisenhower, who had served as Assistant Chief of Staff, was chosen to become Commanding General, European Theater of Operations, effective June 25, 1942. By that date he arrived in London with members of his staff including Major General Mark W. Clark. Soon the other members of his staff were being selected and dispatched to England for Eisenhower's scrutiny.

Late in July Doolittle was ordered by Arnold to be ready to leave the country—Arnold and Marshall having decided that Doolittle should lead Eisenhower's air force. On August 5 he left for London in company with Eisenhower's long-time friend, Major General George S. Patton, Jr., a brilliant, if erratic, tank commander. By this time Eisenhower had been promoted to lieutenant general and the North African operation was code-named Torch.

On the seventh Doolittle, along with others, including Patton, Eighth Air Force commander General Carl Spaatz, and air strategist Colonel Haywood S. Hansell, Jr., met with Eisenhower, his commander-to-be. "Ike," Doolittle recalls, "took an immediate dislike to me; he had little or no use for me."

It began at their very first meeting. The original conception of Torch would have made it a modest but all-American invasion of North Africa (the French would not be as inclined to fight against the Americans, it was reasoned, as the English). Patton's name had been given to Eisenhower as the ground commander for the operation and Doolittle's for air. Eisenhower, a career officer like Patton, was aware of Doolittle's reputation as a madcap pilot during the twenties and thirties and, of course, he was fully informed on the Tokyo Raid, its consequences (as a staff officer in Army HQ he had prepared several memoranda on it), and its ensuing publicity.

Patton, Doolittle's senior, outlined precisely his intentions for the ground troops for the invasion. When he finished, Eisenhower nodded and turned to Doolittle saying, "Our first job will be to acquire airfields in North Africa."

"General Eisenhower," Doolittle replied (with what he later described as a "stupid lack of tact"), "that is correct. However, those fields will be of no value to us until we have the personnel to man them, until we have fuel, oil, ammunition, bombs, and spare parts."

Eisenhower nodded again, but Doolittle realized almost immediately he had taken the wrong approach. "The statement," he has said, "happened to be correct, but I shouldn't have put it quite that way. I should have said, 'General, that is exactly correct—and as soon as we get those fields we will do these things,' and he should have outlined his plans.

As a result of that gaffe, Eisenhower wired Marshall that he would accept Patton as his ground commander but that "for an airman I would like to have Spaatz, [Major General Walter H.] Frank or [Brigadier General Ira] Eaker, in that order."

Both Marshall and Arnold replied with: "You may have anyone you wish; we still recommend Doolittle."

"This put Eisenhower in a bad spot," Doolittle has said. "It made him dislike me even more because he thought I was being forced down his throat. He realized, too, that if he said, 'No, I don't want him,' and then if anything went wrong with the air effort, he would have always been asked, 'Why didn't you keep Doolittle?—he would have fixed that.'"

Being all but forced into accepting Doolittle, Eisenhower found it difficult to conceal his resentment. Doolittle was eventually placed in command of what would become the Twelfth Air Force, the air arm of Torch. It was not an easy post. "While we were planning the North African operation I could see his dislike while making my presentations. It was difficult not to be upset by it because I could just look at him and see the antagonism."

Both men, resigned to each other, proceeded with their planning—Doolittle sensitive to Eisenhower's hostility and Eisenhower unbending and formal. Among the first decisions agreed upon was to build Doolittle's air force, initially codenamed "Junior" and eventually the Twelfth, on a nucleus drawn from Eaker's only recently born Eighth Air Force. Spaatz, the former commander, assumed command of all the American Air Forces in the European Theatre. Eaker had barely begun organizing his air force when, as fate would have it, his most experienced groups, bomber as well as fighter, were drawn from the Eighth or were diverted to Junior. Once this plan for the formation of the Twelfth was put into action, Doolittle returned to Washington to begin assembling his staff; by September 23 he was officially confirmed as commander of the Twelfth Air Force.

He and Allard moved into temporary quarters, along with Patton, in Claridge's Hotel in London. Soon added to Doolittle's staff were Colonels Lauris Norstad (operations), Max F. Schneider (supply), and Hoyt S. Vandenberg as chief of staff. Planning meetings were held daily at Norfolk House in St. James's Square, where Doolittle made his contributions under the baleful eye of Eisenhower. By this time the British had joined Torch, thus making it the first Anglo-American combined operation of the war.

This also resulted in a somewhat clumsy command structure, especially as it applied to air operations. Eisenhower employed two aides to co-ordinate the two air arms—Air Commodore A. P. M. Sanders, Royal Air Force, and Brigadier General Howard A. Craig, U. S. Air Force: Eastern Air Command under Air Marshal Sir William Welsh, with some 450 assorted aircraft under his command and Doolittle's Twelfth, which could muster about 1,200 planes. Their deployment was generally national—Welsh's would assist the British First Army, designated the Eastern Task Force and scheduled to land at Algiers. Doolittle's air force was assigned the task of co-operating with the American II Corps, which had been divided into the Central Task Force, to land at Oran, and the Western Task Force, which would land on the Atlantic coast of Morocco, centered on Casablanca. The French willing, the Allies planned to push eastward along the North African coast into Tunisia. Field Marshal Erwin Rommel and Lieutenant General Bernard Montgomery were at that time engaged in their push-pull desert war farther east in Cyrenaica.

Until airfields had been secured ashore there would be nothing, as Doolittle had so tactlessly pointed out to Eisenhower, for the Twelfth to do. All the initial aerial support for Torch would be contributed by carrier-borne aircraft, mainly British, as well as aircraft drawn from Gibraltar for the action around Algiers.

Doolittle's major work in the early weeks of the Torch planning was organizational: "stealing" units from the Eighth Air Force. He acquired the Eighth's two most experienced B-17 groups, the 97th and the 301st. The term "experienced" was relative since the groups had been flying combat missions only since August and

September, respectively. However, they were the base upon which Eaker had hoped to build his Eighth Bomber Command. Into the Twelfth were also drawn two P-38 fighter groups, two Spitfire groups (manned by American pilots), as well as a number of medium and light bomber units and a transport group.

The deprivation, as he termed it, of the Eighth Air Force and the impact this had on Eaker's planning concerned Doolittle. "Ira Eaker," he has said, "did a superb job with what he had and I penalized him by taking away some of what he had at a time when he already didn't have enough." While the Torch priorities were understood at the command level, the "raiding" by the Twelfth to the detriment of the Eighth led to certain frictions between the two, dividing those who were loyal to Eaker from those who were loyal to Doolittle. This was a problem that would also prove bothersome two years later.

All his time since the return to England from the United States Doolittle spent at the Norfolk House in planning sessions; later he could relax with Jack Allard. He also came to know his colorful new friend George Patton, to whom he continues to refer as "Georgie." Patton, Quentin Reynolds has written, "would stalk up and down the big living room of Doolittle's suite entertaining them all with stories. Patton's first love was probably his ridiculous pearl-handled revolvers, but his second was the hunting knife he always carried with him. His constant fear was that this knife might somehow become dull. While telling the most outrageous stories of his cavalry days, or what his tanks would do once the Navy put them ashore, he would be constantly sharpening the knife on a whetstone he kept with him.

"Doolittle and Spaatz were two of those who were devoted to Patton. They liked his exuberant humor, chuckled at his flamboyancy and relaxed under the stream of his colorful invective, delivered in a high squeaky voice."

About a month before the November date set for the North African invasion Doolittle heard, through Joe Doolittle, that the third of the old Rockwell Field trio, Bruce Johnson, had made a request to join Doolittle's staff. Doolittle had doubts about "the rich man's son," who had been a civilian executive for so long. Besides, he was top-heavy with brass—what was required were pilots, bombardiers, navigators, and gunners who could fire guns (many were found that could not). He could not, however, ignore the request of an old friend. He radioed Washington asking that Johnson be taken into the Air Corps and assigned to his staff; at the same time, he had Allard write to Johnson advising him of the problems he might face, touching on the problem the Air Force had when taking personnel directly from civilian life. The tone of the letter angered Johnson.

Competent people "coming from civil life," he was informed, are not content to do the uninteresting and, to them, unimportant jobs that must be done, consequently they are unhappy and in their discontent cause dissatisfaction and poor morale. "You must realize that you, if you come in, will be put under a much younger (in age) but older in experience and proved competent officer, and you may be there indefinitely. It will be necessary for you to prove your competence by doing little things extremely well. Maybe as a result, you may someday get an important job . . .

"I hope," Allard concluded, "by this time you have heard from Washington and are on your way, but Jim did want you to get this bit of advice which should explain to your satisfaction what we are up against . . ."

Johnson's "first reaction to this letter was outrage." He paced his office, fumed and cursed Allard. "Who in hell did he think he was sitting there in all his pomposity and telling me that I was possibly too old [he and Allard were the same age and Doolittle just a few months younger] and inept to be of value?" Not having heard from Washington, Johnson in a fury packed his bags and headed South.

Doolittle regretted having to send such a letter, but he also felt he owed it to Johnson either to prepare him for what he would have to endure should he decide to join him or to discourage him altogether. Doolittle, under Eisenhower's suspicious glare, was feeling his way around, finding himself as an Air Force commander. There would be little time to minister to an unhappy Johnson. Although not troubled with any self-doubt himself, some of Doolittle's attitude at the time was revealed in an exchange with a young officer who had been assigned to him as an aide.

"Sir," began Clint Frank [a former All-American football star in *his* civil life], "I'm very happy to be your aide, but I must confess I don't know anything about being an aide."

"Son, we're going to get along fine," Doolittle replied. "I don't know anything about being a general."

Perhaps—but the daily, and long, sessions in St. James's Square provided a crash course in the art. By November 5 Eisenhower and some members of his staff were flown in 97th Bomb Group Fortresses to Gibraltar, where his headquarters for the North African invasion was to be established. There was much Allied concern over the Spanish reaction to the activity at Gibraltar, Spain being a kind of silent Axis partner, and how much would be reported to or observed by the Germans. This trepidation was compounded when Eisenhower's plane, upon arrival, was forced to circle the Rock of Gibraltar for an hour before the runway congestion was cleared.

A second flight of 6 B-17s awaited the takeoff signal at Hurn airdrome for the flight to Gibraltar. The plane carrying Doolittle and other members of Eisenhower's staff (including Brigadier General Lyman L. Lemnitzer, Colonel Thomas J. Davis, and Dr. Freeman Mathews, a political adviser) developed hydraulic problems on the runway. The remaining Fortresses continued on to Gibraltar and the Doolittle plane went into the repair shop and was not ready until the next day—when it would have to make the flight unaccompanied.

The next morning pilot John C. Summers and copilot Thomas F. Lohr rather nervously took their positions in the cockpit. They wondered if Doolittle would chew them out for the previous day's near mishap: when the hydraulics went out, their plane nearly crashed into other Fortresses on the line. There were no apparent repercussions and the amiable tone of their trip was established when Doolittle came into the cockpit to study the B-17's controls and instruments, informing the two men that he had never flown a Fortress.

The conversation was interrupted just off Cape Finisterre when four black specks materialized into a four-plane flight of enemy fighter-bombers—twin-engined Junkers Ju-88s. Returning from an early morning Atlantic patrol, the German planes were drawn to the lone aircraft flying toward Gibraltar. Overtaking the B-17, the planes flew alongside as the pilots studied the big bomber (out of which the waist guns had been removed to lighten the plane for its contingent of passengers and their gear). The German pilots must have been curious about a Flying Fortress from which no guns were being fired (only the top-turret, ball-turret, and tail guns were in place).

Upon a signal from their leader, the Ju-88s raced ahead, turned, and came in on the Fortress. Summers whipped the bomber into evasive action, then dived for the water. This made it more difficult for the German planes to attack and made a run from below impossible. Summers' maneuvering brought them through the first pass without a scratch, while the gunner in the top turret fired back at the Germans. The Ju-88s then flew ahead and turned again to come in on the Fortress's nose. Summers again began whipping the B-17 around crazily to keep from being hit, but a 20-mm shell struck No. 3 engine and came crashing into the cockpit.

When the smoke cleared, Doolittle and Summers found that copilot Lohr had been wounded in the arm and that the propeller of No. 3 engine was windmilling, threatening to tear away and making further evasive action difficult. Summers and Lohr managed to feather the propeller, after which Doolittle helped Lohr out of his seat into the navigator's compartment for first aid. He then returned to the cockpit to serve as copilot.

The Ju-88s made another pass without further hits. One of the German planes was trailing smoke and, possibly because of a lessening fuel supply, all four planes decided to break off the engagement. Summers and Doolittle continued on toward Gibraltar while Lohr was attended to by high brass. Lemnitzer, it eventuated, had brought a flask of whiskey (contrary to military rule) and plied the wounded copilot, who arrived at Gibraltar some time later "with a pleasant glow."

For Doolittle it meant catching up with the planning already underway, having lost a day because of the delay in England. Since the Twelfth could not participate in Torch until it had operational airfields, he assigned Allard and Norstad to accompany a combat team invading on D-day. They were then to inform Doolittle, with Eisenhower at Gibraltar, the moment air bases were available. The Allies' particular objective was a complex of airfields in the Oran area, which, according to planning, would be taken by the joint Center Task Force. It was Doolittle's own plan to establish his headquarters at Tafaraoui, which would accommodate B-17s, about fifteen miles inland and to the south of Oran. In between lay La Senia, a French base at which some 55 fighters (Dewoitine D.520s) and about 40 bombers in various stages of obsolescence were stationed. The hope persisted that the French would receive the predominantly American invaders as liberators and would offer but token resistance. The Americans would learn that, like the British, they were not to be welcomed to North Africa by the French.

On D-day, November 8, 1942, although British Fleet Air Arm fighters had successfully strafed the French planes at La Senia, those Dewoitines that had not been destroyed or could be repaired caused serious problems. Troop-carrying Douglas C-47s were attacked by the French fighters and scattered, there were casualties, and three of the American transports ended up interned in Spanish Morocco. Late in the afternoon, after Tafaraoui had been taken by ground troops, Doolittle ordered two squadrons of Spitfires of the 31st Fighter Group, commanded by Colonel John R. Hawkins, to fly from Gibraltar to the Oran area. Flying through and around storms, the Spitfires arrived at Tafaraoui around five in the evening, to find the runways holed and the field under French artillery fire. Hawkins led an attack on the guns and then returned to the field to land on a clear strip. During the landing procedure four Dewoitines circling the field (and apparently mistaken for RAF Hawker Hurricanes) swept in to attack the last few landing Spitfires with their wheels down. One Spitfire crashed with a dead pilot. Immediately three of the already landed but still moving Spitfires took off to drive away the French fighters, knocking down three of the four.

By nightfall fighting had become sporadic, but Norstad and Allard could not yet advise Doolittle that the time had come to establish the Twelfth Air Force at Tafaraoui. That night a lone French bomber came over to drop one bomb on the airdrome, damaging one of the transport planes but none of the Spitfires. And by daylight, when Hawkins could get his Spitfires air-borne again, the field came under attack by French 75s. Almost simultaneously the 31st's ground crews began arriving from the beachheads by truck to begin their improvisational upkeep of the Spitfires with captured French fuel and ammunition. The Spitfires then participated in various missions, ranging from reconnaissance to strafing, there being by November 9 a paucity of operational French aircraft in the area, most of the surviving planes by then having fled to French Morocco. The Spitfires succeeded in turning back a tank column of the French Foreign Legion and silenced the troublesome French 75s that had been molesting their airstrips. They even, because of an error in radio transmission—the word "west" being substituted for "east"—strafed American troops who shot down two of the attacking Spitfires. Although French resistance was weakening, there was clearly much confusion among the Allies.

Doolittle, in a B-17, with Spitfire escort by the 52nd Fighter Group, landed at Tafaraoui in the afternoon of the ninth. The airfield was a shambles—runways were pocked, cannibalized aircraft dotted the area with ground crews siphoning precious fuel from their tanks, smoking wreckage smudged the atmosphere, and now and then a French 75 shell added to the confuson. What was not there were the supplies still on the beach at Oran, particularly spare parts, fuel, and ammunition. Doolittle left the solution to this problem to the capable Colonel Tudor Gardiner (a former governor of Maine) and soon the flow of supplies from Oran to Tafaraoui began; within four days of the Torch landings, the Twelfth Air Force had, in the expression of the time, "found a home."

During those first few days after D-day at Oran the other landings, at Casablanca and Algiers had taken place. Despite French resistance, by November 11, 1942, all three had capitulated to the Allies. The German High Command was quick to react. While the French were fighting their losing battle, the Germans began moving troops and supplies from Sicily into Tunisia on D-plus-1; when the surrender of the French forces came two days later, the total occupation of France was ordered. North Africa had become a full-fledged "theater of war."

Doolittle recalls that "in the early days of the North African Campaign the British had a distinct advantage over the Americans." They had combat experience and the Americans had virtually none, particularly the ground troops. The British had developed an excellent communications network that worked—"Ours was untried and imperfect"—and good intelligence—"good knowledge of the enemy capabilities and intentions. We had virtually none."

He remembered how on one occasion involving the imperfect communications he developed "some gray hairs." The French North African troops had capitulated *after* American fighters had been sent out to strafe those same troops, which were in fact advancing toward Allied lines bent on surrender, not attack. It took a great deal of doing on Doolittle's part and that of his staff to contact the flight leader and cancel the strafing attack on the French troops unsuspectingly heading their way in vulnerable trucks.

"Gradually we learned our job," Doolittle concluded, "and developed good communications and intelligence. General Spaatz, shortly after he arrived in North Africa, installed an excellent communications network which we called 'Red Line.' Not until then did we really exercise complete command over our own units, since we had been dependent on the British for vital communications."

Within two weeks after the invasion Doolittle wrote a summary of the operation for Arnold: "The American carrier-borne Navy aviation at Casablanca, and the British Fleet Air Arm at Oran, did the larger part of the air fighting. By the time the airports were secured, they had destroyed, either in the air or on the ground, the majority of the French aviation.

"[Brigadier General John K.] Joe Cannon, at Casablanca, has done an outstanding job. The 33rd Fighter Group gave air support and the necessary reconnaissance to General Patton's forces. Joe unloaded some 72 aircraft [P-40s] from the [escort carrier] *Chenango* at Port Lyautey. The principal runway had been bombed, and was not usable. The field was soft and 70 aircraft sustained minor damages on landing. Part of these aircraft were moved to the Casablanca airport, and some 35 more were shot off the [British auxiliary carrier] *Archer*.

"Joe now has, in addition to these, a half-dozen B-25s from the 310th Group, and more are coming in steadily. He also has such transports as required, of the 62nd Group.

"In addition to Port Lyautey, there are good fields at Salé, Rabat and Casablanca. The field at Casablanca is large but has no prepared runways, and there are spots that will not hold a B-17. I proved this the other day by landing there and bogging down. Apparently, the small footprint and the high unit loading was more than the sod could stand. It required four tanks to pull the B-17 out so it could take off again. Joe and George Patton have the western situation well in hand and are getting along together beautifully.

"The first airport was secured at noon on D-Day. Twenty-four Spitfires, with Hawkins in command, hopped over from Gibraltar.

"I cannot speak too highly of the work done by these groups. They twice stopped mechanized columns who were attacking the airport at Tafouri [the American version of Tafaraoui] from the south. The ground units had moved forward to take La Senia airport, which is closer to Oran proper. Had it not been for the prompt and efficient action of the Spitfires, Tafouri and our air units would have been lost, and the war at Oran lengthened and made more bloody. One column taken out and routed was the French Foreign Legion, moving in from its headquarters at Sidi-bel-Abbes. Our Fighters destroyed five tanks of this outfit, burned the supplies coming forward, and routed the foot soldiers. La Senia was secured, lost, and secured again. During the process it was bombed by our people and shelled by the French. We have finally moved to La Senia in addition to Tafouri, and are rehabilitating it.

"The necessity for marrying ground and air forces on the field of battle precluded the training and study necessary to secure perfect collaboration. In spite of this, the cooperation was of the highest order, and in only two instances were mistakes made. On one occasion, we were directed to attack an enemy column east of La Macta, on Arzeu Bay. The airplanes flew over the column to the west, which was actually ours. The ground forces, being light on the trigger, cut down on the airplanes. The planes, feeling, in spite of the American appearance, they must be French troops, started to strafe them. Fortunately, our tanks were not as vulnerable as the French, and no damage was done to our ground troops, but two of our planes were shot down by our people.

"As a matter of fact, an operation of this kind promptly separates the sheep from the goats, and I am happy to report that all of our people showed up well, and most of them were superior.

"Two of my principal worries were the concentration of aircraft on Gibraltar, and the long flight down from the United Kingdom in the season of bad weather. Gibraltar is now pretty well cleaned out, and to date, far less difficulty is experienced in flying the aircraft down.

"When I was last in Casablanca, there were about 4,000 air people ashore; yesterday, at Oran, we have 14,000 men and about 1,000 officers. These are stationed at La Senia and Tafouri.

"The fight has moved to the eastward. In order to get the Hun out of Tunisia and occupy this area before he can, we will have made available to the Royal Air Force, to [Lieutenant] General [K. A. N.] Anderson's [British First] army, as many of our units as they can use. This arrangement, under which these airplanes are made available, is for the British to assign the missions, but we operate the airplanes.

"We must keep the Straits of Gibraltar open and provide fighter cover, and later submarine protection, for our convoys along the north and west coasts of Africa."

Besides overseeing the organization and establishment of an air force, Doolittle had to provide men and planes for missions to hinder the German investment of Tunisia—and he had to continue to "sell myself to Eisenhower." While Doolittle's handling of his forces was effective and impressive, his excursions into the unorthodox earned the Eisenhower ire with regularity.

It was while he was still at Oran and Eisenhower was at Gibraltar that Doolittle saw his first Spitfire IX, the latest model in the series. His airman's curiosity, as always, urged him to test the plane in flight, which he did. He took off and enjoyed a brief airman's holiday, luxuriating in the solitude of flight and in the feel of the fine, winged instrument that he himself controlled. For a few moments he relaxed in the pure joy of flying.

Immediately upon landing he was informed that Eisenhower requested his presence at Gibraltar (later Doolittle learned that Eisenhower had called him while he was up testing the Spitfire and had so been informed). Doolittle did not remain in Oran long —just long enough to have the Spitfire checked over; he then headed the plane northwestward across the Mediterranean. Eventually he spotted two cruisers below, one Italian, the other British, exchanging gunfire. He nosed the Spitfire down for a closer look only to be met by antiaircraft fire from both ships (all seamen were notoriously nervous about aircraft and rather negligent about their identification). With black puffs bursting around him, Doolittle pulled away and continued on to the airstrip at Gibraltar. Upon landing he hurried to Eisenhower's office, saluted in a military manner, and waited.

"I understand," Eisenhower began, "you have been up in a Spitfire looking for Germans." This was not precisely true, but as Doolittle would later comment, "I wouldn't have minded."

Doolittle replied, however, to the true portion of Eisenhower's statement: "Yes, sir, a new airplane—a Spit IX—just came down and I wanted to try it out."

"Listen, Doolittle, you can either be a major general [the first intimation to the victim that he was up for promotion] in charge of my air or you can be a second lieutenant and you can go fly Spitfires looking for Germans. I can fix that tomorrow—which do you want?"

"I'd rather be a major general handling your air."

"All right," Eisenhower snapped. "Stay at it!"

The flight back to Oran was without incident, but it took Doolittle a full year to convince Eisenhower that he was not just another "fly boy."

This understanding came in time and Doolittle himself grew fond of the rather strictly paternal Eisenhower and "had a great respect for him. He was unique as a military man in his ability to get people with diverse interests to work together for the accomplishment of a common cause. His problems with the British and French were sometimes very difficult, indeed."

On November 17, 1942, Eisenhower, in reply to a query from Marshall, replied, "Promotion of Doolittle is fully justified and I recommend it be accomplished at once. Apparently my fault that Doolittle has not been recommended since November 8, but it was my impression that you had already planned his promotion to take effect shortly after initiation of TORCH. It is appropriate to announce his promotion as a result of leadership in actual battle command as well as in organization Twelfth Air Force."

Doolittle was officially made a major general on December 15, 1942. Despite his approval, Eisenhower continued to harbor reservations: to Arnold he wrote that he regarded Doolittle as "stronger as a field commander than he is as an organizer" and to Lieutenant General Frank M. Andrews, Commander of the American forces in Europe, he indicated that he felt Doolittle had "established himself as a commander and, although he had to learn the hard way, he has learned something of the responsibilities of high command." This same paternalism surfaced even when Eisenhower recommended Doolittle (in the summer of 1943) for the Distinguished Service Medal; the award citation contained the curious statement that Doolittle had shown over the past year "the greatest degree of improvement of any of the senior

United States officers serving in my command." By this time, it might have been said that Doolittle had succeeded in selling himself to Eisenhower: the latter's letter to Doolittle regarding the DSM opened with the words, "Dear Jimmie." (Parenthetically it might be noted, although chronologically misplaced, that Eisenhower appears never to have readjusted his personal view of Doolittle as anything but a kind of Peck's Bad Boy; he delighted in telling the "looking for Germans in a Spitfire," story long after Doolittle hoped he had forgotten it.)

Much the same reaction greeted the unexpected arrival of Captain Bruce Johnson in North Africa in November, shortly after the headquarters of the Twelfth had been moved eastward from Tafaraoui to Algiers. Seething under the Doolittle-Allard rejection, he had practiced a little guile on Doolittle's liaison officer in Washington (where Doolittle's wire requesting Johnson's induction was not to be found). A half-truth here and a bit of brazening there and soon Johnson found himself armed with two packets of mail for Doolittle headed for North Africa. He arrived at Maison-Blanche, a village just outside Algiers, after more than fifty hours of aerial hitchhiking, using the two sealed packages marked "Major General J. H. Doolittle" as tickets.

These secured him a car and driver at Maison-Blanche that brought him into the Doolittle headquarters driveway simultaneously with another car that happened to be carrying Doolittle. "I put on my steel helmet, adjusted my web belt complete with sidearm and walked over to the alighting officers. Jim Doolittle regarded me in complete amazement as I saluted him and said, 'Sir, I report for duty. I am instructed to give you this packet.' Handing him the package (which might have contained canceled laundry tickets for all I know), I accepted his receipt."

Upon recovering, Doolittle instructed his friend to report to Allard, whose office was in the Shell Building in Algiers, and, after a "Brucie, what the hell are you doing here?" reception, Johnson was absorbed into Doolittle's staff as assistant headquarters commandant. The old Rockwell Field trio was reunited.

The reunion, once Doolittle adjusted to it, was salutary, for after hours the three friends, shedding military trappings became "Jim," "Jack," and "Brucie." They could discuss, argue, even disagree without rancor and, in the case of the two "junior officers," with impunity. The presence of two old friends provided Doolittle with various outlets in a time of stress.

He also unburdened himself in letters to Joe, to whom he wrote regularly. Her replies were encouraging, newsy, and frequently amusing. At the same time, however, she too had taken on additional burdens. "I wanted to help," she said, "and I felt if I kept very busy I wouldn't have any time to think. With young Jimmy and his father both overseas, and John at West Point, it was very difficult not to think of personal things—and I didn't believe I had a right to, so I tried to keep awfully busy."

She discussed this with her friend, Mrs. Henry H. Arnold, who suggested that Joe concentrate her energies on the home front, because of her vast number of civilian friends in industry, arts, and science. Joe Doolittle's war work began simply enough, with factory visits, where she was pleased to see the large number of women factory workers in aviation.

Her duties broadened to include that of radio personality (a job which lasted some fourteen months) on the CBS series "Broadway Matinee"; in her segment of the show, sponsored by the Owens-Illinois Company, she regularly gave "Uncle Sam's message to the women." She also, during the war, made a tour of Shell refineries, as a morale-boosting mission. But most of her work consisted of defining the war to women; she would time her visits when she sensed that there was restlessness brewing and slanted her talks to women to explain "what we had to do on our part to save [for the war effort]. There were discomforts but nothing compared to that of the British and all the other women on the other side endured.

"We have had so much here that we don't react very well when we're not getting things."

Her most rewarding, if at times heartbreaking, work came about when the Air Corps established its first Rehabilitation Center in what had once been a school at Pawling, New York. Dr. Howard Rusk, who, with the rank of colonel, was the chief of the convalescent training program of the Air Surgeon's office, urged Joe Doolittle to work at the Pawling center—in this he was joined by Mrs. Rusk. Although knowing she lacked any psychiatric or medical background, Joe was eventually persuaded by the Rusks to join the center as a counselor even though she also protested a lack of experience in that also.

It was soon learned that not only the patients required rehabilitation—their families did too. Joe Doolittle, practically overnight (experts warned it would take six weeks), established courses for the wives of the patients at Pawling. The women selected their own courses of study, which ranged from nursing (an essential, particularly if their husbands had suffered battle wounds) to charm. She found, too, that many of the patients expressed an interest in the study of art as well as crafts—"pottery and things."

It was challenging work and what with putting in as much as eighteen hours a day, Joe Doolittle had little time to think of personal things while the men in her family were off to war.

Doolittle was also confronted with a myriad of problems and put in long hours: the war in North Africa in the first month and a half had moved eastward more rapidly than had been planned. Supplies could not keep up with this movement. There was more than enough confusion in sorting out the command structure: one of Johnson's duties was "the promotion of harmonious Anglo-American relations . . ." The chain of command frequently ran through ground commanders before reaching Doolittle and ground commanders were not always equipped to utilize air power wisely.

In the initial planning for Torch it had been decided that the Twelfth Air Force would be concentrated in the west, but the fighting moving eastward ruled otherwise. Doolittle very quickly abandoned the original deployment, realizing that the climax of the war in North Africa would come in Tunisia (already filling up with German troops, equipment, and aircraft). He subdivided the vast North African battleground into sections, assigning to each both a fighter and a bomber command, obviating the confusion that often resulted from demands for aerial assistance over the vast desert areas. Thus the move from muddy Tafaraoui to Maison-Blanche near Algiers. Doolittle's B-17s were moved to Maison-Blanche, as were the medium bomber groups, which were soon joined by the P-38s of Colonel Thayer S. Olds' 14th Fighter Group. While this put the German installations in Tunisia within reach of Doolittle's bombers and fighters—the reverse was true also. Algiers and Maison-Blanche suffered severe bombing attacks, night raids on the air base being especially destructive. Reluctantly, by November 22, Doolittle was forced to move the B-17s back to Tafaraoui out of reach of the German bombers.

The fighting in North Africa was primarily a ground war with air power employed tactically to assist the foot soldiers and vehicles. The intranational dealings at Eisenhower's level made it also a political war—and, being the first of its kind, it was characterized by muddle. And when the winter rains came, Doolittle's airfields were reduced to mud, severely curtailing aerial operations. Morale dipped (and ground troops complained that the only aircraft they ever saw were German or Italian, which operated from all-weather fields). By the first of the year (1943), losses had risen as German reinforcements accumulated in Tunisia, from which forward Allied bases could be reached. Allied supply lines, stretched along the coast of North Africa, all but dried up.

Because he wanted to experience missions first hand, and because it would be good for the morale of tired and discouraged crews, Doolittle frequently flew bombing missions. He moved among the various bases of his command, often flying his personal B-26 Marauder—even this had its public relations element, for inexperienced pilots continued to have trouble with this "hot" airplane; but if "the Old Man" flew it, obviously it was a worthy plane.

It was about this time that Doolittle fulfilled the promise he had made to Sergeant Paul Leonard as the two sat near the wreckage of a B-25 on a Chinese hillside the past spring. Leonard had remained for a time in the China-Burma-India Theater following the Tokyo Raid; in June of 1942 he was recalled to the United States to become Doolittle's crew chief. When Doolittle was placed at the head of the Twelfth, Leonard accompanied him to England and to North Africa. Keeping his promise led to Doolittle's "greatest personal tragedy of the war."

He, Allard, and Leonard boarded a B-26 for a flight to a recently captured airfield near Youks-les-Bains, Algeria, not too distant from the border of German-held Algeria. The date was January 5, 1943, and Doolittle was due in for a conference with various ground commanders. Upon landing, Doolittle and Allard left for a nearby command post, leaving Leonard in charge of their plane.

Around midnight the German bombers came over the field; Doolittle found it impossible to get back because an ammunition dump, on the road between the command post and the airfield, had been hit "and ammunition was exploding all over the place."

The following morning Doolittle managed to get out to the field and found that Leonard had moved the plane, but there was no Leonard. Evidently, judging from the spent shells around the turret, Leonard had shot at the attackers until the ammunition ran out. Nearby Doolittle found a filled-in bomb crater—filled in, that is, by a second bomb blast. Searching in the crater Doolittle soon worked out what had occurred. Out of ammunition, Leonard had dived into the bomb crater only to suffer a direct hit. In the rubble Doolittle found "all that remained of the wonderful boy who had tried to cheer me up in China in my saddest moment." It was just the left hand, shattered at the wrist—the wristwatch still in place.

"He was a good friend of mine," he said to anyone who happened to be near, then turned and, with Allard following, returned to the B-26, which had been cleaned of the debris, bomb fragments, and sand that had been blown over it during the raid. It appeared to be undamaged, but Doolittle made a careful visual inspection to be certain. Allard noted that he was businesslike, though grim; the death of Leonard had affected him deeply. There was, however, no time for grieving—the two men were due back at Maison-Blanche.

Doolittle meshed the ignition and the engines burst into life; he released the brakes and began "walking" the B-26, trailing clouds of sand, through the pockmarks and scrap metal on the air strip, toward the runway.

"Think she's all right?" Allard finally broke the silence, referring to the plane.

"She's all right," Doolittle assured him and soon had the plane hurtling along the runway, past the wrecks that had been hit, past the bomb craters and work crews, and lifted it gently off the runway.

"Seems okay," Allard said.

"She's okay," Doolittle replied and flew westward for Maison-Blanche.

The December 1942 rains had frustrated Eisenhower's hopes for the taking of Tunis; these same rains glued down the planes of both the Twelfth Air Force and Eastern Air Command. At the same time, the Luftwaffe and the Italian Air Force, enjoying

TOP: European tour, 1930: Doolittle as dual salesman for Shell and Curtiss-Wright, a job that took him to twenty-one countries from April through July. He is accompanied by two pilots lent by the Army: Captain John K. Cannon (with helmet and goggles) and Lieutenant James E. Parker; and William F. Goulding (to Cannon's left), of Curtiss-Wright. (Parker is barely visible to Goulding's left.) Some years later, during World War II, Cannon took command of the Twelfth Air Force in North Africa, succeeding Doolittle, who assumed command of the Fifteenth in Italy. In the early 1950s Cannon, with the rank of lieutenant general, headed the Tactical Air Command. DOOLITTLE COLLECTION. ABOVE: The Curtiss-Wright lineup in Germany, c. April 1930. The planes represented four types: reconnaissance, observation, advanced trainer, and pursuit (later called fighter). Although the Luftwaffe was *sub rosa* in 1930, the Germans already had their own ideas on these types of warplanes. DOOLITTLE COLLECTION

Doolittle and Cannon discussing flying with an unidentified German pilot. The subject of aviation cut across national boundaries and political ideologies. DOOLITTLE COLLECTION. The Laird Super Solution, designed for Doolittle by E. M. "Matty" Laird for entry in the 1931 Bendix Trophy race. Photo was taken at the Laird plant at Wichita, Kansas. The interplane struts were replaced shortly after by a simpler, streamlined I strut. DOOLITTLE COLLECTION

Refueling stop, Bendix Trophy race, 1931. After takeoff from Burbank, California, Doolittle led the field to Albuquerque, New Mexico, and Kansas City, Missouri, for refueling, and on to Cleveland, site of that year's National Air Races. Doolittle was the winner. Then, after refueling again, he took off, to continue on to Newark and establish a new coast-to-coast record. DOOLITTLE COLLECTION

Doolittle's arrival at Cleveland af[ter] winning the 1931 Bendix race, attending to the refueling of the Super Solution, and takeoff for N[ew] York for a crack at a new transcontinental record. U. S. AIR FORCE

Doolittle back in Cleveland after winning the Bendix race and setting new transcontinental record, with son Jim, Jr., and Joe. In a single day—September 4, 1931—he covered more than 3,500 miles (and won $10,000 in prizes) and, although the photograph is of poor quality, his fatigue is evident. It was, however, temporary, for soon after, Doolittle flew on to St. Louis to attend a party.
DOOLITTLE COLLECTION

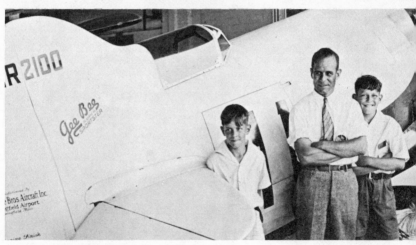

TOP: Doolittle studies his bent Super Solution, after a wheels-up landing at the Laird plant at Wichita, Kansas, in August 1932. The previous year's Bendix winner had been greatly modified, to include, among other things, retractable landing gear. The gear did, indeed, retract, but would not lower when Doolittle had to land and he was forced to crash-land. Though he was uninjured, damage to the plane precluded its participation in the 1932 National Air Races. DOOLITTLE COLLECTION. ABOVE: When word of Doolittle's crash landing reached Springfield, Massachusetts, home of Granville Brothers Aircraft, Zantford D. Granville offered Doolittle the use of their Gee Bee R-1 racer. Here Doolittle stands before the plane in Cleveland with sons, John (left) and Jim, Jr. This was undoubtedly the most unpredictable plane Doolittle ever flew; in less skilled hands it often proved fatal. DOOLITTLE COLLECTION

TOP: The Gee Bee warming up before the Thompson Trophy race, Cleveland, September 5, 1932. In this plane Doolittle had already set a new landplane speed record in the Shell speed dashes. A Gee Bee R-2, flown by Lee Gehlbach, placed fifth in the Thompson. U. S. AIR FORCE. ABOVE: Doolittle rounds a pylon in the 1932 Thompson Trophy race in which he placed first with a speed of 252.686 m.p.h. COURTESY R. H. KNOBLOCH, THE WINGS CLUB

The Doolittles during their trip to China, here in Peiping (Peking) in May 1933. They have been met by General Linson E. Dzau of the Chinese Air Force; Mrs. John Jouett, whose husband, a U. S. Air Corps colonel, was then serving as an unofficial adviser to the Chinese Air Force; and film producer Mark L. Moody.
DOOLITTLE COLLECTION

the benefits of all-weather airfields in Sicily and Sardinia, as well as the fields in Tunisia at Sidi-Ahmed, El Aouina, Sfax, Sousse, and Gabes, could transport men and supplies as well as strike at the hapless Allied troops also mired in the mud. The Stukas, once a laughing matter, reappeared as a new menace, striking from their base at El Aouina, a five-minute flight from the muddy battlefront.

The winter boredom eventually got to Doolittle, who enjoyed a joking relationship with one of the British members of the air staff, Group Captain John Alexander "Speedy" Powell. A colorful bomber pilot, Powell exuded an air of insouciance and that English affinity for offhand peculiarity so often favored by novelists. Powell had even made his screen debut in a film, *Target for Tonight*. As described by Quentin Reynolds, "Powell had an English accent you could cut with a crumpet; he also had about every decoration the British awarded their combat fliers."

Powell good-naturedly took much ribbing about his accent, being surrounded by Yanks. Even Doolittle joined in. "I wish you'd find a mess of your own," Doolittle told him one day. "Either that or learn to speak basic English. That accent of yours is apt to corrupt my men."

"It will do them good to listen to pure English, ol' boy," was the group captain's reply to the general. Powell became one of the welcome favorites at Doolittle's well-stocked—by the adept, often light-fingered Bruce Johnson—mess.

It was during a spell of weather when the planes were grounded that Powell approached a glum Doolittle with, "Weather's jolly good west."

"We're not fighting anyone west of here," Doolittle replied scowling.

"You are obtuse," Powell retorted. "I'm talking of England, ol' boy. Jolly England. We'll have to hang around here another week or so, sitting on our respective arses. But the sun is shining in Merry England. We could hop in a Wimpy [a Wellington bomber] and be there in no time."

Tired, bored, still affected by the death of Leonard, Doolittle reasoned a little diversion might do some good.

"Why not, Speedy," he replied.

"My aircraft is fueled, sir!"

They splashed to the airstrip in a jeep and climbed into a

Wellington which, *sans* bomb load, ammunition, and full crew, lifted off the field very easily. With Powell at the controls and Doolittle dozing in the copilot's seat, the plane soon crossed over the Mediterranean and passed over the shores of occupied France. Doolittle slept peacefully as, according to Reynolds, Powell "roared out a lusty chorus of the the unexpurgated RAF song 'All Day Long We Haven't Flown Above Five Hundred Feet . . .'"

Crossing France at night they were greeted by antiaircraft fire, the proximity of which awakened Doolittle as Powell kicked the controls to present a difficult target. "The Frogs," he explained. "Stupid beggars, don't know who we are. Their flak is really wizard, what?"

Clear of the antiaircraft zone, they proceeded on to England with only one further incident. Doolittle was again awakened by the plane's gyrations, to be told by Powell, "Only a Hun fighter, laddie. Nothing to fret about." Only the light from which Powell was racing turned out to be the planet Venus, not a German fighter. They landed safely at a bomber base in southern England and within two hours were in London, checked into Claridge's, and ready for "fun and games."

As they were about to leave for a night on the town, Doolittle said, "I'll tell the desk where we're going, in case Jack [Allard] or Larry [Norstad] want us."

Powell brightened and said, "Glad you told HQ where we're staying, ol' boy. Forgot to tell them myself."

"What! I didn't tell them we were leaving. They must be going crazy wondering what happened to us. I'll get a message off right away!" The communiqué relieved the tension in Twelfth Air Force Headquarters; much refreshed, Doolittle and Powell returned to North Africa three days later.

Some time after, when Doolittle's heavy bombers began reaching out from Africa for targets in Italy, Powell, whose experience had been primarily with British night bombers, was given the opportunity to hitch a ride aboard a B-24 on a day bombing mission. Powell, as a guest observer, did not fly the plane (he had, in fact, never piloted a Liberator). After bombing, the plane began its run for home when a direct flak hit killed the pilot and navigator, seriously wounded the copilot, and knocked out two engines besides chopping up a wing and the tail.

Uninjured, Powell lifted the pilot out of his seat and began familiarizing himself with the controls and, with the great plane shuddering and barely aloft over the Mediterranean, directed its shattered nose toward Africa.

When the plane was long overdue, Doolittle became concerned, and as time stretched—and the chances for the plane grew slimmer—he was forced to consider the B-24 carrying Powell and the American crew as missing. Dinner time in the officer's mess was cheerless without Powell and the mess attendant, following the custom, removed Powell's chair from the table, leaving the traditional space. Doolittle, unable to eat, left the table for his office to shuffle papers and keep himself occupied.

Around midnight he and Allard were astonished to see a rumpled, rather ragged Powell limp into their office. They then learned that their irrepressible friend had taught himself how to fly the B-24, pulled it up on its two remaining engines until the third engine expired. Within about a half mile of the African coast the overtaxed fourth engine gave out and Powell flattened the glide to crash-land onto the beach. He pulled the wounded copilot out of the plane and then went off in search of help and hospitalization for the survivors of the crew. "A bad show, laddie," Powell commiserated.

Doolittle immediately recommended Powell for the American Distinguished Flying Cross for his remarkable part in bringing back the survivors of the B-24 crew. The medal was approved, and, sad to say, arrived at Doolittle's headquarters two days after "Speedy" Powell had not returned from another bombing mission.

If the North African campaign did not function smoothly according to military or political plan, it was the forge in which the Anglo-American weapon that would defeat the Axis was shaped. There were frictions, based generally on unfounded prejudices, but in time a mutual trust and respect, as well as healthy questionings, grew as British and American officers and men worked together with surprising, though hardly perfect, harmony. Powell's presence at Doolittle's headquarters had contributed to an appreciation of the British fighting airman; his death left a personal vacuum.

Christmas 1942 in North Africa was not a joyous season; the Anglo-American advance from the west into Tunisia was bogged down. Further east and to the south, in Tripolitania, the legendary "Desert Fox," Field Marshal Rommel, was being forced back into

Tunisia by Montgomery, who by December 25 occupied Sirte, about halfway between El Aghelia and Tripoli. Still, both elements of the Allied forces that day were a long way from Tunis.

Their convergence upon the Axis forces did not contribute to a clarification of command lines and the function of the various air forces, however small and overtaxed. The nature of the North African war had afforded little opportunity for the employment of the heavy bombers in what was termed "strategic bombardment" —there being few targets for that type of bombardment. (This would blossom into full fury in Europe within a couple of years.) On Christmas day, Doolittle, anticipating an eventual unbogging of his air force, wrote to Spaatz a few of his ideas on how best to use the Twelfth when the time came to drive the Axis out of Africa. His plan was to concentrate "on docks, marshalling yards, stores, boats, airports and airplanes, in not only Tunisia, but Sardinia [the great island air base directly north of Tunisia] and Sicily as well [also a source of Axis supply pouring into Tunisia]." Only then, he suggested, should the bombing be turned on "all concentration of troops and, if necessary, the cities of Tunis and Bizerte, using high-altitude precision bombing, low-altitude bombing, torpedoes and strafing."

The impending convergence of the Allies—it was assumed and hoped—created further problems for Eisenhower. The French had joined the British and the Americans, but not without demands of a political, jurisdictional nature (i.e., General Henri Giraud refused to permit French troops to serve under British command); the French were also woefully equipped and depended upon British-American supplies and equipment. The "division of labor" between the various air forces in North Africa was a headache also: who was responsible for what? Eisenhower was naturally most occupied with the ground war and tended to depend more and more on his senior air officer, Spaatz, who divided his time between England and the Mediterranean.

By the first of the year 1943, plans for a general reorganization were under way to simplify or expedite the overlapping command structure (and perhaps to assuage the French). Spaatz was brought from Britain to command what by mid-February would be called the Northwest African Air Force (NAAF), thus bringing all the Allied air forces in North Africa under one command —the Twelfth, the Eastern Air Command, and the Western Desert

Air Force (mixed British and American) that had been aiding
Montgomery's push toward Tunisia. Doolittle, as commander of
the Twelfth, would then be head of the Northwest African Strategic Air Forces (NASAF), thus enabling him to implement in general the suggestions he had submitted to Spaatz on the previous
Christmas.

This also meant that between him and the skeptical Eisenhower
there was airman Spaatz, who did not share Eisenhower's skepticism. During those December-January days when it was possible
to fly, Doolittle concentrated his heavy bombers on the harbors of
Bizerte and Tunis and, when necessary, upon Rommel's supply
ports, Sousse and Sfax to the southeast. Initial losses were en-
couragingly light, but in time, as the supplies built up in the Axis
camps, the B-17s encountered heavy flak concentrations as well as
the formidable Focke-Wulf 190 fighters.

It was, in fact, not a clean-cut war (if such exists); the quick,
decisive Tunisian victory had eluded the Allies. Rain and mud
were added irritants; morale was low. On January 14 Roosevelt,
Churchill, and their staffs—plus two all but irreconcilable French
leaders, neither of whom contributed to the smoothness of the
meetings, Giraud and General Charles de Gaulle—met at
Casablanca, in French Morocco, to discuss the future conduct of
the war. (It was here that, among other decisions, the combined
bomber offensive and the concept of "unconditional surrender"
were initiated.)

On the following day Doolittle prepared a memo, marked
"Confidential" and entitled "Work of the Twelfth Air Force."
Perhaps the timing of the memo was coincidental, but while the
Allied High Command wrangled at Casablanca to determine what
would happen to their troops, Doolittle in his memo told his men
what *had* happened to them.

It complied with standard Army form, complete with the usual
"SUBJECT" and "TO:" headings and numbered paragraphs. Paragraph 1 was a simple one line statement: "I am writing this letter
to let you know that I am proud of you."

He then proceeded to set down for them what his airmen undoubtedly already knew but were not aware that any member of
the Top Brass had noticed or was willing to admit: "You and I
know that the Twelfth Air Force was faced with tremendous problems when it arrived in North Africa. Expected equipment did not

arrive, was incomplete, or wouldn't work. Officers and men alike lacked training and experience in the type of warfare with which we were faced. The conventional type of Air Force organization was not adaptable to the theater. We arrived in the rainy season and the mud made airports impossible and living conditions unpleasant. The move to the eastward was more rapid than had been planned and the Twelfth was obliged to move forward, fighting, far ahead of schedule and under most difficult conditions.

"In spite of all obstacles, you have done a job. I address you members of combat crews, and I include too, the ground crews, the services, who by their arduous efforts under adverse conditions made your achievements possible. In order to meet a threatening situation, you have been obliged to fly long missions over highly defended enemy territory, under extremely difficult operating conditions. To the best of my knowledge and belief, you have flown more missions under such conditions than were ever accomplished before. In the past two months you have dropped thousands of tons of bombs, shot down or destroyed hundreds of enemy aircraft, and damaged many more. We have had losses, too, but the enemy has paid a price of more than two to one for every airplane we have lost. This record against an experienced enemy, operating from established bases is better than good—it is damned good."

Other portions of the memo summed up the decorations earned by the men of the Twelfth Air Force; Doolittle explained the general organization of the unit, he even described their aerial battleground—"from French Morocco in the west to Tunisia, a thousand miles to the east. We have airdromes stretching from one end to the other of this thousand-mile front. Our units are actually based on some twenty of these fields. Many other airdromes are now stocked and ready for use and a great many more are being improved, particularly in the forward area, to accommodate our constantly increasing force."

Doolittle also conceded that "So far in this campaign, combat crews have not had adequate rest and relief," but he also honestly informed them that "I am not going to tell you that hereafter you will automatically be sent to a rest camp, or be relieved of operational duty, after flying a certain number of missions or hours." He then outlined a possible plan to accomplish just that.

He summed up, in Paragraph 10, stating that the Twelfth "has done a magnificent job under almost insuperable difficulties . . . I offer my congratulations to every officer and man in the outfit which I am very proud to command."

Within two days the ground war began to stir as the American II Corps began its advance east toward Sfax on the Tunisian coast, which, if successful, could place a wedge between the forces led by Colonel-General Jürgen von Arnim in the north and Rommel in the south. On January 18 the Axis forces, Italian and German, struck back, which, although the counter attack petered out by the end of the month, was ominous. By this time Rommel had abandoned Tripolitania and had withdrawn into Tunisia. The fighting revealed weak points in the Allied line which Rommel was quick to note.

Weather hampered Allied aerial operations, but Doolittle's own combat missions of early February reveal a stepping up of activity after the winter lull. On the eighth he flew as copilot on a B-26 mission; his second mission for that same day was aborted by engine trouble. The next day he took his place in the right-hand seat of a B-17 of the 301st Bomb Group; on the tenth he led a shipping strike in a B-25 of the 310th Group; three days later he flew with the 17th Group (B-26s) on yet another strike—the targets were harbors, shipping, supply lines, airfields. An important target, Palermo, on the north coast of Sicily, a vital shipping point between Italy and Tunis, was successfully visited on February 15. As the Fortresses of the 77th Bomb Group left the area, Doolittle could see a large ship in the harbor disgorging smoke and the dock area was left a shambles. And so it went on—on February 23 Doolittle flew along as a guest in an RAF Wellington to strike at Bizerte.

With the Allied effort concentrated closer to Tunisia, headquarters of the Twelfth (or more properly, NASAF) was ordered to Constantine, some 200 miles east of Algiers. Bruce Johnson was sent ahead to arrange for staff quarters. By this time Spaatz, too, had been ordered to North Africa. He was to coordinate the operations of the various Allied forces operating in North Africa; the over-all command of Allied aerial operations in the Mediterranean were under Air Chief Marshal Sir Arthur Tedder.

Spaatz ranked Doolittle, and it was Johnson's delight to seek out more luxurious quarters for his boss than could be found by Spaatz's own headquarters advance man, Colonel Harold B.

Willis. This became their own private war and a source of irritation, for the duration.

In Constantine Johnson found a splendid mansion, the property of a wealthy and influential Frenchman, which he was certain could not be equaled by Willis. It was perfect for Doolittle, since he wished to house the entire headquarters staff under a single roof for more efficiency. The Frenchman would not bow to military persuasion, but Johnson, with civil intervention, managed to get the owner to relinquish the mansion, provided he and his family could continue to live in the cellar.

"The security involved in this was too great a risk and I leaned on him hard, finally gettting him to agree to move out completely," Johnson has written. "But when Jim arrived and heard the man's tale of woe, his kind heart would not allow the hardships this old bastard painted to the skies. So, with one move, he blew all my security precautions out the window and told the man that he and his family could live below . . ."

An even greater menace to the security of the new headquarters at Constantine erupted during the new move. After a late January–early February lull, von Arnim and Rommel struck.

The two-pronged blow fell upon the American sector of the line in Tunisia, beginning with von Arnim's *Frühlingswind* ("Spring Wind") on February 14, 1943, in the north and Rommel's *Morgenluft* ("Morning Air") two days later in the south. The plan was to accomplish no less than a breaching of the American line, then moving northward to cut off the British and French, thus isolating the Allies in one Tunisian pocket. Both Constantine and Bône (also an important Allied air base) on the Algerian coast were objectives of the concerted attacks.

The inexperienced Americans soon proved to be no match for the toughened troops of Rommel's Afrika Korps and von Arnim's panzers. Gafsa, about 20 miles behind the American lines, fell the first day and its forward air base was abandoned; the next day, the line bending nearly 60 miles, saw the loss of the fighter bases at Fériana and Thélepte. It was about here, on February 17, that Rommel turned his forces northward so that he and von Arnim could converge and bring *Frühlingswind/Morgenluft* to a climax. This was to occur at a place named Kasserine Pass.

That day the two airfields were evacuated, the assorted P-39s, P-38s, and Spitfires were flown to rear bases and then 60,000 gallons of fuel were dumped, rations burned, and eighteen aircraft destroyed to deny them to the oncoming enemy troops. During the hectic days of the evacuations, weather, of course, permitting, the harassed airmen flew bombing and strafing missions.

Ground troops fought in Eisenhower's words, "a series of ineffective though gallant delaying actions on the way back toward Kasserine Pass, a spot clearly indicated as one to be strongly held." The defenses did not hold and on February 21 Rommel's tanks broke through the Pass and began heading for Tebessa to the west, beyond which lay one of the surviving airfields at Youks-les-Bains, and northward toward Thala. From crowded Youks, missions were mounted in poor weather to assist the ground troops who were beginning to dig in for counterattack. At the same time, British troops were rushing down from their sector to aid the Americans near Kasserine.

Doolittle's heavy bombers were too often hampered by poor weather, but on the critical day of the battle of Kasserine Pass the weather broke a little; even so, B-17 flights that day were unsuccessful. Three missions returned to their bases without dropping their bombs and one group apparently lost in the clouds and with navigators untried and confused, strayed 100 miles away from Kasserine Pass and dropped its bombs on Souk-el-Arba, well within Allied lines. The bombing killed several Arabs, wounded a number of them, and destroyed considerable property. "We had to act fast to avoid disagreeable consequences," Eisenhower would later write in *Crusade in Europe*. But it proved to be no serious problem: "We had already learned that the native population would amicably settle almost any difficulty for money . . ."

This was expeditiously done and Eisenhower, who had moved his headquarters from Gibraltar to the St. George Hotel in Algiers, could give full attention to the battle which, by February 23, was obviously turning around; the Axis push was running out of steam and soon they were being bombed and strafed as they fell back from Kasserine. Rommel and von Arnim had lost their gamble, which would prove to be the last major attempt by the Axis in Tunisia. Ill, dispirited, and disillusioned by Hitler and his orders "to fight to the end," Rommel abandoned North Africa within two weeks of the battle at Kasserine. His once fabled Afrika Korps was turned over to von Arnim. To the south, facing Montgomery, were German and Italian troops under General Giovanni Messe.

But the tide had turned and the presence or absence of the celebrated Desert Fox no longer mattered in North Africa.

With the Axis forces being squeezed into a constricting corner
of Tunisia, the conduct of the war assumed a businesslike neat-
ness. The primary job of Doolittle's Strategic Air Force was to interfere with the shipping—perhaps as high as 3,000 tons of
supplies a day—coming in from Sicily. The sea traffic from
Tunisia, too, must be stopped. This blockade would place a strain
on the Luftwaffe and the Italian Air Force. At the same time, the
Allied heavy bombers would strike enemy bases whenever possible, and the Coastal Air Force, under Air Vice Marshal Hugh P.
Lloyd, would protect Allied shipping in the Mediterranean with
antisubmarine patrols as well as shipping strikes.

By late February Nazi convoys moving into Tunisian ports were
attacked by high-altitude B-17s, even as far east as the Lipari Islands, north of Sicily and, for the Axis, ominously close to Italy.
On February 15 Doolittle led a mission, with the 97th Bomb
Group, over Sicily where the port of Palermo was struck. Toward
the end of the month he dispatched the heavies to the island of
Sardinia, just north of Tunisia, where Cagliari was hit. And so it
continued, with the Germans shuttling supplies and men into
Tunisia, and the Allies raising havoc. One of the most spectacular
raids on Palermo occurred on March 22 when two dozen Flying
Fortresses of the 301st Bomb Group bombed, blowing up some
thirty acres of dock area, sinking four merchant ships, and blowing two others out of the water onto the dock. During this same
period Doolittle also concentrated on the various ports of Tunisia
—Bizerte, Tunis, and Sousse.

The Germans had developed a system of air transport—a fleet
of about 500 aircraft, employing principally the old war horse
Ju-52 and the giant Me-323, some times two flights a day origi-
nating in Naples, staging in Sicily, and then crossing to Tunisia.
Doolittle was aware of this reinforcement shuttle and kept a wary
eye on the mass troop movements. Although a plan had been
made to deal with a sizable concentration of these transports, the
plan was canceled when the Kasserine Pass battle erupted.

Because the British had broken the German High Command
code—the so-called "Ultra Secret"—the Allies were able to read
most of a Nazi commander's orders, even those coming from
Hitler, before they arrived in a Nazi command post. Thus were

the transport schedules known down to the last number, including fighter escort. The temptation was to jump the gun, of course; instead, many an aerial convoy was permitted through unharmed with the hope that a worthwhile target would materialize. This operation was given the code name Flax.

The word came through Ultra that a mass flight had been planned for the morning of April 5 and preparations were immediately initiated for an interception.

While Ultra gave the Allies a certain leverage over the Germans, there were also disadvantages. When exploiting the information, the Allies had to be certain that the Germans would not suspect the source in any way. Fake reconnaissance planes were dispatched and made to appear to have spotted a convoy or a flight of transport planes, as if by accident or pure good fortune. The fake spotter planes frequently flew in poor weather and were lost, and a good number were destroyed by Luftwaffe escorts.

There was also a personal, restrictive, disadvantage for Doolittle. Having been informed of the existence and function of Ultra, he was advised by its "keeper," Group Captain F. W. Winterbotham, to stop flying missions with his men. It was a general rule that anyone who knew about Ultra was not supposed to expose himself to the possibility of falling into enemy hands. It was assumed that, if drugged, a captive could reveal the existence of Ultra and lead to its abandonment.

Doolittle, nevertheless, continued to fly missions. Weighing his chances, he reasoned that the effect on the morale of his crews was greater than the probability of his falling into German hands. (Patton, also in on the Ultra secret, refused to remain in behind-the-lines headquarters, preferring to be up front with his troops.) Meanwhile, plans for a new Flax mission had been formulated.

On the morning of April 5, a patrol of more than two dozen P-38s intercepted a large formation of at least 50 Ju-52s, with an escort of Me-109s, FW-190s, and even a half dozen vulnerable Ju-87s just off Cap Bon, at the northeastern tip of Tunisia. Below them, in the Mediterranean, were about twelve Axis merchant vessels. The Lightnings swept into the attack. Meanwhile, B-25s, flying low, struck at the supply vessels, blowing up a destroyer of the convoy; above, the P-38 escort dealt with the air cover, claiming 15 Axis planes. B-17s, with Spitfire escort, bombed the Tunisian reception centers at El Aouina and Sidi-Ahmed with fragmentation bombs. Those transport planes that did break through would have little to come to. Co-ordinated with these several attacks were others, by B-17s and B-25s, upon the staging centers in Sicily.

Flax proved to be devastating to the Axis, with a probable loss of 200 aircraft, about 40 of which were destroyed in the air; Allied losses amounted to 3 shot down and 6 missing. What with the turn of tide against the Axis in North Africa, its supply and reinforcement run to Tunisia had to be continued, despite losses. All through April the decimation continued and on the eighteenth reached a climax in what came to be known as the "Palm Sunday massacre." Three squadrons of the 57th Fighter Group, plus one squadron (the 314th) of the 324th Fighter Group of the Ninth Air Force, flying P-40s, encountered a "gaggle of Geese" off the Tunisian coast. While the Spitfire escort dealt with the German escort above, the P-40s whipped into the "Geese" (Ju-52s, of which there were estimated to be 100). At least 50 (as high as 70 were claimed) of the Ju-52s were shot down, as were 16 of assorted escort aircraft at a cost of 7 to the Allies.

Doolittle's B-17s had begun striking more distant points, nearly 100 dropping bombs on the docks, marshalling yards, and airfields at Naples early in April. A great blow was also dealt the dwindling Italian Navy when the Fortresses bombed Sardinian ports and sank the *Trieste* and damaged the *Gorzia,* both heavy cruisers. By mid-April severe attention was paid those ports in Sicily that might afford evacuation havens for Axis troops escaping Tunisia—provided they could get away safely from their aerial tormentors.

By April 20 practically all of the Luftwaffe that had been based in Tunisia had slipped off to Sicily, which brought them little respite as Sicilian fields were battered by Allied bombers and fighters. By early May the Luftwaffe retained but two airfields in Tunisia on Cap Bon, while ground troops were squeezed into a small pocket on the northeastern tip—hemmed in by the British First and Eighth Armies, French troops, and the American II Corps, under its new commander General Patton. The Afrika Korps surrendered on May 11, with von Arnim himself captured the next day. Messe managed to hold out a little longer, capitulating on May 13. Torch was over. The Allies were decidedly established in the Mediterranean.

Soon Bruce Johnson, now a lieutenant colonel, was dispatched to Tunis to set up a headquarters and find housing for Doolittle and staff. He succeeded in finding a school that could be used for headquarters, with housing facilities for many of the staff, and three fine houses all in a row for Doolittle and his immediate staff. Johnson, as usual, took pride in outwitting his rival Willis whose accommodations for Spaatz came nowhere near Doolittle's for comfort and luxury. Such niceties were lost upon Doolittle, who would settle for a place to rest—and read mysteries for relaxation —and an efficiently functional headquarters.

During the seven months of Torch, he had managed to keep from upsetting Eisenhower's equanimity too much—although hearing about Doolittle's bombing missions caused some discomfort. Doolittle himself was upset when he read a column by Drew Pearson which made a point of how a great aviation hero was being mistreated by Army brass and relegated to a minor role as head of something called a "strategic air force." The stateside papers had been full of stories about General Montgomery, General Eisenhower, General Patton, of course, even Rommel, but very little about General Doolittle. An item such as Pearson's, though unfounded, might have caused Eisenhower to lose his famous grin for a time. Doolittle had no idea who the source might have been; he felt compelled to write Spaatz, denying the Pearson allegations, concluding with "I have the best job in the Air Force; strategic bombing is the Air Force."

Spaatz had seen the article and said nothing, knowing as he did that it did not represent Doolittle's view at all, but since Doolittle had brought it up, he, in turn, replied, closing with the words, "I would not trade you for anyone else to be in command of the Northwest African Strategic Air Force." As for Eisenhower, not a word.

Out of Torch had come an effective air force which had performed a myriad of tasks under difficult conditions. Its green crews were battle-hardened and would prepare and instruct those who would follow. While true strategic bombardment against the Axis had not yet been fully tried, the interdiction of shipping and air transport and other missions were indications of what was yet to come. Of equal import was the demonstration by the Allies, particularly British and American, of their capability for working together, despite certain basic differences. North Africa was also the proving ground of the theory of air-ground co-operation without yoking air power to ground commanders.

With North Africa won, the next large prize, with intermediary stops, was Mussolini's Italy. Before this would occur, Doolittle would have his chance to prove the efficacy of strategic bombardment.

Sixteen

Before the invasion of Italy, even as the planning proceeded, there came a time for reassessment as well as for looking ahead. As a commander Doolittle could not, of course, spend all of his time flying missions with "the boys." There were staff meetings he had to attend, as well as his own conferences and "critiques." Then, too, there was the time spent "flying the desk" and interminable paper work, some of it made less onerous by Vandenberg, his chief of staff, as well as by Allard and Johnson.

In his own planning, Doolittle had arrived at certain conclusions. There had been vaunting predictions of the miracle of American production, with the promise of aircraft in numbers that seemed at the time astronomical. (Hitler and Goering dismissed them as impossible; they were wrong again.) But the preoccupation with things, machines and not men, impelled Doolittle to set down a few observations which he addressed to Major General Barney Giles, then assistant to the Chief of the Air Staff, and whose major concern was personnel. On May 24, 1943, Doolittle wrote:

As an old development and production man . . . , I am convinced that the airplane production curve has now crossed the crew production curve and that unless something is done about it, the present unbalance between airplanes and crews will become worse instead of better. The reason for this is that while mass production methods are readily available to increase the production rate of aircraft, this is not true of combat crews. The airplane part that previously required an hour to fabricate might well be stamped out at a rate of a thousand per hour with suitable mass production machinery. This is not true of personnel. It takes just so long to teach an individual to fly, bomb, navigate or shoot. The rate can be stepped up somewhat by improved instructional methods. It can be doubled by doubling the number of schools. It can never be put on a mechanical mass production basis. I think we might as well face this problem now and base our airplane production not on the maximum amount of aircraft we can build, but on the maximum number of crews that can be developed to most efficiently utilize them. We can either continue with the present airplanes and develop the inevitable surplus, some of which may be utilized in the OTU's [operational training units] and some of which may be given to any of those Allies who may develop crews to manage and man them, or, alternately, we may divert part of our production to the tooling up and manufacture of new and superior aircraft and thus automatically reduce the quantity and increase the quality of those aircraft we are producing.

Doolittle, as often as he could, tested the aircraft firsthand and became acquainted with his crews on the ground and in the air. His views were based as solidly on practice as on theory; there was no place for luck in his scheme of things. He did not deny the existence of chance, but maintained that "the chap that plans the best and works the hardest has the best luck." But the random machinations of fate could not be denied. As an example of this Doolittle was apt to recall "the most unsuccessful mission I ever led."

Intelligence reported the presence of three Italian warships— two heavy cruisers and the battleship *Roma*—in the harbor at La Spezia, Italy, almost directly north of Tunisia. These ships could pose a serious threat to Allied supply lines in the Mediterranean and Doolittle was determined to get them. The mission was approved and Doolittle and his staff "planned well" and "worked hard," and no less than three bomber groups—one per ship— were assigned the task, more than 100 B-17s. The bombers were

armed with 2,000-pound demolition bombs and 1,400-pound ar-
mor-piercing bombs. The plan called for the planes to come in at
right angles to the ships in the harbor and simply blow them out
of the water. The mission was scheduled for June 5, 1943.

The flight out was uneventful—over the Mediterranean, past
Sardinia, and Corsica, to the Ligurian Sea. In the lead plane
Doolittle cheerfully noted the light flak and the three sitting ducks
below in the harbor. The three groups emptied their bomb bays
onto the ships, the water churned, geysered, and bubbled under
the massive attack. The great formation wheeled about and
Doolittle led them back to North Africa.

To his chagrin, reconnaissance photos taken after the mission
revealed that one of the cruisers had been missed altogether, the
other had had a turret blown off, and the *Roma* remained in its
berth as if nothing had happened (a single bomb pierced the deck,
went through the ship, and came out the bottom without exploding). In short, nothing had come of the mission. "It was something that *couldn't* happen," Doolittle remarked in surprise. But it
had. And to his further chagrin, later, after Italy had withdrawn
from the Axis to join the Allies, the *Roma* pulled out of port and
headed for Malta to be turned over to the British, when near
southern Italy a single German plane swooped down upon the
battleship, dropped two bombs, and sank it. (He would later learn
that the bombs were radio-controlled; at the time, however, it was
rankling.)

Within a week of the ineffectual mission to La Spezia, the strategic application of air power would be impressively demonstrated
as an overture to the invasion of Sicily. On May 13, the day that
Messe surrendered and ended the fighting in North Africa, ships
of the Royal Navy began shelling the tiny Mediterranean island of
Pantelleria. The island, about forty square miles of volcanic rock,
lay in the pathway between Tunisia and Sicily. Garrisoned by Italian troops it was vaunted as their Gibraltar or Malta—which, in
fact, was not true. Still, it was strategically placed, what with its
airfield, to interfere seriously with the next phase of the war in the
Mediterranean. Reconnaissance revealed at least a hundred gun
positions emplanted in its cliffs and rocks. It had but one true harbor, which would make amphibious landings a hazardous thing. A
radar station on the island could detect the movement of ships
and aircraft; its many caves along its rocky shores provided a

haven for submarines and torpedo boats. Intelligence estimated a garrison of some 10,000 Italian troops, as well as 600 German. Pantelleria would clearly not be an easy island to take from the sea. To the south, another strategic though less formidable island, Lampedusa, posed a similar threat.

A plan, code-named Corkscrew, was evolved which would attempt to take Pantelleria, as well as Lampedusa, from the air. After the initial naval shelling, the aerial attack began on May 18 with nuisance raids by medium bombers and fighter bombers upon the port of Pantelleria and Marghana airfield in the northern section of the island. This pounding, co-ordinated with a naval blockade, continued for practically the rest of May. Doolittle moved in his B-17s on June 1, with the concentration of bombs falling upon gun emplacements and the shore batteries. The Fortresses, accompanied by other aircraft, continued this hammering until June 6—D-minus-5.

An even greater bombardment lashed at the hapless troops on Pantelleria with the initiation of a round-the-clock (although the term was not yet in popular use) attack, growing more powerful each day as the time for the Allied landing attempt drew near. On June 10 the sky over Pantelleria was so congested with aircraft that bombers frequently circled waiting their turn to bomb. Some 1,100 sorties delivered 1,571 tons of bombs on that single day.

Reconnaissance photos, taken regularly, revealed great destruction wreaked upon the airfield, with consequent almost negligible interference from enemy aircraft (which might also have come in from Sicily and Italy but did not). When landing parties did come ashore, more than eighty enemy planes were found, in various stages of damage, at Marghana.

On June 8 and 10 leaflets were dropped calling for the surrender of Pantelleria, but with no response from the military governor, Vice Admiral Gino Pavesi. D-day followed on the eleventh, with the arrival of troops of the British 1st Infantry Division that had embarked the night before from Africa. Simultaneously the island continued to be battered through the night and the next morning by aircraft and the heavy guns from the Allied ships off shore. The assembled, scurrying landing craft were ready to begin their rush for the beaches when several reports came in just before noon that a white flag had been seen flying from a hill, suggesting surrender—although no official word had come through yet. The invasion proceeded and during the landings a number of FW-190s and a handful of Me-109s appeared, to be driven off by Allied fighters.

The British troops waded ashore to minimal resistance, some scattered and a flurry of small-arms fire and a recalcitrant donkey that bit one British soldier. By 5:30 in the afternoon surrender ceremonies were underway in the vast underground hanger at Marghana. Further missions against Pantelleria had been canceled and attention switched to Lampedusa, which capitulated on the following day (although not officially to the single RAF pilot who, having developed engine trouble, was forced down and blithely demanded the island's surrender). After the fall of Pantelleria the heavy bombers turned again to the airfields of Sicily—code-named Husky—the next objective.

Since Pantelleria had been virtually taken by air power, when questioned by the press on the day of surrender, Doolittle proudly said so. From this it might have been inferred that the use of strategic bombardment could very well have determined the future of the war—or, at least, that was how Eisenhower interpreted it. He prepared a rather curt memo to Spaatz referring to Doolittle's "quoted statement made to the press" and the fact that it had "escaped proper action by the censors"; he concluded with: "It is highly unwise, therefore, to issue statements that generalize and develop a doctrine of war from incidents that happen in our theater." Eisenhower ultimately decided to file the memo rather than send it, giving Spaatz its substance verbally. Whether it was because Doolittle had gleaned some personal publicity, thus perhaps wounding a few egos, or because he had spoken out on the proper use of air power, thus wounding the remaining egos—of ground troops and seamen—that Eisenhower reacted so strongly, is not known, since he chose not to make a great issue of it. But for Doolittle it meant working hard again to resell himself to Ike.

Figures, however, proved the truth of Doolittle's statement—his Northwest African Strategic Air Force had dropped 80 per cent of the bomb load on Pantelleria, the Tactical Air Force (under Air Vice Marshal Sir Arthur Coningham) provided 18 per cent, and the naval forces, 2 per cent. Doolittle would later write of it as a "combined Naval and Air victory," a gracious comment considering the percentages.

By July 10, when the invasion of Sicily began, Pantelleria was a functioning Allied air base, home of the U.S. 33rd Fighter Group and its P-40s.

Doolittle succinctly described the Sicilian operation. "A part of Strategic's contribution to this operation," he wrote late in 1943, "was the careful herding of a large part of the Axis air force into a small area of eastern Sicily and then destroying it there. The method was simplicity itself. There were a limited number of airfields in Sicily. We started on those in the west, destroyed as many planes as possible on the ground (the concentration was high and dispersal poor) with fragmentation bombs, then 'post holed' the fields with demolition bombs until they were no longer usable. The remaining enemy planes were forced to move eastward, securing operational fields in the Gerbini area. An all-out air offensive then destroyed many of these planes and drove most of the rest out of Sicily. The almost complete freedom from air opposition experienced by our ground troops spoke highly for this operation and for the effective cover furnished by the Tactical Air Force."

The prelude to the invasion of Sicily began late in the evening of July 9, 1943, when troops of the British 1st Airborne Division and the American 82nd Airborne Division, after being towed in gliders from North African bases, were cut loose in the general vicinity of Syracuse, on the southeastern coast of the island. At the same time, American paratroopers were to be dropped in the Licata-Gela area in the west on the Gulf of Gela. The operation did not go as planned. The pilots of the tow planes—Dakotas, the British designation for the Douglas C-47s—were inexperienced in night operations and the British glider pilots unfamiliar with the operations of the predominantly American-made gliders. High winds, too, interfered. Consequently, troops were scattered widely over the landing areas (of the 137 gliders released at Syracuse, 12 came down in the landing zone, 56 were scattered, and 69 splashed into the sea).

The main Allied landings began at 4:00 A.M. on the tenth and the tough battle for Sicily erupted. Thirty-eight hard-fought days and nights followed as Patton, leading the American Seventh Army, and Montgomery, leading the British Eighth, raced each other for Messina on the northeastern tip of Sicily and just across the narrow Strait of Messina from the toe of Italy.

During the height of the battle for Sicily Doolittle led a mission that was as historic as it was controversial: an aerial attack on Rome. By mid-July it was obvious the the Allies' main objective was Italy and that Sicily was being secured as a staging area and for its air bases. Although the Italians had just about given up, the Germans had not and reinforcements were being transported from Germany itself, as well as drawn off other war fronts, by rail to repel an Allied invasion of Italy.

The great hub of the Italian rail system was centered in two marshalling yards, the Littorio and the San Lorenzo, at Rome. Rome as a military objective confronted Eisenhower and his staff with serious moral decisions. It was the very heart of world Catholicism and any destruction of religious shrines would bring universal condemnation. Rome was also a storehouse of classic architecture and priceless art treasures—their loss would arouse multitudes, cutting across religious and political lines. However, while the Allies agonized over this, the Germans poured more reinforcements into Italy. On June 15 the mission to bomb the marshalling yards near Rome was authorized.

Eisenhower delayed the mission until the heavy bombers could be spared from the Sicilian campaign. Meanwhile, studies were made of the location of the marshalling yards, as well as of some airfields which could also be hit, vis-à-vis Vatican City and other religious sites. Crews were carefully trained for the mission, with Catholics given the option of excusing themselves from it.

There were four areas on the target map boldly outlined in white, with white block letters identifying them as "Vatican City, S. Maria Maggiore, St. John Lateran and St. Paolo Basilica"; all four bore the legend: MUST ON NO ACCOUNT BE DAMAGED.

The fact that the marshalling yards were a good distance from central Rome made for some simplification. Enemy headquarters in central Rome would not be attacked because of their proximity to the off-limits portions of the maps.

Before the mission was well under way, leaflets were dropped warning the Italians of the impending attack (this at the same time served to alert the Germans that the American bombers were on the way).

Doolittle selected the veteran 97th Bomb Group to lead the mission—158 B-17 Flying Fortresses of NASAF—flying himself as copilot with the group's commander, Colonel Leroy Rainey. In addition, B-24s of the Ninth Air Force, some 112, joined in the mission, as did several groups of B-25s, B-26s, with P-38 escort—a total of about 500 aircraft, the most massive mission up to that time.

Reginald Thayer, then a navigator with the 97th Group, "will alway remember the briefing for that mission. There were the usual comments by the Intelligence Officer, the Communications Officer, the Armaments Officer, the Meteorology Officer, etc. as for any other mission.

"But early in the briefing, the Group C.O., Col. Leroy Rainey, disclosed the target and introduced Doolittle. As Rainey began his remarks no one in the briefing tent knew that the target that day was Rome, and none of us noticed Doolittle standing quietly and unobtrusively at the rear of the tent in his flying suit. Rainey's words went something like this: 'Gentlemen, about a year ago a guy named Tojo stuck his neck out and about four months later a man named Doolittle slapped him down with the first air raid on Tokyo. Today we are flying the first air raid on Rome and General Doolittle will be leading us. I am pleased to present General James Doolittle.'

"At this point General Doolittle walked up to the front of the tent and very calmly reviewed the mission plan with us. I don't specifically remember much of what he said except for one thing. In discussing alternative targets in the event that Rome was obscured by clouds or bad weather, he very calmly said, '. . . but we'll hit the primary target.'

"Something about the way he said that, firmly but without a touch of braggadocio, convinced me that morning that Doolittle would lead us to Rome, regardless of weather, flak or fighters—and that's just what he did. Listening to him I somehow *knew* that we would find the target, hit it and get back.

"I never was one to scoff at flak, but I was so confident on that mission that I looked with scorn on a modest flak barrage that was thrown up at us as we crossed the coast of Italy going in. I think it was near an Italian naval base at Civitavecchia (but I can't swear to that after 31 years). I have a faint recollection of wondering why we had been routed to cross the coast at that point. However, we sailed right in, hit the target and had no losses in our group.

"I'm convinced that Doolittle's comments at the briefing were a major factor in the accuracy of the bombing that day and the safe return," Thayer concluded.

In the morning of July 19, the Fortresses attacked the railway yards at San Lorenzo, while the Liberators dropped bombs on the Littorio, causing serious damage to tracks, rolling stock, workshops, and nearby factories; the only damage to a religious shrine occurred when some bombs fell off target and landed near the basilica of San Lorenzo, noted for its twelfth-century frescoes. Later in the day the medium bombers bombed airfields in the vicinity of Ciampino and the Littorio, also causing serious damage.

The Axis response was all but negligible, with about 30 enemy aircraft making half-hearted attacks on the bomber formations. Flak was more of a problem, being both concentrated and disconcertingly accurate. Despite this, of the 500 plus aircraft participating in the Rome bombing that day, only 2—a B-25 and a B-26 over Ciampino—were lost.

To counter the obvious Axis propaganda that would immediately ensue, reconnaissance photos were taken as soon as the smoke cleared to prove that, excepting the accident at San Lorenzo, only military targets had been attacked. The greater outcries, in fact, came from the United States and Great Britain; Pope Pius XII himself voiced a calm suggestion that all belligerents give serious thought to "the safety of peaceful citizens and of religious and cultural monuments." While the bombing did seriously interfere with Axis rail operation (coupled with the results of a similar attack on the Naples marshalling yards, it blew a 200-mile hole in the Italian rail system), it had a wider political effect. Mussolini, who had been away from Rome conferring with Hitler on the worsening Sicilian situation, returned to the appalling sight of smoke rising from San Lorenzo, the Littorio, and Ciampino. It was a portent, for both King Victor Emmanuel III and the Italian people had become disenchanted with Mussolini, the war, and their pugnacious Allies, the unyielding Germans. Within the week Mussolini was driven out of office.

Mussolini's fall did not end the fighting in Sicily, for the Germans, though withdrawing, resisted tenaciously. But by August 17, 1943, Sicily fell when Patton led his troops into Messina, winning the race with his rival, Montgomery. The Germans declared martial law in Italy, which would render that war-sick country a great battleground. That the airwar was expanding was demonstrated by two missions flown on the same day that Sicily became Allied territory. The first was a great double-pronged mission mounted from Britain by Eaker's Eighth Air Force: the costly Regensburg/Schweinfurt attacks, which had reached deep inside the heart of Germany itself.

The second mission was carried out by Doolittle's own NASAF and diverted attention momentarily from Sicilian and Italian targets by striking at a growing concentration of German aircraft near Marseilles, in southern France. A total of 180 Flying Fortresses dropped fragmentation bombs on the airdromes at Istres/Le Tube and Salon, destroying nearly 100 aircraft and damaging several more as well as various buildings and workshops.

On September 3, the day of the British invasion of Italy (codenamed Avalanche) Doolittle summerized the evolution in the employment of air power since the initial groping weeks of his coming to North Africa. He wrote to his former Chief of Staff, Brigadier General Hoyt Vandenberg, who had left in August for Washington to become Deputy Chief of Air Staff. (He would later return to Britain as Deputy Commander-in-Chief, Allied Expeditionary Air Forces. Replacing Vandenberg as Doolittle's chief of staff was the very able Brigadier General Earle E. Partridge.)

"The air battle is becoming interesting," Doolittle wrote. The German enemy, he indicated, "realizes that if we are successful in invading Italy, we can establish air bases and attack vital military manufacturing facilities in Southern Germany. Apparently fearing this, he is fighting desperately. His fighters are far more aggressive than we have previously found them [the recent bloody missions to the Ploesti oil fields in Romania from North Africa and the Regensburg/Schweinfurt from Britain were still fresh in Doolittle's mind]. He is using aerial bombing and rockets extensively. Yesterday, a half dozen rocket planes got through the fighter escort and attacked the bombers which had finished their bombing and were down on the deck. The enemy fighter raised their noses and lobbed a half dozen rockets in—without damage—before our fighters closed in and dispersed them. Sixty to seventy enemy fighters attacked the escort—they *always* attack now—and shot down six. Three more are missing. The P-38s shot down 23 enemy fighters.

"Every day brings its air battle and while we are more than

breaking even, the Hun has the advantage of initiative (against escort fighters), fighting over his own territory, and the inherent advantages in a short-range fighter over a long-range fighter. Our losses will increase until the Hun is knocked out."

This last was as true in the air as on the ground; during the delaying battle of Sicily, German troops were brought into Italy from Austria, France, and the Fatherland itself. Although Italy surrendered on the day of the invasion (the official announcement not being made by Eisenhower and Mussolini's successor, Marshall Pietro Badoglio, until September 8), these movements portended a hard, long war ahead in what Churchill liked to call (and perhaps even seriously believed was) "the soft underbelly of the Axis."

The name of Patton was curiously absent from the role of Allied commanders who led the Italian invasion; it was his rival Montgomery who opened the battle by moving across the Straits of Messina in Sicily into the "toe" of Italy at Reggio. Eisenhower had taken Patton out of the limelight because of the still unpublicized "slapping incident" which occurred during the height of the battle for Sicily. Under stress himself, Patton had visited an Army hospital and, upon learning that an enlisted man had been admitted without a battle wound, was alleged to have struck him with his gloves and generally raised a great deal of commotion, shouting and cursing at the "yellow bastard."

The incident occurred on August 10, 1943, and was kept "within the military family," as put by General Sir Harold Alexander, Patton's immmediate superior. Eisenhower concurred, and besides ordering Patton to apologize to all concerned, from the man who had been slapped through the hospital staff, he took him out of circulation and exiled Patton to Palermo, ostensibly to head a military government. (It was not until November that newspaper columnist and radio commentator Drew Pearson aired the story and an immediate hue and cry for Patton's skin erupted in the United States. This was what Eisenhower had anticipated and feared when he "exiled" Patton, but he also recognized Patton's capabilities as a commander and felt Patton's apologies and a long period of calm was enough. He did not offer up "Georgie's scalp," sincerely feeling that "Patton is indispensable to the war effort.")

Patton, meanwhile, fretted out his exile in Palermo, guiding his staff over the historic battlefields of Sicily and doubting his indispensability. Meanwhile the war in Italy, no longer the "soft under-belly," dragged on and the old warrior grew restive and sullen.

Some inkling of his mood and personality was revealed to Doolittle later in the Italian campaign. It was after Doolittle had settled in at Bari on the Italian mainland that he had occasion to fly to Algiers. Since he would be passing over Sicily, it occurred to him that he might just "drop in and see Georgie."

He radioed the control tower at Palermo, informing them that he was about to land and would they notify "General Patton that I am landing immediately and would like to pay my respects."

Doolittle then moved into a landing pattern, brought his plane in, and taxied up to the line. "Just as I did George came driving up in his jeep.

"Well, he stepped out of his jeep, this big, tremendous guy and threw his arms around me, with tears as big as watermelons running down his cheeks."

Patton lifted the smaller Doolittle and sobbed, "I didn't think anybody would come to see a son of a bitch as mean as I am!"

The two friends visited and it was good for Patton who did feel desolated and harassed (Eisenhower seemed to be ignoring him and there were voices crying for his dismissal). The situation was, of course, temporary, for Eisenhower had plans for Patton (as well as Doolittle) in the future. Doolittle has observed, "Ike used Georgie Patton very much like a chap would use a pit bulldog. When there was a fight, he would say, 'Georgie, go whip 'em.' Then as soon as the fighting was over, Ike was inclined to collect Georgie and get him out of circulation because Georgie said just exactly what he pleased. Quite frequently—well, I would say that almost always—in my mind he was right. Quite frequently, it would have been better if he had not said it."

It is unlikely that it would have cheered Patton, had he known that when he entered Messina, followed shortly by Montgomery, the Mediterranean became a second-class theater of war. Having taken Sicily, the Allies were not in harmony on the next move. The British preferred continuing in the Mediterranean by moving into Italy; the Americans demurred: having cleared the Mediterranean, it was their belief that it was time to move directly upon Hitler via the English Channel into France. There was, eventually, a compromise. Italy would be invaded, thus forcing Hitler to draw troops out of France and Russia; it would then become a war of

containment with high priority on troops and supplies then divert-
ing to Overlord, the projected cross-Channel invasion of Europe
in the spring of 1944.

An important objective of the Italian invasion was the complex
of airfields grouped around Foggia in southern Italy. An air force
there would be capable of striking important strategic targets in
various Nazi-held countries as well as Germany itself. A fore-
shadowing of this came on October 1, 1943, the day both Foggia
and Naples fell to the Allies, when for a third time (the first: the
oil fields at Ploesti, August 1; the second: the aircraft factories at
Wiener Neustadt, Austria, August 13), a heavy bomber mission
was mounted from the Mediterranean. This was undertaken as
part of the Combined Bomber Offensive (codenamed Pointblank),
a plan which would co-ordinate the missions of the RAF and the
Eighth Air Force, based in Britain, with the air forces based in
North Africa to apply heavy pressures from two directions on Germany's war production centers which, in turn, would place a strain
on the defenses of the Fatherland.

The October 1, 1943, mission from North Africa was primarily
aimed at the Messerschmitt complex at Wiener Neustadt in Austria, which was to be attacked by five B-24 groups. At the same
time, four B-17 groups of 12th Bomber Command were
dispatched to attack fighter plane factories in Augsburg, Germany.
The Fortress formations, because of thick overcast, could not
bomb as briefed; instead they dropped on secondary targets in
Germany and Italy. The five Liberator groups had no trouble
finding Wiener Neustadt and unleashed some 187 tons of
explosives on the Messerschmitt works, sowing effective areas of
destruction and damage through assembly shops, storage facilities,
and rail lines servicing the factories.

While this presaged what was to come for Germany, it also
grimly foreshadowed the intensity of the resistance the American
bombers and fighters would meet. Heavy German fighter opposition came up to meet both formations, about 60 planes against
each, with the Liberators further harassed by heavy flak. The P-38
Lightning fighter escort managed to keep the enemy fighters away
from the Fortresses, although 3 were lost. The B-24s were harder
hit by fighters with 37-mm cannons mounted in the wings and
with rockets, such as those to which Doolittle referred in his letter
to Vandenberg. As a result, 14 Liberators were shot down. The

precise numbers of enemy fighters destroyed was not determined, although the P-38 pilots claimed 8. The mission, particularly against Wiener Neustadt, was successful, despite the rather heavy losses; at the same time, it contained lessons for all combatants.

Almost the moment Foggia fell into the hands of the Allies, on October 1, Bruce Johnson was off for Italy to find quarters for Doolittle and his burgeoning staff. To his dismay, Johnson was met by his rival, Colonel Willis. "Every apprehension I had came true," he would recall. "When I reported to him in Foggia, he showed me the selected sites. His (General Spaatz's) were big and comfortable, mine (General Doolittle's) were bombed to the point that extensive repair would be necessary . . . There wasn't one damn thing left in Foggia that wasn't blown to hell or too small."

After relieving himself of a few tart comments to Willis, Johnson set out in a jeep "with a map of the countryside and went on tour" along the eastern coast. Seventy miles southeast of Foggia he came upon Bari, on the Adriatic Sea. The city was generally untouched by bombs and contained hotels and dwellings that Johnson felt would do just fine. He came upon an impressive building, which he soon learned had once housed the high command of the Regia Aeronautica (Italian Air Force), but found himself confronted with even more of an obstacle than Colonel Willis—a British commander—for Bari was in the hands of the British.

"The British commander wasn't even civil about it," Johnson commented later, having requested the building. "He simply laughed and said no."

When he returned to North Africa, "still so mad that I stuttered for the first time in years," Johnson reported the incident. He recalls that Doolittle merely "squinted at me across his desk and then said he would see what he could do about the situation." Before long, Johnson was involved with elaborate plans for moving their headquarters to Bari. Meanwhile, Doolittle and Partridge were dividing their efforts between the various combat operations and the organizing of yet another air force. On November 1, 1943, the Fifteenth Air Force was activated at Tunis, Major General James H. Doolittle commanding. The Fifteenth flew its first mission on November 2, back to Wiener Neustadt from Tunisia.

The primary mission of the Fifteenth Air Force had been

defined as "the attainment of air supremacy through counter air force operations and the destruction of the enemy's aircraft production." The Messerschmitt plant at Wiener Neustadt was just such a target, but it was clear that such targets provided a most active "counter air force operation." Attacking aircraft industry targets generally gave the term a double meaning. The fact that the Allies were concentrating on aircraft installations obviously meant that they hoped to eliminate as much of the German home defense system as possible before beginning an all-out airwar against Germany. Consequently, aircraft targets were savagely defended by the Luftwaffe. An attack, if all went well, on a Messerschmitt, Focke-Wulf, or Junkers factory could mean potential Nazi defense aircraft were destroyed before ever leaving the ground. At the same time, the great air battles such attacks brought about resulted in the destruction of German planes in the air—if bomber gunnery was good.

The Me-109s, FW-190s, Me-110s, and Ju-88s swarmed up to meet the mixed formation of 112 Fortresses and Liberators, shooting down 5 of each, with an additional Fortress reported missing. Claims of enemy fighter kills were high, the Americans reporting no less than 56 destroyed (it was estimated that between 120 to 160 German fighters attacked the American bombers). The Fifteenth Air Force would claim the mission as an outstanding event; despite the heavy fighter attacks, more than 300 tons of bombs fell into the target area, wiping out an assembly plant and two hangers and causing damage to another shop and hanger in addition to other damages.

The mission was an auspicious debut for the new air force, although in fact it was new only in name and on paper. It had, in fact, been created from the Twelfth Air Force's bomber command (eventually the Twelfth became a tactical air force), so that the changeover had readily been accomplished. Formation of the Fifteenth Air Force, a new strategic arm to operate out of Italy, was the idea of General Arnold who was seconded by Spaatz. Objections came from Britain, from both the RAF Bomber Command head, Air Chief Marshal Arthur Harris, and from the U. S. Eighth Air Force commander, General Ira Eaker. Forming a new strategic air force meant that Eaker's own bomber command would suffer, as it had when the Twelfth had first been formed. With the Eighth Air Force finally coming into its own as a formidable striking force, Eaker could not endorse the concept of another air force to do what he and Harris "round-the-clock" could do from England.

Doolittle sided with Arnold and Spaatz, basing his view on the weather factor. Nearly twice as many operations could be made out of Foggia during the winter months than could be made out of English bases. Eaker countered with the view that weather over bases was not as important to missions as weather over targets (this was before the advent of "blind bombing"). On the other hand, lifting off from and landing on fog-enshrouded bases could be risky.

Both Harris and Eaker believed that a concentration of air power in Britain would contribute to the success of the planned invasion of Europe (Overlord) and the Combined Bomber Offensive (Pointblank), whose immediate objective was the elimination of the Luftwaffe by any and all means.

Arnold, Spaatz, and Doolittle prevailed and the Fifteenth came into being. Six days after its initial mission to Wiener Neustadt, Doolittle flew to Gibraltar to meet with Tedder, Spaatz, and Eaker. Eaker gracefully accepted the realities and joined in the discussions on how the operations of the Eighth and the Fifteenth could be co-ordinated, particularly as they pertained to Pointblank. It was agreed that it would take time before the new air force would be able to become a full partner in Pointblank (partly because it was liable to being drawn off to strike tactical targets in Italy). But as soon as possible, the Fifteenth Air Force would attack such Pointblank targets as those at Wiener Neustadt, Augsburg, Budapest, and Regensburg (all aircraft factories) as well as ball-bearing factories in Turin, Stuttgart, and Schweinfurt.

On November 8 Doolittle returned to Tunis, where preparations were under way for the move to Italy. The day was an anniversary. Just one year before he had arrived in North Africa with the Twelfth Air Force; soon he would be leaving with the Fifteenth— the move was set for December 1. Meanwhile, he continued to schedule missions, both strategic, such as striking again at German-held airfields in France, and tactical, in support of the land battle in Italy, by bombing enemy lines of communication.

Bruce Johnson was busy preparing the quarters at Bari for Doolittle and his staff. One member, however, would be missing: Allard, who was seriously ill with phlebitis. Although he managed for a while to conceal his worsening condition from Doolittle, it became necessary around the time of the move to Italy to fly him to England and then to the United States for hospitalization.

On December 1, 1943, Doolittle was established in his vast office at Bari. It was a busy port city with a population of about 200,000; the port itself was crammed with Allied ships, unloading supplies, ammunition, and other cargo. Doolittle and Partridge had barely settled into their luxurious quarters when, to everyone's surprise, the Luftwaffe came calling. In the night of December 2/3 a formation of 3 aircraft passed over the city, dropping "window," strips of metallic foil that would confuse ground radar. Then about 30 Ju-88s dropped parachute mines and bombs across the city and harbor. Chance as much as anything caused the bombs to fall into two ammunition ships in the harbor. The resulting detonations also blew up adjacent ships and great fires soon enveloped the harbor.

The explosions blew out the windows in Doolittle's quarters and glass littered the floor. Partridge, observing the havoc in the harbor, was impressed with the "beautiful fireworks," but both he and Doolittle were more impressed with the luck of the Luftwaffe. It took three weeks to clear up the harbor; seventeen ships had been destroyed by the fires that followed the explosions. About a thousand men, soldiers and sailors, had been killed or injured. Hospital supplies in the ships had been lost, as were some 10,000 tons of steel plank. The dock area was a shambles.

The success of the German attack on Bari was not all luck, however. Allied defenses had been caught napping—the most important radar station had not been operating that night and the "window" took care of the rest; telephone communications had been poor; and, as a British historian indicated, "the defence arrangements suffered from being under too many authorities." Thus night fighters had not intercepted the raiders, nor had antiaircraft fire disrupted them. The Luftwaffe returned in the night of December 13/14, but without the spectacular results of the earlier raid. It was, in fact, the last sizable bomber mission undertaken by the Luftwaffe in 1943. By the end of the month there were less than 30 operational German bombers remaining in the Mediterranean. Most of the others had been withdrawn to Germany.

While the Luftwaffe pressures may have diminished in Allied-held Italy, vexations, sometimes from way out in left field, would pop up. During this period Doolittle received word that certain eager city fathers of Los Angeles were vigorously promoting a scheme to change the name of Los Angeles International Airport to Doolittle Airport. They were opposed by the then mayor, who undoubtedly wished the name of the city to stay. He wrote Doolittle asking him to oppose the idea also. Doolittle discussed this minitempest with his chief of staff, Partridge, and both agreed they would side with the mayor. Doolittle then answered His Honor's appeal by informing him that it being the custom to name airports for dead aviators, he wasn't "yet willing to make that sacrifice."

In Washington Joe Doolittle, too, fielded her share of problems from the Los Angeles area. Metro-Goldwyn-Mayer, planning to film *Thirty Seconds over Tokyo,* approached her for permission to have Doolittle portrayed by Spencer Tracy. She referred the studio to the Air Force, feeling that neither the Tokyo Raid nor Doolittle, at the time, were "owned" by her; whatever the Air Force decided would be fine with her. Permission was granted and M-G-M agreed to pay $50,000 into a fund for the Air Force Aid Society. Almost immediately after, Joe began getting calls (she characterized is as "hounding,") from another film studio offering her $250,000 if she would withhold permission from M-G-M. The experience was a revelation to her—and an education in Hollywood economics and ethics. But Metro produced the film. Doolittle, meanwhile, had his own problems to face in a less-than-sunny Italy.

By the end of that dismal December, Doolittle was ordered out of Italy. The winter stalemate had set in along the Gustav Line, the German defense line that ran across Italy between Rome and Naples, one of whose strong points was Monte Cassino, site of a sixth-century Benedictine monastery. Poor weather curtailed both the ground and the air war.

On January 3, 1944, Major General Nathan F. Twining assumed command of the Fifteenth Air Force. Doolittle, accompanied only by Partridge and an aide, had already flown to England.

Seventeen

On January 6, 1944, Doolittle became commander of the Eighth Air Force. It was a challenging position, but not an enviable one in the light of the personal-political situation in which it placed him. There was real pleasure in knowing that he had succeeded in "selling himself to Ike," though none in, even inadvertently, appropriating the job of the very able Ira Eaker.

An outstanding commander and superb airman, Eaker received his commission in 1917. Like Doolittle, he participated in early Billy Mitchell-inspired, historic flights that promoted both the air service and aviation. One was a Pan American Good Will Flight that began at Kelly Field, Texas, on December 21, 1926, and ended at Washington, D.C., on May 2, 1927, after visiting more than twenty Central and South American countries. Then a captain, Eaker was pilot of the *San Francisco,* one of the five Loening amphibians that had made the trip. As a major he was chief pilot in January 1929 of the *Question Mark,* a Fokker C-2 trimotor, in which a new endurance record was established. For nearly a week the *Question Mark* circled over Los Angeles (and dramatically refueled in the air) until engine trouble forced it down after more than 150 hours aloft. In command of the flight was Eaker's good and lifelong friend Major Carl Spaatz.

Unlike Doolittle, Eaker had made a career in the Army Air Service, managing at the same time—during the Depression doldrums—to earn degrees in both journalism (in post-Second

World War years he would be a widely read columnist) and the law. Soft spoken, courtly, Eaker demonstrated an impressive organizational skill and a fine sense of command and at the same time inspired deep loyalties. These unique qualities enabled him to create a great air force, practically out of nothing, during the early, tumultuous days of the war.

Eaker had built the Eighth Air Force from its very beginnings as Eighth Bomber Command in England in 1942, when its first strategic mission consisted of a striking force of 12 B-17s; he had suffered through its growing pains, the early heavy losses before the advent of long-range escort fighters; he had fought for men and machines, and on Christmas Eve 1943 managed to mount a mission of more than 700 bombers. Having achieved this massing of air power, Eaker was informed that he would be replaced by Doolittle and transferred south to command the Mediterranean Allied Air Forces. His disappointment was revealed in a letter to Arnold when Eaker wrote that it would be "heartbreaking to leave just before the climax."

But leave he did, for an immutable decision regarding personnel had been made long before. Initially, the cross-Channel invasion was to have been commanded by a Briton, but as American production had supplied the preponderance of both means and men, with huge numbers of American soldiers "invading" Britain, even the staunch Churchill agreed to an American commander for Overlord. That American, all agreed, was to be Eisenhower (General Marshall had been considered, but it was felt he was more essential to the Washington scene).

When Eisenhower accepted the command he stipulated that he would bring certain members of his staff with him, including as his "chief air man" the English Air Marshal Tedder and as top American commander General Spaatz. The latter two selected Doolittle, with Eisenhower's approval, to head the Eighth Air Force. But Eaker was very popular with his own men as well as the British, and two of his top officers made it plain that they preferred not serving with Doolittle, who approved their transfers when they applied for them.

As for the English, Eaker's popularity began right at the top, as Doolittle soon learned. One of his first official acts was to pay a courtesy call on the King, George VI. Doolittle was ushered into the King's office in Buckingham Palace. The King entered, sat down, indicated that Doolittle should also be seated. "We sat there for a little while with neither of us saying anything." Doolittle felt that any conversation should be initiated by the King, but that appeared not to be forthcoming.

"Finally after quite a while—and the King didn't say anything —I broke the silence by saying that I was very pleased to be in England, that the treatment my people and I had received was of the highest order, that the relationship between our troops and the British was excellent and felt that one of my primary jobs was to maintain that fine relationship that existed between the British and the Americans."

In response to this the King, who had a slight stammer, said, "We're c-c-c-certainly sorry to lose Eaker!"—which, Doolittle remembers vividly, "left me a little nonplussed."

Further "nonplussing" followed when he paid his first visit to his British counterpart, Air Chief Marshal Harris of the RAF's Bomber Command. The soul of decorum and military courtesy, Doolittle entered Harris's office, snapped a salute, and announced himself. Harris acknowledged his presence and then returned to shuffling papers on his desk, leaving Doolittle standing and waiting (and fuming just a little). The papers neatly piled, Harris finally turned to his guest, and the two men, Doolittle finally seated, had a reasonably pleasant visit. Just as he was leaving, Doolittle said to Harris, "Anytime you wish to see me, Sir Arthur, you will always be welcome at my office." As they worked closely, all formalities eventually dissolved and they became "Bertie" and "Jimmy."

Doolittle was further "nonplussed" to learn that the British, with their fondness for "hush-hush" and "cloak-and-dagger," gathered intelligence on friend and foe alike. A close personal friend of Doolittle's, correspondent and writer Bill Courtney, came by one day and informed him that a certain friendly person who looked in on Doolittle now and then was actually a British Intelligence officer. Doolittle tested the individual by making "an interesting but not precise statement" on the next look-in. Since British and American intelligence agencies were working together closely, Doolittle had his own Intelligence Officer check on the Doolittle dossier the British kept—and there recorded was the statement.

There were other fascinating entries. It was Doolittle's practice to invite senior officers in his command to a weekly meeting in his mess so that "we could get to know each other better and discuss mutual problems." About a thousand British WAAFs (Women's Auxiliary Air Force personnel) worked in the Eighth Air Force Headquarters. In keeping with his custom, he invited the WAAF senior officers to these meetings in his mess also. His dossier contained this entry: "Doolittle must like the ladies as he frequently has them, including WAAFs, at his quarters." Also interesting was Harris's contribution to the Doolittle dossier: "Doolittle is entirely dependable but is more difficult to deal with than Eaker."

Whatever his personal disappointment, Eaker remained in England until mid-January to assist during the period of transition. On New Year's Eve he met with Doolittle, Spaatz, and others to discuss the reorganization of the Eighth Air Force. Spaatz's official role was that of commander of the U. S. Strategic Air Forces in Europe, the major function of which would be to co-ordinate the operations of the Eighth and Fifteenth Air Forces in what would be the American contribution to the Combined Bomber Offensive. Major General Frederick L. Anderson, former commander of the disbanded Eighth Bomber Command, acted on behalf of Spaatz in the strategic operations of the Eighth and Fifteenth. The nucleus of Doolittle's own staff also came from the former Eighth Bomber Command. Organizationally and operationally, Doolittle inherited a powerful, functioning air force unlike the pragmatically shifting forces he had been given in North Africa. There he had begun from scratch and built, at times inprovisationally, until the Twelfth had become an air force, only to be transmuted into the Fifteenth (which would come into its own during the spring of 1944). The Eighth Air Force, no longer drained by the exigencies of the Mediterranean campaign, was indeed mighty.

Doolittle was to have no less than twenty-five heavy bomber groups under his command, plus fifteen fighter groups. The tactical Ninth Air Force, independent of the Eighth but also stationed in Britain, could provide an additional eighteen fighter groups, if needed, for escort. In addition, there were the most important, but generally unsung, supply, maintenance, and other service units. In January 1944 there was a total of more than 5,000 American combat aircraft in Britain.

In his New Year's message for 1944 General Arnold stated his estimation of how things stood at home and what would be expected from the American airmen in Europe during the coming year.

a. Aircraft factories in this country are turning out large quantities of airplanes, engines and accessories.

b. Our training establishments are operating twenty-four hours per day, seven days per week training crews.

c. We are now furnishing fully all the aircraft and crews to take care of your attrition.

d. It is a conceded fact that OVERLORD and ANVIL [the invasion of Southern France, later renamed Dragoon] will not be possible unless the German Air Force is destroyed.

e. Therefore, my personal message to you—this is a MUST—is to, *"Destroy the Enemy Air Force wherever you find them, in the air, on the ground and in the factories."*

Doolittle concurred with Arnold's message, underscoring his own views in a letter to Brigadier General Uzal G. Ent, then commanding the Second Air Force, a training command in the United States that provided crews to the Eighth and other air forces. The most formidable weapon was still the German single-engine fighter, he wrote Ent on January 2, 1944. "All rocket guns, aerial bombings, self-propelled missiles, etc. are a means to an end, namely, to loosen up our formations and cause stragglers so that the single-engine fighters can come in for the 'kill.' "

He stressed the need for tight formations, saying that these afforded "mutual fire support" and "co-ordinated offensive tactics by our fighter escorts to prevent the Hun's rocket and other trick aircraft from getting within range of our formations and the avoidance of stragglers by slowing down . . . Don't throttle away from your cripples.

"The speed of bombardment formations en route to and from, and particularly when departing from the target area, must be reduced to the extent necessary to insure that the slowest airplane is able to maintain its proper place."

(This was an innovation, for the tendency was to bomb and

"get the hell out." Aircraft unable to keep up with the formation were left behind, generally to be finished off by the Luftwaffe. Tight formations had been the rule—whenever possible. Now Doolittle would hammer away at it, plus the idea of using the entire formation, with all its firepower, to protect the cripples.)

Doolittle wrote to Patton (who would be set free from Sicily by the end of January), comparing the riches of the Eighth with the poverty of the Twelfth. "Down there," he wrote, "the problem was to make something out of nothing. Up here it requires an equal or greater amount of ingenuity to effectively utilize the almost unlimited resources at our disposal. Down there, when you were not 'under the guns,' any modest success was apparently appreciated. Up here miracles are confidently anticipated. Have been a little slow in getting my miracle department organized, but hope for the best."

Even more pervasive a problem than the Luftwaffe because of its unpredictability was the weather, whether over the targets or over the English bases. Hardly had Doolittle settled into his office at High Wycombe, Buckinghamshire, before he was confronted with that enigma. On January 11, 1944, after a period of poor weather over Germany the Air Force meteorologists promised a clearing over several aircraft industry targets at Oschersleben (Focke-Wulf), Halberstadt (Junkers), and Brunswick (three Messerschmitt plants). To hit such objectives visual sighting was a prerequisite, as previous radar bombings through overcast had proved.

No less than 663 bombers in three massive formations (one of B-24s and two B-17s) took off from their East Anglian bases, escorted by several groups of P-47 Thunderbolts and P-38 Lightnings, six squadrons of Spitfires, and one group of P-51 Mustangs which met them over the target areas. Takeoff and assembling in the air were complicated by poor weather over the bases. The weather held, however, over Germany, so the mission was still on. But as the formations approached their objectives, the weather closed in, obscuring the target areas of the 2nd (B-24s) and the 3rd (B-17s) Divisions—and that weather was headed for England. This could make landings a serious problem, especially for crippled bombers.

The 1st Division (B-17s) was within 50 miles of its objective, Brunswick, when Doolittle, taking all factors into consideration, made his decision: he sent out a recall for the 2nd and 3rd Divisions. All aircraft, except for a wing of B-17s from the 3rd Division (whose commander felt they were deep enough into enemy territory to go the rest of the way) and the 1st Division, swung around and headed for home, dropping their bomb loads on assorted targets of opportunity in western Germany. Of the original 663 bombers that took off that morning, only 238 succeeded in bombing their primary targets (139 at Oschersleben, 52 at Halberstadt, and 47 at Brunswick). While the bombing accuracy was good, even effective, in spite of the reduced forces, the aircraft that accomplished it suffered a mauling from the Luftwaffe.

The formations were met by over 200 single- and twin-engined German fighters—in such numbers, partly, because the bombers appeared to be heading for Berlin. The only escorts that were able to provide the bombers any protection to the target area were the 49 P-51s of the 345th Fighter Group. The German twin-engined fighters broke up the bomber formations with rocket fire, and then the single-engined Me-109s and FW-190s swept through. A total of 60 B-17s were lost that day at a cost of 39 German fighters (although the bomber crews claimed more than 150).

It had not been a very good day for the Allies; the weather closed in and canceled operations for several days. A break finally seemed to come on January 24, but again the elements turned capricious and Doolittle ordered another recall. This earned him a reprimand in the form of a "suggestion" from Spaatz: "No recall [is to] be issued by ground headquarters after [our] entering the enemy coast. In order to preserve the integrity of the Air Commander, it would be wise to keep him advised of changing weather conditions wherein he could not receive the fighter cover promised him, and leave the decision up to the Air Commander as to what course of action he should take."

In his biography of Doolittle, on which he was given much assistance by Jack Allard, Quentin Reynolds gives a more dramatic version of this incident. According to Reynolds, Spaatz summoned Doolittle to his office and opened the conversation with the bristling words, "It looks as though you haven't the guts necessary to run a big air force." When queried about Reynolds' version of this encounter, Doolittle said, "Don't recall Tooey's exact words and agree while the quoted words don't sound like him, that was the 'spirit' of his comment." Despite his respect and affection for

Spaatz, Doolittle said he had a problem containing his temper—but managed to, continuing to maintain that his decisions were based on personal experience and upon the fact that he did not want to gamble with the lives of men in the weather they had experienced. He added that Spaatz dismissed him with a rather curt "That will be all."

Spaatz, in short, was not convinced that Doolittle's decisions had been correct—and he was also anxious at this time to get on with the Pointblank operation, which was to eliminate as much as possible of the Luftwaffe and the German aircraft industry in preparation for further strategic bombings and the invasion of Europe. He was understandably concerned since the recalls affected the Pointblank timetable. Doolittle felt Spaatz unduly influenced by his meteorologists—one of them being his old friend, Dr. (now Colonel) Irving Krick of the meteorologically misguided cross-country flight of 1934. Doolittle had not forgotten that flight and continued to view Krick with some suspicion, summing up with, "Krick was an excellent meteorologist but like most, erroneously considered meteorological prognostication as more of a science than the art it was."

Within a few days after the second recall, Doolittle had the opportunity to put his point across to Spaatz about English weather and its prognostication. He and Spaatz had planned a flying visit to several bases in England in *Boots,* Spaatz's B-17, piloted by Lieutenant Colonel Robert Kimmel. The first day they visited a few bases, ending up for the night as guests of the 92nd Bomb Group at Alconbury, in Huntingdonshire. The next morning, about to leave, they checked with the weather man and, assured the weather was fine, they then walked out into a pouring rain.

Doolittle studied the lowering clouds and said, "Let's head for home."

Instead they took off to visit more bases and on the way to the third, Duxford, near Cambridge, which housed the 78th Fighter Group, found themselves ten minutes out of Snetterton Heath, completely enveloped in English weather. True, the weather was clear at 18,000 feet, but as Quentin Reynolds would observe, "there were no airfields at 18,000 feet."

The fog was too thick for Kimmel to locate the base so he decided to drop down to hedgehopping level, hoping to find a spot to land the Fortress. This, while hazardous, was the only solution.

As Kimmel gingerly brought the great plane down all three men peered into the mist for a likely place to set down. Kimmel found a clearing that appeared to be unblemished by wiring, livestock, or other impedimenta. It was not a large field, but Kimmel guided the plane in by skillfully sideslipping; the single problem was a stone wall that lay in their path, but Kimmel managed to bring *Boots* to a jolting stop without a collision.

Spaatz and Doolittle stepped out of the plane, studied their predicament, and suspiciously studied the darkening clouds. Spaatz spoke first, "You were right, Jim."

"I hate uncalculated risks," Doolittle replied, "even with a pilot like Bob Kimmel at the controls. And remember, Tooey, most of the kids flying our heavies don't have the experience of a Bob Kimmel."

Doolittle would make that point even more emphatically, if a bit indelicately, later in the year. Spaatz, accompanied by Eisenhower, visited High Wycombe one day and Doolittle briefed the two on a bombing mission then in progress. Spaatz, somewhat mystified, asked why they were striking the secondary target.

"Because," Doolittle replied, "the primary is socked in."

Spaatz countered with the information that Colonel Krick had assured him the primary was clear.

Doolittle double countered with, "Colonel Krick is full of shit."

As Doolittle tells it, "There was an awed hush and then I was asked why I had made that statement. I said, 'We just talked with a pilot who is in a fighter plane over the target.'"

Doolittle then explained how the problem of the target weather had been solved. Colonel Budd J. Peaslee, who had once commanded the 384th Bomb Group, had conceived the idea of sending out a fast fighter plane before the bombers took off, to reconnoiter the various targets and to keep the air commanders informed as they penetrated deeper into Germany. Doolittle supported the plan and approved the formation of the First Scouting Force, which had been "born in the tormented mind of a bomber commander," in the words of Peaslee (who neglects to say he was the bomber commander), "when his formations were broken up by unpredictable weather conditions along the target route. Many bomber missions had been ruined by these circumstances, aerial collisions had frequently occurred with heavy and useless loss of life. The responsibility of aborting a force of 800 bombers that might do great service to the Allied cause over critical targets was not one to be taken lightly."

Once he had Doolittle's backing, Peaslee proceeded to organize the First Scouting Force, selecting eventually former bomber pilots who would fly the scout plane (the P-51D was employed). A wingman, a fighter pilot, generally accompanied the scout and was provided by the 385th Fighter Squadron (of the 364th Fighter Group). The results of the work of the First Scouting Force very quickly proved the validity of the concept in terms of missions accomplished, lowered accident rate, and, most importantly, lives saved.

Not all of Doolittle's decisions made while he commanded the Eighth Air Force were as well received; there were two which he regarded as "important but very unpopular." One concerned the standard number of missions required of air crews which was twenty-five. By early 1944 certain patent changes had come about: the number of fighter aircraft available to the Eighth and the Ninth Air Forces had increased and the number of bomber losses were reduced. Thus, as Doolittle reasoned, crews had a "much better chance of making a full tour. It took about ten missions before a team really became first class. Adding five missions to the crew's tour [of twenty-five], in fact, resulted in not a fifth, 20 per cent, but fully 33⅓ per cent improvement in the effectiveness of a crew. You were keeping them when they had gotten best."

The crews did not appreciate the percentages, feeling instead that it affected their chances of making it. Doolittle could understand their feelings, but effective crews were hard to come by and green crews still required the usual number of missions to shake down. However, the survival rate and the general improvement in bombing efficiency proved Doolittle correct. So correct that the standard tour was subsequently increased to thirty-five missions.

Another controversial decision earned Doolittle the epithet of "killer." This occurred shortly after his arrival in Britain during a visit to Eighth Fighter Command Headquarters at Bushey Hall, a few miles northwest of London. Accompanied by the commander, Major General William E. Kepner, he visited the operations room to listen in on, and observe on maps, a mission then in progress. He could hear the fighter and bomber commanders in cryptic radio conversation, and even a German intercept that indicated that the bombers were off course.

Kepner radioed Colonel Glenn Duncan, commander of the 353rd Fighter Group: "Are you with bombers?"

"Affirmative," Duncan replied.

"Are you on correct return track?"

"Negative." Off course as they were, the P-47s escorting the bombers were low on fuel. Duncan was soon heard saying to the bomber commander, "I am sleeping in my bunk tonight; will change course."

"Thanks and me, too," replied the bomber leader.

But shortly after Duncan led his Thunderbolts onto the correct return track, the bomber formation came under German fighter attack.

Doolittle then asked, "What will he [Duncan] do?"

"He will return," answered Kepner, "and attack the GAF [German Air Force] though he may have to ditch in the Channel."

Soon the radio crackled with cheers from the bomber crews as Duncan's Thunderbolts returned to the scene and drove off the German fighters. Then Duncan's voice was heard again, "I am turning again and won't be back because I may have to swim."

"O.K.," acknowledged "B" Wing commander, "and thanks."

Kepner was quite pleased with what the new commander of the Eighth Air Force had just heard—"a superior performance by a fighter group escort"—and invited Doolittle into his office. On the wall was the motto of Eighth Fighter Command:

OUR MISSION IS TO BRING THE BOMBERS BACK

Doolittle studied the sign for a moment then said, "From now on that no longer holds. Your mission is to destroy the German Air Force."

Kepner was stunned. He had been arguing for months to free his fighters from the bombers, and here in a fraction of a moment Doolittle was unleashing them. "I could hardly say anything for a few seconds," Kepner has written. "I was overjoyed. That was precisely what I wanted to do. As I recall, I said, 'Thank God, we can now operate like fighters ought to.'"

Following a discussion of future operations and the change in the fighters' mission, Doolittle was ready to leave. Glancing again at the motto, his parting words were, "Take that damned thing down!"

The implications of Doolittle's decision might be gleaned from Kepner's view of the function of the fighter: "A fighter plane is one hundred per cent offensive. Its only final success lies in 'attack and conquer,' individually or collectively in teamwork. It combines the cavalry charge, the power maneuver, and the Hitler blitz, provided it has freedom of local decision as an individual or, as we used them, in flights of two, and mass assault action by units in mutual support. The action must flow through the enemy's weakness to finally destroy him where he is incapable of counterattack. Surprise and destruction of the enemy are necessary for success. This result it cannot accomplish when spread thin everywhere over extended areas that move with the speed of flight. In this situation it is strong nowhere. It can only deter and hinder to a limited degree enemy fighter plane attacks; it cannot stop them. Our fighter forces must destroy the enemy before they reach their target. In the Eighth Air Force during World War II the target was our bombers."

When Kepner announced the Doolittle decision to his fighter commanders, it was warmly greeted with cheers. When filtered to the bomber leaders, however, the reaction was unanimously negative. The divisional, group, and squadron commanders, Kepner recalls, "all lit into me with loud protests. It was as if I was personally destroying our own bombers." Doolittle, too, was subjected to protests. "The bomber commanders were all very distressed," he remembers, and they approached him "individually and in groups to tell me I was a killer."

The distress was understandable in the light of the bomber commands' previous experience when the loss rate of aircraft was in direct proportion to the lack of fighter protection; unescorted or meagerly escorted missions were often chewed up by the Luftwaffe. But by early 1944 both bomber and escort formations were larger—and the P-51 was capable of flying as far as Berlin (as could the P-47s and P-38s with additional fuel tanks). Bomber crews had become accustomed to the comforting proximity of the "little friends" (this was especially true of the veterans of early battles, now group commanders and higher). If the fighters were off racking up their own victories, what would happen if some of the Luftwaffe came in from another quarter?

Doolittle and Kepner argued that all fighter victories would mean that correspondingly fewer enemy fighters could get at the bomber formation, including even fighter planes destroyed on the ground. Nor was the plan to have fighters ranging all over the sky, virulent with "ace fever." It would be possible to assign several fighter groups to each mission, some of which would fly in the vanguard and along the flanks to "destroy the German Air Force" wherever it could be found. Meanwhile, other groups would fly with the bombers, though high above, on call for any assistance.

"It took a long time for the bombers to accept the idea," Kepner recalls, "if they ever did really. They did of necessity improve their own gunnery."

Doolittle stuck by his decision, which proved itself. Once again he had taken the calculated risk and it had worked. Later in the war, when the Luftwaffe was all but eliminated from the air, the Allied fighters applied their hunting technique closer to the ground, against airfields with sitting-duck aircraft, trucks, electrical installations, canal boats, even locomotives.

Destroying the Luftwaffe was the major theme of Doolittle's initial campaign for the Eighth Air Force, code named Argument, a co-ordinated series of attacks by the Eighth and Fifteenth and the British Bomber Command against high-priority targets, most associated with the aircraft industry, in Germany. These missions would come to be called "The Big Week," February 20–25, 1944. Late in January Arnold had written to Spaatz, "Can't we, some day and not too far distant, send out a big number—*and I mean a big number*—of bombers to hit something in the nature of an aircraft factory and lay it flat?" The Big Week (the epithet was coined by contemporary newsmen, not the Air Force) was Spaatz's reply to the query.

The Week opened the night of February 19/20 with a contribution from the British who bombed Berlin and Leipzig, the latter associated with the aircraft industry. February 20, in the American camp, dawned dubiously with clouds and icing conditions over the English bases of the Eighth Air Force and heavy cloud over the targets in southern Germany of the Fifteenth. Besides, the situation in the Italian campaign diverted Eaker's heavy bombers to the beleaguered Anzio beachhead. The Eighth, meanwhile, was poised with more than 1,000 bombers ready to go and an escort of seventeen fighter groups from both the Eighth Fighter Command and the Ninth Air Force.

The ultimate decision lay with Spaatz, who was forced to balance the risks with the objectives of Argument, which, he hoped, could be concluded by March 1. When he said "Let 'em go," he was ordering Doolittle to launch the largest allied air mission up to that time. What with good fighter escort, the work of the RAF the night before, and improved weather conditions, the opening phase of The Big Week for the U. S. Strategic Air Forces (despite the absence of the Fifteenth) began auspiciously. Of the more than 1,000 bombers dispatched, 941 bombed their targets, a high proportion with great effect. Although great losses were expected, only 21 bombers and 4 fighters were shot down.

And so it continued for five additional days, through February 25, with one day off for the Eighth because of weather on February 23. Doolittle was grateful for the bad weather, for it gave his crews a chance to rest after three days of mounting tension. This was especially welcome following the misfortunes of the previous day when unexpected clouds over England caused mid-air collisions, after which 3rd Air Division commander, Major General Curtis E. LeMay, canceled his part of the mission. This left only the 1st Division to join with the Fifteenth Air Force, in its first large scale participation in The Big Week. The 2nd Division had also dropped out of the mission because of weather. Consequently, the Eighth lost 41 bombers and 11 fighters, the Fifteenth lost 15, and bombing results did not match those of the two previous days.

The final two days of the Week provided the opportunity for coordinated operations by all three of the strategic air forces, which included a nighttime visit by RAF's Bomber Command to dreaded Schweinfurt, the ball-bearing center. The Eighth also bombed Schweinfurt, on February 24, and on the following day wound up the Week by sharing a critical target with the Fifteenth —the Messerschmitt complex at Regensburg. On this final day, Doolittle managed to get up no less than 738 Fortresses and Liberators; of these, 31 were lost. The Fifteenth fared worse than the Eighth, having less fighter protection and being particularly victimized by the Luftwaffe. Of its 176 bombers dispatched, 33 fell to German fighters. The Week closed with an RAF night bombing of the main Messerschmitt plant at Augsburg, which had also been hit by the Eighth the previous day.

On February 26 the weather turned sour and rang down the curtain on The Big Week. Allied public relations men, with aid from newsmen, gave it its name and made rather large claims for its impact. To the men who had fought through it at all levels—including ground crews that worked night and day—it had, indeed, been a big week. But the Allied High Command, including Doolittle, was more guarded, less given over to premature celebration. In six days the Eighth Air Force had lost 137 heavy bombers, the Fifteenth, 89; in addition, 28 fighters had gone down. The loss average was not prohibitive: roughly 6 per cent. (It was not long after The Big Week that Doolittle made his two most unpopular wartime decisions, increasing missions and unleashing the fighters.) In human terms this represented about 2,600 casualties, dead, missing, and wounded. The question in Doolittle's mind was, was it worth it?

Photoreconnaissance revealed that while the German aircraft industry had not been "laid flat," it was in serious trouble. No one was more aware of that than the Luftwaffe. The major objective of the co-ordinated onslaught was clear to them, necessitating hastily assembled conferences.

In *The Luftwaffe Diaries* Cajus Bekker describes the impact of The Big Week: "In Luftwaffe Command consternation reigned; there was despair amongst the leaders of the aviation industry. At the Ministry of War Production, and the office of *Generalluftzeugmeister* [Erhard] Milch, conference followed conference. Orders were issued to all concerned to take extreme measures to save the remnants of the vital fighter production industry and get it going again.

"Initial reports from the individual plants encouraged little hope. At the Gotha works the destruction was such as to prevent all production for six to seven weeks. Yet at Erla [a Me-109 assembly plant] in Leipzig 160 damaged aircraft, salvaged from the ruined workshops, were in most cases found, astonishingly, to be repairable. At Regensburg the Messerschmitt factory was so devastated that it was first decided not to resurrect it, but to start up afresh on another site. Then it was discovered that the vital machine tools had suffered less than had been feared, many needing simply to be freed from the rubble that had fallen on them. Four months later the works had fully regained their former output. As for Messerschmitt, Augsburg, it resumed production on March 9th—i.e. only two weeks after the 'double blow' [by the Eighth and Fifteenth Air Forces]."

The full extent of the damage to the German aircraft industry was not known to the Allies until after the war, of course. Though not lasting, it had been disrupting, since it did force the Germans to disperse their factories, which produced nothing while being rebuilt. Nor was the impact only immediate, for the aircraft that were *not* built would *not* be flying over the Normandy beachhead in June. The intense air battles, too, took their toll of experienced Luftwaffe pilots, including, in the words of the commander of the fighters, Adolf Galland, "our best squadron, *Gruppe* and *Geschwader* commanders. Each incursion of the enemy is costing us some fifty aircrew. The time has come when our weapon [the Luftwaffe] is in sight of collapse."

The sequel to The Big Week, once the weather broke, was the opening of the American daylight assault on Berlin in early March of 1944. Doolittle looked forward to leading this "first," having led the first bombing raids on the two other Axis capitals. But that was not to be; because he had participated in the planning of the coming Normandy invasions, he was forbidden to fly any mission over enemy territory.

Disappointed, he had used his wiles on Spaatz, much as he had on Arnold in connection with the Tokyo Raid, and Spaatz had reluctantly granted his permission. Doolittle was delighted until word had reached Eisenhower and the word from him was final. Lieutenant General (as he was by March 1944) Doolittle would confine his flying—if he must fly—to the British Isles.

Doolittle made it a practice to fly every type of aircraft in his command, including British aircraft such as the de Havilland Mosquito, whose almost all-wood construction he found fascinating. He also personally checked out any aircraft which was giving any trouble—"my engineering background enabled me to analyze situations in the field when we didn't have factory representatives or other people to check the problem."

It was during this period that the Lockheed P-38 Lightning evidenced a tendency to catch fire in flight and this troubled Doolittle. Accompanied by his aide, Captain Thomas Barrineau, Doolit-

TOP: Lieutenant Colonel James Doolittle and Air Cadet James Doolittle, Jr., meet in 1941 at Kelly Field, Texas, where the younger Doolittle was earning his wings. Later, during World War II, he would fly both medium bombers and fighters in two theaters of war, the Pacific and Europe. DOOLITTLE COLLECTION. ABOVE: John, Doolittle's younger son, c. 1943, won a West Point appointment and was graduated after the war ended, in 1946. He later served in Korea and then Vietnam as a bomber pilot. DOOLITTLE COLLECTION

TOP: Joe Doolittle in wartime and h[...]
cherished tablecloth signed by num[...]
great figures in aviation (and whose [...]
signatures she carefully embroidere[...]
the cloth). While her husband and s[...]
served in the military during the Sec[...]
World War, Joe Doolittle indefatiga[...]
visited defense factories, spoke to [...]
American women at luncheons (and [...]
radio) and did other morale work wi[...]
servicemen and civilians. DOOLITT[...]
COLLECTION. CENTER: Aboard the [...]
aircraft carrier *Hornet* en route to T[...]
April 1942. Doolittle, the captain of [...]
Hornet Rear Admiral Marc A. Mits[...]
and crews participate in a ceremony [...]
Japanese medals that had been awar[...]
Americans were affixed to the 500-[...]
bombs for delivery to Japan. U. S. A[...]
FORCE. BOTTOM: Most of the crew [...]
B-25 Mitchell a/c No. 40-2344: Lie[...]
Henry A. Potter, navigator; Lieuten[...]
Colonel James Doolittle, pilot; Staf [...]
Sergeant Fred A. Braemer, bombar[...]
Lieutenant Richard E. Cole, copilo[...]
Navy Lieutenant Henry L. Miller, w[...]
helped train the Raiders. Staff Serg[...]
Paul J. Leonard, engineer-gunner, [...]
present for the photo. U. S. AIR FO[...]

...ril 18, 1942: Takeoff for Tokyo. ...use the *Hornet* had been spotted ...by a Japanese picket boat, it was ...ecessary to launch the Mitchells ...ne 600 miles distant from Japan, ...0 farther away than planned. The weather was grim, the Pacific choppy, and the *Hornet* tossing. ...oolittle, in the first plane, led the ...offs and fifteen aircraft followed ...n off the slippery, rocking deck.

U. S. AIR FORCE

RIGHT: A despondent Doolittle contemplates the wreckage of his B-25 on the China mainland the morning after the Tokyo Raid. When this photo was taken by Sergeant Paul Leonard, Doolittle had no idea of the whereabouts of the other 15 crews and was certain his mission had been a total failure. U. S. AIR FORCE

LEFT: Post-Raid relaxation with Joe back in the States. To his surprise, Doolittle learned that the mission had succeeded and had been a morale booster for the United States. Though it accomplished little militarily at the time, the Raid triggered the decisive battle at Midway. To Doolittle's further surprise, he was promoted to the rank of brigadier general and awarded the Congressional Medal of Honor. PHOTO BY LOWELL THOMAS

The first reunion of the Tokyo Raiders in North Africa one year later, April 18, 1943. Doolittle invited as many participants as possible who were stationed in North Africa and held his first party in a farmhouse. Not all of those pictured actually flew the mission; some took part in the preparations for the Raid. *Front row, left to right:* Major William Bower, pilot, crew No. 12; Major Travis Hoover, pilot, crew No. 2; Doolittle; Lieutenant Colonel Harvey Hinman; Captain Heston C. Daniel; Captain Thomas Griffin, navigator, crew No. 9. *Back row, left to right:* Captain William Pound, navigator, crew No. 12; Major Rodney Wilder, copilot, crew No. 5; Captain James Parker, copilot, crew No. 9; Major Ross Greening, pilot, crew No. 11; Major Joseph Klein; Captain Griffith Williams, copilot, crew No. 15. Unidentified man stands to Williams' right. U. S. AIR FORCE

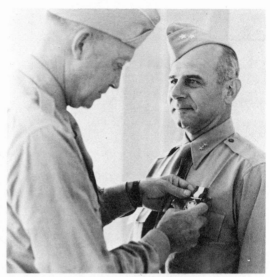

TOP: Eisenhower bestows the Distinguished Service Medal on Doolittle for his service in North Africa, 1943. U. S. AIR FORCE. CENTER: Greeting members of a USO troupe visiting North Africa to entertain GIs stationed there: Frances Langford and Bob Hope. U. S. AIR FORCE. BOTTOM: North Africa, December 1942. Climbing into the cockpit of a Spitfire; one such adventure got him into trouble with his superior, Dwight D. Eisenhower. DOOLITTLE COLLECTION

TOP: Major General James H. Doolitt[le,]
commander of the Eighth Air Force, [...]
U. S. AIR FORCE. CENTER: Visiting w[ith]
Major General William Kepner,
commander of the VIII Fighter Comm[and]
in England, shortly after being transfe[rred]
from Italy to head the Eighth Air Forc[e,]
1944. Doolittle's decision to free the
fighters from escort duties with the
bombers, Kepner believes, spelled di[saster]
for the Luftwaffe and led to its defeat[. U. S.]
AIR FORCE. BOTTOM: General Carl
Spaatz, commander of the U.S. Strat[egic]
Air Forces in Europe, and Doolittle, [now a]
lieutenant general discuss a bombing
mission with crews of the 303rd Bom[b]
Group, England, 1945. U. S. AIR FO[RCE]

eneral George Patton and Doolit-
ve in Washington, D.C., in June
5, a month after the war ended in
rope. Before leaving for other as-
nents (Patton returned to Europe,
e he died after an accident in Deer, and Doolittle, with the Eighth
orce, went to the Pacific), the two
de a joint speaking tour to remind
untrymen that the war was not yet
pletely over. The outspoken Pat-
requently salty comments greatly
enlivened the tour.

AIR FORCE. SECOND FROM TOP:
dcasting *Broadway Matinee*. Joe
oolittle interviews the President's
ife, Eleanor Roosevelt, February
944. DOOLITTLE COLLECTION.

D FROM TOP: In the cockpit of a
B-29 Super Fortress, the aircraft
h which the Eighth Air Force was
equipped on being assigned to the
fic. Fire-bombings by planes like
devastated Japanese cities; Super
ses also carried the atomic bombs
roshima and Nagasaki, to end the
he war was over before the Eighth
ance to participate, and Doolittle
flew home in a B-29.

AIR FORCE. BOTTOM: Doolittle,
nmander of the Eighth Air Force,
is successor as commander of the
fteenth Air Force, Major General
an F. Twining. U. S. AIR FORCE

TOP: The Doolittles chatting w[ith] one of Joe's "boys" and his w[ife] at the twenty-eighth annual reunion of the Tokyo Raiders a[t] Cocoa Beach, Florida, in April of 1970. U. S. AIR FORCE PHOTO, COURTESY C. V. GLINES. CENTER: Richard A. Knobloch, president of the Wings Club, reads the special citation presented to Joe Dooli[ttle] on the occasion of the club's thirty-third annual dance, October 21, 1975. Knobloch, a[retired U.S.A.F. brigadier general, was copilot of a/c 40-2247, crew No. 13, and brought back the only photographs taken during the Tokyo Raid. THE WINGS CLU[B] BOTTOM: The first Wings Club Distinguished Achievement Award was presented to James Doolittle on October 21, 1975, [in] New York. With the trophy in the background are Pilot Doris Renninger, manager of the Wings Club, Joe and Jimmy Doolittle, and Richard A. Knobloch, president of the club[.] THE WINGS CLUB

tle drove out to an air depot where he could find a P-38; the plan was to see if he could manage, perhaps by backfiring the engine and other mechanical means, to induce a fire. The big twin-boomed fighter was readied and Doolittle took off into the rather foggy air. He didn't have a long wait: "On the takeoff it backfired and caught fire. By this time I was airborne and the fire was spreading fairly rapidly, but I felt that I had best try to make a hundred-eighty [turn], another hundred-eighty, and swing in and land.

"The weather was quite bad, although I could keep the field in sight while I made the turns; the fog was sufficient, at the same time, so that I couldn't see far enough ahead in case of a crash-landing to make sure I didn't crash into a house, or something of that kind.

"I was successful in getting the P-38 back. I immediately called the fire department on the field and as I landed the fire was going pretty good. I stopped and got out of the plane. By that time the fire wagon was there and they drenched the plane and, except for the fire damage, saved it.

"I didn't learn a great deal except these things didn't have to be backfired—they backfired themselves."

Obviously some changes were necessary in the fuel system and soon the defect was corrected.

Guns, too, were a problem that Doolittle looked into, although the root was often human. "We will appreciate better-trained gunners," he informed Major General Robert B. Williams, former commander of the 1st Air Division, later transferred to Colorado Springs to lead the Second Air Force, the huge training command. Doolittle analyzed the reasons behind the inaccuracy and the burned-out guns of combat crews. The Luftwaffe tended to concentrate on an individual group, overwhelming the bombers with persistent attacks which, Doolittle pointed out, "are so prolonged and frequent that the gunners are squirting their guns like hoses and soon go past the point of accurate and effective fire. Recent tests have confirmed this. As you know, in a prolonged burst or in too frequent short bursts, the barrel gets too hot and tumbling, followed by dribbling and cooking, results."

He illustrated with his own personal experience. "I was flying home in the P-38 the other day shooting at the waves. Five of the guns ran out but one was still firing. It continued to fire, but the bullets were not kicking up splashes in the vicinity of the waves at which I was shooting. As a matter of fact, it appeared that the bullets were not going out of the gun at all. On banking up, it was found that they were actually coming out of the muzzle but were dribbling out and falling down into the water." This he believed is what occurred when the bombers were under concentrated attack. Gunners continued firing until their overheated weapons were rendered ineffective.

Doolittle had begun to take steps with his commanders to correct the problem. "It is very difficult, however," Doolittle observed, "to tell a gunner not to fire when he is being attacked. On the other hand, if he does fire too frequently, his fire loses all effectiveness. The solution is to waste no fire after giving an occasional squirt to indicate that you are on the job (preferably with headlight tracers), then hold your fire until the Hun closes in . . . It may be necessary to periodically force-cool the guns. As you know, the best way to do this is to point the gun forward and pull back the bolt so air can blow through the inside of the barrel. This will be easy to accomplish with all except the tail guns and the radio operator's guns."

Doolittle's day-to-day solicitudes were not always technical. On the same day he landed the blazing P-38, he had planned to make another visit, since he made it a habit to call at various installations in his command when he happened to be in the area. Having overseen the dousing of the Lightning, he climbed into his staff car and said to Barrineau, "Tom, let's go over to the hospital while we're here"—there was one near the air depot.

The two men found the office of the surgeon in charge and Doolittle, after some preliminary conversation, inquired if there were any particular problems that he might help solve. Whereupon the surgeon launched into a rather long dissertation. He opened with the statement that he had trouble "getting people to realize that under three conditions it was undesirable to attempt to rehabilitate an individual for further flying duty. It was far better to send him home because nobody ever got over any of these experiences." He then enumerated them for Doolittle and Barrineau.

The first and most gruesome, while it did occur, was quite rare. A piece of flak slams into the cockpit and decapitates the pilot (or copilot), the head falling into the copilot's lap, and then, bloodied and with the eyes of the pilot leering up at him from his lap, he has to assume command of the plane, bring it under control, and fly it. "This kind of shock can never be gotten over," the doctor concluded.

A second experience was immersion in the North Sea; few crews survived that unless they were found almost immediately. They either drowned or froze to death. "If a man survives the shock to his whole system of that immersion in freezing water, he should be sent home."

The third condition, he continued, warming up to the subject because it was obvious he had the general's sympathetic ear, was "fire in the air. Whoever this happens to, regardless of who he is, should be sent home. He is of no further use to the organization!"

By about the middle of this statement Barrineau had begun plucking at the surgeon's sleeve trying to warn him off pursuing the fire theme too far. But he finished and Doolittle replied, "I agree with you on the first two, but can't quite agree with you on the third because I just had a fire in the air." He conceded, however, that his reaction to the situation might be different from that of a less experienced, younger pilot. But it seemed at times to Doolittle that just about everyone tried to keep him on the ground.

As commander of the Eighth Air Force—"flying his desk"—he contended with dozens of problems totally unrelated to logistics, operations, or even flight. These were war stories that Doolittle refers to as "human rather than humorous."

For example, one day two English women, mother and daughter he soon learned, were ushered into his office. The younger had been selected to speak for both. She inquired about a certain sergeant; Doolittle had an immediate check made and found that the man had been ordered home.

In Doolittle's words, the following explanation was given: "We wondered why we hadn't been seeing him. I work in the daytime, my mother works at night, and he was very kindly spending some time with each of us between missions. We live a couple of miles away. He found it increasingly difficult to visit us both as often as we would all like because of the distance and the long walk required. So we loaned him our bicycle; he then found it possible to spend more time with both of us. We are both pregnant as a result of his ministrations and we came to see why he had stopped visiting. We see now that the reason is that he's gone home.'

"I said, 'Well, I would like to acquaint you with some of the rights you have under the law . . .'

" 'Oh, no, no, no—don't misunderstand," she told me, 'We don't want to cause the sergeant any trouble; we would just like to get our bicycle back.' "

A related, but grimmer, incident was sent to Doolittle for action: "There was a boy who had been visiting a British family," he recalls. "He visited them on Christmas Eve and had Christmas dinner with them—the husband was a night watchman. As he was leaving the woman invited the boy back, after the husband left. So he returned and was in bed with his hostess when a neighbor woman happened to step into the house.

"At this point the hostess began shouting that she had been raped. This made a rather difficult thing to deal with: here was a boy who not only accepted kindness from this family, but had violated the confidence of the husband and was actually accused by the neighbor of rape. I could not ignore it although I felt that the boy was as much raped as rapist.

"So I had to explain to the British that the boy was being disciplined and was being sent home—and I sent him home with a request that leniency be shown and that the very severe sentence that I had given him be immediately commuted when he got home. I had to fulfill American obligations to Great Britain and I had to take care of the boy and had to see that he was not victimized by his hostess and the neighbor. Well, everything came out all right.

"These were some of the little things that come up to a commanding officer and sometimes try him sorely. Some of them were humorous and some were tragic."

As commanding officer Doolittle routinely visited air bases to award medals or to celebrate the completion of a round—100, 200—of missions. This was considered good for *esprit de corps* and generally perked up the group (this was especially true of Doolittle who had been the boyhood hero of the aviation enthusiasts among the men). Certain visits were not always as ceremonial.

When a group suffered unusual combat losses it was mandatory to call at the base in hopes of boosting morale. The 100th Bomb Group, one of the Eighth's hard-luck units, often suffered from concentrated Luftwaffe attacks and, consequently, heavy losses. After three bad missions in a row, the 100th, Doolittle believed, had more than earned a special visit from The Old Man. The morale problem, he has explained, could be serious after such a string of losses. Replacements had to be expedited to the group, for one thing, because "the vacant seat at the table was real bad." The visit from high brass was another.

The losses of the 100th had been so bad that Doolittle urged Spaatz to accompany him to Thorpe Abbots, where the group was stationed, for dinner. There would be some relaxing drinks and the two air leaders had prepared brief speeches of encouragement as after dinner boosters. In the early evening Doolittle and Spaatz ("Tooey" to Doolittle and other long-time friends) arrived at the base and were taken into the Officer's Club.

"We were up at the bar having a drink when a little second lieutenant came up to me. (Tooey was then a four-star general and I was a three-star.) The lieutenant poked his finger at my chest—he was about half drunk—and said, 'You think we don't know what you're here for, dontcha?'

" 'Well, I'm here to discuss your problems and express regret that you've had these bad attacks and see what we can do about making things a little better.'

"Again he stuck his finger in my chest, where it almost disappeared—Tooey of course, who was strictly military, was getting more and more incensed. For the third time he poked and then said, 'Let me tell you something, general: we know what you're here for, you're here to improve our morale and lemme tell you this, if there is anything in this goddam world that will ruin our morale it's a couple of goddam generals comin' around trying to fix it.' "

Spaatz, as Doolittle remembered, was "fit to be tied" and "I had to grab Tooey and take him away (I was amused to beat hell at this little kid)." Spaatz, a West Point graduate, a great leader, and a fine gentlemanly officer, was a stickler for military courtesy and found it difficult to hear such talk from a subordinate, drunk or not; nor was he happy with the young lieutenant's fingerly familiarity. Doolittle managed to soothe him and the dinner went off with no further incident.

The 100th, obviously, did not lack plucky second lieutenants; morale was not the problem. They had merely been subjected to the Luftwaffe technique of concentrating on a specific portion of the bomber formation. This generally served to break up the defensive pattern of the group's formation, enabling the German fighters to get at the other bombers. Thus a single group or squadron would suffer—and the Germans, too, were aware of the effect of empty places in the mess hall. There were those who believed the erroneous legend of the Bloody Hundredth—that the Luftwaffe harbored a personal grudge against the group because of an inadvertent violation of the "code of the air" (a 100th plane, with wheels lowered—although the crew was not aware of it—which was a signal of surrender, opened fire on its Luftwaffe escort).

The evening ended with Spaatz pacified and Doolittle chuckling now and then on the way back to his quarters. Perhaps there was something about the effect of the "little second lieutenant" on Spaatz that recalled the trials and tribulations of a certain Colonel Burwell at Rockwell Field, ages ago.

Around this time, March 1944, the American aerial Battle of Berlin began, the first attack occurring on March 4 despite deteriorating weather and unfavorable bombing conditions. Most of the bombers either turned back or hit targets of opportunity, but the 95th and 100th Groups, a mere 29 planes altogether—continued on and dropped bombs for the first time from American planes on the German capital. The London *Evening Standard* noted the historic, but not very effective, event with an editorial headed ALLIES OVER BERLIN. The bombers had been escorted directly to the target area by P-51s, the sight of which, Goering would later admit, made him realize that a German victory was no longer possible.

When the Eighth returned to Berlin in force (660 planes attacking) on March 6, they were met by large formations of German fighters, including twin-engined aircraft obviously drawn from night-fighter units. The result was a climactic battle, with American bomber losses reaching 69; 11 of the escort fighters were destroyed also. As Adolf Galland would later write, "The Reich's defenses could only muster about 200 fighters and destroyers against this force. Our losses were almost twice as high as those of the Americans." Inexorably, though it cost time and losses, operation Argument was decimating the Luftwaffe.

Some of the weight of the burden of mounting these missions was lightened for Doolittle, personally at least, with the rather unexpected return of Jack Allard to the Eighth Air Force Headquarters. Although he had improved after the hospitalization for phlebitis, the Army physicians were doubtful about his complete recovery and had even recommended his discharge. Allard apparently prevailed upon his friendship with Arnold, who assigned him back to the Eighth as a brigadier general and Doolittle's chief of staff. (General Partridge would later command the 3rd Air Division, replacing LeMay, who, in turn, was sent to the Pacific.)

In preparing Doolittle for the arrival of his old friend, Arnold had written that Allard's medical chances appeared to be poor. "He knows this too," Arnold noted, "but he says that if he has to die, he'd rather die over there with you and the Eighth Air Force than a hospital. I know it's an insane thing to do, but I'm sending Jack back to you." Weak, pale, and fifteen pounds lighter than he was when he had left, Allard reported in for duty. (He would serve with Doolittle until the war in Europe was over, although plagued by his illness. Allard in fact survived the war.)

The old Rockwell Field triumvirate was rounded out with the arrival of Colonel Bruce Johnson from Italy. Ever since Doolittle had left Bari, Johnson had bombarded all concerned with transfer requests, one of which was finally granted in March 1944. He arrived, by a B-24 that had made various stops before landing in Britain. With him Johnson carried a twenty-five-gallon jug of wine and a crate of oranges acquired in Algiers. Once again Johnson was appointed as official headquarters commandant.

Johnson's first assignment, once he had settled in, was to find suitable quarters for Doolittle and staff within a fifteen-minute drive of Eighth Air Force Headquarters. Early in the search Johnson ran into trouble when he innocently tried to requisition the fine home occupied by Sir Arthur Harris, chief of the Bomber Command. He persevered until he found Mill House, adjacent to the Thames, close to High Wycombe, and the property of one Mr. G. T. Frost. "It was a beautiful estate with a big house and several lovely outbuildings including a red-brick caretaker's cottage by the big iron gate . . . How to get it was another thing entirely."

After the Harris incident, Johnson was more cautious, but when he explained his problem to Mr. Frost an agreement was reached. The next day he brought Doolittle and members of the staff to inspect the new quarters. "I watched Jim's face for any reaction . . . He kept as solid a poker face as any you would see in a barracks game, thanking his new landlord and taking his leave. On the way back in the car, he looked at me with a dead pan and said, 'Bruce, I told you fifteen minutes from headquarters. That place is twenty!'"

It was during this period that Doolittle had his most pleasant surprise, a call from Captain James H. Doolittle, Jr., who, having served a tour of duty in a medium bomber squadron in the Pacific, had transferred to the Ninth Air Force as a B-26 pilot. Father and son spent some pleasant times together, as Doolittle visited Eighth Air Forces bases, Jim, Jr. accompanying. (Later Doolittle would have the proud pleasure, substituting for Ninth Air Force commander General Vandenberg, of awarding his son the Distinguished Flying Cross, earned for missions over enemy-occupied Europe.)

This was a pleasant diversion from the monumental chore of reorganizing the Eighth Air Force in anticipation of what would almost universally come to be called "D-day," the start of the Allied invasion of Europe. Meanwhile, a certain routine had evolved. Doolittle and his chief of staff (Partridge and later Allard) would be driven from Mill House by 6:30 A.M. to High Wycombe, about seven miles away. After a quick breakfast, they would attend briefings for the day's missions and then review the results of the missions of the day before. After lunch—generally a good one, thanks to Johnson's scrounging talents for both chefs and food—the afternoon was spent at headquarters at paper work. By late afternoon the initial information for the next day's missions would begin clicking through the teletype machines and various aspects of the operations come under discussion, from weather prospects to fighter escort assignment, with Doolittle questioning this decision or that, making suggestions, and generally shaping the final form of his air force's mission.

He would keep in touch with the day's mission—and battle—by radio from the various combat leaders and by interception of the German defense radio communications. Then he might drive to one of the bases to meet the incoming Fortresses or Liberators after the mission was over.

By 6:00 P.M. he would be back at Mill House for dinner. The staff at High Wycombe would still be at work on the many details of the next day's mission, with Doolittle immediately available by phone; he was also in instant reach of Spaatz. After dinner there might be a movie, perhaps shown for guests and visitors, and then talk into the evening—shop talk. By midnight Doolittle would be abed, phones close at hand.

During this period—March, April, May 1944—Doolittle was capable of launching massive missions comprising literally thousands of aircraft per mission. While the assault on Germany did not erase the German aircraft industry (paradoxically, the production of German aircraft actually increased because of dispersal and the more efficient production methods introduced by Albert Speer, Minister of War Production, and the dynamism of General Milch), the Luftwaffe suffered serious attrition in both aircraft and, more critically, experienced pilots in combat against the bombers.

Doolittle's decision to unleash the fighters was having a drastic effect on the Luftwaffe.

Doolittle has regarded this as the most important military decision he made during the Second World War. In agreement, General Galland, the Luftwaffe fighter commander, underscored the devastating effect of Doolittle's order on the hapless Luftwaffe in his book, *The First and the Last* (1954): "Only now did the superiority of the American fighters come into its own . . . Wherever our fighters appeared, the Americans hurled themselves at them. They went over to low-level attacks on our airfields. Nowhere were we safe from them; we had to skulk on our own bases. During takeoff, assembling, climbing, approaching the bombers, once in contact with bombers, on our way back, during landing, and ever after that the American fighters attacked with an overwhelming superiority." Interestingly, Galland erroneously attributed the decision to Spaatz, Doolittle's superior.

The Eighth and Fifteenth Air Forces, literally and freely, roamed the skies over Germany, with only intermittent Luftwaffe resistance. The Germans were forced to conserve their fighter force and defend only the most important targets. German Major General Walter Grabmann summarized the situation as it was in May of 1944: "The Americans had reached the stage of enjoying complete air mastery over the Reich. The total number of fighters we still had left represented, at best, less than half the number of escort fighters the Americans used on a single raid. The latter thus no longer had to bother about special maneuvers to mislead the defense. Their fighter preponderance was such that, in fine weather particularly, they could send out whole formations in advance to shatter the Germans before they were in position . . ."

As D-day impended, the Allied air target priorities shifted from the Luftwaffe to railway centers and coastal defense installations and airfields within a 130-mile radius of the selected landing beaches. More definite strategic targets deeper within Germany or in occupied countries were oil, synthetic fuel, and hydrogen works. Closer to home were the so-called Crossbow targets, the recently discovered launching sites for rocket missiles in France and Belgium. These missiles—the V-1 and V-2 rockets—would later cause senseless havoc in southern England. Crossbow targets did not readily lend themselves to heavy bomber attacks, and by May, Doolittle had informed Arnold that, for that job, Mosquitoes were "the most effective type of aircraft." His hope was to concentrate on the more important, and more vulnerable, strategic targets.

Meanwhile, the German propaganda machine was announcing the existence of a tide-turning miracle weapon, which caused concern in the Allied camp. The presence of the launching sites, pointing in the general direction of Britain, was especially disconcerting to the British. The American commanders preferred pursuing the strategic goals, rather than diversions to V-sites. However, whenever possible Doolittle would send the heavies to Crossbow targets. While the V-sites were not totally put out of business, they were not able to interfere with the Normandy invasions on June 6, 1944.

Doolittle literally had a front row seat for the drama of D-day. He and his deputy commander, Pat Partridge, took off early in the morning to observe the heavy bombers' contribution to the day's battle. Each man flew a P-38, the most distinctive, and therefore most readily identified, Allied fighter; flying over ground and naval units was invariably an invitation to disaster. In P-38s they could be assured of a reasonable safety factor.

Some of the Eighth's heavies had been assigned the task of bombing just inland from the invasion beaches, to soften up the German defenses for the push inland. It was not an ideal day for an invasion nor for bombing, as Doolittle and Partridge soon learned—the bombing would have to be done through a solid overcast. This necessitated moving the bombline further inland to make certain that no bombs would fall on Allied troops. This typical weather hitch meant that the German forces were not as "soft" —vulnerable—as they might have been had the weather been clear.

"When we saw 'Bombs Away,' we realized they had bombed with radar through the overcast," Doolittle recollected, "and that there was nothing more that we could see, so I then decided to go down to fly along the beaches." The two P-38s were pointed toward England and heading homeward when Doolittle spotted the break in the overcast that he had been seeking and dived through. At that moment Partridge ran out of fuel in one tank, and as he bent down to switch to the other, he lost sight of Doolittle. The hole too was gone and Partridge continued on to England.

Below the overcast Doolittle had a panoramic view of all of the Normandy beaches and the Channel dotted with practically every type of ship. "It was a terribly sensational thing," he recalls. As he swooped almost directly over the beaches he could see the Allied landing craft (LSTs) bring their cargoes of men and equipment ashore—he saw one ship struck by several German shells and blown up, scattering its contents, men and supplies, in a terrible explosion. "The invasion was a most spectacular operation, beautifully carried out by our ground troops—magnificently, with consummate courage."

For an hour Doolittle traversed the beaches, from the American Utah and bloody Omaha beaches in the west to the British Gold, Juno, and Sword at the eastern end—and back again, watching the great spectacle of Overlord, come at last. He did not see one German aircraft.

Achieving a beachhead on June 6 was no walk-in, but in the critical initial stages the absence of marauding German aircraft was contributory to the success of the invasion. When Eisenhower assured the troops that the only aircraft they would see on D-day would be their own, it was a simple statement of fact not a boast. The Eighth's bombers, besides dropping warning leaflets to the French civilian population, assisted tactically by destroying bridges and closing roadways to deny the Germans access to the beachheads. Fighters of both the Eighth and the Ninth strafed various targets inland and provided air cover over the Channel for the invasion fleet. Medium bombers struck at coastal batteries as well as at transportation targets. The RAF joined in clearing enemy resistance from the air and the areas in and around the battle zones. By early evening, when Doolittle was back on the ground in England, he was confident that the Allies had returned to Europe to stay; he had also returned with the first eyewitness report for Eisenhower.

It happened that when Eisenhower and his staff moved into France later in the summer, Doolittle was left as the senior American officer in England, burdening him with social responsibilities which at times required deft management. A formal visit by the King and Queen to High Wycombe did nothing for Doolittle's peace of mind. He realized that the royal pair would have to be met by the headquarters commandant, Bruce Johnson, who, when excited, tended to stammer.

The King also stammered; how sensitive might he be to Johnson's tendency? Doolittle summoned Johnson into his office and said, "Brucie, you can't meet the King." Johnson's eyebrows shot up inquiringly; Doolittle continued, "If he were to stutter and you were to stutter, we might have an international incident. He might even think you're mocking him."

Johnson would not accept this. "Boss, it's my job to meet the King and I should meet him." Doolittle decided not to push.

"O.K., Brucie," he replied, "but don't open your mouth." Which is how it was done, although to his chagrin, Johnson later learned that he had fractured some rule or other in the protocol. He wisely chose to be the Queen's escort, leaving Doolittle to converse with the King. During the escorted tour of the headquarters Johnson was concerned with always placing the Queen where she would be visible to the great numbers of invited guests, military and civilian, as well as to the press. A long path to the reception hall was flanked by a wall, thus when Johnson escorted the Queen, he walked to the right of the Queen (he being then next to the wall) so she could be seen by the guests.

"It was not until later that I was told that I had committed the most grievous of all faux pas," Johnson wrote later. "No one, but no one, ever walks on the right side of royalty. Jim had caught my mistake instantly and, in order not to embarrass me even further, had multiplied the mistake by doing it himself [i.e., walking to the right of the King].

"The following morning the front page of a London newspaper

had a large picture displaying my crime to all and sundry. The reporters were kind to me in the story, however, never mentioning that I had committed a social sin of monumental standing."

The transgression appears to have had no effect upon the British-American alliance. Further, before he left for Buckingham Palace, the King made Doolittle a Knight Commander of the Order of the Bath. Doolittle immediately wrote Joe, informing her that he was now officially "Sir James" and that she was "Lady Doolittle." Her response was succinct: "It will take more than the King of England to make me a lady," in keeping with her aptitude for viewing all things in perspective.

The most fascinating Briton Doolittle met was the Prime Minister, Winston Churchill. Although a confessed "Former Naval Person," Churchill was also knowledgeable about aviation and liked to be kept informed on the progress of the air war. Thus, after Eisenhower left for France, it was routine for Doolittle to make a weekly visit to Number 10 Downing Street and a monthly visit to Churchill's country estate Chequers, a few miles from High Wycombe. Generally present at these monthly meetings was Doolittle's English counterpart, Sir Arthur Harris, of Bomber Command.

Doolittle recalls his first visit to Chequers: "We would have a few drinks, supper and see a movie. Then we'd discuss the joint British-American air effort in which the Prime Minister was extremely interested. On this first occasion I made the great mistake of accompanying the Prime Minister in his frequent glasses of brandy. I soon realized that his capacity was much greater than mine and that I was in the home of the Prime Minister modestly in alcohol.

"Well, this didn't quite shock me sober, but it shocked me to a point where I realized I had to be quiet, but that before becoming quiet and making it too obvious, I should say something that would be a little unusual and then lapse into silence, drink some black coffee and reachieve sobriety.

"So I thought for a while and finally came up with a very, very fine statement. When I made this statement to the Prime Minister, he said, 'Splendid, Jimmy, splendid! I shall use that tomorrow in the House of Commons.' To this day I haven't the faintest idea what I said."

Doolittle was beset with more serious problems than that of

royal etiquette or keeping up with the P.M.'s alcoholic tolerance. After D-day he had to strain to keep his strategic arm from being wasted on tactical solutions to the problems of ground commanders in France, who would transform the Eighth Air Force, given the opportunity, into field artillery with wings (a mistake the Germans had made and for which they had paid heavily).

The term "precision bombardment" is relative and such bombing eludes pure achievement. Dropping tons of metal and explosives under frequently trying conditions—fighter attacks, flak, poor weather, fear—was rarely accomplished with "picklebarrel" accuracy. For the Normandy invasion, control of the Strategic Air Forces had passed to Eisenhower; his headquarters therefore had first call on the heavy bombers should the need for them arise in connection with the fighting in France.

Once the beachhead had been secured, the next phase of the battle would be the breakout and the beginning, it was hoped, of the race for Berlin. To prepare for the breakout a plan (Cobra) was devised by Eisenhower's staff to employ the heavy bombers as a massive, flying field artillery to bomb in advance of Allied troops. This plan did not give Doolittle any joy, and all precautions were taken in the planning to avoid accidents.

On July 24, 1944, the Eighth Air Force's three air divisions—more than 1,500 planes—were dispatched to St.-Lô, where the Germans were putting up tremendous resistance. Before the planes arrived at the target area poor weather caused the lead groups to turn away from the primary target. The operation was canceled at ground headquarters on the scene, but it took time for the message to travel to Britain and back again to the bombers over France. Further misadventures occurred: one bombardier, startled by something striking the turret in which he was poised, inadvertently, by reflex action, toggled his bombs and hit a forward airfield of the Ninth Air Force at Chipple, destroying two American planes and damaging several others.

Another bombardier in a lead aircraft, having trouble with his bomb release mechanism, accidentally released a part of his bomb load whereupon the remaining planes in the formation followed suit, as was the practice. These bombs, released far short of the target area, fell into the position of the American 30th Infantry Division, killing sixteen men and injuring over sixty.

The next day Cobra continued, opening with strafing attacks by fighter bombers of the Ninth Air Force and followed later by 1,500 heavy bombers, B-17s and B-24s. Various errors led to a repeat over St.-Lô of the previous day's tragedy—again the men of the 30th Division suffered—and more than a hundred men died, including Lieutenant General Lesley J. McNair, and some 380 were wounded. While these massive bombings did assist in clearing the breakthrough area, the cost to American troops was high; it was obvious that this was not the way to use heavy bombers. Even so, Eisenhower would later say that it was impossible to "convince the Army that the battle of St.-Lô had not been won as a result of the support given by the Eighth Air Force."

Eisenhower's chief of staff, Brigadier General Walter Bedell Smith, did not agree. Immediately after the second misfortune he confronted Doolittle, blaming him for the poor performance. The two men exchanged some rancorous words, Doolittle making his point with, "Goddamit, Beedle, we shouldn't even have been there!"

Smith turned frosty and made a comment about "orders being orders," and that it was Doolittle's job to comply. Doolittle, heated, went into the consequences of abusing the function—through stupidity—of strategic bombardment.

Furious, Smith cut the argument short with the announcement that he was "going to Ike."

When he left, Doolittle called Spaatz, informing him that he soon might very well need a new commanding officer of the Eighth Air Force. Spaatz, moving quickly, got to Eisenhower first and was able to explain away the clash as the result of two different personalities abrading each other. Eisenhower's reaction was to write Doolittle a reassuring letter, saying in part, "I know how badly you and your command have felt because of the accidental bombing of some of our own troops by a portion of the Eighth Air Force during your preparation for the recent jump-off of the First Army [commanded by Lieutenant General Omar Bradley].

"Naturally," Eisenhower continued, "all of us have shared your acute distress that this should have happened. Nevertheless, it is quite important that you do not give the incident an exaggerated place either in your mind or in your future planning . . ."

Eisenhower quoted a portion of a letter from Bradley on the ultimate effectiveness of the bombing, despite the casualties, and concluded: "The work of the Eighth Air Force over many months in this Theater has been far too valuable to allow the morale of the organization to be dampened by this incident." He also continued to maintain that it was feasible to employ elements of the Strategic Air Forces in support of ground troops "under proper circumstances."

The letter was reassuring although it revealed that Eisenhower would continue to divert the Eighth from its primary mission if he and his staff believed it necessary.

Doolittle hoped that time might solve the problem, but he also presented his views to those who would listen sympathetically and intelligently. Shortly after the St.-Lô misbombings and the Smith incident, he wrote Arnold that Germany's sole means of prolonging the war was "by interfering with our strategic bombing effort." He was prophetic in predicting how that might be accomplished. "We are convinced that he [the enemy] hopes to have, in the very near future, a considerable number of jet and rocket-propelled aircraft with performance substantially superior to anything we have." He correctly deduced that the reason so few Luftwaffe planes were encountered was because they were being conserved for intermittent massive reactions to the bomber forces.

Meanwhile, the Eighth Air Force was being used to fight German ground troops in France and only occasionally to destroy the jets before they got off the ground in Germany. On September 28 he wrote to Spaatz on the issue. "Bad weather and the diversion of the Eighth Air Force from strategic targets to direct support of the ground forces has caused us to get far behind where we would like to be in our destruction of munitions in being and the German productive capacity for aircraft, oil, armament, tanks, motors, motor transport and other military equipment and supplies.

"If the war is to be won presently, this is not a point of great importance. If the war is to go on for any considerable period, the difficulty of eventually winning it and the personnel losses it will entail will be substantially increased as a result of having permitted German manufacturing capacity this comparative respite from bombing."

Doolittle reminded Spaatz that with the approaching winter and its contrary weather there would be fewer possibilities for strategic bombardment. The Luftwaffe, he noted, was "gradually increasing in strength and aggressiveness" and while the Luftwaffe was suffering from a lack of trained pilots and a fuel shortage, it was still a threat—"their present policy is to attack infrequently, without warning, in force, thus overwhelming individual units. This assures them maximum effectiveness with minimum fuel consumption and losses . . ."

He returned again and again to the role of the Eighth, bluntly stating that "there is a strong tendency to utilize the strategic air effort to win individual battles to the detriment of eventually winning the war." The ground Battle of France had, as far as Doolittle could see, supplanted the air Battle of Germany.

Whenever the bombers could be drawn away from France or from futile attempts to destroy the rocket launching sites, Doolittle turned again to the factories and oil facilities of Germany and occupied Europe, joined in this endeavor by the Fifteenth Air Force.

Within a month after he had written Spaatz, Doolittle received a typical letter from his old friend George Patton, rushing the U. S. Third Army across France:

My dear Jimmy,

This is to inform you that those low bastards, the Germans, gave me my first bloody nose when they compelled us to abandon our attack on Fort Driant in the Metz area.

I have requested a revenge bombardment from the air to teach those sons-of-bitches that they cannot fool with Americans. I believe that this request will eventually get to you, and I am therefore asking that you see that the Patton-Doolittle combination is not shamed in the eyes of the world, and that you provide large bombs of the nastiest type, and as many as you can spare, to blow up this damn fort so that it becomes nothing but a hole.

With warm regards, I am as ever,

Devotedly yours,
G. S. Patton, Jr.

Doolittle's reply, combining the formal with tongue-in-cheek, was, in effect, a polite "No," with an explanation (almost invariably required by ground commanders):

Dear General Patton:

Am just in receipt of your letter of 19 October and have

directed our A-2 Section to "case the joint" and our A-3 Section to plan the best method of attack—this in order that we may be ready to give you 100 percent service upon receipt of clearance from higher headquarters which establish our priorities.

You appreciate the fact that you have given us a pretty tough job. I doubt if the largest bombs that we have available are big enough to properly crack the thick cement emplacements at Fort Driant. Maybe we can do better with deep penetration projectiles. It may prove desirable to make the attack with fire. All of this we are studying.

In any case, you may be sure that we refuse to allow the nasal proboscis of our favorite field commander to be sanguinated by those, as you so subtly put it, "improper offspring of a long line of illegitimates."

Sincere best.

As ever,
J. H. Doolittle

In a concerted Allied attempt to get the ground war moving again, following an autumn check at the Rhine, the forts around Metz, which would include Patton's bête noire, Fort Driant, were subjected to artillery fire in addition to attack by fighter-bombers (most often P-47s), medium bombers, and roughly a thousand heavies. Vengeance-bound Patton took the precaution of insisting that no aerial bombing should be attempted within four miles of his troops. Although the ground offensive moved forward again, the use of the heavies upon the forts, as Doolittle predicted, accomplished little. (Eventually Metz was simply by-passed and encircled.)

Doolittle continued to decry the diversion of his forces and began to predict the re-emergence of the German fighter forces, whose factories, assembly plants, and airfields had been neglected in favor of the Allied rush to the Rhine; he even had gone so far as to criticize, though mildly, the ill-fated Market-Garden operation in Holland (a predominantly British undertaking) because it too had drawn the bombers away from their primary mission.

Ground-air co-operation was better achieved by tanks and P-47s in radio communication, but even that could go wrong. This occurred in December to Patton, who was moving ahead so rapidly that his tanks were mistaken by Allied planes for the enemy and sorely strated by mediums and fighter-bombers. As Reynolds aptly put it, "Patton's cry of rage filled the whole European theater . . ."

Spaatz, the diplomat and a man who was wise to the Patton penchant for mouthing the impolitic, suggested that he, Doolittle, and Vandenberg visit Patton, apologize, and generally soothe him. Spaatz and Doolittle boarded a twin-engined Beechcraft C-45, with the latter at the controls, and, accompanied by Vandenberg also flying a C-45, hurried to Patton's field headquarters. They very quickly calmed down their unpredictable friend and spent the evening with him.

The next morning they left for England, Doolittle taking off first with Vandenberg close behind. Doolittle was suddenly startled to see tracers flashing by. He assumed they had come under German fighter attack since they were near the front lines. He nosed the Beechcraft closer to the ground, Vandenberg still following, when he realized that the tracers were coming from ground positions held by Patton's trigger-happy troops. Doolittle took violent evasive action until they were out of the range of the troops.

Spaatz's most printable comment was a laconic, "Damn it, Jimmy, if we'd waited one more day, Georgie would have had to apologize to us," since it was now Patton's turn to explain an attack by "friendly" troops. While Spaatz tended to view the incident with characteristic mordant humor, had the troops been more accurate, the loss of three of the highest Allied air commanders in Europe would have been a serious one.

Upon arrival in England Spaatz immediately phoned Patton to inform him of what had occurred. Patton's reply was a loud, bellowing laugh; turnabout, in his curiously conceived book, was fair play.

A more grave turnabout soon followed, with the sudden, unexpected German counterattack in the Ardennes which came to be known as the "Battle of the Bulge." It was Hitler's last, futile, and rather mad attempt to drive the Allies away from the German border. The initial assault came before dawn on December 16, under the cover of impossible flying weather. Striking through the weakly held, wooded Eifel region of the Ardennes, which was covered with snow and shrouded with fog, the German forces began pushing back some six American divisions along a 70-mile front. The unexpectedness and the impact of this offensive was stunning.

If the weather hampered Allied air operations, it also kept the Luftwaffe, which was to have played a major role in the offensive, from contributing immediately to the breakthrough. Not all of the tired, surprised American troops fell back, and while the German attack was shattering, it was not as successful as Hitler and a few of his commanders had expected. For the first week, continuing foggy weather contrived to limit any aid to the desperate Allied ground forces from the Eighth and Ninth Air Forces, although full advantage was taken of any break in the weather.

The first real break occurred on December 24, with the dawning of the first of four days of good flying weather. While this brought out the Luftwaffe, it also unleashed the American P-47s and P-51s, often in dual roles as fighters and bombers. C-47s, laden with supplies, began making drops on beleaguered American positions. Eighth Air Force and Ninth Air Force bombers—mediums and heavies—united to wreak havoc among the German panzer units.

A study made by the British Air Council and based on contemporary German documents reveals the effect on Hitler's great plan: "The bombing of roads and railways in the rear was so successful that the supply situation, already bad, became catastrophic. Yet, so great was the need of the forward troops for protection that the Luftwaffe was compelled to leave Allied heavy bombers unmolested during the attacks on rear supply and communications areas, while attempting to provide defense against Allied close-support aircraft for their armored spearheads. . . . Bad weather which set in again on December 28 gave both the Luftwaffe and the German Army a badly needed respite, but the damage was done."

These were tumultuous days and nights for Doolittle, who had to keep one eye on the situation maps and the other on the weather. The success, however limited, of Hitler's offensive had a depressing effect in the Allied camp; if Hitler could spring such a surprise, it was obvious the war would not end by spring 1945—and where had he gotten all those planes?

Even the ever ebullient Doolittle, tired, concerned, revealed something of this effect in a letter to Joe, written after Christmas 1944:

Colder weather, shorter days, and soon another year gone. How time flies—and this in spite of the constant desire to get the job done and return home to loved ones. Sometimes tired, particularly when things go wrong. Rested, refreshed and exhilarated when things are going smoothly. Responsibility! Responsibility to God, nation, superiors, contemporaries, subordinates and self.

Command, regardless of its size or importance, carries with it both responsibility and opportunity. Responsibility to superiors and subordinates. Opportunity to utilize one's attributes and ability. It is difficult but necessary to exercise command in such a way as to assure respect and loyalty of subordinates and the confidence of superiors. To strive to avoid engendering antagonism and annoyance and establish approbation, admiration and even affection. The last objective is rarely achieved, particularly among our contemporaries.

I sometimes think that when this is all over I'd like to run a peanut stand. Would want it on a quiet street where there wouldn't be too many customers to interfere with my meditations. Actually, after a week's rest I imagine I'd be restless and looking for work and responsibility again.

Doolittle's mood was not lightened when on New Year's Day 1945 the Luftwaffe again sprang out of nowhere in surprising numbers, to lacerate Allied airfields in Holland, Belgium, and France. Before the day ended some 156 Allied planes had been destroyed (36 American). This was a chilling and even discouraging development—since those in the Allied camp were unaware of the fact that this was just another wasteful, last-ditch measure that contributed nothing to the war except tragic prolongation. In addition, the Luftwaffe lost more aircraft that day than they had destroyed; the planes could be replaced but not the pilots, both veteran and the undertrained.

By the end of January the Bulge had been flattened out, but Allied plans for a spring offensive and the hoped-for victory in Europe had to be revised. Doolittle's concern was with getting back to strategic bombardment and anticipating the advent of German jet fighters in numbers, along with increasing numbers of conventional Me-109s and FW-190s. There was a multiplicity of targets: it was even seriously suggested that the Air Forces con-

centrate on the wiping out of Hitler's mountain lair at Berchtes-
gaden, in Bavaria. (To what strategic, or even, tactical end?
Doolittle enquired.) Or why not a joint British-American effort to
destroy every inch of Berlin in a massive daylight raid; this plan
was nipped in the bud by Spaatz and others, with objections to
morale bombings. And so it went until control of the Strategic Air
Forces finally reverted again from Eisenhower's headquarters to
the Combined Chiefs of Staff and, thus, back to the air commanders. But the autumn problems of the ground forces, of
course, had interfered with a complete reversion, although a systematic attack on German oil targets was initiated; other targets
were German railways, ordnance, and motor vehicles—none especially susceptible to successful destruction by bombardment.

But Doolittle's nagging concern was the German fighter, and as
early as mid-November 1944 he was willing to set aside the strategic goal for another all-out effort against the Luftwaffe, which
chose to lie low but came out in force from time to time at great
cost to the Eighth. The Allied air commanders had no idea that
these unexpected and generally appallingly costly forays were but
an indication of the Luftwaffe's dire straits: it faced a shortage of
pilots and fuel.

A general air of pessimism permeated the various Allied headquarters when 1945 began; taking the Battle of the Bulge at face
value, as well as the sudden mass emergence of the Luftwaffe,
the more gloomy predicted that the war—which all had expected
to be over by the spring—could grind on until the following year.

Thus when General (Frederick) Anderson commented that the
increase in German oil production and in manufacturing jets,
missiles, and ball bearings because of the diversion of Allied
bomber forces to the ground war, the strategic picture was "very
sad," Doolittle agreed "one hundred per cent or more."

During January Doolittle dispatched three quarters of his strategic force to assist in the ground war and most of the remainder
to oil targets inside Germany, with telling effect. In this he was
again at times joined by the Fifteenth Air Force—when it was not
engaged in bombing transportation targets in Italy and other German-held countries. While not purely strategic, these bombings by
both Air Forces would have a decided impact that would contribute to bringing the German war machine to a grinding halt.

On February 3, 1945, Doolittle sent 1,000 Fortresses to bomb

Berlin, the first attack in two months. The prime target was Berlin's vast transportation system. On the same day the 2nd Division's Liberators, 400 in all, sought out oil and rail targets in the Magdeburg area. P-51s not only served as escort (and with effect; the 21 bombers lost fell to flak, not to the Luftwaffe), but also went down to the deck to strafe railway installations. The bombing of Berlin, especially since it ranged through all of Berlin, was questioned in the foreign press and labeled as a "terror raid" on "innocent civilians."

The fact was that bombings on such transportation centers would confuse, even cut off, the flow of enemy supplies and troops to fronts in both East and West and was, in part, an aid to the Russians. The bombings also interfered with German withdrawals from both fronts. Unfortunately, however, most rail centers were situated in great population centers, such as Berlin, Leipzig, and Dresden. This last city became the symbol of Allied "terror bombing" after it was attacked, upon a request from the Soviets, on February 13–14 and was transformed into a seething inferno, resulting in a great number of civilian casualties and widespread destruction in residential areas. As a rail center it was also finished.

On February 22, the U. S. Eighth and Fifteenth Air Forces and British Bomber Command literally ranged all over Germany striking at targets that had never been hit before, mainly transportation targets. Fighters again escorted as well as strafed. The plan, code-named Clarion, was designed to demonstrate to all of Germany that the skies were now owned by the Allies. It was hoped that this would affect the morale of the German people— always an unknown quantity and a "target" the American air commanders rejected. A second Clarion mission took place the following day, again with little Luftwaffe opposition and with the loss of only 2 B-17s by the Eighth (out of a force of 1,193). The transportation network was mangled, but the morale of the German people revealed no signs of cracking.

The German war machine was cracking, however, although Hitler refused to read the portents in the sky. His senseless, self-destructive continuation of what was clearly a lost war only heightened the slaughter and the desolation. There was hardly a corner of Nazi Germany safe from bombing or strafing. The neat concept of strategic bombardment no longer obtained; the fate of

dozens of German cities, and their hapless populations, was tragically sealed.

Doolittle himself described in 1945 the technique employed at
the time as it had applied back in 1944 to but three industrial
cities, Magdeburg, Kassel, and Zeitz: "The first two are illustrative
of the normal type of collaboration in which American heavies destroy the major industries on the fringes of the city and the RAF
destroys the city proper with the substantial number of factories
situated in the urban center. This combined effort results in a virtual elimination of the city as an armament producing center.
Thus, in Magdeburg, the Eighth operated on the top priority synthetic gasoline plant at Rothensee, the Krupp plant at Buckau
making tanks, guns, shells and other weapons, the ordnance depot
at Friedrichstadt where these weapons were collected for dis-
tribution to the 6th Panzer Army and other units in combat on
the Western and Eastern Fronts, and the Junkers factory turning
out the newest engine powering the FW-190.

"The RAF followed this by the destruction of the urban area.
This final phase not only destroyed the houses of the factory
workmen and interrupted vital military industrial transport, but
more important still, destroyed a very large part of the remaining
factories in this highly developed industrial center. In an armament city of this kind, most of the industries are inter-dependent
one upon the other, using common sources of power, raw materials and transport, with many smaller plants making parts for
final assembly of war material in the larger ones.

"The combined Allied attacks result in the virtual elimination of
the city and its industrial environs as a major producer in the German war economy.

"Kassel is another example of the same coordination, with the
difference that the RAF, in a night area attack, also destroyed a
factory on our priority list of precision targets, the FW assembly
plant at Kassel/Bettenhausen.

"In recent months, and coincident with greater versatility in
RAF operations, Bomber Command and the Eighth have been attacking identical targets. The RAF, having reduced the production
of the synthetic oil plants in the Ruhr to minor proportions by attacks during the summer and autumn of 1944, began in December
to help us with the campaign which we started last spring against
the major synthetic plants lying much deeper in Germany. Zeitz is

a good example of this. We knocked it out in late May 1944 and kept it from any substantial production until November 1944. Then in January, the RAF put it out for another three months.

"Even more recently, the Eighth and the RAF have been engaged in a joint assault on the vital rail and water communications of Western Germany. The RAF, by a series of accurate attacks, has blocked the Dortmund-Ems Canal and the western part of the Mittelland Canal, while the Eighth has twice breached the aqueduct at Minden. These waterways were used for bulk transport, including coal from the Ruhr and parts for prefabricated U-boats too large for shipment by rail. On the railways, we have been working on the same list of targets comprising major marshalling yards, bridges, viaducts, and other key points. Damages and the progress of repairs are carefully watched and co-ordinated attacks are made against these targets which have the greatest current importance.

"This program, which is too ambitious for either Air Force to tackle alone, has made systematic operation of the railroads impossible. The economic traffic from and within the Ruhr, which is doubly important since the loss of Silesia [which had fallen to the Russians in the east], is being strangled and military movements in the area east of the Rhine become slower and more hazardous every day."

By the end of February 1945 the German economy was in ruins, a ruin that would have its strategic effect only in the future —but Germany as a war-making nation had no future. However, it had stock-piled materials in the past that were still being used in the chaotic present. The rocket and jet fighters that Doolittle had cautioned against since the previous summer materialized menacingly in the spring of 1945.

Their initial appearances were tentative, undecisive; but the effect on Allied air force crews was one of apprehension. It was a neck-wrenching experience to watch either the Me-163 rocket fighter or the Me-262 jet fighter flash through a bomber formation with incredible speed. It was disconcerting to see a dot in the distance enlarge into a deadly aircraft in an instant and, within practically the same instant, become a distant dot again. Or to see such aircraft "playfully encircling the slower P-51s, making a few attacks and eluding the Mustangs without apparent difficulty," as was documented in Craven and Cates's *The Army Air Forces in*

World War II. This first real encounter occurred during the mission of March 3, 1945, the jets accounting for 3 bombers and 6 fighters before leaving the scene.

The toll was not spectacular, but the first performance of the jets, Me-262s of *Jagdgeschwader* 7 was unnerving. With their appearance, a new day had dawned in aerial warfare; even the fleet and deadly Mustang could not overtake the extraordinary twin-pod Swallow, with a speed of more than 500 miles an hour. Mysteriously, however, after this first major test run with the jets, the Luftwaffe chose to lay low for a while (the Allies were not aware of the reason, the paucity of experienced pilots and the fuel shortage); to the nervous bomber crews it appeared like another diabolical German super weapon they had read about in aviation pulp magazines of the 1930s.

But bombing missions continued, with an almost random selection of targets, primarily to disrupt the German transportation system. One unusual mission was mounted by Doolittle on March 12 at the request of the Russians, who wished the Baltic port of Swinemünde bombed to interfere with possible German army reinforcements for the Eastern front coming in by sea. Doolittle complied, subtracting some 671 bombers from other missions of the day. Because of 10/10 cloud cover, which made visual bombing impossible, the bombers used the H2X (a form of radar) to accomplish the mission. Certain that the Eighth had done a fine job, Doolittle asked the Russians if they would be so kind as to furnish photos of the bomb damage, since the Eighth had not been able to photograph the bomb strikes.

Curiously, the only reply from the Russians minimized the damages and no photographs ever arrived. However, the RAF flew over Swinemünde to make reconnaissance photos and reported "substantial damage." Attempts to co-ordinate operations, or to co-operate, with the Russians invariably proved to be frustrating. The general, if not always expressed, attitude became: if you have Russia for an ally, you don't need an enemy.

The sparse Luftwaffe fighter operations during early March were ominous; obviously the Germans were conserving fuel for a major confrontation. The lull was finally broken during a bombing mission to Berlin on March 18, again to accommodate the Russians who were pushing eastward toward the German capital, when the Luftwaffe met the Eighth Air Force bombers and fighters ferociously—and with chilling numbers of the dismaying jets.

When orders for the Berlin mission came down from Spaatz's headquarters, Doolittle had already scheduled a number of short-range operations against targets inside Germany. These were scrubbed and a full-scale mission was set in motion. It was to be the most massive daylight attack on Berlin of the war: 1,250 heavy bombers escorted by fourteen groups of P-51s.

Despite the poor weather, which necessitated bombing through clouds with H2X, the Me-262s of JG 7, 37 in all, rose up to meet the American invaders. The attacks were described as "aggressive," and at least one observer reported being attacked by a formation of no less than 36 jets at a time. The Swallows ranged through the entire bomber stream, eluding the Mustangs with ease and shooting up the bombers. Before the battle ended, 36 heavies had gone down—and an additional 16 were so damaged that they crash-landed behind the Russian lines (some of these had been damaged by flak, which was also heavy that day). Five P-51s were lost, to complete the day's toll. The full impact of the jet fighter upon a conventional combat formation was rammed home that March 18, 1945.

As early as the previous August Doolittle had begun planning his counterjet campaign. The problem could be dealt with strategically by bombing jet-producing factories and airfields. Tactically, methods would have to be devised whereby the now outclassed Allied fighters might cope with the much faster Me-262.

When more jets appeared, although less aggressively, on the two days following March 18, Doolittle asked to meet with Air Chief Marshal Tedder, Eisenhower's deputy commander, to discuss his plan for an all-out attack on the Luftwaffe, with emphasis on jet bases. Tedder agreed to the plan and the Eighth, with aid from Bomber Command and the Fifteenth, systematically attacked at least fifteen airfields in northwest Germany. These missions contributed also to the planned crossing of the Rhine on March 24, when another heavy attack on German airfields was launched. By the close of March there were few strategic targets left in Germany and Eisenhower spoke of a "whipped enemy." The enemy, however, neither agreed to nor admitted this truth and the air war continued, with another visit to the suburbs of Berlin on March

28. A stand-down followed because of weather on the following day and then on March 30 some old and hated (though now low priority) targets, invoking the initial troubled days of the Eighth, came up again. The place names—Wilhelmshaven, Bremen, Hamburg—recalled those early days of heavy losses with small effect, when the Eighth engaged in its war on the U-boat. The attacks, however, went unchallenged (except at Hamburg, where jets appeared but did not attack) and bombs tumbled onto the U-boat installations as they never had in the history of the Eighth. Some stray bombs at Wilhelmshaven spilled into the harbor and accounted for no less than 19 German ships.

When April began the system of target priorities meant very little: the Fifteenth Air Force shifted to assisting in the land battle; Harris of the RAF Bomber Command asserted that he had practically run out of targets; the Eighth mounted but ten strategic missions during the month. The jet fighters continued to meet the bombers, but with little result—on one mission it took some 30 Me-262s to destroy a single B-17.

There was concern now in the Allied camp about the extent of destruction in Germany by aerial bombardment and its effect upon the advancing Allied armies. On April 12, at an Allied Air Committee conference, Doolittle stated that all fighters should be ordered to stop all strafing, since troops then inside Germany were likely to be Allies.

Two days later he said good-bye to both Allard and Johnson, the former because his phlebitis had flared up seriously enough to necessitate sending him home for hospitalization. Johnson went along to see Allard into the hospital in Washington. Accomplishing that, he then checked in with Arnold. Johnson's secondary mission was to be briefed on the future plans for the Eighth Air Force once the war in Europe ended.

Two days after that, April 16, 1945, Doolittle received a message from Spaatz which began: "The advances of our ground forces have brought to a close the strategic air war waged by the United States Strategic Air Forces and the Royal Air Force Bomber Command . . .

"All units of the U. S. Strategic Air Forces are commended for their part in winning the Strategic Air War and are enjoined to continue with undiminished effort and precision the final tactical phase of air action to secure the ultimate objective—the defeat of Germany . . ."

The missions had become almost random: from April 4 to the sixteenth bombers carried 2,000-pound demolition, incendiary, and napalm bombs by the thousands to eliminate a particularly stubborn German garrison in the vicinity of Bordeaux, by-passed during the race across France. At the end of the month, on the twenty-fifth, Doolittle called on the Eighth to bomb its last industrial target of the war, the Skoda factories at Pilsen, Czechoslovakia. The mission made the crews unhappy, for before the bombing occurred a warning was sent out to Pilsen to spare casualties among the workers (despite this, five were killed). Air crews, however, regarded this as a sign that their leaders had greater concern for the safety of civilian workers than their own. But neither fighter nor flak interfered with their dropping 500 tons of bombs into the Skoda works to very devastating effect.

The Eighth's final missions of the war in Europe were totally unwarlike: mercy missions in May to Holland, dropping food to the Dutch, and the evacuation of prisoners of war as the Allied armies overran prison camps. Even the ground crews, who had worked so hard in England—30,000 of them—were given an air tour of devastated Germany to see what air power had wrought.

Bruce Johnson, meanwhile, had more work to do once his mission to Washington had been concluded. From Washington he had been flown to Peterson Field, Colorado, to study at first hand a giant aircraft he had never seen before: the Boeing B-29 Superfortress.

On May 7, 1945, five days after the German forces had capitulated in Italy, Germany surrendered unconditionally at Eisenhower's forward headquarters at Reims. The Third Reich had collapsed into a rubble of smoking ruins, a grisly finale with overtones of madness. Hitler, his world crumbling around him, committed suicide in his Berlin bunker on April 30, after appointing Admiral Karl Doenitz as his successor (deliberately by-passing Luftwaffe Reichsmarschall Hermann Goering), clearing the way for the final surrender.

The signing took place in a small schoolhouse with Colonel General Alfred Jodl, weeping, and Admiral Hans von Friedeburg signing for Germany; General Walter Bedell Smith signed for the

Allies and generals Ivan Susloparov and François Sevez, signed as witnesses for Russia and France, respectively. General Spaatz was present at the surrender as a representative of the American Air Forces.

The following day, May 8, was proclaimed V-E day by Prime Minister Churchill and President Harry Truman, who had succeeded to the presidency on the death of Franklin Delano Roosevelt in April. Upon the ratification of the surrender by the German High Command, and what remained of the government, in Berlin on May 9, the war in Europe officially ended.

But the war was not over for Doolittle; he had been ordered to take the Eighth Air Force to the Pacific.

Eighteen

For the first time since he had come to England in July of 1942 (excepting a brief flying visit that same year "to iron things out"), Doolittle was going home for an extended stay. On May 10, 1945, he turned over what remained of the Eighth Air Force in Britain to its new chief, Major General Kepner, former commander of the Eighth Fighter Command. Doolittle had become a popular figure in England and his departure was marked by one London newspaper, the *Evening Standard,* with the declaration DOOLITTLE TELLS OF PLANS TO WIN OTHER HALF OF WAR . . .

This statement had been made not by Doolittle, but by an Eighth Air Force officer while drunk in a pub frequented by newspapermen. Inadvertently, Doolittle once again—as he had with Eisenhower—was stepping off on the wrong foot and that one in his mouth; only in this instance he himself was completely innocent. Someone sent the newspaper to his new supreme commander, General Douglas MacArthur, who was generally, and understandably, piqued by the article's implications. (Reynolds, in his biography of Doolittle, quotes a London headline as reading: DOOLITTLE TO SHOW MACARTHUR HOW TO WIN THE PACIFIC WAR. While this may have been a distortion, it is how MacArthur translated it.)

Doolittle, meanwhile, happy to be on his way and unaware of the claims made for him by a well-intentioned, but not totally responsible friend, headed homeward accompanied by his son Jim, for a reunion with Joe Doolittle. By mid-May the senior Doolittles snatched a little "R&R" (rest and recreation) in Florida, as Doolittle called their brief respite, for he knew that the Army Public Relations Office had already made plans for him before his departure for the Pacific.

There was serious concern in Washington that the end of the war in Europe would bring about a public apathy with the war that still remained to be fought. So an idea was conceived by the Public Relations Office to remind the American people of the war in the Pacific.

Since both Doolittle and Patton were native Californians, they were requested by the War Department to make joint appearances and speeches in their home state. Their reunion in June was well covered by the press. Patton did not disappoint the photographers, who swarmed over Buckley Field, Colorado, to cover the event. He wore a gleaming helmet, a beribboned and starred battle jacket; a special belt with a round, medallionlike buckle was burdened with a pearl-handled pistol at his right side. Jodhpurs, glistening boots, gloves, and a swagger stick completed the costume.

Doolittle was less flamboyantly attired, in standard summer uniform and a rather floppy cap, the "crusher," popular among aircrews.

Their tour almost instantly revealed that Patton presented special problems in public relations. Even in Europe he had made some upsetting statements about war in general and the Russians specifically that had disturbed Eisenhower, who already had his hands full trying to keep peace among the Allies. Patton's penchant for saying bluntly precisely what he had on his mind carried over to the States as well: speaking before a girl's organization he informed them that they would undoubtedly qualify to serve as nurses in "the next war."

The Army felt a little constraint might be appropriate and wherever possible had a monitor (often in the stage's prompter's box) to keep an eye and ear on Patton to spot any symptoms of imminent indiscretion. If these were detected in time, the monitor would cut off Patton's microphone, thus sparing the Army embarrassment. The ploy did not always work.

Doolittle and Patton made a colorful team, of course, and to the Army it was worth the risk of a Patton gaffe to present them together. "Georgie would always give them a fire-and-brimstone talk, which I usually felt was a little too severe," Doolittle remembers. "So if he talked first, I generally tapered off a bit, made it a little quieter. If I talked first, why Georgie would pep it up a bit."

On one occasion they appeared together at the Hollywood Bowl and were accompanied by Joe Doolittle and Mrs. Beatrice Patton, who were seated on the stage with them. Doolittle spoke first, reminding the large audience that the war was not over and that the same spirit that had ended the war in Europe, undiminished, would bring an end to the war in the Pacific. In conclusion he said, "Ladies and gentlemen, I would like to say we have two very lovely ladies here with us who, if General Patton and I have achieved any success whatsoever, are largely responsible for that success with their constant support, understanding and affection."

Whereupon the two ladies were introduced, took their bows to tremendous applause, and Doolittle turned from the podium as Patton approached for his speech. Just as they passed, Patton said into the microphone, "You son-of-a-bitch, I wish I'd thought of that!" This boomed over the PA system and filled Hollywood Bowl with another "Patton incident," though a relatively minor one.

Eventually Doolittle and Patton went their separate ways. In July Patton returned to Europe to take up duties in the occupation of Germany, where he continued making blunt statements, most of them very uncomplimentary to the Russians. He was still at it until, tragically, he died following a jeep accident in December 1945.

Doolittle, after Patton left, continued with his speaking tour traveling up to Seattle, home base of the Boeing Aircraft Company which produced two of the war's outstanding aircraft, the B-17 and the B-29. Doolittle would take the opportunity to study the latter, the Superfortress—a very heavy bomber—that was to be his air weapon once the Eighth Air Force was established in the Pacific.

By the first week of July he joined Bruce Johnson at Peterson Field, Colorado, where Johnson had been overseeing the selection of a crew for Doolittle's personal B-29 for the transfer to the Pacific. Their flight plan took them eastward to Washington, D.C. first. Johnson left Peterson in a B-17 carrying replacement parts for Doolittle's Superfortress in which Doolittle was to follow later. By July 9 both planes were at Bolling Field, near Washington, and Doolittle attended to the final details for the flight.

The next morning both planes took off, flew to Newfoundland, refueled there and then continued across the Atlantic to Britain. They remained there only for a couple of days—during which Doolittle managed a side trip to France where he picked up two cases of champagne (gifts for MacArthur and his air chief, General George Kenney) and a bottle of old Napoleon brandy for Admiral Chester Nimitz, commander of the Pacific fleet. They left England on July 12 bound for Cairo; from there they flew to Kharagpur, India. A long flight of thirteen hours brought them to the Philippine Islands, where they were greeted by Kenney on July 15.

The next day they left for their final stop. Flying generally northward, they brought their two bombers down at Kadena Air Base, Okinawa. On July 16, 1945, the Eighth Air Force was officially established at Okinawa (on that same date in the United States at Los Alamos, New Mexico, a new type of bomb had been tested with frightful success).

With the arrival of Doolittle and Johnson at Okinawa the Eighth had arrived in the Pacific: two men and their crews and two bombers. The Eighth had been transferred, as the record puts it, "without personnel, equipment, and combat elements." Some groups of the original Eighth Air Force had remained in Europe as part of the occupation forces, others had begun flying back to the United States. Veteran crews were dispersed, some were sent to schools for transitional training, from the B-17 to the B-29. Doolittle, in short, was beginning from scratch.

Johnson never forgot his first sight of Kadena, then in the process of being bulldozed and manhandled into the semblance of an air base. A feeling of "absolute dismay" gripped him. "It was one of the sorriest looking spots in the world." It dawned on Johnson that they were a long way from the amenities of High Wycombe or the delights of Piccadilly: "The proposed site for our headquarters lay ten miles northeast of Kadena, a flat section of land that butted into a large coral hill on the north. One section of the area was full of Okinawan burial mounds and I could see that much of the old cemetery would have to be moved—reverently, I hoped—for us to have the space that we needed. As it now stood, the whole area was a sea of mud."

Doolittle recalled Johnson's initial experience in that delicate project: "The Okinawans buried their dead in large urns above ground. Brucie's natural curiosity caused him to remove the lid of one of the urns and look in. He was eyeball to eyeball with a tremendous spider who, with family, also inhabited the urn. It was a fine lesson in reverence for the dead."

Meanwhile, even as the new B-29 crews were being processed through the staging center at Peterson Field in Colorado, Doolittle and Johnson were confronted with the problem of having housing ready for them when they arrived in Okinawa. Johnson immediately organized all available hands into labor gangs, including members of "our own headquarters enlisted group and a few officers who were unwillingly pressed into service on the wrong end of a shovel."

Doolittle lived in a tent; he had come full circle—it was like reliving the North African campaign all over again, down to dining on unpalatable K-rations. Johnson befriended a group of Seabees (Navy construction battalion engineers), who managed— "where they found it, I never enquired"—to scrounge up a good-sized refrigerator (a Navy "reefer"), which Johnson placed in their headquarters. "I kept it under full-time guard once we had it working."

In addition to the paucity of luxuries, let alone comforts, they were frequently bombed by hit-and-run Japanese nuisance raids. Until their men and planes arrived, Doolittle and Johnson whiled away their evenings at cribbage. Johnson's tent was near Doolittle's and the evening's game would begin when Doolittle shouted, "Brucie, come on over!"

He had seen to it that he brought several of his old Eighth Air Force reliables with him. Besides Johnson, there were Partridge, now a major general, as deputy commander, and Thomas Barrineau, now a major, as aide.

While they were settling in, the war moved inexorably toward a climax. General LeMay's B-29s were incinerating Japanese industrial cities. To the southwest of Okinawa, in the Marianas group, on an island named Tinian, a rather mysterious, close-mouthed unit, the 509th Composite, equipped with special Superfortresses, was poised for an undefined, secret action.

A few days later, on July 20, General Spaatz arrived at Guam, also in the Marianas, to assume command of all U. S. Strategic Air Forces in the Pacific. He was, in effect, General Arnold's deputy, for in keeping with his intentions of not letting the B-29s fall into the wrong, i.e., other than Air Force, hands, Arnold, through the Joint Chiefs of Staff, retained control of the long-range bombers. As he himself put it, "MacArthur yelled for the B-29's; Nimitz wanted the B-29's; Stilwell and Mountbatten wanted the B-29's—all for tactical purposes." Arnold, of course, ranked all those who raised their voices.

Kenney, MacArthur's very capable airman, was vocalizing, too. He did, however, understand airpower and wished to acquire very heavy bombers also, to supplement the B-24s he was then using. During a trip to the United States he had collared Arnold and got him to consent to open up the Convair B-32 production line which would enable Kenney to acquire a fleet of those giant bombers. The war ended, however, before the B-32s were ready for combat.

Even as Doolittle's forces grew (the Eighth was not scheduled to reach operational status until February 1946), the mysterious 509th Composite made its first strike with a lone B-29. The *Enola Gay* dropped the first atomic bomb on the city of Hiroshima on August 6, 1945. When it became clear that the Japanese would not capitulate, despite the horrors of Hiroshima, a second atomic bomb fell on Nagasaki three days later. The next day word came from Tokyo that Japan was willing to surrender provided that the Emperor would not be touched or restrained in any way. On August 14 Japanese representatives agreed to unconditional surrender. August 14, 1945, would officially be V-J Day. The war was over.

The Pacific war ended before the Eighth's Superfortresses could participate; however, long-range P-47s of the Eighth Air Force, based on Ie Shima adjacent to Okinawa, had flown several missions over Japan. A group of B-29s had arrived at Kadena, but had not yet "comfortably settled in" when the second atomic bomb was dropped. Almost immediately after, Doolittle was called by an officer urging him to mount an Eighth Air Force B-29 mission. The war would be over within the next few days, he was told, and if he wanted to "be able to say that Eighth Air

Force bombers had participated in the bombing of Japan, he'd better get a mission off at once."

Doolittle's answer was that if the war was really over, he did not plan "to jeopardize the life of one crew member" merely to add another historic date to the chronicle of the Eighth Air Force.

He was pleased, however, to participate in the official surrender ceremonies that were to take place September 2 in Tokyo Bay aboard the battleship U.S.S. *Missouri*. His return to the scene of the Raid was tinctured somewhat by a little contretemps that occurred that day. Having arranged for his transportation from Okinawa to Tokyo, Doolittle invited Major General Ennis Whitehead, commander of the Fifth Air Force, who happened to be visiting at the time, to accompany him.

Upon landing in Japan, Whitehead had some details he wished to attend to before they boarded a boat for the *Missouri*. Despite Doolittle's importunings for speediness, Whitehead became so involved with his projects that they found, when they arrived at the dock, that their boat, the penultimate one, had already left. The remaining boat was assigned to MacArthur. In order to reach the *Missouri* they would have to steal a ride—uninvited—in MacArthur's craft.

The frostiness in the air was obvious, although Doolittle believed neither apology nor explanation would have cleared the air. They were permitted aboard, but it was evident that MacArthur was not pleased. Doolittle was philosophical. As with Eisenhower, he had not endeared himself to MacArthur—perhaps some of the unfortunate British newspaper articles had had some effect. Doolittle was certain that MacArthur assumed that he, Doolittle, was responsible for the tardiness which had almost upset the surrender ceremonies.

Despite the uneasiness of the occasion, the ceremonies proceeded with great dignity, carried off with solemn poise and statesmanship by MacArthur. "I had a great respect for General MacArthur," Doolittle has written. "While it is true he had a great self-confidence—he was entitled to it. He was good! He was a great military leader, tactician and strategist.

"He did not, I am afraid, have the same confidence in me."

If the small breach in etiquette caused Doolittle some anxiety, it was nothing compared to Joe Doolittle's V-J Day experience. Between her speaking tours she returned to the Pawling Rehabilitation Center. When it was learned that many of the patients revealed certain of their problems, feelings, and doubts to her that they did not confide to members of the medical staff, it was decided to send her to Fort Logan, Colorado, for a special course in aviation psychiatry.

It was while she was at Logan that Joe became aware of a familiar face among the patients there that seemed to appear and disappear—a rather eerie experience. Finally she sought out the young man, who wore his cap low over his face, and recognized a former Pawling patient whom she had thought had been released. The young man had crashed in the Philippines in the early days of the war, and although he had managed to elude the Japanese, he had witnessed many atrocities. After his rescue, he had broken down mentally and been sent to Pawling.

Obviously he had not recovered, for it was necessary to return him to a mental institution, for which he was ashamed—which explained his attempts to keep Joe from seeing him. Once his disguise had been penetrated, he again talked with her. "He was after me to have Jimmy send for him—Jimmy was in the Pacific by that time. The boy's whole idea was 'to kill Japs.'"

Joe Doolittle had quarters in the Officers' Club and it was her practice to leave her door open for several hours each day should any of the patients wish to talk with her. She was resting in her rooms in the evening of V-J Day when the young man who had so fervently hoped to kill Japanese appeared at her door. Celebrants had apparently given him a drink. He rushed into the room, tackled Joe, and announced that he was going to kill her.

The sounds of scuffle brought some doctors into the room. They were able to restrain the patient who was placed in a strait jacket. (Some time later he did commit suicide.)

With these two disparate V-J Day experiences, the Doolittles had a right to believe that the Second World War was officially over for them. Not quite, for Doolittle had one more uncomfortable experience to endure.

The war, having come to a spectacular close, required a newsworthy exploit as a dramatic coda—or so it seemed to someone (no one knows who) in Washington. Why not bring the curtain down on the bloody drama with a peaceful flight of B-29s from the Pacific to Washington, D.C., nonstop if possible? And why not have the colorful Jimmy Doolittle lead the flight?

As anxious to get home as to lead the flight, Doolittle immediately began making plans for it. General LeMay, veteran commander of Europe and the Pacific, was to pilot one of the other planes.

The aircraft were prepared for the flight by the removal of all unnecessary equipment to save weight and to enable the installation of the required extra fuel and oil tankage. Crews would be reduced to an absolute minimum—even personal luggage was to be carried in an extra plane that would take another route (the "historic" B-29s would take a great circle route) to Washington.

General Spaatz by this time had returned to Washington leaving Doolittle, now the senior Strategic Air Forces officer, in command at Guam. It was here that Doolittle received a message from MacArthur suggesting that Kenney, MacArthur's senior air officer, make the flight as a passenger in one of the planes. Doolittle replied that the stripped-down planes could simply not carry any additional weight and therefore recommended against carrying any passengers. It is possible that Doolittle sensed that once Kenney, who was his military superior, came aboard, he might then automatically be in command of the flight.

This may have been a subconscious, or perhaps conscious, surfacing of the more or less friendly Pacific v. Europe rivalry. Doolittle recalled some of the good-natured exchanges between Spaatz, the European air commander, and Kenney, the Southwest Pacific air commander. The latter offered to come over and introduce some of his successful innovations, particularly close-in dive bombing, to European airmen. Spaatz's reply was a rather caustic, "If he wants to help win the war in Europe, he can take on the German fighters and flak and send us the Japanese fighters and flak." The truth of this riposte was demonstrated by a famed Pacific airman, Major Thomas G. Lanphier, Jr., one of the major participants in the mission that ended the brilliant career of Japanese Admiral Isoroku Yamamoto.

Lanphier, upon completion of his tour in the Pacific, was sent home to serve as an instructor. Hoping to acquire a better understanding of the demands of European training techniques, he had himself tranferred to the ETO (European Theater of Operations) for a while. Among other things, he flew missions with Colonel Hubert Zemke's 56th Fighter Group. Zemke asked Lanphier to come along on a dive-bombing mission to observe and to suggest improvements. Lanphier, who had been accustomed to flipping bombs into a jungle at barely treetop height, was surprised to see the P-47 Thunderbolts let loose at six or seven thousand feet. As for the target, "they missed the hell out of it." For the next mission, led by Lanphier, Zemke assigned two wingmen to make the attack along with the Pacific veteran.

Lanphier put the Thunderbolt into a dive and plunged at the target. It was then he learned about the difference between Japanese and German flak. He also understood why Zemke's dive bombers released at what he regarded as too high an altitude. Vicious flak ripped up all three of the P-47s (although all returned safely) and Lanphier's had the additional distinction of having a cylinder from the engine shot away. He landed back at the 56th's base and laconically told Zemke, "I guess it won't work here."

The war was finished, but the intratheater rivalry continued. Doolittle was eager for his Eighth Air Force to close the drama with a flourish and MacArthur determined to have his own airman, Kenney, provide the colorful finale.

The day after Doolittle had informed MacArthur that he did not recommend Kenney's making the flight, word came literally out of the blue, from Washington, that he would proceed home by the regular route and that Lieutenant General Barney M. Giles, Arnold's deputy, would lead the 3-plane flight. Doolittle was naturally very disappointed and wondered exactly what had happened. (Years after the war, after Arnold's retirement, Doolittle asked his former chief what had occurred and Arnold could only say that he had been away from his office at the time and the decision had been made in his absence.)

So, accompanied by a fuming Bruce Johnson, who blamed the fiasco on MacArthur, Doolittle flew home in the "baggage plane." The trip "was uneventful except for an engine failure" (the B-29 made a good deal of the flight then on three engines). They took off from Okinawa on September 12, landing at Kwajalein on the sixteenth, where Doolittle was presented a samurai sword by the island's commander, Brigadier General Lawson H. Sanderson, U. S. Marine Corps. The sword had been given to Sanderson by the Japanese commander of the island when he capitulated.

The flight continued uneventfully. On September 19, 1945, Doolittle set the big bomber down at National Airport, across the Potomac from Washington. Among the many in the great crowd there to greet him was Joe Doolittle.

A succession of reunions followed and the Doolittles were soon caught up in a revived social life. Doolittle enjoyed a reunion with both his sons, John then a West Point cadet and James, Jr., a captain and returnee from Europe. In New York John Allard, still in uniform and with his health somewhat improved, arranged for a party at the Lexington Hotel. The Doolittles' suite was crowded with old friends—aviators, military men, former colleagues from Shell. The party which spilled over into an adjoining suite reunited the Rockwell Field trio yet another time.

Alex Fraser, of Shell, managed to get Doolittle away from the din for a few moments; there being practically no quiet spot in the Lexington, including the lobby, where Doolittle attracted admiring attention, Fraser simply commandeered a cab, ordered the driver to "go anywhere," and proposed that Doolittle give some thought to returning to Shell as vice president. It was an attractive offer and Doolittle agreed he would probably return to Shell, but there was still work to be done while he remained in uniform. (Just the same, he would have to give serious thought to his postwar career, for he had doubts about the advisability of remaining in the peacetime Army.)

They returned to the sound-racked rooms at the Lexington; manager Charles Rochester had sent some entertainers in from the hotel's dining room—a group of Hawaiian singers complete with throbbing ukuleles and romantic songs of the South Seas.

Later, a special party was held at "21," which included the Rockwell Field trio, Joe Doolittle, John Doolittle, Mrs. Allard, and Mrs. Johnson. Bruce Johnson, Jr., an Army lieutenant just returned from Europe, completed the party. Columnist Louis Sobol reported a notable incident: Doolittle proposed a toast, then ordered the elder Johnson to rise, and pinned a Bronze Star on his chest. "It [was] probably the first time in history that a presentation of a military honor has been made in a restaurant," Sobol concluded.

The Doolittles returned to Washington, settled into an apartment at the Carlton, while Doolittle rounded out his tour of duty with the Air Force. The shooting war was finished, but the "cold war" loomed on the near horizon. There was trouble even closer to home, a flaring up of the internecine imbroglio between the services, with a special enmity between the Navy and the Air Force.

Doolittle set out on a cross-country lecture tour—what he termed his "Chautauqua circuit"—appearing before various civic groups to speak on the war and for a separate Air Force, a belief that he had never abandoned since his Baker Board minority report of 1934. He interrupted his tour in November to appear before the Senate Military Affairs Committee. While he had been away from Washington certain Navy men, who opposed a separate air force, made rather extreme claims for the Navy's contribution to the winning of the war. Speaking at Annapolis, Vice Admiral Marc Mitscher, from whose carrier *Hornet* the Tokyo Raid had been launched, rather categorically stated that "we must not for a moment lose sight of the fact that our carrier supremacy defeated Japan."

Admiral Chester Nimitz, in the same month, told a gathering at the Waldorf-Astoria in New York that it was sea power "alone" that had compelled Japan to sue for peace.

These were curious statements in light of the efforts of the ground as well as air forces during the war. Incensed, Doolittle fired off a memo to Arnold saying, "Any statement which ignores or belittles the magnificent contribution to victory in Japan made by the B-29s does not give all of the facts and depreciates the sacrifices of the heroic B-29 crews who attacked the Japanese mainland at a time when the Japanese Air Force was still a potent factor.

"I believe that teamwork won the war, and that each agency— land, sea, and air—did its job well . . ."

When he appeared before the Senate committee, Doolittle stressed that point. Secretary of the Navy James Forrestal leaped to his feet, evoking the mood of the Billy Mitchell trials, to accuse Doolittle of "unseemly conduct" and of course, of disrespect for senior Naval officers.

Doolittle reported the encounter to his former chief of staff and good friend Partridge: "I testified last Friday and called forth a sharp rebuke from Secretary Forrestal. It's a little difficult to understand this, since all of the four letter words had been edited out of my talk. I was delighted to have Secretary [of War Robert P.]

Patterson back me up a few days later. General Spaatz testified yesterday [November 12, 1945] and General Eisenhower today. Both gave excellent testimony. The Army is anxious to bring this thing to a conclusion as quickly as possible; the Navy is endeavoring to drag it out. The Senate Military Affairs Committee is apparently entirely sold not only on an autonomous and co-equal Air Force, but on a single Department of National Defense. We presume that House Military Affairs Committee hearings will take place after the first of the year. It's going to be more difficult to sell these people. We feel, however, that the least we can get out of it will be a separate Air Force. The problem is then going to be getting all land-based air under one agency."

Having had his say in Washington, Doolittle resumed his lecture tour which carried him to Oakland, California, and back east to West Point, with intermediate stops at St. Louis and Buffalo.

He returned to Washington to what was virtually a desk job, with emphasis on public relations. He willingly raised his voice in favor of a separate Air Force and a single Department of National Defense, but in considering his own future, his mind returned to the offer of Alex Fraser of Shell. On December 14 he achieved the age of forty-nine, still the youngest lieutenant general in the Army (and the only Reserve Officer to attain that rank), but he realized that his temperament would not accommodate itself to the politicking of the postwar Army.

The war over, he must turn to other responsibilities. He accepted Fraser's offer in the spring of 1946, with the proviso that, when needed, he was on call for duty with the Air Force. By mid-March the Doolittles moved into a spacious Fifth Avenue apartment in New York and Doolittle took up his duties for Shell in the RCA Building, in Rockefeller Center, as vice president.

Nineteen

A viation, as it had during the course of the First World War, progressed tremendously during the Second. Great strides were made in aircraft design; more powerful, more efficient engines were developed (not to mention the introduction of the jet engine); a network of airlines covered most of the globe. Transoceanic flight, particularly across the Atlantic, had become commonplace. The day of the romantic flying boat, and even the twin-engined transport, was over. Wartime transport aircraft, such as the Douglas C-54 Skymaster and the Lockheed C-69 Constellation, were converted into peacetime passenger airliners; even the Boeing B-29, with modification, was transformed into the Stratocruiser. It was, however, the introduction of an operational jet aircraft that would have the greatest impact on postwar aviation.

Among Doolittle's multiple duties as a vice president of Shell was to keep a sharp eye on the aircraft industry, its progress, and its needs as related to the petroleum industry. He was senior adviser to the board of directors on all aviation matters and undertook special assignments from the president or the board whenever he felt he could be helpful.

His role was flexible, for Shell readily recognized his value as a public relations representative—there were few people in aviation, if any, who were not Doolittle's friends or acquaintances. His long experience in engineering also made him an invaluable technical adviser in areas not confined to aviation. Despite these various roles in the Shell organization, it was also understood that whenever Doolittle's services were requested by agencies of the United States Government, including the Air Force, Shell would come second; and Shell concurred.

Thus was Doolittle the executive born, the popular chairman of the board, the trustee—the solid citizen, no longer the madcap pilot of legend (which, in fact, he had never been). His wartime fame as the leader of the Tokyo Raid clung to him more than did the years as the chief executive of the mammoth Eighth Air Force; even his prewar stint as a Shell executive, which had helped prepare him for his work during the war, was obscured by his reputation as an adventurer. He was, in fact, a celebrity much in demand for personal appearances, speeches, and interviews. He was also, although under salary to Shell, aviation's general spokesman—"Mister Aviation," in the apposite phrase of newspaperman Joseph F. Oravec.

If his demeanor was less sportive than it had been in his air pioneering days, he remained the same approachable, informal, sunny personality. The transformation from "General" to "Mister" was easily accomplished; more frequently he was addressed simply by his first name (he discouraged the use of his military title in business).

In April 1946, while on a South American tour for Shell, Doolittle learned that he had been elected to the board of directors. He had also returned to active flying, inducing Shell to acquire an Army surplus B-25, to be used as a flying laboratory for testing new products and as his own private transport, as there were cities still not served by the growing airline industry.

During this period he also served his annual Reserve stint with the Air Force and continued to fly various military aircraft, checking out eventually in such postwar jets as the Boeing KC-135 Stratotanker (the military transport variant of the Boeing 707), B-47, and B-52, all bombers, and the North American F-100 Super Sabre, a fighter-bomber. Doolittle continued to fly these aircraft until his retirement from the Air Force.

Commercial airlines could, within a few years, take him just about anywhere he needed to go and, finding this convenient, Doolittle did less and less of his own flying. Not keeping in flying trim, he knew—and had been tragically demonstrated by too many old-timers—could be dangerous and, after his retirement from the Air Force, he stopped flying altogether in 1961, as an active pilot (though, on occasion, he might spell a pilot in the cockpit for a few miles).

Doolittle had barely settled back at Shell in 1946 when his first call came from Washington: Secretary of War Robert Patterson asked him to serve as chairman of the Board on Officer/Enlisted Men Relationships. It was more popularly known as the Doolittle Board, or, unpopularly, as the "G. I. Gripe" Board. The study was initiated in response to public reaction to the war and the growing antimilitarism in the nation.

Public complaints had mounted concerning the inequities, real or imagined, of the military system. As Doolittle would explain to C. V. Glines, "You must remember that this occurred shortly after the end of World War II which we thought was a war to end wars. The public was fed up with the military, fed up with war, fed up with discipline." Consequently, following the hearings, the board made recommendations to the Secretary of War to ease up some on what had been regarded as de rigueur military discipline and military courtesy, even in such small matters as saluting. "The report was fairly well accepted at the time," Doolittle told Glines, "but was bitterly criticized later."

Some of his most vehement critics were friends among the military, who accused Doolittle of contributing to the breakdown of a proper system of military discipline. "The fact was," Doolittle recalls, "that nobody would come forth and testify for retention of a strong disciplinary system. The pressure was all from the other side."

There were also family repercussions, for both the Doolittle sons were then in military service and their lives were made uncomfortable by superior officers who resented the findings and recommendations of the Doolittle Board. When, later, Doolittle was scheduled to receive one of his many special awards, the Awards Committee could not find one Air Force officer willing to serve as guest to present the certificate to Doolittle. Eventually they were forced to seek out the Navy and found Admiral Arleigh Burke delighted to serve.

The following year, 1947, Doolittle had the satisfaction of seeing the birth of an independent United States Air Force, with the appointment of Stuart Symington as the first Secretary of the Air

Force and Doolittle's friend Carl Spaatz the first Air Force Chief of Staff. For Doolittle it was a fulfillment of a long-held dream. A patriot and an exponent of air power, he strongly believed that the United States should maintain a powerful military stance, with a powerful independent air arm, in a world turning cold with a new kind of war.

In 1948, the year the cold war turned quasi-incandescent, Doolittle was asked to serve on the prestigious National Advisory Committee for Aeronautics (NACA), then under the progressive chairmanship of an MIT aeronautics professor Dr. Jerome Hunsaker. The membership of NACA consisted of representatives from the Air Force and Naval Air Service, the Smithsonian Institute, the National Bureau of Standards, and the Weather Bureau, as well as a number of private citizens who would be "acquainted with the needs of aeronautical science, either civil or military, or skilled in aeronautical engineering or its allied sciences."

NACA had pioneered countless advances in aviation since its inception in 1915; by the time Doolittle became a member, especially under Hunsaker's guidance, the committee had begun the study of guided missiles. These studies eventuated in, among other innovations, the ablative (i.e., "wasting away") nose cone, the hypersonic glider, and the lifting glider, as well as those configurations that would come to the fore in an entirely new flight age: Mercury, Apollo, and Gemini. By 1956 Doolittle himself served as chairman of NACA (he was still employed by Shell; NACA members were not paid for their services). Later, in the wake of the Russian launch of the satellite *sputnik zemlyi* ("Fellow Traveler of Earth"), American activity in space was galvanized. He was the last chairman. NACA became NASA (National Aeronautics and Space Agency) in 1958, with the advent of the space age.

By 1951, the furor caused by the recommendations of the Doolittle Board in 1946 had abated enough for Hoyt Vandenberg, his former chief of staff of the Twelfth Air Force period and now Air Force Chief of Staff, to have Doolittle appointed his special assistant for science and technology. From time to time Doolittle would revert to serving as Lieutenant General J. H. Doolittle while assisting Vandenberg, who had succeeded Spaatz, in implementing the terms of the new Air Force Organization Act signed by President Truman in September. Doolittle, according to Vandenberg's memorandum, would be handed "Problems in connection with this Air Force reorganization of mutual concern to the Air Materiel Command and the Air Research and Development Command which cannot be resolved by mutual agreement between the two Commands. [These problems] will be forwarded with a clear statement of each of the conflicting views to me for decision through General Doolittle, who will study the problems and make recommendations to me. Similar action will be taken on problems arising in the Air Staff which cannot be resolved by mutual agreement between the Deputy Chief of Staff, Materiel, and the Deputy Chief of Staff, Development."

In short, Doolittle became a high-level trouble-shooter during the growing pains phase of the new independent U. S. Air Force. This, plus his work in between for Shell, kept him literally on the run. His great desire was for the formation of an air force second to none. Consequently, he did not attend to his personal needs in this hectic period, and on one of the few stopovers at his New York home he found he had broken out in a rash—a new development for him. A visit to a doctor informed him that he was suffering from shingles, a virus infection of the nerve ends. As Quentin Reynolds put it in his biography, this "came as a complete shock to Doolittle. He'd never known that he had any nerves."

The further explanation was that his system had merely rebelled against the strain to which Doolittle subjected it. Joe Doolittle insisted that her husband have a thorough physical checkup. Doolittle agreed, provided his assistant at Shell, H. Frank Brown, would come along and be subjected to the same examinations since he had seconded Joe in her demands.

The two men flew out to the Lovelace Clinic in New Mexico, where Doolittle's friend Dr. Randolph Lovelace and Dr. Samuel White, probed, tested, and otherwise gave him the full treatment. Dr. Lovelace informed Doolittle that he was in excellent physical shape, that all he required was a rest. "Stay here a month," he was told, "and absorb some sun; then you'll be as good as new."

Doolittle suspiciously asked, "What's wrong with me?"

Lovelace answered, "Organically not a thing."

Whereupon Doolittle replied, "In that case, I don't need a rest. Come on, Brownie, let's pack." The next day they were back in

New York at their respective desks. Doolittle, however, did heed his friend's advice and spent a less strenuous month than usual.

The next extracurricular request from Washington was not long in coming—this time in February 1952, from the White House. A letter followed a phone call and began with a Trumanlike "Dear Jim." In part it stated the problem: "For some time now, I have been seriously concerned about airplane accidents, both commercial and military, that have occurred in the take-off and landing of aircraft, especially in heavily populated areas. I have been concerned about the loss of life and I have been concerned about the anxiety in some of our cities [no less than three accidents had occurred that winter at Elizabeth, New Jersey]. I have decided to set up a temporary President's Airport Commission to look into the problem of airport location and use.

"I am delighted that you are willing to serve as Chairman of the Commission, and hereby appoint you as such. Mr. Charles F. Horne, the Administrator of Civil Aeronautics, and Dr. Jerome C. Hunsaker, Head, Department of Aeronautical Engineering, Massachusetts Institute of Technology, will serve with you on the Commission."

He was to be "Dr." Doolittle again. Truman further explained in his letter that what was needed was "a study that is both objective and realistic." The President, because of the problem's urgency, hoped that Doolittle and company might complete that study "within ninety days."

Doolittle and his colleagues went to work immediately. They mailed detailed questionnaires to the mayors of more than a hundred cities with airports. Doolittle himself visited thirty major airports to study firsthand their locations and operating conditions and to observe the safety features that existed or should be introduced.

About midway in the preparation of the report he was visited by Truman's adviser on aviation matters, Major General Robert W. Burns (who had served under Doolittle in the Eighth Air Force as commander of the 351st Bombardment Group). His visit coincided with a current controversy over which should be the major airport serving the nation's capital—Friendship (now Baltimore—Washington International) near Baltimore, or National Airport in Washington.

Burns delivered a message from the President, who suggested

that he would like the report to reflect the President's desire that National Airport should be the selected airfield.

"Bobby," Doolittle replied, "we never discuss any particular field in this report. I want to be objective and in the report we will say what we feel are the proper conditions under which an airport should be built and under which it should operate.

"But, if the President wants me to change that philosophy and to be partisan in this affair, then I will turn in my suit and he may get another chairman."

"You want me to tell the President that?"

"Yes."

Whereupon Burns left Doolittle's office and the subject never came up again.

The report, which ran to 116 pages, was completed within the prescribed ninety days and published under the title, "The Airport and Its Neighbors." It contained recommendations pertaining to all aspects of airport safety (as well as the safety of its surrounding populated areas), from the placement of runways to control departures and arrivals to the type of landing gear best suited for crosswind landings. The work immediately became the bible on airport location and utilization and remained so until the introduction of the larger, faster jets that introduced somewhat different problems requiring different solutions.

Gratified with a job well done by his commission, Doolittle happily returned to the less politically charged milieu of Shell, where he would remain for six more years in the dual role of vice president and director. The year following his service as chairman of the President's Airport Commission, Doolittle, as was customary with him, began planning for the future and a return to his and Joe's native California by purchasing some property in Carmel. In this spectacularly beautiful setting Doolittle hoped to build a home (although he never did), a base for the two of them from which they could travel from time to time and where he could store his hunting and fishing tackle.

Indefatigable, he was not seriously considering retirement— just a retreat out of the public eye and the bustle of the business world. But it was impossible, for in 1955 he began serving as chairman of the Air Force Scientific Advisory Board, whose function was to advise the Air Force on the latest developments in flight, now truly entering a space age, and to evaluate long-range planning. Doolittle followed in illustrious footsteps: the first chairman had been Dr. Theodore von Karman, a world-renowned aerodynamicist and pioneer in the field of missiles, and Dr. Mervin J. Kelly, an engineer prominent in industrial research. Dr. Doolittle was the third chairman. At the same time, he also served as a member of the President's Foreign Intelligence Advisory Board. This began a new phase of hyperactivity, for the next year he was appointed chairman, also, of the National Advisory Committee for Aeronautics, joined the advisory board of the Smithsonian's National Space Museum—in addition to making a round-the-world trip with Joe.

The global tour in 1956 was undertaken because Doolittle had been asked to serve as American representative (and the first airman) at the Coral Sea ceremony in Australia commemorating the great aerial-naval battle of May 1942 in which the Japanese were prevented from landing troops at Port Moresby, New Guinea, by Allied carrier aircraft. (Surface ships did not exchange any shots, making the battle of the Coral Sea the first carrier v. carrier battle in history.) The Doolittles, with Colonel Peter Taylor as their helpful and engaging aide, had an "absolutely delightful" round-the-world trip, with the Coral Sea ceremony, celebrated with Australian and British representatives, as the highlight.

The next year, 1957, found Doolittle appointed to the President's Science Advisory Committee. After his election, the new President, Dwight D. Eisenhower, held a White House reception for this committee which was made up of, in Doolittle's words, "some of the most competent scientists in the United States—and Doolittle." The committee's chairman escorted Eisenhower through the reception line, introducing the various distinguished members, including a few recipients of the Nobel Prize. The President and the chairman then came upon Doolittle. Eisenhower stopped, studied his former maverick general, and exclaimed, "Jimmy! What the hell are you doing with this group?"

The same question, every now and then, had occurred to Doolittle. His life seemed to have become a succession of cross-country flights, board and committee meetings, creamed chicken dinners and luncheons, and strange, but distressingly similar, hotel rooms. The notion of actually putting down roots, preferably in their own home state of California, became increasingly appealing as time passed.

Shell ordinarily retired its senior executives at the age of sixty; upon reaching fifty-nine in December 1955, Doolittle asked to be transferred to his and Joe's favorite city, San Francisco. The request had been granted and the Doolittles moved back to California. Although he was busy, Doolittle did not find his work load too demanding and he and Joe began enjoying their new life in a relaxed and restful San Francisco. They could even begin to plan building their dream house on their Carmel property.

This idyllic life had scarcely begun for the Doolittles when it was shattered in April 1958 by a family tragedy—the death by suicide of their oldest son, Jim, Jr. He had chosen to remain in the Air Force after the close of the Second World War only to find himself the victim of resentment or envy. From time to time he was assigned to serve under a career officer who harbored anti-Jimmy Doolittle sentiments and took it out on the son. But Jim, Jr., accepted this and persevered. During the Korean War he served as a fighter pilot; after his tour of duty, he returned to the States and became a fighter instructor. Still later he became a test pilot at Edwards Air Force Base, with the rank of major.

Serious marital problems led to a divorce and the breakup of his little family; his son, James Doolittle III, moved to San Antonio with his mother. Jim, Jr., eventually remarried.

The final contributing cause of his death was never known; he left no note, nor had he discussed his service or personal problems with his parents or friends. But an accumulation of these problems led to despondency and depression and to his suicide in that bleak spring of 1958. His son, James III, notably, has followed in the footsteps of both his grandfather and father. He was a fighter pilot in Vietnam and later served as an instructor in fighters with the hope of eventually becoming a test pilot.

The impact of their son's death on the Doolittles was stunning. Shortly after, Doolittle, in a rare personal statement, revealed a little of its aftermath: "Only when someone very near and dear to one leaves does one appreciate the stark tragedy of death," he wrote. "Even then, nature tends to cushion the initial shock, and the thought 'he is gone' does not carry the later realization of finality and permanence that comes only with the final indisputable understanding that 'We will *never* see him again.'"

That inexplicable void could never be rationalized by the Doolittles, but there was solace in the presence of Jim, Jr.'s, sons.

Their younger son, John, a West Point graduate, a veteran of the Korean War and, later, Vietnam as a bomber pilot, remained in the Air Force until March 1975. His children, too, brought welcome vivacity and diversion.

The Doolittles, as they had for years, could depend upon one another for support, although the death of Jim, Jr., so incomprehensible and irrevocable, distressed and grieved Joe long after. But time, warm friendships, and activity served to make the loss eventually bearable.

By the winter of 1958 Doolittle's retirement from Shell would become official; he had been permitted to stay on beyond the set date—1956—to complete some projects he had initiated upon his arrival in San Francisco. Doolittle was in no mood for retirement and so, when the period of extension ended, he was cheered when he heard from an old friend, Fred Crawford, head of Thompson Products in Cleveland, suppliers of a variety of components to the automotive and aircraft industries. Crawford asked Doolittle if he would be interested in joining a newly formed company known as TRW Incorporated.

TRW, Crawford explained, had been the brainchild of two very gifted scientists, Dean Wooldridge and Simon Ramo, who had been initially employed by Howard Hughes. Deciding to form their own company to work in the aerospace industry, they left Hughes, taking a good number of their associates with them to form the Ramo-Wooldridge Corporation. "They had good ideas," Doolittle has said, "and competent people—but no financial backing." This was solved by the merger with Thompson, resulting in TRW (Thompson, Wooldridge, and Ramo).

Thompson was named chairman of TRW, Ramo vice chairman, and Wooldridge president; they established a subsidiary which would explore the fields of space and missiles called Space Technology Laboratories (STL). It was this branch of TRW that Crawford hoped Doolittle would join as chairman of the board. To be able to remain active was most attractive, even more so because he would continue to be associated with flight and defense, and made it easy for Doolittle to make his decision. When he left Shell in December of 1958, though he continued to be associated with the firm as a director until 1967, to join STL, Doolittle resigned from all of his governmental advisory boards as well as all of his Air Force associations to avoid possible accusations of conflict of interest, since TRW products were used by various government agencies and, of course, the Air Force. He chose however to remain with the National Aeronautics and Space Council, assuming since it served all of American aviation and space industries, it was neutral. (Even so, this inspired press innuendos that only proved to be irritatingly petty.)

His resignation at the time from the Air Force Scientific Advisory Board prompted a disappointed reaction from a friend, also a member of the board, the eminent nuclear scientist Dr. Edward Teller, who wrote: "Maybe you don't realize yourself how deeply unhappy a great number of your good friends are about your resigning from the chairmanship of SAB. In my experience the SAB is the only group of scientists that is giving effective and sane advice to our Government. That it is so is due to a very large measure to your effective leadership, which has been exercising its influence as long as I have been on the SAB . . ."

Having made his decision, Doolittle proceeded as planned. He would have liked very much to have remained on the SAB, but preferred not being placed in the position of advising the Air Force (as chairman of SAB) to make purchases from Space Technology Laboratories, which he served in the same capacity. He could rationalize his decision without excessive soul-searching: STL would be capable of making tremendous contributions to the national defense as well as the projected man-in-space program. His own contribution to these could be made as readily in California, as head of a unique organization of scientist-executives, as in Washington.

On New Year's day 1959, after divesting himself of all possible "conflict of interest" connections, Doolittle and Joe found temporary quarters in Los Angeles and eventually they rented and finally bought a comfortable home in nearby Santa Monica on a quiet, wide street within an easy walk of the Pacific, where they still live. Though unpretentious, the house is generously roomy; the front yard is sedately green—the expansive backyard is a riot of lush flora. The fauna includes one dog—a German shepherd—and a couple of perky cats of undetermined background.

The rooms of the house are packed with memorabilia accumulated throughout a busy, full lifetime (and the gathering continues). The collection ranges from exquisite gifts from the Orient to hunting trophies, the latter on display in the basement game room. In the basement also is Doolittle's workroom for he still loves to fashion objects of wood, to tie his own flies for fishing expeditions, and generally to tinker. The workroom is dense with tools and gadgets, but not cluttered: each item has its place.

Besides the hunting trophies, the game room also houses Doolittle's numerous flight trophies, plaques, awards, certificates, etc. The room also serves as a tiny theater for occasional film screenings. One small room in the main part of the house is set aside for Doolittle as an office and contains a desk, a cabinet in which his gun collection is stored, a book case, a globe; among the wall decorations is a poster-sized periodic table such as is used in college chemistry classes.

The hallways adjacent to Doolittle's office which lead to the basement or out to the sunroom and garden are covered with signed photographs of Doolittle friends in practically every field of human endeavor—from the arts to, of course, aviation. There are captains of industry and statesmen (among the latter is a Karsh portrait of Churchill); there are great military leaders and pilots dating back to the barnstorming era of flight—literally hundreds ("actually 450," Doolittle has commented in the interests of precision) of photographs of some of the remarkable people whose lives have touched Doolittle's. Bookshelves appear to ramble through the house and are stuffed with volumes on a variety of subjects (the kitchen bookcases are filled with Joe's collection of cookbooks). The bulk of these mementos, some of which (at the time of this writing) have already been disposed of, will be deposited in the Smithsonian's National Air and Space Museum, the Air Force Academy, or the Library of Congress.

Probably the primary characteristic of the Doolittle home is its ambiance of informality and comfort. Interesting, too, is the fact that their next door neighbor is Bill Downs, their old schoolmate from Los Angeles Manual Arts High School. The Doolittles form lifelong friendships. They are close to Joe's sister, Grace, and her husband, "Andy" Andrews; also living within an easy drive are Doolittle's favorite cousin, Emily, and her husband, Ronald McNamee, a retired Army colonel. Jerome Simson, a schoolmate dating to Doolittle's rough-and-tumble Alaskan days, lives in nearby Arcadia, representing another unbroken tie—and there are dozens of friends from various chapters in the lives of the Doolittles with whom they are still in touch.

The house in Santa Monica is Joe Doolittle's first permanent home since her marriage in 1917 to a bumptious second lieutenant with few prospects.

Retirement time brought Doolittle into a final confrontation with the military brass—this time with an old friend, General Emmett O'Donnell, Jr. Some time early in 1959 O'Donnell, then associated with the Air Force personnel office, called Doolittle and informed him, "We have a problem."

"What problem?" Doolittle inquired.

"You are the only reserve officer, in any service, to have reached three-star rank. We have no policy on how to handle your retirement."

"What would you do if I were in the regular service?"

"You're over sixty—we'd retire you."

"All right, retire me."

"You are eligible," O'Donnell then informed him, "for retirement pay."

"Well, I don't need any retirement pay; I'm quite self-sufficient and don't choose to go on the government tit."

"All right," O'Donnell replied, "you don't have to take it."

"Wait a minute," Doolittle interjected. "What I would like to do is have a right to my government pay in the future, so that if at some future time I should come on hard times and need my military pay, I would like to be able to put in for it at that time—not retroactively; anything I might lose in the meantime is all right with me."

"Sorry," O'Donnell told him, "we can't do that. Take it or leave it."

"I'll take it," Doolittle answered. "But what I want done is to have my retirement pay sent to the Air Academy Foundation so I won't have to pay income tax on it." Later, he chose to divide this amount between the Foundation and the Air Force Aid Society—and so it has gone since 1962.

Doolittle's severance from the Air Force did not end all of his associations with it; both he and Joe number dozens of good friends among Air Force men and wives. The same year he left the service, he became a member of the Air Force Space Systems Advisory Group; also, at the request of the Air Force and TRW, he joined the board of the Aerospace Corporation—which was a rival of TRW for Air Force business! No one raised a hue and cry of conflict of interest, all parties having agreed upon Doolittle's objective integrity.

Doolittle could not regard their home as a place in which he would go soft while his arteries hardened and yet he had to face the inevitable. In December 1961 he would turn sixty-five, the mandatory retirement age at TRW—and the thought of retirement was anathema to Doolittle. Still, his several concurrent chairmanships left him little time for Joe, the other members of his family, or friends.

His association with TRW's Space Technology Laboratories grew as the operation itself expanded and was transformed into the Systems Division of TRW—of which he was appointed director. In its final nominal evolution it has become, simply, TRW Systems. After retirement from TRW Doolittle continued to serve as a consultant from 1962 through 1965. (When Apollo 11 first placed men on the moon in July of 1969, among the major contributing contractors to that historic event was TRW Systems.)

When he might have been expected to retire officially and finally from all business activities, Doolittle became instead a director and member of the executive committee of the Mutual of Omaha Insurance Company, with an office in Los Angeles. From here, under the capable eye and the gently efficient hand of Donna Roop (who had worked with him at TRW), Doolittle continues to keep up a wide correspondence and a heavy personal appearance schedule. He has, in the 1970s, curtailed his speechmaking—a chore he has never relished, although he is a well-organized, pungent public speaker.

When Doolittle is "at home" he drives into Los Angeles from Santa Monica in the morning, parks his car in the basement-garage of the Mutual building, and walks up to his office on the seventh floor. He never uses the elevator—not because he has lost faith in technology. He feels—and his physician concurs—that it is good exercise and keeps him in trim. If he happens to be accompanied by a visitor, however, Doolittle thoughtfully ushers the individual into the elevator for the eight-flight trip up or down.

One of the Doolittles' strongest, and warmest, postwar associations is with a very special group of men, the Tokyo Raiders. One of the promises Doolittle had made before they left the *Hornet* on April 18, 1942, was for the biggest party they had ever known when they gathered in Chungking after the mission. Because of the dispersal of the crews and his own early recall to the United States, that party never occurred.

On the Raid's first anniversary Doolittle was in North Africa with the Twelfth Air Force. So on April 18, 1943, a small, informal reunion was held in a North African farmhouse, with only a few of the Raiders present. The rest, those who had survived or were not imprisoned or interned, were serving in other Air Forces around the world. It was not until after the war ended that Doolittle could keep his promise of a full-scale party.

The first Tokyo Raiders reunion of any real proportions took place on Doolittle's forty-ninth birthday, December 14, 1945, at the McFadden-Deauville Hotel in Miami. All of the surviving veterans of the Raid who could, descended upon the hotel and had such a memorable time that a consensus decreed that it should become an annual event. Having spent well over $2,000 on the celebration, Doolittle could not see himself financing such a revel indefinitely. There was full agreement on that point also, and a committee was formed, a chairman elected, and plans for future reunions formulated.

Setting up the organization and preparing for a series of Tokyo Raid reunions was time consuming so 1946 was skipped (the only other hiatus occurred in 1951, when many members had returned to active duty in Korea). In 1947 the reunions began in a planned, but no less boisterous style. Once again the ribald, pleasure-seeking crews gathered at the Deauville. The night watchman later filed a report in which he declared that he had never before experienced such a night.

"I let them make a lot of noise," he reported to the hotel's manager, Warren Freeman, "but when about fifteen of them went into the pool at 1:00 A.M. (including Doolittle), I told them there was no swimming allowed at night. They were in the pool until 2:30 A.M."

Admitting to a degree of apprehensive inadequacy, he came upon vociferous, bathing-suited Raiders in the halls up to 5:30 in the morning. "The Doolittle boys added some gray hairs to my head," he lamented to his boss when he turned in his report. Freeman immediately took the watchman's account to Doolittle— and requested an autograph. He located all the other Raiders he could—those who were capable of using a pen—and had them sign the report also and kept it as a prized souvenir of their memorable celebration.

In the three decades or so since the first reunion the three-day gatherings have become much more subdued than the 1947 frolic. Time has also diminished the circle—some members have died. And, while the reunions continue to generate good feelings, affection, and companionship, they are a good deal more serene than they once were. The Doolittles are, as always, the honored—loved would not be an inappropriate word—guests, for Joe Doolittle regards the Raiders as much her "boys" as they are her husband's. In keeping with their more dignified demeanor, by 1963 the gang of former hotel-wreckers were incorporated as the Doolittle Tokyo Raider Association; the practice of awarding Air Force units recognition for safety was begun. With permission from their Boss a scholarship for deserving engineering students was established bearing his name (the Association is not by any means wealthy and the deficit in the Doolittle Scholarship is made up by donatons from private citizens and industry).

It has become a tradition at each reunion to drink a toast to those Raiders who have died. Their silver goblets are kept in a special display case which is brought by the Reunion Committee for the ceremony; the case also holds a bottle of brandy which will not be opened until that day when only two of the Raiders remain. The survivors will drink a final toast to their dead and, as C. V. Glines has written in his fine study of the Tokyo Raid, "a glorious chapter in aviation history will close forever."

At a recent reunion Doolittle happened to be standing behind some of his boys who were replacing their goblets into the display case after the toast. They were speculating on the symbolism of the goblets and the brandy. Doolittle overheard one of the men say, "It wouldn't surprise me a bit if the old son-of-a-bitch turns out to be one of the last two." Doolittle was amused and flattered, "even though the lad had used an appropriate adjective."

Doolittle's attendance at the Tokyo Raider reunions is not his only diversion. A born outdoorsman and sportsman-hunter from boyhood, he has, since leaving active military service, spent a good deal of time in the wilder parts of the world.

The term "sportsman-hunter" is deliberately used. To Doolittle's mind there is a tremendous gap between this type of hunter and the inconsiderate despoiler who is destructive and wasteful of wild life as well as the property of others. "A gamehog," he firmly believes, "is not a sportsman. He is the same thoughtless, selfish slob who throws bottles, cans, and allied trash through the countryside."

Cognate with Doolittle's love for hunting is a preference for the simplicity such activity affords "away from the crowds," in the company of other sportsmen, informally garbed in rugged clothes, cooking their own meals, telling tales, and breathing clean, forest-scented air.

That rugged environment—mountains, frigid streams, snow-encrusted slopes—has provided Doolittle with an occasional brush with gratuitous adventure. One of these occurred some time in the late forties or early fifties when he hired the colorful—and number one—glacier pilot, Don Sheldon, to transport him to bear country (this was, of course, long before it became illegal to search for game by air).

Sheldon's little light plane was based at Talkeetna, Alaska, near Mount McKinley and it was from there they took off. They had not been flying long before they spotted a moose in the snow below them that had evidently been killed by a bear. Sheldon set the plane down in the snow close to the moose so that they could make camp and await the return of the bear. Upon alighting from the plane Doolittle was a bit disconcerted to see that the skis of their plane had broken through the crust and were deep in snow. Visions of living on bear meat—or ripe moose—until rescue immediately took some of the joy out of the hunt.

But Sheldon, a veteran of northern skies and snows, appeared to be unconcerned and the two men set out for the spot where they had seen the moose carcass. Meanwhile, the processes of nature had been at work; the "varmints," as Doolittle calls them—the scavengers—had already begun to share the bear's kill. Having ascertained that it had been a bear, Doolittle waited. When the bear returned the varmints moved to their perimeter while it gorged. Doolittle got in a clean shot and the bear was his.

Leaving the rest of the moose to the varmints, Doolittle and Sheldon skinned the bear and dragged the heavy hide to the plane. Doolittle again faced the nagging problem of sunken skis. But Sheldon, unperturbed, donned his snowshoes and began stomping the snow in front of the plane. Doolittle joined in and before long they had created a reasonably solid runway for takeoff.

Sheldon then introduced a rather sour note. Once the trophy of the hunt was placed in the plane, he would be unable to take off carrying additional weight, namely Doolittle's. But again Sheldon was undismayed—as always, he had a plan: he would take off from their improvised runway, turn around, and come skidding back along the surface of the snow. Doolittle had only to grab a wing strut as the plane passed by, clamber along the strut, over the landing gear, and into the cabin—simple as that.

Because he was in good physical condition, Doolittle did not find the plan too unreasonable. He watched Sheldon lift off the runway, luckily without breaking through the crust. The plane turned and headed back for Doolittle who had to keep his eyes on the rapidly approaching skis, propeller, and the crucial strut. With a roar the plane bore down on him; his timing had to be precise. He grabbed at the speeding strut, held fast, and as Sheldon climbed above treetop level, managed to work his way into the cabin, losing only his hat during the exploit.

Doolittle campfire tales are legion and might fill a volume alone. He is not above telling stories on himself. One such occurred during a sheep hunt in northern Alaska. On the trail of a bighorn, Doolittle was fording a freezing glacial stream when he slipped and fell. Sputtering, he climbed out and dried out his rifle and his soaked clothing before continuing the hunt. Only then did he realize that he was still on the same side of the stream. To Doolittle this exemplified his "consummate stupidity."

More revealing of the man was another experience—the setting in this instance was in the mountains of southern California. With his friend Leonard Gillman, then chief of the Western Division of the U. S. Border Patrol, Doolittle was once more hunting the wily bighorn. ("Gil," he will say with emphasis, "is a wonderful man— the sort of chap you want with you when you're in a pinch.")

Having hired an Indian guide, Doolittle and Gillman set out in that order of march. They were seeking an elevated vantage point from which they could get a good vista of the area and had begun to climb up a very precipitous slope rising some 500 feet above them. Their guide had succeeded in reaching the top and had climbed over the rim, with Doolittle not far behind and Gillman bringing up the rear. The cliffside afforded only the meagerest of hand- and footholds; both Doolittle and Gillman clung tenaciously to any small protuberance.

Doolittle had gotten within a foot of the top, "just hanging on" with all fours, and was reaching for the rim to pull himself over.

Then both feet and the one hand grasping the cliff held only air and he began slipping down the face of the slope. From that moment on each man reacted with remarkable, and characteristic, instinct.

"I came by Gil," Doolittle has related, "and there was a *tremendous* tendency to reach out and grab him, but I didn't. I wasn't going to take him down and get him hurt also [a 500-foot fall could also have proved fatal]. As I went by, he swung his arm out and grabbed me by one arm—and as he did, I was moving fast enough so I tore him loose. And there we were, both of us going down this precipitatous slope."

Gathering momentum the two men continued their plunge when suddenly Gillman reached out again to snatch at a tiny bush— "about an inch around and a foot high growing out of a rock"— which actually held and stopped their fall. Undaunted, "we got organized again," as Doolittle put it, "and made it to the top of the ridge" to continue with their hunt.

While his outdoorsmanship has been of great importance to him in the years since he had decided to curtail his workload, much of that time has also been devoted to conservation. Doolittle will not hunt an endangered species, of course; he is active in curbing the irresponsible hunter, he is concerned with ecology—and primarily with man.

Approaching eighty, Doolittle fills many roles except that of "senior citizen." He is too busy with his full and precise schedule (set down in a small notebook he always carries) to be overly conscious of the calendar and the passage of time. He is not preoccupied with aging, believing that only with the accumulation of years does the individual acquire, finally, wisdom. A conservative in politics, he is a progressive in philosophy—flexible, he is always willing to listen to an opposing point of view.

Doolittle is unperturbed by the so-called generation gap; there is none for him. Nor does he believe that with age, wisdom descends as a matter of course. While no cynic, he is not convinced that all men are basically good—or even equal, there being a multitude of variations physically, mentally, morally, and emotionally. "Some people are more moral than others," he will point out while speaking to a gathering of businessmen, or Boy Scouts, or a friend. "I am satisfied that some people are basically good; others are basically evil. Most of us lie in between, creatures of our environment, and are not consistently the same."

Doolittle is unpredictably consistent (and vice versa); his mind is not closed. His decisions are based on facts, carefully weighed, not on prejudice. Though a graduate engineer, he believes there is a fallacy in "learning about things, not people." In this area, he has been active since 1959 when the Harry Frank Guggenheim Foundation initiated an investigation in the field of "Man's Relation to Man." When his old friend, Harry Guggenheim, who had sponsored the historic blind-flight experiments in 1929, asked him to serve as a director of this study, Doolittle was delighted to accept and is active to this day.

As Guggenheim stated, some time before his death in 1971, mankind "has failed to keep pace with the extraordinary progress of this era in science, engineering, medicine and surgery, agriculture, industry, transportation . . . and other fields of human endeavor." The study was begun to explore this problem and is seeking to determine what motivates man so that human relations can be improved. To accomplish this the Foundation provides funds for a wide range of research projects engaging teams of anthropologists, psychiatrists, and sociologists, many of them young and others eminent specialists in their respective fields.

Doolittle believes that this continuing study will prove to be a valuable contribution to mankind's knowledge of itself and that this contribution, in the form of papers and books, will be an enduring monument to his friend and what he calls "the thoughtful utilization of riches."

He and Joe, he feels, are rich—"in friendships." Not to mention honors. Rarely a week goes by without an invitation for Doolittle to appear for some award or other—there are even a town in Missouri and a street in Alameda, near the Oakland airport, named for him. What Doolittle enjoys best about these ceremonies is that it generally provides the occasion for reunions with their many aviation friends. He has retained that "little bit of mischief" that had enlivened the life of Colonel Burwell at Rockwell Field a half century ago. He delights in a playful relationship with Joe, gently teasing and at the same time touchingly attentive and considerate. She, as always, not only holds her own but is ever ready with a riposte if necessary.

A quite active social life keeps them busy, together or separately. Doolittle travels a good deal, appearing at business dinners or as the guest of honor at a tribute, often accompanied by Joe. She, less the traveler than he, keeps up with the lives of a wide circle of friends by phone and letter. She makes regular calls to shut-ins; and still hears from several of her "boys" she knew at the Pawling Rehabilitation Center during the war.

The Doolittles are rich, too, in their own family life, there being a number of grandchildren as well as great-grandchildren. Their oldest son, James, Jr., left them James Doolittle III, at this writing an Air Force officer, and Jeffry Allen, and two adopted sons, John Michael and Eric (the latter the son of his second wife). John and Priscilla Doolittle have presented them with five grandchildren: Josephine (now Mrs. Paul D. Crane and mother of Paul, Jr., and John Merrill), Jonna (Mrs. Steven Hoppes), Penelope (Mrs. George E. Jones and mother of Jennifer and Michelle), and the twins, Patrick John and Peter James.

A family gathering at the Doolittle home in Santa Monica can be an energetic experience. While Grandfather Doolittle may evince a preference for tussling with the younger boys, the several young ladies keep him on his mental toes, not only with the strange music they bring with them into the generally quiet household, but also with the same teasing banter that their grandmother so effectively employs to keep Doolittle's sense of perspective in perfect alignment.

Doolittle knows fully who he is and what he has accomplished and so is capable of seeing himself objectively and with a sense of humor. He has a wealth of stories in which he comes off with egg on his face. He has been hearing encomiums for years and accepts them with dignity, but he still enjoys a joke at his own expense. Recently, when he was selected to receive the first Wings of Man Award from the Society of Experimental Test Pilots, he heard one of the society's founders and vice president of Eastern Airlines, Scott Crossfield, refer to him as no less than "the world's greatest aviator." Crossfield was followed by Bob Hope who proceeded to say of Doolittle: "He's contributed a lot to aviation. He wrapped sandwiches for Lindbergh. He set the compass for Douglas Corrigan . . ."

Not long after this event the Doolittles made a long postponed journey. Doolittle wrote of the trip to a friend saying, "Joe and I are going . . . to Alaska in late September. Up the inside passage by boat and from Skagway to White Horse by train. It's a trip that I promised her some sixty years ago. She has been *very* patient."

When Lieutenant James H. Doolittle, reformed roughneck with minimal expectations, first proposed marriage to Josephine Daniels in December 1913, one of the promises he made to her was that they would make a leisurely trip by boat to Alaska.

As they boarded ship at Seattle, after a flight from Los Angeles, to depart for their first port of call, Ketchikan, Joe turned to her husband and said, "Doolittle, you are a man of your word."

Appendix

SUMMARY OF PROFESSIONAL CAREER

United States Army Air Corps, 1917–30.

Major, United States Army Air Corps Reserve, 1930–40.

Manager, Aviation Department, Shell Petroleum Corporation, 1930–40.

Major, United States Army Air Corps, 1940.

Lieutenant Colonel, 1940.

Brigadier General, 1942.

Major General, 1942.

Lieutenant General, 1944.

Commanding General, Twelfth Air Force, North Africa, 1942.

Commanding General, Fifteenth Air Force, Italy, 1943.

Commanding General, Eighth Air Force, England, 1944.

Commanding General, Eighth Air Force, Okinawa, 1945.

Vice President, Shell Oil Company, 1946–58.

Director, Shell Oil Company, 1946–67.

Chairman of the Board, Space Technology Laboratories, Inc., 1959–62.

Director, Space Technology Laboratories, Inc., 1959–63.

Director, Thompson Ramo Wooldridge, Inc., 1961–69.

Consultant, TRW Systems, 1962–65.

Director, Mutual of Omaha Insurance Co., 1961–.

Trustee, Aerospace Corporation, 1963–69.

Vice Chairman, Board of Trustees, Chairman, Executive Committee, Aerospace Corporation, 1965–69.

Director, United Benefit Life Insurance Company of Omaha, 1964–.

Director, Tele-Trip Company, Inc., 1966–.

Director, Companion Life Insurance Company of New York, 1968–.

Director, Mutual of Omaha Growth & Income Funds, 1968–.

AVIATION FIRSTS AND OTHER ACHIEVEMENTS

First cross-continental crossing in less than 24 hours, 1922.

Winner, Schneider Trophy Race, 1925.

First to execute outside loop, 1927.

First "blind flight," 1929.

Winner, Bendix Trophy Race, 1931.

New transcontinental record, 1931.

Winner, Thompson Trophy Race, 1932.

World's Landplane Speed Record, 1932.

AWARDS

Mackay Trophy, 1926.

Spirit of St. Louis Award, 1929.

Harmon Trophy, Ligue International des Aviateurs, 1930.

Guggenheim Trophy, 1942.

International Harmon Trophy, 1940, 1949.

Wright Brothers Trophy, 1953.

Fédération Aéronautique Internationale Gold Medal, 1954.

Silver Quill, 1959.

International Aerospace Hall of Fame, San Diego,
 California, 1966.
Aviation Hall of Fame, Dayton, Ohio, 1967.
Thomas D. White National Defense Award, 1967.

Horatio Alger Award, 1972.
Conservation Hall of Fame, 1973.
Wings of Man Award, Society of Experimental Test Pilots, 1973.
Bishop Wright Air Industry Award, 1975.

DECORATIONS

Congressional Medal of Honor
Distinguished Service Medal, with Oak Leaf Cluster
Silver Star
Distinguished Flying Cross, with two Oak Leaf Clusters
Bronze Star
Air Medal, with Three Oak Leaf Clusters
Official Order of the Condor (Bolivia)
Yon-Hwei, Class III (China)
Knight Commander, Order of the Bath (Great Britain)
Grand Officer of the Legion of Honor and Croix de Guerre,
 with Palm (France)
Grand Officer of the Crown, with Palm and Croix de Guerre,
 with Palm (Belgium)
Grand Commander (Poland)
Abdon Calderón, First Class (Ecuador)

APPOINTMENTS

Member, Army Air Corps Investigating Committee
 (Baker Board), 1934.
Chairman, Secretary of War's Board on Officer/Enlisted Men
 Relationships, 1946.
Member, Joint Congressional Aviation Policy Board, 1948.

Adviser, Committee on National Security Organization, 1948.

Chairman, President's Airport Commission, 1952.

Chairman, President's Task Group on Air Inspection, Stassen Disarmament Committee, 1955.

Chairman, Air Force Scientific Advisory Board, 1955–58.

Member, President's Foreign Intelligence Advisory Board, 1955–65.

Chairman, National Advisory Committee for Aeronautics, 1956–58.

Member, Advisory Board, National Air Museum, Smithsonian Institution, 1956–65.

Member, Defense Science Board, 1957–58.

Member, President's Science Advisory Committee, 1957–58.

Member, National Aeronautics and Space Council, 1958.

Member, Plowshare Committee of the Atomic Energy Commission, 1959–72.

Member, National Institutes of Health Study, 1963–65.

Member, Air Force Space Systems Advisory Group, 1963–.

EDUCATIONAL ACTIVITIES

Massachusetts Institute of Technology Corporation, Life Member.

University of California, Member, Engineering Advisory Council, 1957–66.

HONORARY DEGREES

(NOTE: Doolittle earned his M.S. in 1924 and Sc.D. in aeronautical science from the Massachusetts Institute of Technology.)

University of California, Doctor of Laws.

University of Michigan, Doctor of Engineering.

Clarkson College of Technology, Doctor of Science.

Brooklyn Polytechnic Institute, Doctor of Engineering.

Waynesburg College, Doctor of Military Science.
Northland College, Doctor of Laws.
University of Alaska, Doctor of Science.
Pennsylvania Military College, Doctor of Science.

ASSOCIATIONS

Honorary Fellow, American Institute of Aeronautics and Astronautics.
Fellow, Royal Aeronautical Society.
Fellow, American Astronautical Society.
Member, American Petroleum Institute.
Member, Society of Automotive Engineers.
Member, American Society of Mechanical Engineers.
Member, Air Force Association (President, 1946).
Member, National Aeronautical Association.
Member, Order of Daedalians.
Member, Order of Free and Accepted Masons (33d Degree).

CLUBS

National Aviation Club, Washington, D.C.
Lotos Club, New York.
Wings Club, New York (President, 1955).
Explorers Club, New York.
Boone and Crockett Club, New York.
The Bohemians, San Francisco.

TOKYO RAIDER ROSTER

(NOTE: Crews and aircraft are listed in order of takeoff. Crews, with ranks as of April 18, 1942, generally listed in this order: pilot, copilot, navigator, bombardier, engineer/

gunner—with exceptions noted. The Air Force serial number is indicated for each plane; the birthplace of each Tokyo Raider follows his name. All returned from the raid except as indicated by the following code numbers: 1—Killed on bailing out of plane; 2—Executed by Japanese; 3—Died in Japanese prison; 4—Imprisoned by Japanese, released after war; 5—Died of injuries in crash landing of plane; 6—Interned by the Russians. As this is being written, May 1975, there are fifty-two of the eighty original Raiders living. Raid-connected deaths are footnoted. This material has been taken largely from the best book on the Raid, *Doolittle's Tokyo Raiders,* by Carroll V. Glines, Lt. Col., USAF [Ret.], D. Van Nostrand Company, Princeton, N.J., 1964.)

1. **40–2344**
Lt. Col. James H. Doolittle, Alameda, Calif.
Lt. Richard E. Cole, Dayton, Ohio.
Lt. Henry A. Potter, Pierre, S.D.
S/Sgt. Fred A. Braemer, Seattle, Wash.
S/Sgt. Paul J. Leonard, Roswell, N.Mex.

2. **40–2292**
Lt. Travis Hoover, Melrose, N.Mex.
Lt. William N. Fitzhugh, Temple, Tex.
Lt. Richard E. Miller, Fort Wayne, Ind.
Lt. Carl R. Wildner, Holyoke, Mass.
Sgt. Douglas V. Radney, Mineola, Tex.

3. **40–2270**
Capt. Robert M. Gray, Killeen, Tex.
Lt. Jacob E. Manch, Staunton, Va.
Lt. Charles J. Ozuk, Vesta Heights, Pa.
Sgt. Aden E. Jones, Flint, Mich.
Cpl. Leland D. Faktor, Plymouth, Iowa.[1]

4. **40–2282**
Lt. Everett W. Holstrom, Cottage Grove, Ore.
Lt. Lucian N. Youngblood, Pampa, Tex.

Lt. Harry C. McCool, La Junta, Col.
Sgt. Robert J. Stephens, Hobart, Okla.
Cpl. Bert M. Jordon, Covington, Okla.

5. 40–2283
Capt. David M. Jones, Marshfield, Ore.
Lt. Rodney R. Wilder, Taylor, Tex.
Lt. Eugene F. McGurl, Belmont, Mass.
Lt. Denver V. Truelove, Clermont, Ga.
Sgt. Joseph W. Manske, Gowanda, N.Y.

6. 40–2298
Lt. Dean E. Hallmark, Robert Lee, Tex.[2]
Lt. Robert J. Meder, Cleveland, Ohio.[3]
Lt. Chase J. Nielson, Hyrum, Utah.[4]
Sgt. William J. Dieter, Vail, Iowa.[5]
Sgt. Donald E. Fitzmaurice, Lincoln, Neb.[5]

7. 40–2261
Lt. Ted W. Lawson, Fresno, Calif.
Lt. Dean Davenport, Spokane, Wash.
Lt. Charles L. McClure, St. Louis, Mo.
Lt. Robert S. Clever, Portland, Ore.
Sgt. David J. Thatcher, Bridger, Mont.

8. 40–2242 (the only aircraft participating which landed intact, in the U.S.S.R.)
Capt. Edward J. York, Batavia, N.Y.[6]
Lt. Robert G. Emmens, Medford, Ore.[6]
Lt. Nolan A. Hernson (also bombardier), Greenville, Tex.[6]
Sgt. Theodore H. Laban (engineer), Kenosha, Wis.[6]
Sgt. David W. Pohl (gunner), Boston, Mass.[6]

9. 40–2303
Lt. Harold F. Watson, Buffalo, N.Y.
Lt. James M. Parker, Houston, Tex.
Lt. Thomas C. Griffin, Green Bay, Wis.

Sgt. Wayne M. Bissell, Walker, Minn.

T/Sgt. Eldred V. Scott, Atlanta, Ga.

10. **40–2250**

Lt. Richard O. Joyce, Lincoln, Neb.

Lt. J. Royden Stork, Frost, Minn.

Lt. Horace E. Crouch, Columbia, S.C.

Sgt. George E. Larkin, Jr., New Haven, Ken.

S/Sgt. Edwin W. Horton, Jr., North Eastham, Mass.

11. **40–2249**

Capt. C. Ross Greening, Carroll, Iowa.

Lt. Kenneth E. Reddy, Bowie, Tex.

Lt. Frank J. Kappeler, San Francisco, Calif.

S/Sgt. William L. Birch, Calexico, Calif.

Sgt. Melvin J. Gardner, Mesa, Ariz.

12. **40–2278**

Lt. William M. Bower, Ravenna, Ohio.

Lt. Thadd H. Blanton, Archer City, Tex.

Lt. William R. Pound, Milford, Utah.

T/Sgt. Waldo J. Bither, Houlton, Me.

S/Sgt. Omer A. Duquette, West Warnick, R.I.

13. **40–2247**

Lt. Edgar E. McElroy, Ennis, Tex.

Lt. Richard A. Knobloch, Milwaukee, Wis.

Lt. Clayton J. Campbell, St. Maries, Idaho.

Sgt. Robert C. Bourgeois, Lecompte, La.

Sgt. Adam R. Williams, Gastonia, N.C.

14. **40–2297**

Maj. John A. Hilger, Sherman, Tex.

Lt. Jack A. Sims, Kalamazoo, Mich.

Lt. James H. Macia (also bombardier), Tombstone, Ariz.

S/Sgt. Edwin V. Bain (gunner), Greensboro, N.C.

S/Sgt. Jacob Eierman (engineer), Baltimore, Md.

15. 40–2267

Lt. Donald G. Smith, Oldham, S.D.

Lt. Griffith P. Williams, Chicago, Ill.

Lt. Howard A. Sessler (also bombardier), Boston, Mass.

Sgt. Edward J. Saylor (engineer), Brusett, Mont.

Lt. Thomas R. White (medical officer-gunner), Haiku, Maui, Hawaii.

16. 40–2268

Lt. William G. Farrow, Darlington, S.C.[2]

Lt. Robert L. Hite, Odell, Tex.[4]

Lt. George Barr, Brooklyn, N.Y.[4]

Cpl. Jacob DeShazer, West Stayton, Ore.[4]

Sgt. Harold A. Spatz, Lebo, Kans.[2]

HONORARY MEMBERS

Lt. Henry L. Miller, USN, Fairbanks, Alaska.

Mr. Tung-Sheng-Liu, Wei-Tying, Kiangsi, China.

Mr. Richard Pittenger (public relations adviser), now of Los Angeles, Calif.

Mr. Steven Leonard (legal adviser), now of Washington, D.C.

DOOLITTLEISMS

NOTE: During the writing of this book, conversations, taping sessions, letters, and Doolittle's jottings set down by the authors not so much for publication as for guidelines to his thinking and views, resulted in a number of succinct observations on various subjects. While all of these did not work into the text, it seemed that they deserved to be preserved somewhere. Unpolished at times, they do reveal certain aspects of the Doolittle character and philosophy that may have been overlooked in the main text.

THE BORE

A bore is a person who monopolizes the conversation talking about himself when you want to talk about yourself.

INTELLIGENCE AND WISDOM

Intelligence is the ability to acquire and use knowledge. It is ordinarily acquired through books and experimentation. It deals largely with things—inanimate objects. Wisdom, which is closely allied with judgment and "common sense," is usually acquired through living, observing, analyzing, and remembering. It deals largely with the animate—particularly with people.

EXCELLENCE AND AGGRESSION

Those of us who have a desire to excel, to get to the top of the heap, are ambitious and are generally aggressive or become aggressive. There can be little criticism of the desire for excellence —particularly if that excellence is to be used in the service of our fellow man—but aggressiveness can be good or evil, depending upon how, when, and for what reason it is employed.

The real problem is to avoid selfishness—which may be closely allied with aggression—because it is inherently bad. We are all selfish to some degree. It is largely instinctive and most of us have to be continually on the alert to avoid it. We have, actually, to lean over backwards.

You can't have consistent excellence without incentive.

ENVIRONMENT AND THE SPORTSMAN

A periodic change of environment is not only desirable but necessary. Necessary to clear out the mental cobwebs, open up the mind—and rejuvenate the body.

I love the outdoors—the mountains, the desert, the jungle, the sea, lakes and streams.

I am a sportsman, hunter, and fisherman.

Unfortunately some hunters are not sportsmen and give all hunters a bad name.

To my mind the sportsman:

1. Adheres, rigidly, to the letter and spirit of the law.
2. Respects the rights and property of others.
3. Takes all game in fair chase.
4. Knows and practices the rules of safe gun handling.
5. Knows the capabilities and limitations of his firearm—or bow and arrow—and stays within them.
6. Handles his weapon skillfully in order to make sure, clean kills.
7. Never leave a wounded animal to suffer. (Many hunters have been killed following a wounded, dangerous big-game animal into thick cover to make the *coup de grâce*).
8. Practice conservation rigidly—and help finance it.

RELIGION

Though I am not a regular church-goer, I am convinced that a universe as complex and as orderly as ours—from the microcosm to the macrocosm—could not have just happened. It had to have some purpose, some supreme control—far greater than the mind of man—behind it.

This "control" may be called God or, in other lands and cultures, by a variety of names.

ON RETIREMENT

I have often pointed out the importance of not taking on too many chores upon retiring. There are so many good things that need doing within the area of one's cognizance that one is inclined to take on more than he can do well—and there is no personal satisfaction in a job poorly done.

The optimum is a good work load where one can continue to serve rather than take from society and still not be under undue pressure—with time to enjoy some leisure, hobbies, avocations, etc.

On the other hand, if a well and active person retires to complete inactivity, he is inclined to become a cranky old man—or die of boredom.

A PHILOSOPHY OF LIFE (excerpt from a speech upon receiving the Horatio Alger Award, New York, October 27, 1972)

America always has been and still is a land of opportunity. Sometimes other people, coming in from less-favored nations, appreciate this better than we do.

All that is required for success here—for progress and service —is health and a willingness to work intelligently and diligently.

I have a very simple philosophy of life. I believe that we were put on this earth for a purpose. That purpose is to make it, within our capabilities, a better place in which to live.

We can do this by painting a picture, writing a poem, building a bridge, protecting the environment, combating prejudice and injustice, providing help to those in need, or in thousands of other ways. Just so we serve.

We should unselfishly serve our fellow man, our Nation and our Deity. If we do, then our time on earth will have been worthwhile, well spent. And when our time comes to go we can go happily and peacefully, in the knowledge that we have accomplished God's purpose.

A FAVORITE QUOTE

A very wise man once said, "The mind is not a vessel to be filled, but a lamp to be lighted."

ON ATTITUDES TOWARD YOUR FELLOW MAN

Live.................... 0%
Live and let live......... 50%
Live and *help* live........ 100%

Bibliography

1. *Biography*

   Glines, Carroll V. *Jimmy Doolittle, Daredevil Aviator and Scientist*. New York: Macmillan, 1972.

   Reynolds, Quentin. *The Amazing Mr. Doolittle*. New York: Appleton-Century-Crofts, 1953.

2. *Autobiographies with Doolittle References*

   Arnold, H. H. *Global Mission,* New York: Harper, 1949.

   Johnson, Bruce. *The Man With Two Hats*. New York: Carlton Press, 1968.

3. *The Tokyo Raid*

   Glines, Carroll V. *Doolittle's Tokyo Raiders*. Princeton, N.J.: D. Van Nostrand, 1964.

   Lawson, Ted W. (ed. by Robert Considine). *Thirty Seconds over Tokyo*. New York: Random House, 1943.

   Merrill, James M. *Target Tokyo*. New York: Rand McNally, 1964.

4. *Histories*

   Bruno, Harry. *Wings over America*. Garden City, N.Y.: Halcyon House, 1942.

   Craven, W. F., and J. L. Cate, eds. *The Army Air Forces*

in World War II. Chicago: University of Chicago Press, 1948–58. 7 vols.

Freeman, Roger A. *The Mighty Eighth*. Garden City, N.Y.: Doubleday, 1970.

Goldberg, Alfred, ed. *A History of the United States Air Force 1907–1957*. Princeton, N.J.: D. Van Nostrand, 1957.

Guggenheim, Harry F. *The Seven Skies*. New York: Putnam, 1930.

Hansell, Haywood S., Jr. *The Air Plan That Defeated Hitler*. Atlanta, Ga. Privately printed, 1972.

Peaslee, Budd J. *Heritage of Valor*. Philadelphia: Lippincott, 1964.

Vorderman, Don. *The Great Air Races*. Garden City, N.Y.: Doubleday, 1969.

Author's Note

The bulk of this book is based on materials gathered by the senior author during a friendship of several decades. The book was begun in the early thirties, set aside until World War II, when it was set aside again at Doolittle's insistence. That the Tokyo Raid might have appeared to be exploited did not appeal to him and he thought the timing was bad. Thus, the book was not picked up again until late in 1972, when the junior author was introduced.

The most reliable, and often the most objective, source on Doolittle is, of course, Doolittle himself—and his carefully kept records. On two occasions, in March and August 1973, extended interviews were taped in his Santa Monica home and his Los Angeles office. A further photo-hunting and checking visit took place in November 1973. Over the period of January 30, 1973–May 1, 1975 (when the main text of the book was completed), a copious, if random, correspondence supplied the answers to questions, particularly those in which two versions of the same tale by two or three different writers did not jibe. Generally it eventuated that the Doolittle version, if not so colored, was more fascinating.

Many close to Doolittle were most helpful, particularly Josephine "Joe" Doolittle, an extraordinary lady, indeed; her sister, Grace and brother-in-law, L. S. "Andy" Andrews, were both generous with their memories and time. Doolittle's cousin Emily (Mrs. Ronald McNamee) was a delightful source of early

Doolittleiana—as well as Americana. Mr. and Mrs. Jerome Simson, of Arcadia, California, provided a friendly setting for a discussion of Nome school days. One of the Doolittle's oldest friends, William "Bill" Downs, provided insights into the scrappy Los Angeles—and later—Doolittle.

A special nod must go to Miss Donna Roop, of Mutual of Omaha, Los Angeles. As the General's secretary, she dealt with the various letters, schedules, and meetings with grace, humor, and unflurried efficiency.

Others who have contributed to the work are aviation writer Richard S. Allen, Albany, N.Y.; Robert R. Allen, Golden, Colo.; Don Bane, Systems Group of TRW, Redondo Beach, Calif.; Stephen N. Bower, TRW Inc., Cleveland, Ohio; Walter Cate, 1361st Photo Sq., AAVS (MAC), Arlington, Va.; Jacqueline Cochran, Indio, Calif.; Virginia Fincik, also of the 1361st Photo Squadron and a long-time good friend and aide; Herbert O. Fisher, Kinnelon, N.J.; C. V. Glines, aviation writer, Doolittle Tokyo Raid archivist and friend, McLean, Va.; R. H. Hodges, Major, USAFR; Lieutenant General William E. Kepner, USAF (Ret.), for a comprehensive, informative letter; Claudia M. Oakes, NASM, Washington, D.C.; Robert C. Reeve, Anchorage, Alaska; Miss V. Shrubsall, Air Historical Branch 5, Royal Air Force, London; and Reginald Thayer, once a member of the 97th Bomb Group (H), Palisades, N.Y.

The Magazine and Book Branch, Public Information Division, Department of the Air Force, Major Shirley J. Bach, Chief, and the National Air and Space Museum, Smithsonian Institution, Washington, D.C., have helped immeasurably and willingly as always.

Index